Socrates Comes to Wall Street

Thomas I. White
Loyola Marymount University

PEARSON

Boston   Columbus   Indianapolis   New York   San Francisco
Hoboken   Amsterdam   Cape Town   Dubai   London   Madrid   Milan
Paris   Montréal   Toronto   Delhi   Mexico City   São Paulo   Sydney
Hong Kong   Seoul   Singapore   Taipei   Tokyo

Editor in Chief: Ashley Dodge
Program Editor: Priya Christopher
Editorial Assistant: Malini Bhattacharya
Managing Editor: Amber Mackey
Program Manager: Carly Czech
Senior Operations Supervisor: Mary Fischer
Operations Specialist: Mary Ann Gloriande
Art Director: Maria Lange
Cover Designer: Kristina Mose-Libon, Lumina Datamatics, Inc.
Cover Image: Paul Panasevich/Fotolia, Emin Kuliyev/Shutterstock
Full-Service Project Management and Composition: Sudip Sinha/Lumina Datamatics, Inc.
Printer/Binder: LSC Communications, Inc.
Cover Printer: LSC Communications, Inc.
Text Font: PalatinoLTStd, 10/12

Credits and acknowledgments borrowed from other sources and reproduced, with permission, in this textbook appear on pages 307–312.

Library of Congress Cataloging-in-Publication Data
White, Thomas I.
  Socrates comes to Wall Street / Thomas I. White. — First edition.
  ISBN 978-0-205-94807-9 — ISBN 0-205-94807-3   1. Business ethics.
2. Corporations—Moral and ethical aspects.   3. Corporate governance—Moral and ethical aspects. I. Title.
  HF5387.W493 2016
  174'.4—dc23

                                                    2014039796

ISBN 10: 0-205-94807-3
ISBN 13: 978-0-205-94807-9

10 2023

Dedication

To W. Michael Hoffman

Vir omnium horum.

TABLE OF CONTENTS

Two students, Natalie and Sergio, join the conversation to underscore the issue of the rights of future generations. At issue is the CEO's bank's support of ExxonMobil plus the executive's public denial of global climate change. Sergio reviews the scientific evidence for global warming. Did ExxonMobil violate either of two basic moral principles: *do no harm* or *treat others appropriately*?

Continued discussion of climate change, ExxonMobil and the CEO's public statements. Description of the military consequences of climate change. Socrates challenges the CEO to produce a full analysis of the ethical character of the actions of ExxonMobil and the executive. The CEO applies both teleological and deontological approaches.

Focus shifts to Socrates' concern about the CEO's public statements about the economy. What is the 'job' of the economy? Does a 'rising tide' actually 'float all boats'? Natalie presents evidence for a mixed picture. Since World War II, the U.S. economy has generally done very well. However, the benefits have not been evenly distributed.

Does the U.S. economy do its 'job' as well as most people think? Socrates presents evidence about poverty rates, quality of life, tax rates, tax revenue from corporations, government spending on infrastructure. Citing Milton Friedman, Socrates asks whether the current concentration of wealth in the United States constitutes a threat to freedom? Discussion of the positives and negatives of global capitalism.

Examination of the role of intellectual frameworks and unstated assumptions in shaping our observations—and the "facts" that result. Sergio describes an example from marine mammal science. Socrates claims that the lens through which business is typically viewed is a set of ideas with the strength of religious beliefs, and he challenges Natalie to identify them. She describes the "Business Creed" and argues that the data challenge the accuracy of these beliefs. In fact, she concludes that the data about how the economy actually works are far from how the "Business Creed" says it should work. In fact, the economy operates so much for the benefit of a small number of people that she claims that the data could even support the idea that "a giant con" is being perpetrated.

Chapter 25   Business, Ethics, and Ideology (continued)   261

Socrates describes the alleged "confidence game" ('The Sheriff of Nottingham') in which the goal is to benefit the rich at everyone else's expense. Challenged by Socrates to come up with an alternative set of rules and values that would govern how business is done, Natalie describes the "Village Creed." The CEO responds. Socrates reveals that there was never any question whether the CEO would be offered the new job. He explains that he was the person who originally recommended the CEO for the post, and he encourages the executive to accept.

Chapter 26   Epilogue   273

The executive accepts the position. Now in London, site of the new post, the CEO reflects on the experience with Socrates.

PREFACE

This is a deliberately provocative book written in the spirit of Socrates' claim that "the unexamined life is not worth living." Accordingly, this book challenges readers to question a number of basic assumptions about business, corporations, and the workings of contemporary free-market capitalism in a global economy. As a business ethics book, its primary focus is on the ethical character of actions these ideas produce.

This book critically examines perspectives and practices that are taken as "givens" in most American business schools and corporations. For example:

- The purpose of a business is to generate maximum profit for shareholders.
- Wealth generated by business will "trickle down" throughout the rest of the economy to everyone's benefit. That is, "a rising tide floats all boats."
- Contemporary free-market capitalism invariably promotes maximum individual freedom.
- CEO compensation in the range of hundreds of times more than that of average employees is ethically appropriate.
- Corporations have very limited responsibility for any harm their actions may bring to people now or in the future.
- It is ethically acceptable for businesses to keep their tax bill as small as possible, even if it means they pay no taxes at all.
- Ethics is a largely subjective, even arbitrary matter, rather than a technically sophisticated way to describe actions, their consequences, and assess risk.
- A rigorous and sophisticated ethical analysis need not be part of decision making in business. Abiding by the law and consulting mission statements, lists of corporate values and one's corporate ethics office are more than enough to guarantee that a company's actions are ethical.

Beliefs such as these are challenged in this book simply because they are "common coin" in the United States and are rarely questioned in business schools and corporations. (If this book were being written in a socialistic economy, its target would be contrary assertions.) The heart of Socrates' challenge is to ask ourselves whether ideas that we're *absolutely certain* are true are, in fact, backed up by facts and logic. Moreover, no attitude is so sacred that it is excluded from scrutiny. Indeed, the *more* sacred it is, the more important the need to examine its validity. Accordingly, the opinions of the book's characters are designed to be challenges to the reader, not expressions of my own position on any particular issue.

Aside from claims such as those just noted regarding business and the economy, this book hopes to encourage broader scrutiny about business and ethics in the wake of two events: the 2008 meltdown, and the ongoing concentration of the nation's wealth in the hands of a very small percentage of the population.

Given what should have been learned from the 1929 stock market crash and the savings and loan debacle of the late 1980s, the most recent collapse of the economy—which put us on the brink of global disaster—was avoidable. It was the product of greed, deception, irresponsibility, ideology, and a failure to pay attention to warning signs. To make matters worse, the "fix" favored the very industries and executives who were primarily responsible for the disaster. The average homeowner, small business, or employee who suffered most will bear the costs of this disaster for decades to come in terms of lost income, increased debt, and a postponed and more difficult retirement.

At the same time, the vast majority of the population has seen their net worth shrink while those at the top of the economy have achieved stunning levels of prosperity. Most disturbing, some would argue that this wealth is being used to advance policies and an ideology fundamentally antithetical to America's long-standing commitment to the common good.

It is my hope that this book will encourage the next generation of business leaders to be more astute about the implications of their actions and to act more prudently and more fairly than we have seen in the recent past.

A Note to Faculty About Options

This book is designed so that it can be used comfortably by faculty in either philosophy departments or business schools. The more technical discussions of John Stuart Mill and Immanuel Kant are concentrated in Chapters 13, 14, 15, and 17. While the cases discussed in these chapters (Apple/Preview, a gun company) illustrate important ethical issues, the chapters that follow do not depend on anything in them (except for a short section at the end of Chapter 21). If you consult the chapter descriptions in the Table of Contents, you'll see that many individual chapters (or two chapter sets) can stand alone.

Except for trying to approach business ethics through a Socratic dialogue, the only originality this book claims lies in two ideas designed to be controversial—that "ROI" should also be understood to mean "return on infrastructure," and that viewing certain workings of the economy through the lens of a "confidence game" works disturbingly well.

ACKNOWLEDGEMENTS

As is the case with any book, this work is the product of the support of many individuals. Pride of place goes to Jeff Herman, my agent, on whose expertise and professionalism I have relied for the last 30 years. A number of colleagues read various drafts of this book and provided sage feedback and encouragement: Kenneth Goodpaster (University of St. Thomas), W. Michael Hoffman (Bentley University), Barney Rosenberg (Meggitt PLC), the students of my ethics classes at Loyola Marymount University, and the anonymous readers engaged by Pearson to read the original manuscript. Kirsten Nordblom's exceptional work as my Associate Director of the Center for Ethics and Business has saved me countless hours that otherwise would have gone to putting out fires. The team from Pearson—Ashley Dodge, Priya Christopher, Carly Czech, Reena Dalal, Susan Hartman, Brooks Hill-Wilton, Nancy Roberts, Nicole Suddeth, Molly White—skillfully shepherded the project from beginning to end. Finally, I am particularly grateful for the patience and support of my wife, Lisa Cavallaro, who has the thankless task of being married to someone who likes to write so much. Of course, any weaknesses in the book are entirely my responsibility.

Thomas I. White
Redondo Beach, CA

1

Socrates Arrives

We were the latest company to find ourselves in the crosshairs of the Feds, the media, and our customers. The details of what happened don't matter. All that counts is it was a "perfect storm" of bad news. Almost overnight, we'd become the company everyone loves to hate.

It was bad enough I was supposed to appear before a Congressional committee the day after tomorrow. But some comments I made earlier today were being played over and over on the internet and on every news program.

Here's what happened. As I walked out the door of my gym in my sweats, some reporter ran up and stood right in front of me. Someone had tipped her off I was there, and she was trying to get a scoop.

She shoved a microphone in my face. "Being hauled in front of a Congressional committee must be a new low point for you as one of the country's most prominent CEOs. How do you plan to respond to these charges? What's your defense going to be?"

OK, I was caught off guard and didn't stop to think. I also didn't take the time to notice she'd brought a cameraman, who was shooting our exchange.

"Defense? What do you mean?" I virtually spat out my words. "Look smart ass," I continued, in my most arrogant voice, "everybody knows that business is about making money. We didn't break any laws! We didn't lie, cheat, or steal! We didn't do anything wrong!" Then I turned my back to her, got into the back seat of my Mercedes limo, slammed the door, and told my driver to take off.

It wasn't my proudest moment. I lost my cool. And 5 minutes later, the video was on CNN, MSNBC, you name it. The video went viral immediately. There I am in sweaty workout gear insulting a young, professionally attired reporter. We're toe to toe, and I'm 6 inches taller than she is, yelling down at her. I look like a jerk—over and over again for millions of people to see.

But she *did* have it all wrong. I'm not being "hauled in front" of the committee; I'm testifying voluntarily. There are no "charges"; I'm going to answer questions. And I don't need a "defense" because I haven't done anything wrong.

At least I recognized immediately I'd messed up and that it was going to be a public relations disaster. As soon as I got into my limo, I called Phyllis, our head of PR. I explained the situation and told her she needed to find me a spin doctor. *Fast!* I needed to talk to someone who could keep me from saying something stupid in Washington.

So you can't blame me for thinking that the guy in the charcoal Armani suit waiting for me in front of company headquarters was the consultant Phyllis had contacted. OK, I should have been amazed that even she could have someone there only 10 minutes after we talked. But I've gotten used to her doing the impossible. As I got out of the car, he stuck out his hand and said, "I gather you could use my help." Who else would he be?

I returned a couple of calls as we made our way through security and up to the top floor. As we headed toward my office, I turned to my executive assistant. "Marie, I'm going to be in conference and don't want to be disturbed."

"There's coffee, tea, and bottled water over there." I pointed to the antique mahogany sideboard on the other side of the room. "Let's get down to business."

I sat down behind my desk, rearranging some files to clear some space. "I have to say how impressed I am you got here so quickly. I assume you saw that disastrous interview. But my real concern is the Congressional hearing. As you know, we're getting hammered in the press, and now there's talk of investigations. I want to find a way to get the heat turned down. We're having trouble getting our message heard. That's why I need your help."

I leaned back in my chair and looked straight at him. "I really screwed up in that interview. I was completely wrong. I should have noticed the camera. And I admit it was stupid to call the reporter 'smart ass.' I'm not going to bullshit you with some silly excuse. And you don't need to think I have a precious ego that needs protecting.

"I know it's no excuse, but I felt bushwhacked. I didn't expect to be interviewed right after a workout. But I honestly meant what I told her. Business is about making money. We didn't break any laws, lie, cheat, or steal. We didn't do anything wrong.

"Because our problems have been the lead story on every network recently, I assume you're familiar with the main facts. I can have someone fill you in on the details tomorrow if you want. But right now, I need your advice about how to spin this—especially in Washington. I told Phyllis to get me the top person. I'm sure you've had experience with this sort of thing."

While I spoke, my companion sat and listened carefully. But the longer I went on, the stranger his expression became. First, he looked puzzled. Then, he looked amused.

"I think there's been a misunderstanding," he chuckled. "I'm sorry about laughing. I don't mean to minimize how serious your situation is. But I'm not who you think I am."

"OK, so maybe you're not the *absolutely* top guy. I know this was a last minute thing. But Phyllis wouldn't have called you if she wasn't sure you know what you're doing. So, what do you think? How do we play this?" I grabbed a pencil and yellow legal pad to take notes.

"*Really.* I'm not who you think I am," he repeated. "I'm not a spin doctor. I haven't a clue who Phyllis is. I'm not here because of any phone call."

It's an understatement to say I wasn't thrilled to hear this. I'd just escorted a total stranger I met on the sidewalk through security and all the way into my office. The press—not to mention, my board—would have a field day with this.

Putting down the pencil, I looked at him seriously. "So, if you aren't who you're supposed to be, who are you? And what are you doing in my office?"

"Well, I may not be a spin doctor, but I am someone who can help you. That's why I'm here. I've been reading about your problems and thought you could use a hand. I didn't see that latest interview. But it sounds like you need my help even more than you did before."

While I admired his initiative, this isn't how I do business. "Look, I give you a lot of credit for getting your foot in the door, but this isn't how I hire consultants—not for such an important issue. But I like your style, so give me your card. I'll have my people check you out, and maybe we'll give you a call for something in the future. And I don't want to be rude, but you've got to leave. I need help, but not yours."

He rose up from his chair and headed for the door. "As you wish. Maybe our paths will cross some other time. Good luck with the hit your stock's going to take after your quarterly loss is reported."

I couldn't believe what he'd just said. Only three people were supposed to know about that.

I got up and walked over to him. "Wait a minute. How do you know that?" If nothing else, I wanted to learn how I could have such a serious leak from my inner circle.

He turned back toward me. "How about this? I'll tell you in exchange for your listening to me about how you need my help more than you realize."

I honestly didn't care about why some stranger thought I needed his help. But I couldn't let him leave before finding out how he got such confidential information.

I went back to my desk and sat back down. "OK. I'll listen to you for a few minutes. But first tell me who you are and how you got inside information about my company?"

He settled into the chair opposite me. "Who am I? Well, I'm the guy who, in the last few days, has gotten control of 30% of your company's stock. As far as the quarterly loss goes, in my world, getting inside information is easy. It's what I do."

"Wait a minute!" I sputtered. "*Nobody* owns 30% of our stock. Who are you?"

He pulled out a small, black leather notebook from his pocket and jotted something down with his gold fountain pen. "*Doesn't listen carefully,*" he mumbled as he scribbled. "Another one of your problems—but we can't work on that today."

He looked up and put the notebook down in front of him on my desk. "I didn't say I *owned* 30% of the stock. I said I *controlled* it. I prefer to keep the details of how I do things confidential. But I decided to call in some favors. And there's no point in telling you my name because you wouldn't recognize it. I've worked very hard to remain anonymous. However, I'm a venture capitalist who likes to help promising companies and individuals—people like you. When I see a company that can use my help, I 'arrange things,' shall we say, so I can make things happen—like this conversation. I decided I wanted to talk to you. I thought controlling a sizable chunk of your company's stock would get your attention."

I didn't know whether I felt impressed, mystified, or afraid. If what this guy said was true, he had the power to fire me on the spot. He also had a no-nonsense way about him that made me think he wouldn't hesitate to do so if he wanted to. Of course, he could also be some con artist who knew how to talk his way into situations like this. But I was intrigued. I could grill my staff later to see if one of them actually gave this guy company information. I decided to play along for now.

"OK. You're a combination of invisible man, Gordon Gekko, and puppet master. You're not a spin doctor. And you claim to control enough stock to make me and the company do whatever you want. For the sake of argument, let's say I believe you. Why do I need your help?"

He got up from his chair, walked to the sideboard, got a cup of tea, and stared intently into the china cup for a few seconds. Then he turned to me.

"Here's the situation. I think you can do a lot of good running this company. I think this can be a great example for other businesses about how to operate. Up until recently, you showed real potential. That's why you caught my attention in the first place. But—to be blunt about things—lately, you've been making *terrible* decisions. And you know it. If you're honest with yourself, you'll admit that your decisions haven't felt the way they should. You haven't been trusting your instincts. I bet you've felt like you've been swimming upstream.

"And that bad news about your losses is only the tip of the iceberg. Your company is weaker than you've been telling the analysts and the business press. And you know *that* too."

I hated to admit it, but he was right. Things were worse than we were telling everyone. And I'd been scrambling. Everything had been going along great. We were making money hand over fist. Then, all of a sudden, we had one problem after another. On paper, every decision I'd made looked good. Everyone on my team agreed what we should do. But it always ended up like throwing gasoline on a fire. We were all mystified that things kept getting worse. But we couldn't seem to turn things around.

"The root of your problem," he continued, "is that you've based your decisions on *ideas you don't really believe*. You've been making critical decisions based on what you said to that reporter about *what business is about* and on your claim that *there was nothing wrong with what you've done*. But despite what you think, you actually *don't* believe these things. That's why—despite what you've been saying to the analysts and the business press—your company is sliding so badly."

Now I *really* didn't know what to think. He was on target that things were worse than most people knew. But now he sounded crazy. He's telling me *I don't believe what I say*? I stared at him for a few seconds while I ran this idea through my brain a couple of times. Then I shook my head. We had problems, but his was the stupidest analysis I could imagine. That was it for me. I was done. I decided I *didn't* believe he controlled that much stock. At best, he was a really good con artist.

And just as I was about to tell him to leave, he said something that really got my attention.

"Of course," he laughed knowingly, "you think I'm crazy. What, you don't think I've seen that look before? You don't believe I control so much of your stock. You think it's ridiculous for me to claim that you don't believe what you just said. So I'm going to give you some incentive to continue this conversation for a while. I understand you enjoy betting." He paused to let me take in what he just said.

His comment did more than catch my attention. It troubled me because hardly anyone on the face of the earth knew about this. For years, I'd bet on foreign currency rates for fun. And the way I approached this wasn't "investing"; it was "gambling." But because you can't have a successful marriage and keep secrets about something like this, Bobbi and I agreed on a set amount of money I could play with. If this guy was able to find out something so private, he was someone I couldn't afford to underestimate.

"Your compensation from the company last year was $20 million," he continued. "If I'm who I say I am, you can imagine what I'm worth. We each contribute 2% of our last year's compensation to the pot. Winner takes all. To show that I'm good for it, you can hold this as collateral."

He took something out of his vest pocket and handed it to me.

"A pocket watch?" I said, almost laughing. "*This* is supposed to make it worth my while to talk to you? You're going to have to do a lot better than that."

He sat back down, picked up his notebook, and jotted something down. He read out loud as he wrote, "*Makes snap judgments and doesn't pay attention to detail.*" He looked up and said, "Take your time. I want to check my e-mail anyway." He put the notebook away, pulled out his phone, and started reading.

I looked more closely at the watch. There was something familiar about it. It was a double-open-faced watch with what looked like a display of the Milky Way on the back. "I've seen this before," I said quietly to myself.

"Yes, you have," he said, never looking up from his e-mail, "in Switzerland."

I turned to my computer and did a quick search. The watch was a dead ringer for the world's most expensive pocket watch. It sold at Sotheby's in 1999 for $11 million—to "an anonymous Middle Eastern collector." It was now on display in the Patek Philippe Museum in Geneva. I'd just visited that city, and, because I collect watches, I went to the museum.

"Very clever," I said. "It's an impressive copy. So, not enough for the bet you propose." I put the watch down on the desk in front of him.

"Well, there *is* a copy," he remarked, still staring at his phone. "That's what you saw in Geneva. But I'm wagering the genuine article."

"So you're a jewel thief as well?" I laughed. I couldn't help but be curious at what kind of story he was now going to tell me.

"People like me don't have to steal. No, as much fun as it would be to have the skills of a cat burglar, this was a gift from a friend. He had a copy made so the museum would still have something to display."

I picked up the watch and examined it carefully. It was either genuine or a remarkable forgery.

"You're still skeptical. I understand. Here's my friend's personal number, if you want to call and verify my story. He won't be entirely surprised because you won't be the first person to call to check me out. However, because of the 7-hour time difference, you'll likely get one of his bodyguards."

"So this is real?"

"Absolutely."

"And it was gift?"

"As I said," he smiled.

"For what?"

"A favor. Obviously, a *big* favor. And my friend is a very generous individual. Seriously, if you call him, he'll confirm my story. So, do we have a bet?"

I leaned back in my chair and stared at the ceiling. Two percent of my $20 million was $400,000. $400,000 for one conversation? Not bad. If the watch was real, his collateral was OK. And his clothes were very expensive. This guy was either who he said he was, or he'd done a superb job of dressing the part.

"It's an interesting proposition—*if* you're who you say you are. But how do we have a bet connected with a conversation? Who decides who wins?"

"It's simple. I bet I can show you that you don't really believe what you said to that reporter. You may *think* you believe it now, but after we talk about it, I bet—literally—that you'll see you *don't*. You may have *said* those things to the reporter. But you said them *without thinking*. I wager that if we really dig into what you were talking about, you'll come to the conclusion that you don't believe what you said, after all. And *you'll* be the judge. At the end of our conversation, *you* decide whether you still believe what you just said."

I've always thought that if something looked too good to be true, it usually was. And this felt like one of those times. There must be a catch. I studied my opponent to see what I could learn. The saying in poker is you play the man, not the cards. Realizing I was trying to size him up, my companion just grinned. He was revealing nothing that would give me an edge. Still, no matter what I actually thought at the end of the conversation, if I simply lied, I could win the bet.

As if reading my mind, he added, "Of course, it goes without saying that you'll tell the truth about what you think."

"Right—goes without saying," I agreed, embarrassed that the prospect of so much easy money had me consider lying.

"So, do we have a bet?" he asked.

I still wasn't sure. "You know everything about me, but I know nothing about you. For all I know, the most I stand to win is a watch that might be a copy."

"I can appreciate your doubts. So let's do this in two parts—the equivalent of two hands in poker. The first *hand* deals with your statement about what business is all about; the second, your claim you've done nothing wrong. If you're unhappy after the first hand, we stop. And to add some enticement, if I win the hand and you think I've cheated or that this wasn't in some way completely above board, I'll let you off the hook. You owe me nothing. We shake hands. You never hear from me again. I step away from your company. But that also means you're on your own."

I still had misgivings. But I was also worried about the company. And part of me was curious about what would happen if I let this play itself out. What was this guy suggesting when he said I didn't really believe what I said? *Of course* I believed it, or I wouldn't have said it in the first place. What does a conversation around that idea even look like?

"OK, I'm in," I said, sticking out my hand.

"Great." Getting out of his chair, he took my hand and gave it a firm shake. He nodded approvingly. "Shaking on a deal like you mean it. Very old school. That's a good sign. Let's get to work."

"One more preliminary before we start," I said. "I take it you aren't going to tell me your real name. But I need to call you something. What's it going to be?"

"Well, my closest friends have a nickname for me when I pull stunts like this. How about that?"

"Seems appropriate. What is it?"

"*Socrates*," he answered with a wink.

I had to laugh. Despite the expensive clothes, he had a white mane and beard and piercing eyes. Swap out the hand-tailored suit for a toga, and he'd fit the classic image of the Greek philosopher. "*Socrates*," I said. "That's rich."

2

What Is the "Job" of Business?

"OK, 'Socrates,' " I said with air quotes, "let's not waste any more of my time. How does this work?"

"As I said, we'll do this in two parts. The first *hand* concerns what you said about the point of business. So let's start by making sure there's no misunderstanding. Tell me how you'd describe the purpose of business."

"That's easy. I meant exactly what I told that reporter. The whole point of business is to make money. It's all about profit, ROI, and increasing shareholder wealth. I stand by my words. And that's what I base my decisions on."

"Fair enough," he replied. "And just to be clear. I claim that you don't really believe that's the purpose of business. So let's get into it."

He thought for a moment and then looked directly at me. "Tell me, why do humans live together?" he asked pointedly.

"Wait a minute?" I sputtered, wondering whether "Socrates" was actually some guy who'd lost his marbles. "Why we live together has no connection with whether I believe business is about profit. What does that have to do with anything we're talking about?"

"Look," he sighed. "We're going to be here forever if you don't cooperate. Let me explain. My friends call me 'Socrates' because I use the Socratic method. I ask questions; you answer them."

"OK, it's your show," I groaned.

"So," he repeated, "why do human beings live together?"

"You mean as couples and families?" I asked.

"No," he answered. "Think bigger."

"Cities?"

"Too big. And too modern. Think smaller, and think earlier in our history. Go as early as you can."

"OK," I thought out loud as I continued. "Really early humans. Before agriculture. We aren't even living in one specific place. We're nomadic. The tribe, group, or whatever we call it moves around."

"Why?" Socrates interrupted.

"Why do we move? To follow food sources, I assume."

"No, why do we move *as a group*? Why aren't we operating as *individuals*?"

"For one thing, we're less likely to get killed by a hungry saber tooth tiger. If something comes after us, we have a better chance to survive if there are other people around to help us."

"Good start," he said encouragingly. "Any other benefits?"

"Sure. As I said—help with hunting animals that are bigger and faster than we are."

"Keep going," he nodded.

"There are all sorts of advantages to having other people around," I explained. "Help with raising children. Help with learning what we need to know in order to survive—where the best sources of food and water are, how to hunt and gather, how to make clothes and tools, how to make fire, how to cook, how to deal with injury or disease."

"Good. Now," he instructed, "describe the benefits in one sentence."

"One sentence?" I thought for a minute. "How's this? Living together makes our lives easier, better, more comfortable."

"Excellent!" Then, getting up out of his chair, he walked over to the white board I have in my office and picked up a marker. "Do you mind?"

I waved my hand indicating I had no objection. I scanned my e-mails while Socrates drew something on the board.

"Forgive me," he said when he finished. "I'm a frustrated teacher."

"With a nickname like Socrates," I smiled, "I never would have guessed."

Pointing to his sketch, he said, "It's simple. Our species discovered early on we'd be more successful at surviving if we lived in groups and cooperated with each other. We aren't the strongest or fastest animals on the planet. But we do have big brains. And if we used them in cooperation with other people, we'd have better lives than if we were on our own."

"Fine. And this has *what* to do with my business?" I asked.

"*Impatience*," Socrates murmured, returning to his chair, shaking his head, and jotting again in his notebook.

"Sorry. Living in a group makes life easier. So?"

"*So*, tell me more about what life would be like in those groups. If you lived back then, what would you be doing?"

"Oh, that's easy," I said with a big smile. "I'd be in charge."

He rolled his eyes. "Why am I not surprised to hear you say that?"

"You think I'm joking, but I'm serious. That's what I'm good at. Seeing the big picture. Solving problems. Putting people in the right jobs. Running the show so that everything's more efficient."

"Fine, let's go with that then. Tell me more about what you'd be doing in 'putting people in the right jobs.' "

I thought for a moment. "Some of us will be stronger, some weaker. Some will be smarter. Some will be great with their hands; others, like me, will be terrible at that. We want to leverage our strengths and minimize our weaknesses. So I'll divide up the work and have members of the tribe concentrate on what they do best. Those who are both strong and smart will hunt. We're going to need people who understand how to construct some kind of dependable structures to protect us from the elements. Maybe someone will be very smart, not so strong—*but* is great at looking after people. That person can be our expert in medicine and healing. If someone in the tribe has an excellent memory, their job will be to make sure we have a way to record or preserve the important knowledge and skills we need in order to survive. You get the idea."

As I was explaining this, Socrates got up again and added to his sketch.

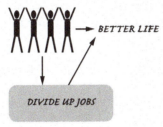

"Good," he said, pointing to the board. "So one of the secrets of our species' success is division and specialization of labor. Each of us doesn't have to be an expert in food, shelter, medicine, and the like to survive. By living in groups and dividing up the work, it's easier for us to get all the critical jobs done dependably and efficiently. We increase our odds of survival and make life easier."

"Right," I nodded.

"Now jump ahead thousands of years to when humans have settled down and live in big communities—communities that are connected in some way and make *societies* or *countries*. How do things work? What do you see?"

"Interesting," I smiled, closing my eyes and making it look like I was gazing into some ethereal mist. "I'm still in charge."

Socrates grimaced. "No surprise there. So, how are you going to arrange things now?"

"Well, the situation we're managing is obviously much bigger. But I'd use the same principles."

"Tell me in detail what you mean."

"Alright, let's start with the basics. We have thousands—even millions—of people who need food, shelter, and the like. So people who are good at farming specialize in that. The people good at medicine do that. And so on."

"But this isn't like before," noted Socrates. "You may still be in charge, but the situation is too big and complicated for you to decide individually who ends up with which job."

"You're right. But I'd handle things the same way I do in my company. I'd have specialized groups handle their own critical function. Each group would have an important job to perform. Then I'd oversee these groups—the same way I oversee the critical functions of my company: product development, operations, sales, marketing, legal, HR, and so on."

"Excellent. And what do you call those?"

"Call what?"

"You're overseeing a society of millions of people. What do you call these smaller groups that are going to handle the important jobs?"

I thought for a moment. "We could call them *organizations*, but that feels too limited. I think we're talking about something bigger than that. Something that refers to, say, a bunch of organizations all in the same area—health, for example."

"You're on the right track. But go at it this way," he advised. "Come back to the present. There are a number of other companies that do the same sort of thing your company does, right?"

"Correct."

"How do you describe what you and your competitors have in common?"

"In common?" I repeated. "I guess I'd say that we're all in the same *industry*?"

"Good. Now, bring to mind all of the industries you can think of."

I took a minute and made a mental list. "Got it. Now what?"

"What do all of the companies in all of the different industries have in common?"

"Well, they all try to make money. They buy and sell. They're all *businesses*. So, the companies may be in different industries, but they're all *businesses*."

"Excellent. And is it fair to say that, as a group, they serve a critical function—that they're one of your groups doing an important job in the society?"

"Absolutely. In my opinion, they do one of the *most* important jobs."

"OK. Now broaden your perspective and tell me about the other groups that need to be there. Look at modern human society. Tell me which other groups do some sort of big job."

"No problem," I said immediately, seeing what he was getting at. "In addition to business, you mean things like *government, education, science, medicine, religion,* and *the arts*."

As I ticked these off, Socrates was back at the whiteboard writing them down.

"Excellent. And—since you're still in charge," he added with a smile, "remind me why you've organized things this way."

"It's the same reason as before. This is the most efficient way to get the important jobs done."

"Good. And remind me why we need these things done."

"That's an odd question," I remarked. "It's obvious. Isn't it?"

"Maybe so. But sometimes it helps to state the obvious. Humor me. In fact, go back to our original nomadic tribe. Give me your simplest, most practical explanation for why the critical jobs need to be done."

"If you insist," I sighed. "The jobs are critical because our survival depends on them. They're also critical because they determine what kind of life we'll have. How comfortable things will be. Whether we get the kind of life we want."

"Excellent," he beamed. (Given how much money was riding on our conversation, I was a little uncomfortable with just *how much* he approved of my answer.) "So now relate that to the groups you identified as doing the *big jobs* in our society. Start with *government*."

The job of government? Socrates had hit one of my hot buttons, which I suspect he already knew. So I was raring to go. "Well, government does a lot of stuff that it's not really *supposed* to do," I said, getting up a head of steam, "For example,"

"Wait a minute," he interrupted, "I already know your opinions about current events—and I honestly don't care. I'm fine with your explanation of what the job of government *should* be. A simple description of the *job* of government is fine with me."

"If you insist. The only thing we need government for is to make and enforce laws (a legislature and the police), referee disagreements (the courts), protect us from external threats (an army), and handle the relatively few things the market can't. And more than anything, government should protect individual rights! That's one of the reasons it needs to keep its hands off of business. That's where individualism flourishes and is rewarded!"

Socrates groaned. "I see you're intent on going down this road. I suppose I shouldn't be surprised because it's certainly been a theme in lots of your public statements. But focusing on that now is going to pull us off track. How about this? You shelve *rugged individualism* for the time being, and I promise we'll come back to it. In the meantime, I want to press ahead so we get the big picture view of how the village is organized."

"I'm surprised a VC like you doesn't automatically agree with me about the importance of individualism. But as long as you go along with my thin view of government, I'm OK with things for now."

He nodded his head. "Agreed. But to keep it short, how about if I just write *order* and *protection*?"

"Sure," I said, as he added the words to his list.

"How about *education* next?" he asked as he turned back toward me.

"Easy," I answered. "The job of education is to let us get the knowledge and skills we need to operate successfully in the present. And for a community to flourish over the long term, young people need to be in a position to take over down the road."

"Good answer," he said, writing *knowledge* and *skills* on the whiteboard.

DIVIDE UP JOBS
BUSINESS
GOVERNMENT: ORDER, PROTECTION
EDUCATION: KNOWLEDGE, SKILLS
SCIENCE
MEDICINE
RELIGION
THE ARTS

"But what about this?" he continued. "What about when the schools in our society treated women and people of certain races differently? Was *education* doing its job then?"

"Not in my opinion," I said, glaring at Socrates in a way that said I was insulted he'd even ask me this question.

"Why not?" he pressed. "The society didn't collapse. For the most part, people got food and shelter. One generation was ready to take over for the next. It sounds to me like education did its job."

"Do you really think," I asked, starting to raise my voice, "that a woman who had to break about a dozen glass ceilings to get to the top is going to say that schools *did their job* when they were discriminating?"

"Of course I don't. I just want to know how you explain their failure."

"Their *failure*? It's obvious. Schools weren't treating everyone the same. They were setting things up so one group could dominate everyone else.

That's not the job of education! How can you have the kind of life you want if you don't have the knowledge and skills to compete?"

"You won't get any argument from me," he smiled. "But that's the second time you've used that phrase. What do you mean by it?"

"Which phrase?"

"*Kind of life*," he said slowly, turning around to add the phrase to the whiteboard. "You used it when you explained why the critical *jobs* that the different parts of a society do are so important. One of the reasons you gave was that they determine the *kind of life* we'll have. What are you talking about?"

BETTER LIFE
KIND OF LIFE

DIVIDE UP JOBS
BUSINESS
GOVERNMENT: ORDER, PROTECTION
EDUCATION: KNOWLEDGE, SKILLS
SCIENCE
MEDICINE
RELIGION
THE ARTS

"I wasn't aware I'd used that phrase, but that *is* what I think. Let me see if I can explain what I mean." I got up and joined Socrates by my bookcase. "When you put me in charge of figuring out who does what, efficiency wasn't the only thing I was thinking about. I had a certain *kind of life* or *quality of life* in mind. Sure, I'd want a life that was physically safe and comfortable. But I'd also like a life where we treat one another properly. People should be treated equally, fairly, and with respect."

"So, you're a *philosopher queen* now," Socrates laughed, pulling a copy of Plato's *Republic* off the shelf and waving it at me. "You're going to organize things so that we have not only food and shelter, but justice and fairness."

"You're mocking me," I replied, walking to the sideboard for a cup of coffee. "But I'm serious," I continued, turning back to face him. "The *job* of these major parts of a society—government, education, medicine, business, science, religion, the arts, and the like—isn't just survival. It's a decent way of life."

"Very nice explanation," Socrates noted, re-shelving Plato. "So, educational institutions that don't support that way of life aren't *doing their job*?"

"Not in my opinion. And, if you remember," I added with a smile, "I'm still in charge."

"So," Socrates said, moving away from the whiteboard and walking toward the window, "just one of two more cards in this *hand*. What about *medicine*? What's its job?"

"Simple. The job of medicine—that is, medical institutions like hospitals, medical schools, clinics, and the like—is to keep us healthy and to help us when we get sick or injured."

"Good," Socrates said, putting *health* on his list as the *job* of medicine.

"But just to clarify something," he said as he turned back toward me, "Let's say we have a privately owned hospital that's extremely profitable—but it's so successful only because it spends less than it should on patient care. Is it doing its job?"

"It's obviously *not* doing its job as a hospital. *But*," I paused and then added, "as much as I hate to admit it, it *is* doing its job as a business. It's making money."

"Sorry," Socrates countered, pointing his finger straight at me, "there's no 'on the one hand, no' but 'on the other hand, yes' in this conversation. I need a straight up *yes* or *no*."

I knew what Socrates wanted me to say. But I thought he was just being stubborn and refusing to look at the complexities of the situation. "This can't be just yes or no," I explained. "It's a hospital *and* it's a business. It's a bad hospital, but a good business. And because it's a bad hospital, the market will make sure it will ultimately go out of business."

"Look, patronizing me as though I'm stupid and don't know how the market is supposed to work isn't going to cut it." He was clearly annoyed with me. "You're missing the point. You're the one who identified a need for taking care of health as one of the major jobs that has to be done in a society. And you were right to identify *medicine* and *medical institutions* as the group doing that job. And you were also right not to distinguish at that point between *profit* and *nonprofit* medical institutions. Because it doesn't matter. So, no splitting hairs. Is the hospital doing its job or not?"

I still thought he was oversimplifying things, but, frankly, I was getting tired of this back and forth. "OK. No. It's not doing its job," I said, deliberately showing my impatience and taking my coffee back to my desk. "Are you happy?"

"Probably happier than you realize," he replied as he leaned back against the wall with a smile. "Now."

"Look, I know we have this bet and that I agreed to handle things your way," I interrupted, "but I really don't think that what we're talking about is going to help me at the hearings. Maybe you find this entertaining, but I find it irrelevant. Let's wind this down."

"Still impatient," he said, shaking his head. "But, lucky for you, finishing this hand is precisely what we're about to do. So, what's the job of *business*?"

"Well, as I told that reporter, the whole point of business is to make money. So that's its job."

"You're sure about that," asked Socrates, now back in his chair with his hands folded behind his head. "I don't want you to cry foul when you lose."

"Look, I know what I believe," I said, getting laughter in reply. "And I haven't heard anything to change my mind."

"Well, not yet," I heard Socrates mutter to himself as he got back up and added *making money* to his list.

BETTER LIFE
KIND OF LIFE

DIVIDE UP JOBS
BUSINESS: MAKING MONEY
GOVERNMENT: ORDER, PROTECTION
EDUCATION: KNOWLEDGE, SKILLS
SCIENCE
MEDICINE: HEALTH
RELIGION
THE ARTS

Then, turning back to me, he said, "Go back to our tribal village. Is *business* there?"

"What do you mean?"

"When you assigned jobs in that society, you identified hunters, healers, and people who knew how to make shelters. You didn't say anything about buying and selling," he pointed out.

"You may not see buying and selling, but that doesn't mean *business* isn't there." I explained. "In such a small group, we're probably bartering. Healers get food from the hunters and, in exchange, provide medical care. Shelter builders contribute their skills and get what they need in return."

"Makes sense," Socrates nodded. "But, if we have a year when hunters easily find food for us while shelter builders have a tough time providing what we need, would it be OK with you for the hunters to put in a couple of hours—while the shelter builders work all day?"

"I *could* explain to everyone that eventually things even out," I said, "because there will be years when the *hunters* will have a more difficult time. But that's not the kind of place I want to live in."

"You mean that's not the *kind of life* you want," interrupted Socrates.

"Right, it's not *fair*. Life in our community will simply work better if we help each other when necessary and if we do things in a way that's fair. Things will be more efficient, and everyone will be happier."

"Sounds reasonable to me," replied Socrates as he added *fair* to the board.

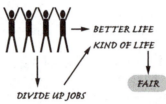

"So in your tribe, we see a primitive form of business in bartering goods and services done in a way that ends up with people getting what they need, keeps the peace, and gives us the *kind of life* you have in mind. In this case, a *kind of life* in which people feel that things in the tribe are done fairly?"

"Right. That's what I'm saying."

"And where's the money?" he asked.

"What do you mean, 'Where's the money?' It's a barter economy, not a cash economy."

"But you said 'business is about making money,' and then you said you could find business in our tribal society. So," he paused, "where's the money?"

"OK," I sighed, impatient that Socrates seemed to be splitting hairs just to give me a hard time. "You want to be picky? What's going on in the tribe isn't *precisely* business because we don't have to worry about profit. We're bartering. We're getting what we need in that way. We don't need cash or profit. So let's call it pre-business because as societies get bigger and advance, they need to develop *business*."

"I've never heard of *pre-business*. But if you insist," he said, shaking his head. "Nonetheless, you *are* saying that *pre-business* and business do the same *job*?"

"Look, you're comparing apples and oranges," I tried to explain. "Forget this tribal society and go back to our bigger, more modern society. The job of business is to make money so we have a more efficient mechanism than bartering. We get the goods and services we need through buying and selling with money."

"Thank you," said Socrates, with a big smile as he added *goods* and *services* to the list.

"What do you mean 'thank you'? Thank me for what?" I asked, wondering what he was up to now.

"You'll see," he said, as he sat back down opposite me looking very pleased with himself. "So you're saying that money isn't profit for the sake of it. It's a *tool* for making sure we get what we need. It's the means to an end, not the end itself. Right?"

"I have no idea why you're sitting there looking so smug," I said, beginning to feel exasperated. "That's what I said. That's what profit does. If you have no profit, you have no goods and services. If there's no business, there's no *stuff* that we need."

Socrates paused, put a finger to his chin, thought for a moment, looked at me, and said, "Humor me for a minute, because I want to make sure I have this right. We live in groups so we can have a decent life. We organize our villages and societies around division and specialization of labor so we get what we need more efficiently. Each of the different *parts* of a society has a *job* connected with some critical need. So far, so good?"

"Sure," I replied, "and why do you like to repeat yourself so much?"

"Humor me." I'm sure he repeated himself just to annoy me. "And the job of business is?"

"I just told you that. It's to make profit so that we get the stuff we need."

"So the job of business *isn't* making money. It's making it possible for us *to get what we need*!" Socrates said with an air of triumph as he headed back to the whiteboard and underscored his point with some additions.

BETTER LIFE

KIND OF LIFE

FAIR

DIVIDE UP JOBS

BUSINESS: MAKING MONEY, GOODS, SERVICES THAT WE NEED

GOVERNMENT: ORDER, PROTECTION

EDUCATION: KNOWLEDGE, SKILLS

SCIENCE

MEDICINE: HEALTH

RELIGION

THE ARTS

"The job of business is about *stuff*, not money!" he continued. "We determine whether business is doing *its job* by whether it's giving us the *stuff*—the goods and services—that we want for a decent life. *Not* whether it's generating profit."

"But you can't have the one without the other," I said, refusing to be pushed around. "You're just splitting hairs." I got up and walked over to where he was standing to make sure he'd listen to me.

"I'm not splitting hairs," he countered, waving a marker in my face. "You're confusing means and ends. Go back to the 'bad hospital but good business' example. In the end, you agreed it wasn't doing its job. Right?"

"Right," I replied, "because the issue was whether it was doing the job of a *medical* institution."

"Which is?"

"Health."

"Well, it's the same thing here," he countered, turning to the whiteboard and punctuating each sentence with a thump on the appropriate line. "*Medicine* meets critical needs for *health*. *Education* meets critical needs for *knowledge and skills*. *Government* meets critical needs for *order and protection*. The critical needs that *business* meets are all of our *basic material needs*: food, shelter, transportation, and the like."

Socrates paused for a moment and then gave me a hard stare as he continued, "And let's look at something closer to home. Businesses like banks and other financial institutions—like the one *you* run—are *supposed* to meet our need for having a stable and secure financial foundation for the entire economy. And if a bank isn't doing that—even if it's making piles of money—*it isn't doing its job!* It's like a hospital that's making money but not curing people.

"We have *business* for exactly the same reason we have *medicine*, *education*, *government*, and the like—to make life easier for us and to meet our needs. That's the job of business, not making money. Business, like every part of society, needs money to operate. And, at least in our kind of economy, business is where profit gets generated. But profit, we might say, is just the fuel for a machine that makes us what we need. And if you think the fuel is the main point and not the machine, you've gotten things backward."

While Socrates paused, I returned to my desk. He stayed silent for a while as a way of letting me squirm in my chair and chew over his words. I could see what he was getting at, but I wasn't ready to concede. Maybe Socrates was right. Or maybe he was just very good at debaters' tricks that made me *think* he was right.

3

What Is the "Job" of Business? (continued)

"I gather from that smug look that you think you've won the first hand," I said after thinking about things for a minute.

"I gather from your silence that you do as well," he replied, returning to his chair.

"I'm not so sure. Why don't you spell it out for me? Remember, our bet isn't that you could get me to change my mind. It's that if I really thought about the details of what I said, I'd admit that I didn't truly believe it. I only *thought* I believed it before I analyzed it."

"You're right. That was the bet, and that's what I think I've shown. Actually, this is pretty simple. The key was when you recognized in our discussion of the tribal village that we organize human communities *in order to get what we need to have a decent life*. Then you used the same principle when you organized our bigger, more modern society. The *job* of every element of society— medicine, education, government, business—is to get us what we need in order to have the *kind of life* we want. Business, like government, should be seen as *working for us*—not the other way around."

"But you said it yourself," I objected. "Profits are the fuel that make this possible. No profits, no stuff. According to you, a business that meets some basic material need but can't make a profit and stay afloat is still doing its job. But that's ridiculous! Surely, its first priority is to stay in business. And it can't do that without making money. A business's survival is critical. That's why profits have to be the primary goal. That's why making money is a business's *job*!"

Now Socrates was the one who was quiet.

"Have you ever been scuba diving?" he asked.

I was sure I'd heard him wrong because this had nothing to do with anything we'd been talking about. "Did you just ask me if

I've been scuba diving? I hope that's just some clever way of admitting you've lost this hand."

"Humor me," he said again. I was beginning to get tired of that expression.

"No, I've never been scuba diving. What does that have to do with anything?"

"I saw a T-shirt in a dive shop in the Florida Keys, 'Oxygen is like sex. It's not important until you aren't getting any,'" he smiled. "*Of course* profits are critical for a business. Just like breathing and eating are critical for staying alive. But you're still confusing means and ends. That would be like saying that, as far as your own life goes, your most important responsibility is to eat and breathe."

"Well," I countered, "you're close. The way I see it, my first job as CEO is actually to stay healthy. Why do you think I was at the gym before being ambushed by that reporter? Job 1: stay healthy. I can't run this company properly if I'm not healthy and in good shape. My brain works better. I can push harder. I can do my job better. I think that's true for everyone—which is why we emphasize health and fitness so much here. And speaking of fitness," I pointed back at Socrates and his, shall we say, somewhat-less-than-buff physique.

"I know," he said apologetically. "I get the point."

"It's the same with a business. Job 1 is to make money. Everything else comes second."

"What about a food company that's very profitable, but is regularly getting warned and fined for unhealthy practices? The fines are manageable—only a percentage of the profits. And they're less than the cost of making the production process healthier and safer. Is it doing its job?"

"But you aren't looking at the bigger picture," I countered. "As long as everyone knows what's going on, that company will eventually go down. 'The market' will make sure it goes out of business. Customers will stay away. Its stock price will slide."

"The company will go under?" he mused. "Maybe yes; maybe no. The market doesn't really worry about whether a business is *doing its job*, the way we understand it. The market looks at whether it can make money. And we both know plenty of companies that can make money but, strictly speaking, *not* provide much in the way of what we need for a decent life."

I sat for a moment and thought. "I think we're at a stalemate. I honestly wouldn't think this food company you mention is doing its job. We take a lot of pride here in providing services that make people's lives better. So I can't support any company which compromises that for the bottom line. Look at our mission statement. We mean what we say there. We're here to make a difference. And it's true, as you pointed out, that I think the reason behind how we organize things in society is to give us the kind of life we want. So, in a sense, I *do* think the job of business is to meet our needs in some way. *However*," I put my hand up to keep from being interrupted, "I don't think you can separate that from the need to make the money that lets a business do that. I still think this is the job of business. But I'm willing to concede that meeting our needs is also the job of business—and that I've always believed that even if I didn't say that in so many words."

"*I* knew you believed it all along," Socrates said, nodding. "That's what brought you to my attention in the first place. I *knew* you didn't really believe that business was *only* about making money. However, that's not how you've been making decisions lately—which is also what brought you to my attention. So, where does that leave us?"

"To be honest, I don't feel as though I've won the hand. I've been so focused on the company's financial problems over the last few months that, frankly, I *have* been running the company as though all that counts is profit. I ignored the rest of our mission statement. I ignored my gut feeling that I wasn't paying attention to something important. However, I don't feel as though I've lost the hand either. If anything, this latest crisis has reminded me just how important it is for us to be making money, to be financially healthy— to be able to hit a rough patch and have the resources to make it through. I don't want us to be one of those companies that crumbles overnight because they're leveraged to the hilt."

"Fair enough," said Socrates, "I said you'd be the judge, and I'm a man of my word. So, no winners at this point. And I appreciate your honesty about admitting what you've been overlooking. You and I really aren't that far apart. After all, your company is providing jobs for thousands of people. You make it possible for people to earn a living, have a home, buy food, raise their children, and the like. You're certainly providing for the basic needs of many people in a direct way. And you couldn't be doing that if you weren't making money. Besides, I'm less concerned about winning a bet than about helping you see things more broadly than you have been lately. So we'll call this hand a draw. *However, . . .* "

Everyone on my staff knows that I hate sentences which include *but* or *however* because 90% of the time they're "good news/bad news" sentences and someone's using the former to soften the blow: "We just announced our best quarter ever, *but* there's someone from the SEC who'd like to see you." So I suspected that Socrates was about to try to put something over on me. The expression on my face apparently told him this.

"For a gambler, you're easy to read," he observed. "I sure hope you don't play poker. I bet you think I'm up to something that will trick you into conceding the first hand."

"As a matter of fact," I replied, "that's exactly what I think you're doing. I also suspect you're trying to make me forget your promise that we'd get back to my point about individual rights."

Again with the notebook. "*Suspicious beyond belief. MAJOR trust issues,*" Socrates muttered, jotting the words down with a sigh. Then, looking up with a steely glare, he said, "I'm going to say this only once. *If I say something, I mean it. I don't play games.* If you can't operate that way, I've overestimated you, and we're done here."

He paused while I looked down at my desk and shifted uncomfortably in my seat. He'd made his point, and he was gentleman enough not to force me to embarrass myself by replying. After a few seconds' pause, he continued, "As I started to say, *however*, we need to look at your concern about individual rights before we go any further so that it's not a sticking point."

I felt appropriately chastened that I'd accused Socrates of breaking a promise just as he was about to keep it.

"OK," he said, waving his hand in the air. "I've read all of your recent speeches. I know this matters to you. But, I think you've lost perspective, which is why we need to talk about this. Make your case."

I got back up, walked over to the whiteboard and gestured at what was there. "If we had a primitive society, I'd be OK with all of this. But a modern, complex society gives us the opportunity to expand our definition of the 'kind of life' we're aiming at so that individuals get to have greater freedom. The overall 'job' of a modern village includes maximizing the rights and freedom of each villager. That's progress. I see it as one of the signs of the evolution and growth of our village. We now have technology and infrastructure that make us less dependent on each other. This means that, as *individuals*, we can spread our wings and take more control over our lives. We get to take advantage of the opportunities economic and technological progress allow us. You were right when you said that the *job* of every element of society is to get us what we need in order to have the *kind of life* we want. Business, like government, should be seen as *working for us*—not the other way around. But, in my opinion, 'working for us' means working to advance the freedom and rights of the *individual*.

"And I'd expect you to be the *last* person to have any objection to this," I said with no amount of surprise in my voice. "As a venture capitalist, you exercise your freedom every day. You take risks, and you get the appropriate rewards for your choices. You've become wealthy through your actions as an individual. You're entitled to enjoy that success. And speaking specifically about the 'job of business,' you're living embodiment of the idea that a big part of the job of business is to provide individuals with the opportunities to use our talents *as we choose* so we get to have the kind of life we want. I think a huge part of the 'job of business' in a modern society is to give us the opportunity to support ourselves and fashion our own lives *as we choose*."

Socrates listened seriously as I spoke. I sat back down opposite him and waited for his answer.

"I appreciate your perspective, and I don't want you to think that I don't take this seriously. You're correct. I'm successful because I made my own decisions, took risks and have been rewarded for that. But, frankly, I came here to talk to you primarily about how you're running your company, not the relationship between the individual and the community. Still, I respect your passion on this matter, so you're entitled to a response. It's not going to be as full as you'd like, but it's all I want to do for now. We can talk about this more later. But for now, let me just suggest a different way to think about things that may at some point let you see things differently. All I ask is that you consider this perspective sometime in the future."

"That seems fair."

"For a VC, I read pretty widely—just for fun. My particular favorites these days include books about the stained glass in medieval cathedrals, Spanish cooking, Harry Potter, anything to do with Sherlock Holmes, and philosophy. What can I say? I'm successful enough that I don't care if my friends call me eccentric. A number of years ago, I bought a used copy of John Rawls' *A Theory of Justice*. To be perfectly honest, what caught my eye was the green cover. I recognized Rawls' name as a Harvard philosopher from when I lived in Cambridge. And I picked up the book because I knew it had created quite a stir when it came out. In any event, Rawls has this idea he calls 'the veil of ignorance.' I've made it into an exercise I do as a check on my own decisions. For me this is a simple way to determine whether something is *fair* or *reasonable*."

"But you said Rawls is talking about a philosophical theory of justice," I interrupted. "What does that have to do with business?"

"It's not so much Rawls's theory of justice but how I use the 'veil of ignorance' as a general standard for fairness or reasonableness. I'm going to oversimplify this like crazy, but for our purposes, it's a thought experiment that goes like this.

"Imagine we're going to create a society. We know there will be differences in wealth, privilege, abilities, talents, and the like. There will be differences that come from how effectively people use their individual freedom. But none of us knows what we're going to be like or where we end up in the society. We don't know whether we'll be rich, poor, smart, stupid, healthy, infirm, or the like. We're completely *ignorant* of anything to do with our future. At the same time, we all get to *agree* ahead of time about whether there will be any limitations or restrictions on the differences. We get to draw up a *contract* that will govern the differences. As a champion of individual freedom, you should recognize that what makes this such a good exercise is that it's all about identifying what we'd *freely agree to*."

"OK, I'm with you so far."

"So let's talk just about wealth," Socrates continued, "but think of it as a metaphor for any of the benefits you get from individuals exercising their freedom. After all, you and I might aspire to wealth, but other people will want to use their freedom to achieve something else. At the same time, we need to be realistic and recognize that some people will be in situations that determine that no matter how much they try to exercise their freedom, it's not going to make much difference in their lives."

"I'm not sure I agree with that last bit. Apparently, I have more confidence in what people can do with their lives than you do."

Socrates crooked an eyebrow. "Duly noted. But remember, I'm not debating you on this. I'm just trying to give you a different perspective. . . . So, if you knew you were going to be remarkably talented and wealthy in this society, what would your attitude about wealth be?"

"That's easy," I answered. "There should be no limits. And everyone is responsible for earning what they need."

"But what if you knew you were going to be stupid and poor. Would you agree to this?"

"Of course not. I'd want something that protected my interests better."

"Precisely. Like what?"

"Nothing less than that the wealth gets distributed equally or at least a major portion goes to alleviate poverty."

"Makes sense. *Now* assume you don't have a clue how you're going to end up. You're trying to cut the best deal for yourself from behind a *veil of ignorance*. What would you be willing to agree to? What kind of a deal would everyone agree to? *Not knowing how things would turn out*, what would every rational, self-interested individual agree to ahead of time?"

"That's easy," I explained. "I negotiate deals like that all the time. You want to minimize the downside (if all of the unpredictable factors go against you) while still leaving room for a good profit (if the unpredictables break your way). So I'd want some linkage between the ceiling and the floor."

"Keep going," Socrates encouraged.

I thought for a minute and then beamed.

"Someone's certainly pleased with themselves," he chuckled. "This better be good, or the fact that you can impress yourself so easily will be embarrassing."

"Let me put it this way," I continued, ignoring the taunt. "To cover my 'worst case scenario,' any 'rising tide' would have to 'float all boats.'"

"And you'd agree to that ahead of time and then take your chances?"

"Yes," I answered thoughtfully. "It would be a rational, prudent deal. If I ended up with lots of talent, I could get rewarded by using it. But if I was the village idiot, I'd be protected from disaster. Given the conditions you lay down, that strikes me as a reasonable and fair agreement."

"Not bad," he said, as I got up to refresh my coffee. "You're not all that far from Rawls. One of his most basic ideas is that any social and economic inequalities need to work to *everyone's* advantage."

"Right. That's what I said. A rising tide has to float all boats. But wait," I continued, "what does that have to do with the 'job' of business and fostering individual freedom?"

"Just this—the veil of ignorance forces you to remove everything that could cause you to tilt the contract you're negotiating one way or another. You have to be completely objective and rational. You have to cover all possibilities. So, logically, you can't promote any particular *interest*. You can't have a *conflict of interest*.

"The problem with everything you've been saying is that you don't even realize how much lack of objectivity you bring to the table. Consciously and unconsciously, your ideas about the job of business and the importance of the individual are shaped by what will protect what you have. You're rationalizing to protect your assets."

I didn't appreciate Socrates dismissing my ideas as rationalizations. But I understood what he was referring to because I'd overheard too many comments about how something about my being a woman was supposed to make me less qualified for a promotion than the men being considered. "She'll want to have children. She won't be available 24/7. She doesn't really 'fit in' with the current team." It wasn't even that these remarks came from guys who, in their hearts, believed that women are inferior. They were uncomfortable because I was 'different.' And they found a way to tell themselves their opinions were really logical and business-related.

"However," he continued, "when we use something like the 'veil of ignorance,' we're trying to neutralize any conflicts of interest. When we get to the end of such a process, when we decide what we'd ultimately *agree* to, the result is *fair*. For me, this is equivalent to a combination of 'worst case analysis' and 'fair dealing.' To use your language, what would I agree to if I assume that the unpredictable factors go against me?"

"OK, that seems reasonable enough. But how does that apply to what we're talking about?"

"You'll see," Socrates winked. "First, the 'job of business.' Then, individual rights."

He settled into his chair in a way that said this would not be a short explanation.

"So, think about what you'd *agree* to as the 'rules of the game' or 'terms of the deal' of any 'business' in our society. Let's go back to our mediocre hospital that makes money."

"Right, our *it does its job as a business but doesn't do its job as a hospital* example."

"Well, that *was* your view," Socrates noted. "Let's see if you stick to your guns. I say that the only reason you came to the *bad hospital but good business* conclusion is that as a CEO, you're too close to things to be objective. But step behind the veil of ignorance and imagine you're a patient who may end up paying for services at that hospital. When you check in, you're given a copy of the 'terms of the deal.' They include this one: 'I recognize that in order for the hospital to turn a profit, it may be necessary for me to receive substandard medical treatment.' Would you sign on the dotted line?"

"Of course not. That could be suicide."

"Would *anyone* sign?"

"Not if they had their wits about them."

"OK, that's an extreme example, but I think it shows where I'm going with this. I say that no matter what kind of business we imagine, no rational person would ever agree to 'terms of the deal' that didn't promise some specific benefit that he or she wanted. No rational person would agree that profit could ever be more important than the good or service that the business is supposed to deliver. Anyone who made such a deal would be a fool."

"So you're calling me a fool for saying the bad hospital is a good business?" I asked, making my annoyance clear.

"No, I'm diplomatically saying that as a wealthy CEO, your perspective is clouded by a variety of factors that make you unable to see this objectively," he explained carefully. "As I said before, I'm not looking to replay this hand or to badger you into changing your mind. All I want is for you to consider this way of looking at things. I say that if we're behind the veil of ignorance and we need to come up with the rules by which business will operate, we'd say that the 'job' of business is to deliver goods and services. Profit is important, but it's only the means to that end. So, bad hospital, bad business."

I wanted to continue the discussion, but Socrates put up his hand. "Let's move on to protecting individual rights in the village. Obviously, making individual freedom sacrosanct can benefit some in the village at other people's expense like when weak banking regulations allow reckless wheeling and dealing that torpedoed the economy or when liberal gun laws let some unstable individual massacre school kids. So, step behind the 'veil of ignorance.' As a rational, self-interested person who didn't know where you'd end up in our village, what would you be willing to freely agree to as a reasonable and fair standard about individual freedom? Take a minute and think about it."

It wasn't difficult for me to imagine best and worst case scenarios. I was very successful at my job, but I'd had a bout with cancer. I also had a daughter. Seeing that I was taking his request seriously, Socrates busied himself with his smartphone.

"Done," I said to get his attention, prepared to announce my conclusion. "People can do whatever they want as long as it doesn't directly or indirectly hurt anyone else in the village. Actions have consequences. I want to be able to enjoy the good consequences of my actions yet be protected from the bad consequences of somebody else's actions."

"Excellent. You're giving us something close to a restatement of the line attributed to Supreme Court Justice Oliver Wendell Holmes, 'The right to swing my fist ends where the nose of the other man begins.' This is at least a general principle we can both agree on. Of course, part of the problem in applying that to real life is how differently people can define 'harm.' For example, some people think that pornography is harmful, while others think that limiting the freedom to make and buy it is harmful. But your principle at least tells us that we've identified a reasonable principle for determining how much individual freedom people are entitled to on the other side of the 'veil of ignorance.' "

Then Socrates eyed me knowingly. "*However*, I know that, as a gambler, you're imagining that you're so smart and talented you wouldn't need a lot of protection from other people's actions. So you could legitimately rationalize a very expansive stance on individual rights."

"I didn't realize I was that transparent," I confessed.

"I've done my homework which is why, when you were thinking, I prepared a little object lesson."

He handed me his phone. It displayed the current balance in one of my bank accounts . . . only most of my money was missing! I was stunned and furious.

"You've hacked my account and emptied it? My balance is *three dollars*! Are you crazy? You casually sat there and stole $80,000 dollars for fun?"

"As I said, it's an object lesson. Let's call it an example of how 'there's always a bigger fish.' We all need protection from people who abuse their freedom. No one's bulletproof.

"One of the things that always strikes me about people—like you—who talk about 'getting government off our backs and out of the way so that individuals and businesses can do what we want'—is how naive you are about real-world risks. We'll set aside for a moment the fact that no one minds when government helps out in times of disaster—natural or economic. The problem is that you romanticize what it would be like if we left absolutely as much as possible to individuals and took a very aggressive position on individual rights. You forget that for many people, they exercise their freedom by giving up any scruples.

"As I just showed you, in real life, there's always a bigger fish. People deserve protection against that. In my experience, Hobbes knew what he was talking about when he suggested that, left to our own devices, we'd be in 'a war of all against all' and that life would end up 'solitary, poor, nasty, brutish and short.' "

He took his phone back from me, made a few taps and looked up. "There. The money's back. I'm sure I got your attention enough to guarantee that you'll think about what I've been saying.

"So, our first hand came to a draw. And that's fine with me, because the next hand is the one I'm really here for."

"What do you mean?"

"However we may debate about 'the job of business,' I am *positive* you don't truly believe what you said about not doing anything wrong in the way your company's been operating. You said that only because you didn't really *think* about what you were saying."

4

Has the CEO Done Anything "Wrong"?

Here we go again with the "I didn't really mean what I know I meant" nonsense. I could put up with that when we debated the "job" of business. That just seemed like an academic discussion. This felt personal.

"I know this is part of our bet," I said, my voice starting to rise, "and I'm willing to play this hand. But I want you to know I resent what you're suggesting. You apparently think I've been doing things I *know* are wrong and that I lied to that reporter when I denied doing anything wrong."

Socrates gave me a disappointed look. "You know, you really need to listen better. I'm not accusing you of knowingly acting unethically or being a criminal. I'm sure that, in your heart, you feel like you're a good and decent person. I'm sure you believed what you said to that reporter. But from everything I've been able to learn about you before approaching you earlier today, I know that if you stop and look at things objectively and dispassionately, you'll agree with me that some of what you've been doing was *wrong*. Look at our last discussion. In the end, you admitted that your 'gut' told you that you were ignoring some important things."

"Right," I countered, "but on this, my 'gut' is fine. We didn't break any laws. We didn't lie, cheat, or steal. My conscience is clear. And I resent the fact that you're accusing me of being a bad person."

"This has nothing to do with 'being a bad person,' " Socrates countered with some exasperation. "You still aren't listening. Do you think it's impossible for good people to do things that are wrong? Or for good people to make errors of judgment? Forgive me for being blunt, but your problem is that you really don't know the first thing about what makes something *wrong*."

I was so insulted I wanted to throw this guy out of my office. But a bet was a bet. So I settled for a frustrated, "Wait a minute! I'll have you know that I got an A in my business ethics course in my MBA program, so . . . "

"*Please!*" he interrupted as he got up to get himself another cup of tea, waving his hand dismissively at me, "Spare me the litany of dead white guys—Plato, Mill, Kant, and the gang. I'm sure you were an excellent student. But if you want to talk about right and wrong from that perspective, you're going to overthink things."

"What do you mean *overthink*? You want to talk about *ethics*, don't you? Utilitarianism? The categorical imperative? Virtue ethics? Philosophers from A to Z?"

"*Not in the least!*" he replied, to my surprise. "Remember that 'Socrates' is just a nickname. I'm a businessman. I look at things from a commonsense, practical point of view."

"Now I'm really confused. We didn't break laws, lie, cheat, or steal. What's a more commonsense point of view than *that* for deciding what's wrong?"

"Well," he replied, pointing his finger at me again as he sat back down, "how about the way you talked about things when you were running our tribal village?"

"What do you mean? I didn't say anything about right and wrong. All I did was to explain how I'd make sure we got everything we needed efficiently—food, shelter, medical attention."

"But this is *exactly* what I'm trying to get you to see in this entire conversation," he said with a smile. "You *think* that's all you were talking about. But you were actually talking about a whole lot more. You were talking about a fundamental standard of right and wrong."

"I don't have a clue about what you mean. I remember what I said. And I didn't say *anything* about right and wrong."

"Let's go back to the beginning," Socrates said with a deep sigh. "Remind me why you arranged things as you did in our tribal village."

I saw no reason to retrace out steps. "It's what I just said. I arranged things so they'd be efficient. But we covered all of that," I shot back impatiently.

Socrates paused to give me a look that said *Suck it up and do as I've asked*. "No," he countered, "you did more than that."

"What do you mean?"

Walking back to the whiteboard, he pointed at his list. "You said you were arranging things 'so we'd be able to get what we need *in order to have a better life*.' Remember?"

"Sure. But that's the same thing. It's . . . "

"And then later," he interrupted, pointing again to his list, "when you organized our bigger, modern society—when I asked you to give me your most practical explanation for why the critical jobs need to be done—you said part of the reason was so 'we get *the kind of life* we want.' "

"OK, so what? I wasn't talking about ethics when I said *kind of life*."

"Yes, you were," Socrates said, cutting me off again. "You just didn't realize it. It's what I said. You're overthinking this."

"I still don't know what you mean." I felt increasingly frustrated and didn't mind showing it.

"Go back to the beginning," he replied patiently. "Tell me what you meant when you said you wanted to arrange things so you'd have a certain *kind of life* in the village. *Which* kind of life?"

I had no idea how to reply.

"Keep it simple and practical," he encouraged. "You're in charge of the village. Tell me how you're arranging things."

I took a deep breath and thought for a moment. "OK, first, I'm making sure that people are in the right jobs so the tribe's critical needs are met: food, shelter, medicine, education."

"Good. And are there any problems connected with assigning everyone their jobs?"

"What do you mean?"

"Think about when you do the same thing in your company. Is everybody always happy with the assignments you give them?"

"No, not always . . . at least not at first."

"What do you mean 'not at first'?"

"Well, I'm a *manager*, not a dictator. If someone isn't happy about an assignment I want them to take on, we talk. We listen to each other. We see what the issues are. We see if we can work things out. Usually, we can."

"Very good," Socrates nodded. "And if you can't? If they don't want the assignment?"

"Then we work something else out, of course."

"You don't try to get your way—and have people do what you think is best for the company—by leaning on them? By suggesting it will hurt their careers if they don't do as you ask? Or by threatening to fire them?"

"Of course not," I replied, feeling insulted. "That's not the way we do things here. We're not that kind of company."

"Not *which* kind of company? Which kind of company *are* you?"

"A good one to work for," I said with pride. "We don't push people around. We treat one another with respect. We do win-win here."

"Excellent!" beamed Socrates.

"I don't know what all the excitement is about," I said, puzzled. "It's just good management. I use a commonsense approach. I treat people the way I want to be treated."

"Exactly!" said Socrates, smiling again. "Now, go back to the village."

"Fine," I said, amused—but still mystified—by Socrates' obvious delight. "We're back in the village."

"Now answer what I asked you before. Which kind of village is it? Which *kind of life* do people experience there? Give me your simplest, most practical description about how people treat each other."

"Simple and practical is easy. We treat each other with respect. We don't hurt each other. And we help one another."

"Great!" said Socrates, beaming again.

"OK, I appreciate enthusiasm. But you really have me puzzled."

He turned to the whiteboard again. "It's not rocket science. The *kind* of life you want in the village is one that's safe, comfortable, and one in which people treat each other properly. You actually started getting into this during our last hand without realizing it when you said the kind of life you were looking for in the village was 'fair,' " he said, pointing it out. "And look at what you just said: 'respect,' 'treating people the way you'd want to be treated.' " He added these to the board.

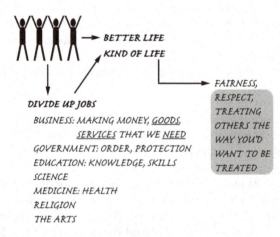

"So, if we expand what you're talking about into something like 'principles to respect when you live in the village,' how do 'do no harm' and 'treat others appropriately' sound?"

"I wouldn't have any problems with that. But so what?"

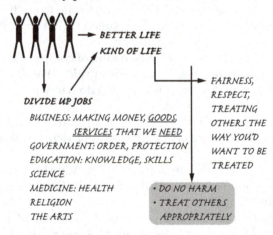

"So *what*?" He nearly shouted into the whiteboard as he wrote down our "principles." "That's what *ethics* is! Principles to live by. If one member of our tribe hurt another member, you'd say it was *wrong*, wouldn't you?"

"Absolutely."

"And if one member treated another unfairly? Also wrong?"

"Of course."

"So there you have it," he continued, as he drew more on the whiteboard. "As I said, your idea about *what kind of life* we want to have in the village gives us a basic *ethical yardstick*, if you will—a yardstick that we can use to measure our actions and determine whether they're right or wrong.

"Think of one side of the yardstick as being marked off in a way that tells us whether we're *doing any harm*: physical harm, emotional harm, short-term harm, long-term harm, harm that can be repaired, harm that can't, and so on. Think of the other side of the yardstick as being measured off in a way that tells us whether or not we're *treating people appropriately*: fairness, equality, honesty, keeping promises, helping people when they need it, and the like."

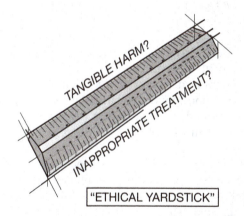

"ETHICAL YARDSTICK"

"So that's all that right and wrong is about for you?" I asked. "*Do no harm* and *treat others appropriately*?"

"I honestly don't see why it has to be more complicated than that."

"Well, in that case, you'd better get ready to pay up," I said triumphantly. "As I said before, I didn't break any laws, lie, cheat, or steal. I didn't do anything *wrong*."

Socrates smiled and then laughed good naturedly. "You really didn't think it was going to be that easy, did you?"

"What do you mean?" I asked, suspecting that he was going to try to weasel his way out. "Those are *your* principles—*do no harm, treat others appropriately*. And I'm fine with them. So, according to *your* ethical yardstick, I didn't do anything wrong."

"Look," he said patiently, sitting back down in front of me, "I'm sure you're being sincere. I'm sure that right now, at least, you truly believe in your heart you did nothing wrong. But you aren't seeing everything that's involved. You're looking at only part of the picture—which is, by the way, one of the reasons your company is in the fix it's in."

"Only *part* of the picture? What do you mean?"

"For one thing," he said pointedly, "if we're talking about whether you did anything *wrong*, you know as well as I do that the fact that you didn't break any laws is irrelevant."

"OK," I conceded. "Ethics 101. *Legal* and *ethical* aren't the same thing. Not every illegal action is unethical; not every unethical action is illegal." My brain was obviously getting muddled because I was so tired. So I got up and started walking around the office.

"Thank you," Socrates said graciously. "I really didn't want to waste our time on that one.

"Of course, that's not to say that whether something's legal or illegal is *irrelevant* to being right or wrong. If something's illegal, it may tell us that an action could hurt someone or treat people inappropriately. If so, it's information we can use in deciding whether what we're doing is *ethically* acceptable. In the same way, if an action is legal, it may tell us something about what counts as *appropriate* treatment toward one another—what kind of actions people are entitled to do—and, therefore, which actions it would be *wrong* for us to interfere with."

"Fine," I conceded. "No more playing the 'I didn't break any laws' card. But I still didn't lie, cheat, or steal."

"You know," he paused, "you say 'lie, cheat, and steal' as though that's all you have to worry about. Lying, cheating, and stealing may all be wrong, but there are plenty of unethical actions that *aren't* lying, cheating, or stealing. There are *other ways* to hurt people or treat them inappropriately than lying, cheating, or stealing."

He stopped for a moment. The way he looked at me felt like he was up to something. He was trying to set me up to make sure I'd lose the hand.

"How about if we start with something small—but very close to home." His tone got more serious. "Then we'll work up to the *bigger* problems."

Now I *knew* he was trying to set me up. I focused to make sure I wouldn't let down my guard. "OK, let's hear it."

He got up out of his chair, paced a bit while he thought and then turned to me. "Let's start with promises. Is it wrong to break a promise?"

"Where are you going with this?" I asked cautiously as I walked over to the window and looked out. I wanted to get a sense of what he was up to.

"You're getting suspicious, which is not a good element to add here. Right now, I just want to see what you and I agree on when we say *treat others appropriately*. Do we want members of the village to keep their promises to one another? As the tribal leader, will you consider it a serious matter if you hear that people are breaking agreements?"

"Certainly we want people to keep their word. At the same time, sometimes things happen that make it impossible to keep a promise. Or sometimes circumstances change in a way that taking care of something that's more important leads to our breaking a promise."

"Agreed. But as a general rule?"

"As a general rule? It's wrong to break a promise."

Socrates got up and added "keep promises" to the whiteboard.

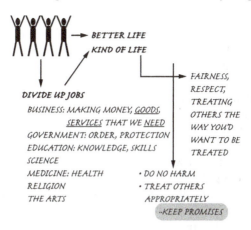

"And to keep things simple," he continued, "can we say that promises, and contracts and agreements are all essentially the same thing?"

"Well, contracts are legal documents that usually contain some penalty for not fulfilling them—however, I agreed to de-emphasize the legal side of things. So, yes, promises, and contracts and agreements are all basically the same—we commit to act in a particular way."

"Excellent. Now tell me what *you* have *promised* the company?"

"Me? What have I promised the company? Let's see. I have a contract with the board, but since we aren't going to focus on legal things, I take it you're referring to something else?"

"Not 'something else' as much as 'something more.' I'm sure that in addition to the specifics in your contract, you have some broad sense of what you've agreed to accomplish when you do your job. The mutual expectation between you, the board, the shareholders, employees, and the like. The tasks everybody figured you could do better than all the other candidates they passed over for the job. Just start ticking off the goals and priorities you have in mind when you make decisions."

"As I said before, I worry *first* about keeping the company profitable and afloat."

"Why? For whose benefit?"

"Isn't it obvious?" I was disappointed Socrates was wasting our time with something so self-evident. "For the benefit of everyone who has a stake in the outcome, of course—shareholders, employees, customers, our vendors." Taking a marker, I added these people to our list myself.

> • *DO NO HARM*
> • *TREAT OTHERS*
>   *APPROPRIATELY*
>   ··*KEEP PROMISES*
>   shareholders
>   employees
>   customers
>   vendors

"In fact," I continued, "the very first line in our mission statement says that 'our chief goal is to serve our clients and stakeholders.'"

"Good," he said approvingly, "But that encompasses lots of people. Does any *one* group count more than the others?"

"You aren't going to like my answer, because this takes us back to the world of law. But since we're a corporation, the *owners*—our shareholders—have to count more than anyone else."

"Shareholders," he repeated. "Why do they deserve such a special place?"

"First, because they own the business. So their 'piece of the action' should come off the top."

"It's true that, technically, they *'own'* the business," he answered, "but let's split hairs here. They own stock. So they may be 'owners' for no more than an afternoon. And if the company goes belly up, they go to the end of the line. . . . By contrast, if I owned a shop that went out of business, as the owner, I'd still have rights to any remaining assets. It's not exactly the same sort of ownership."

"True," I conceded. "But still, the shareholders invest in the company and get no guarantees. And because they'd end up at the end of the line, they're taking the biggest risk. So they deserve the biggest reward."

"Understood," he nodded, as he noted this on the whiteboard. "So no one else goes in that first tier? Just shareholders?"

> • *DO NO HARM*
> • *TREAT OTHERS APPROPRIATELY*
>   ··*KEEP PROMISES*
>   1. *shareholders. biggest risk=biggest reward*
>   *employees*
>   *customers*
>   *vendors*

"I assume you want me to say bondholders," I answered, "but they have more legal standing than shareholders. So I don't put them at the top."

"What about employees?" Socrates asked, choosing to ignore what I'd just said. "Where do they stand?"

"Obviously, I consider them to be important, but they get paid. So they're not up there with shareholders."

"And you consider their salary to be a good return on their investment?"

"What do you mean—'their investment'?" I replied. "We *do* encourage employees to buy stock. And any who do will be in the top tier *as shareholders*. But, otherwise, they're farther down the list. So I don't know what you're getting at."

"I'm getting at the fact that your employees invest something more valuable than what your shareholders invest."

"More valuable than *money*?" I asked, puzzled.

"*Much* more," he replied earnestly. "Look at it this way. Let's say you invest $50,000 in a company and you lose it. What are you going to do?"

"The first thing I'll do is to fire my broker who recommended the stock," I said with a laugh.

"Right, me too," he added with a smile. "But then?"

"Then I'd try to find an investment that would let me make it back."

"So if things go well, you'll replace what you lost. You'll end up back where you were."

"Right. I'm not ahead. But I'm not behind. I'm even."

"Good. Now consider the situation of an employee who's worked for you for 15 years. The company goes under, or maybe you just decide to downsize and eliminate his job. He's out of work. He's 55. Let's be candid about his future. He's screwed. He's not going to get another decent job. Now he's really regretting that he decided to work for you, rather than for your very successful competitor. What about him?"

"Well, first, I hope that 10 years ago he had the good sense of talking to a financial planner about how to prepare for something like this."

"Why?"

"I'm surprised you'd even ask that? He was taking a risk. No one guaranteed him the company would survive. We didn't promise long-term employment—not even if he was doing a great job. We're an at-will employer. There are lots of scenarios where he could have ended up without a job."

"I understand," nodded Socrates. "He had no guarantees. He was taking a risk—with his *time*, with his *life*. He invested his time and talents in your company."

"Right, for which he was *paid*—and *generously*, I might add. We pride ourselves in paying above market rates to attract the best people."

"That may be, but you're missing the point. You're ignoring his incredibly steep 'opportunity cost.' When you lose money on an investment, you have the possibility of replacing it. When it turns out your employee made a bad bet by working for you, it's *absolutely impossible* for him to get the *time* back."

"Right, and that's unfortunate. But that's life. We can't do time travel," I quipped. "I can't change the laws of physics."

"No, you can't. But you *can* recognize and appreciate the fact that he's invested something more valuable than money."

"And if I do, what does that mean? What are you asking me to do?"

"Right now, all I'm asking is that you recognize and appreciate the fact that shareholders aren't your only 'high risk' investors. Employees have invested and risked the most important thing any of us possesses—the irreplaceable days of our lives. So when it comes to who's in that first tier of the people to whom you owe the most in the *promise* you're making, I think employees need to be there as well. And I believe you need to think about how to recognize that on a practical level.

"Of course," he continued, as he started writing more on the whiteboard, "maybe I have it wrong," his words thick with irony. "You did say you paid people *generously*. If, *like you*, your employees make enough to be *independently wealthy* after a year or two, they can go to the end of the line."

"Very funny," I countered, not at all comfortable with his tone as he started talking about my salary. "Let's say I take your addition to my promise 'under advisement,' " I said, taking a marker and adding "maybe" to the whiteboard.

> • DO NO HARM
> • TREAT OTHERS APPROPRIATELY
> ⋯KEEP PROMISES
> 　　1. shareholders. biggest risk=biggest reward
> 　　1. employees. even bigger risk MAYBE
> 　　customers
> 　　vendors

When I turned back around I could see Socrates looking at some numbers in his notebook. I had a feeling that he was laying a trap for me.

5

Has the CEO Done Anything "Wrong"? (continued)

We both sat back down. "Let's go back to your promise. Tell me again what you *promise* to do here as CEO."

"That's simple. I promise to manage the company in a way that will make as much money as possible. That's why I worry so much about the bottom line."

"And where do *you* fit into all of this?"

"What do you mean?"

"What about *your* interests? How much do they factor into your decisions?"

"I'd like to keep this job," I laughed. "So if the company's not profitable, that won't exactly help me. The more money the company makes, the more likely it is I'll stay on. Of course, since we believe in 'pay for performance' around here, part of my compensation is linked to the price of our stock. So I have direct incentive to promote the interests of our shareholders. But otherwise, as I regularly tell everyone, I'm an employee, just like everyone else. And we all have basically the same job. To make life better for other people—our investors and our customers. And when we do that, we'll make life better for ourselves as well."

"So, if we take all of that as your *promise*, how are you doing? How well are you keeping your word?"

"Well, like everyone else in this industry, we've had some rough times. But we got through it better than most. For one thing, we're still standing, while some giants in our industry fell. And our stock price took a hit for a while. But I took some aggressive actions—I had to let some people go, and I moved some operations offshore—and things started turning around. Except for our most recent problems, I think I'm doing a good job of keeping my promise."

"But you said you had to lay off some people and send some other jobs offshore," he observed. "I don't imagine *those* employees felt that you were keeping your word with them."

"Nobody was happy we had to do this, especially me. But the bottom line took priority. There were professionals on another part of the planet who had the right talents and experience—but who'd work for a lot less. I felt it was my duty to the shareholders to take advantage of that, even if it meant some employees here lost jobs."

"So that's the way your company runs? Whenever you find a reasonable way to cut costs, you do it?"

"Well, that's certainly the way that I *try* to run it."

"Really?" he said, glaring. "You can say that with a straight face?"

Once again, I wasn't happy with the turn the conversation was taking. "Look," I explained, "I know what you're getting at. You're going to say how much the employees needed their jobs, and how hard it would be for them to find work in a down economy, and how they'd get hurt more than the shareholders got helped."

"That's not . . . " he started to say.

"But I really had no options. . . . "

"That's not what I was . . . ," he tried again.

". . . it was a strategy of last resort," I finished.

"*That's. Not. What. I. Was. Getting. At,*" he said firmly, finally getting the whole sentence out.

"It's not?" I asked, surprised. "This isn't about the layoffs and offshore move?"

"No, not really. But it is connected with your *logic* behind the offshore move."

"What do you mean?"

He opened his small notebook. "Let's see," he said flipping through some pages, "last year you earned $20 million. $5 million of that was salary and the rest was bonus and stock."

"Right. Most of what I received was tied to how well I did my job. 'Pay for performance.' Remember?"

"And last year," he continued without looking up, "your British counterpart earned approximately $8 million. About $2 million in salary and the rest in bonus. So you made almost three times more than he did."

"OK," I noted.

"And both operations made about the same amount of money," said Socrates, still ignoring me in favor of his notebook. "But let's expand our perspective, shall we?" He looked up briefly.

"The average CEO of a large company in the United States makes substantially more than the CEO of a large company in the other major industrial countries on the planet.

"In 1965, U.S. CEOs typically made about 24 times that of the average worker in their company. In 1980, it was 40 times more. In 1990, 100 times more; in 2000, 200 times. While the ratio's gotten as high as 500:1, it's currently about 350:1. Historically, the ratio has been lower in the rest of the world. It currently ranges from about 60:1 in Japan to 80:1 in the UK to 145:1 in Germany and Switzerland."

Socrates got back up and added still more to his wall art.

PROMISE: MAKE $ FOR OTHERS

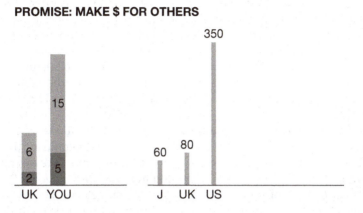

When he finished, he turned and said pointedly, "Pretend for a minute you aren't the CEO, and you're looking at this company from the outside. Why should this company be paying its CEO so much more than its foreign counterparts pay their Chief Executives? Why should it be paying its CEO about 200 to 400 times more than it pays most of its employees?"

Continuing without giving me a chance to answer, he asked, "If this company was *truly* keeping its promise to its shareholders, wouldn't it be paying its CEO—and everyone in the C-suite, for that matter—much less? If nothing else, wouldn't this company go offshore to find a talented CEO who would be happy to work for a more reasonable amount? This company doesn't mind moving 'lower' jobs offshore because it's cheaper. Does the company truly need to pay someone an amount that lets him or her become independently wealthy after only a year or two on the job—and maybe end up fabulously wealthy when they leave or get fired? If an American executive wouldn't agree to run this company for something less, surely there are talented managers in other countries who would. So, as an outside analyst, what do you think?"

I'd heard criticisms of executive compensation before. But, as far as I was concerned, they didn't amount to anything more than "Boo! CEOs make too much money!" I normally wrote it off to some combination of envy, not understanding the responsibilities connected with the position and, more importantly, ignorance about the cost of a very small pool of people who have the necessary talents. It's simple supply and demand. After all, no one forces companies to pay us at that level. It's the board's decision.

But no one had ever brought up the international dimension of the issue to me. A couple of friends of mine who are CEOs of EU companies have commented on it to me over drinks. And my reply has always been, "You are s-o-o-o underpaid! You really need to talk to your boards to get this fixed!"

Socrates was asking me to look at things strictly as an outsider, however. And I've always prided myself at being able to be ruthlessly objective.

"You're awfully quiet," he observed. "I'm sure you're thinking something. Humor me and think out loud."

"OK, I have to admit that *at first glance* you make an interesting point. I just don't think it's as simple as you make it. However, I do sit on some boards. And while there have been discussions about the need to move some functions offshore because of lower costs, I have to admit that there's never been an analogous discussion about the lower offshore cost of executive talent."

"That's not surprising, given who's sitting around the table? Most of your fellow board members are current or former CEOs from U.S. companies. Right?"

"Of course. Given what you need to know in order to exercise oversight of another company, other CEOs are the most qualified people for the job."

"In some ways, yes. In some ways, no," Socrates said. "We can talk about that another time. Right now I'm interested in the *conflict of interest*."

"What conflict of interest? Any potential conflicts are worked out with everyone's legal departments. The boards I'm on all have clear conflict of interest policies. And, as far as I can tell, everyone observes them to the letter. I thought you didn't want to talk about legal issues?"

" '*Limited imagination when it comes to ethics*,' " he said, looking at the ceiling and then writing in his notebook again. "It looks like you forgot we were talking about *ethics*," he reminded me with a hard stare. "This 'hand' is about your claim that you've done nothing *wrong*. Remember? Right now, we're talking about whether you've broken any promises."

"Then I really don't know what you're getting at. My 'promise' for any board I'm on is to make sure the company's being run appropriately—in the financial interest of the shareholders. That's exactly what I do. And I don't have any conflict of interest."

"You're absolutely sure of that?"

"Yes, absolutely. But I take it you see things differently."

" '*Not obtuse (on occasion)*,' " he said smiling, as he jotted in his notebook. "OK, let me help you see the problem. Have you ever been on a board compensation committee?"

"Yes."

"Now I'm sure that everyone around the table goes at this very objectively," he conceded, "but indulge me for a moment. How do you think everyone—you included—would *feel* if someone suggested cutting in half what the company had to pay for a CEO? How would you and everyone else *feel*—not think—if someone suggested bringing in a new CEO from offshore because he or she would do the same job for so much less money?"

"To be completely honest," I admitted, "I'd feel very uneasy about this. One of the first things that would cross my mind is the fear that someone on my board might try the same stunt as a way to push me out."

"Which proves my point," Socrates said. "Your job is to advance the financial interests of *other* people. Any consideration related to *your own* interest is inappropriate. And before you say that you set your own interests aside and are objective, make sure you understand that the whole point of conflict of interest policies is to structure things so that people can't even be *tempted* to choose between two competing masters. Higher CEO compensation helps you. Lower CEO compensation hurts you. You can't deny it. So you have a conflict of interest—as do all of the CEOs around the table. None of you can be as objective about this issue as the people whose interests you're supposed to advance deserve. You may not *intend* to break your promise to promote their interests as much as possible, but I think you *do* break it," he said as he spelled things out on the wall.

PROMISE: MAKE $ FOR OTHERS

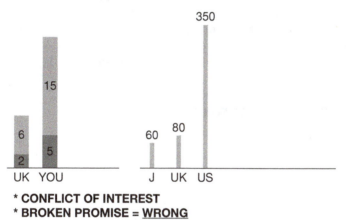

* CONFLICT OF INTEREST
* BROKEN PROMISE = <u>WRONG</u>

Socrates let me sit silently and brood about this for a couple of minutes. It finally dawned on me that the fact that I was debating with myself about this so much told me there was indeed some sort of conflict. If the system were unambiguously structured to make as much money as possible for other people, I wouldn't be thinking twice about how things were done.

"Well, I hate to admit it, but you do bring up some important points. We've never talked about conflict of interest at a compensation committee meeting that way. For the most part, we accept the recommendations of the report from the outside consultant. Everything looks above board and objective. But I'll be the first to admit that when you're doing comparisons—compensation at the board's company versus others—the companies you put into the data pool and those you leave out will affect the outcome. But it's more complicated than that. We need to make sure the CEO feels rewarded and has the right incentives."

"True. And I'm not saying this is the whole story. But does the incentive really have to be getting so much more than that of an offshore CEO in the same industry?"

"I see your point," I admitted grudgingly.

"Meaning what?" he pressed.

"Meaning that at the next compensation committee, I'll bring up your interpretation of conflict of interest and ask everyone what they think."

Socrates pulled out that damned notebook again and started scrawling something, " *'Stubbornly refuses to admit when she's wrong,'* " he said with a frown.

"Wrong about what?" I asked feeling very insulted.

"We're talking about whether you did anything *wrong*, remember?" he said, exasperated. "I don't think you *treated others appropriately*. Put your CEO hat back on. For me, the bottom line of our discussion about your compensation is that you *broke a promise* to truly run the company in other people's interests. You were blind to the *conflict of interest* involved when—against the background of artificially inflated CEO compensation in the U.S.—you, as a CEO, help set the compensation for another CEO. I also think it's *seriously unfair* that you earn 200 to 400 times more than most of the people who work for you—especially when compared to the rest of the world. And I haven't heard anything to make me think otherwise," he said, adding still more to the whiteboard.

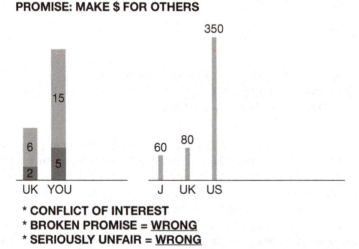

PROMISE: MAKE $ FOR OTHERS

* CONFLICT OF INTEREST
* BROKEN PROMISE = WRONG
* SERIOUSLY UNFAIR = WRONG

"But my salary is set by market forces and negotiation," I pushed back. "The market has apparently decided that U.S. CEOs are worth more. We're probably more productive. The board made me an offer. I accepted. I'm keeping my side of the contract. And fairness cuts both ways. I don't think it would be fair to expect me to work for less than what the market has decided I'm worth."

"Market forces?" he laughed, mocking me. He pointed to my bookcase. "I see you have a copy of Graef Crystal's *In Search of Excess*. So we both know how 'market forces' started to get manipulated in the 1980s by a variety of players to drive up CEO compensation. And more productive?" he scoffed. "Not according to the research I've seen. In one 10-year stretch studied, aggregate compensation paid by public companies for the top five executives grew from less than 5% to more than 10% of aggregate corporate earnings—with no equivalent increase in performance to justify the $350 billion involved. So if all you can do is respond with some disingenuous appeal to 'market forces' and 'productivity,' you're either blind, stupid, arrogant, or pigheaded!" His voice rose as he ticked off his litany of insults.

Clearly angry, Socrates got up, walked over to the window, stared out for a minute and then took a deep breath. Now calm, he turned around.

He pointed at the whiteboard. "We need to go back to the village. Do you recall that as leader you said you'd want to arrange things so we'd have *a decent life* and *the kind of life we want*?"

"Of course."

"And do you remember you agreed that people treating each other fairly and keeping their agreements with each other were part of that?"

"OK, go on."

"So, let's say that the people in the village make you leader with the understanding that you'll try to make sure we get a decent life, you'll look out after everyone, and make sure everything is done fairly."

"Fine."

"Would they think you're keeping your word if you arrange things so that you live in luxury, while they live much more modestly? In fact, some of them even have to struggle to get food and shelter. Would they think it's fair? Look at it from the point of view of an average villager."

It wasn't hard to see where Socrates was going. I was insulted that this was now about how much money I made. I felt this was out of bounds, so it was time to leave this topic behind. "Fine. If I were in their shoes, I wouldn't be happy with things."

"So apply this to your company."

I was annoyed that he kept pushing. "You've made your point. I know what you want me to say. If I were an outsider—like you—I'd probably have some serious reservations about how I (as CEO) have been doing things."

"Just 'serious reservations'?" Socrates asked, an edge again showing in his voice.

"Serious reservations. That's all you're getting at this point," I answered firmly, making it plain the subject was closed. "Move on to another topic."

Socrates paused, deciding how to respond to my resistance.

"You know, you may be able to avoid difficult topics with the people who work for you with that 'serious reservations' crap," he said pointedly. "But when you try to pull it with me," he flipped through his notebook again. "Ah yes," he said as he cast a disapproving glance my way. "Your net worth—dispersed in a variety of legal but interesting investments and locations."

I was stunned. "How did you get that information?" I demanded. "You couldn't have gotten it legally!" I said angrily.

"Maybe yes; maybe no," he said calmly, ignoring my anger. "As I said, I occasionally call in favors. This one was to let me see how scrupulous you are in how you handle your personal wealth. And that's scrupulous from an *ethical* perspective not a *legal* one."

"And what did you find?"

"That while I'm sure you could defend what you do, I doubt that everyone would agree if the details were made public which I, of course, would *never* do. So back to our discussion."

The implied threat was enough to remind me that my partner in this conversation had the power to fire me. I'd agreed to a serious discussion, and he was going to hold me to it. I put my hands up in a sign of surrender. He nodded and continued.

"I say you broke your promise to run this company in the financial interest of other people. You didn't break your legal contract. But, ethically, you broke your promise. You said that those layoffs were 'a strategy of last resort.'"

"And they were," I said, as I started to get up so I could be nose to nose with him on this.

"Right now, you just sit down, listen, and don't interrupt," he said sharply, pointing at my chair. He waited until I complied before continuing.

"You've been CEO for the last five years and have been generously rewarded. You're independently wealthy. You never have to work another day in your life. You may *want* more money, but you don't *need* it.

"The way I see it, under those circumstances, if you were *really* going to keep your promise, you would have done something like decrease your compensation in the last couple of years and made sure that money went to one of your profit centers. *You*, don't forget, are *not* a profit center. Are you telling me that your company couldn't have found a way to turn a profit from an extra few million dollars of capital?

"That's what a real leader would have done. A real leader wouldn't have said, 'I guess we have to get rid of some of the people who could make us some money.' She would have said, 'We have people who aren't making money for us right now, but who can. We've invested in them. Let's put them where they can generate some profit.' And a real leader would have let everyone know that was precisely what she was doing—taking a cut in her own pay to save other people's jobs and to make the company more profitable. Do you have any idea how much loyalty that would have generated? The bottom line here is that if you say your first priority in managing this company is making money for other people, I expect you to act like it." He punctuated his speech by thumping his fist on my desk and looking me straight in the eye.

I wasn't sure how to respond—although that didn't matter because it was clear Socrates wasn't interested in what I had to say. And he wasn't going to tolerate anything that sounded like disagreement. A different side of my visitor had emerged—hard-nosed, a rule breaker, aggressive. If this were baseball, I'd say that I'd just been brushed back with a 100 mph fastball thrown as a warning. If the pitcher wanted, the next one would be in my ear. Socrates' lecture was a stern reminder that the person sitting opposite me controlled 30% of my company's stock, held my future in his hands, and was seriously unhappy with aspects of my performance. I decided to sit quietly for now and see what else was on his mind. I was sure he wasn't finished.

"And one more thing," he said after pausing, "Whether you 'deserve' the money or not, your employees probably resent it. One of the companies that I'm a board member of surveyed its employees about what they thought were the biggest ethical issues at the company. Executive compensation topped the list. Last year, you and your cronies got raises of 30%, while your employees ended up with 2%, if that. Who do you people think you are, sixteenth-century Florentine nobility? Tell me *that* doesn't undercut a CEO's effectiveness as a leader!

"Let me tell you a story you aren't going to like," he continued, apparently set on driving his point home even further. "Every now and then, you remind me of another CEO with whom I had a conversation like the one we're having. I thought he had a lot of promise. So he and I talked, and I tried to give him advice of the same sort I'm giving you. A few months later, he called and said he was giving a talk on ethics to some business students. He wanted me to attend because he was sure I'd be impressed."

"You must have been pleased," I remarked. "It sounds like you got through to him."

"That's what I thought at first. But in the course of his talk, he made a big deal about what he learned as a boy from the fact that his father always gave money back if he got too much change at a store. 'I learned right and wrong from my Dad—that you never accept what isn't yours,' he said. 'I'm proud to say that I've never accepted anything that I didn't work for or that I didn't deserve.' But here's what he *didn't* say. He'd made $35 million the preceding year, which was about three times what other CEOs of similar sized companies in his industry were making. Shareholders were complaining because that was also the first year the company had ever gone into the red. This guy was giving a talk on *ethics* and he didn't have a clue that his own situation was rife with ethical problems. I came to the conclusion that he was ethically blind."

"So what happened?"

"Let's just say that he was lucky he'd gotten that $35 million and he was smart enough not to ask for a severance package."

6

Has the CEO Done Anything "Wrong"? (continued)

Apparently deciding to let his point settle in, Socrates took a minute to browse the titles in my bookcase some more and to examine my Boston Marathon medal.

"Let's shift gears," he continued, turning toward me. "Let's explore other aspects of how well you do with *treat others appropriately*. How about the perspective of *women* in your organization? Would they think you're treating *them* fairly?"

"Well," I said proudly, "I'm sure they'd say that this is a perfect place for women to work. Obviously, looking at me, they'd know the sky's the limit at this company!" After being hammered about my compensation, I guessed he decided to give me a break and let me talk about something he could compliment me on.

Almost as though he was reading my mind, Socrates said, "PR drivel!" dismissively. "I'm serious," he continued. "This isn't a 'gimme.' I want a real answer."

"You're kidding," I said, not being able to hide my astonishment. "You're asking a female CEO what women in her company would say about how women are treated?"

"Yes," he said with a hard glower, "I am."

"So you don't think 'very well' is the obvious answer?"

Saying nothing, Socrates pulled out that damned notebook again.

Mumbling as he looked for the right page, he finally stopped. "Here it is. Women make up about 50% of the population, and hold about 50% of all management and professional positions. But only 15% of the Fortune 500 board members are women."

He closed the notebook and looked up. "And how many women are on *your* board?"

"Other than me? None," I had to admit. "But it's not from my lack of trying. We're looking for active or retired CEOs, and there aren't many women who fall into that category."

"No kidding," he observed, looking at the notebook again. "Only 3% of the Fortune 500 companies have female CEOs. And there are hardly any women to be found anywhere in the C-suite—fewer than 10%."

"Right, it's a talent shortage. When more women like me have made it to the top, this will be a non-issue."

"A talent issue. You believe that?" he scoffed. "You honestly believe that?"

"Of course," I replied seriously. "The talent isn't there. We've searched."

"But if there's such a shortage of female leadership skills," he asked, "why is it that women account for about 25% of all college and university presidents in the U.S. and about 50% of the presidents of the Ivy League? Why that 'talent gap' between business and education?"

"Well, I've never looked into that," I answered, "but the most logical reason is that women have been in higher education longer than they've been in business."

"Sounds good, but it's wrong. Try the fact that there's more of a 'glass ceiling' in business as an explanation. Any 'talent shortage' *now* comes from the fact that the women of my generation in business didn't get a fair shot. An entire generation was aggressively recruited into business after the women's movement. But then they were bypassed for all of the really top slots."

I thought for a moment. "Maybe yes; maybe no—to borrow your phrase. I honestly didn't know there weren't more women on boards. But I think it's more complicated than just the 'glass ceiling.' Besides, what does this have to do with my performance?"

"I'm glad you asked," said Socrates. "First, I'm really a fanatic about this sort of thing. Whenever I go to a meeting of any consequence, I make a point of looking to see which groups are *and aren't* represented—women, African-Americans, Latinos, Asians, and so on. I expect good leaders of organizations to do the same. Either you didn't do that at your first board meeting, or, if you did, you didn't care about what you saw. You've been CEO for five years. I think that if you honestly took *fairness* and *equality* seriously, you'd have made some aggressive moves to make your board more diverse."

I nodded that I understood, and said, "And? You said 'first,' so I assume there's a second."

"Actually, there's a *third* as well." He smiled. I groaned.

"So second, there's at least one study that shows that Fortune 500 companies with the highest representation of women board directors and women corporate officers, on average, achieve higher financial performance than those with the lowest. If you're going to keep your promise to run the company in the most profitable way possible, I'd say that a board that's all white and male could be a financial liability. This looks to me like another example of *not keeping your agreement.*

"And as long as we're talking about your board and keeping your agreement, what's the deal with your being CEO and Chair of the Board?"

"What do you mean? Things work really well this way. Everything goes smoothly. You have a problem with *that*?"

"I have a problem with keeping a board from doing a big part of its job."

"Now you're making no sense. The board is there to give me advice when I need it. I actively seek out my directors' opinions on things. I really value their input. I have a very talented board and that's definitely helped the company while I've been CEO and Chair."

"And?" he pressed.

"And what?"

"They give you advice and you're smart enough to take it. Fine. But what about the rest of their responsibilities—the ones that you keep them from doing?"

Socrates obviously didn't like the blank stare I responded with. He sighed, got up, walked around, glanced back at me, and just said, "Think!" Then he stared out the window and sat back down. Looking back at me, he made a kind of "keep going" signal with his hand and looked at me intently. He was going to wait me out on this one, but I didn't know what he was after. Then he reached for that damned notebook again.

"Lives in a bubble. Probably believes her publicists' press releases about her. Has a really sweet gig and says it's 'good for the company.'" He sighed again, looked up and said, "Remind me whom you work for?"

"We've done this before," I replied impatiently. "Why don't you just tell me what you want me to say."

"No," he said with quiet exasperation. "This one is too important. This one is more than just about not keeping your agreement. It's about the kind of hubris that can cost lots of jobs and huge piles of cash. So, whom do you work for? Whose interest have you agreed to put first?"

"The shareholders," I answered. "But you probably want me to include . . . "

"No," he interrupted, *"shareholders* is fine. It's their company, right?"

"Right."

"And how do they get to make sure you and your management team are running the company the way you've agreed to?"

"Through the board, of course."

"Correct." Then he leaned toward me so I wouldn't miss what was coming. "A board that's chaired by the very person who's supposed to be evaluated. A board that you've done your best to stack with people who will let you do what you want. What part of *objective oversight* and *conflict of interest* don't you understand?" he almost spat out dismissively.

Now he was getting insulting again. "You really don't . . ."

"You own stock in other companies," he said flatly, interrupting me.

"You know that."

"And I also know that you wouldn't tolerate it if those CEOs' performance was evaluated in anything less than the most objective, independent, and rigorous way."

"True," I conceded.

"So don't your shareholders deserve the same as you? Independent directors who can do their job of oversight with maximum autonomy? There's a reason, you know, that 'best practices' in corporate governance call for the CEO and Chair to be separate. No one can objectively evaluate themselves. It's hubris, pure and simple."

"Fine," I said. "I'll think about it," making it clear by my tone that this was as much as I was going to concede right now. I was really feeling pushed around by Socrates, but I was having a hard time figuring out how to argue back. "Go on," I sighed, "I'm sure you aren't done."

"You're right," he said, getting up to pace around again. "But before we get to the *serious* stuff . . . "

"*Serious* stuff?" I interrupted. "You're suggesting that what you've been accusing me of isn't *serious*? That I'm gouging the company with what I earn? That I'm perpetuating discrimination against my own gender? That I'm not keeping my promise to run the company as well as I can? I'm undermining the board? You don't call those things *serious*?"

"As I was saying," he shot back sternly, "before we get to the *serious* stuff, I want to be clear about where I think we've arrived. You may not have lied, cheated, or stolen, *but*, from an ethical perspective, your actions have definitely fallen short. You've clearly broken your promise. Intentionally or not, you've advanced your own interest inappropriately. You didn't even recognize the conflict of interest you had. And you certainly aren't doing such a good job in making sure that your company respects ideas of fairness and equality as much as it should." Going back to the whiteboard, he made another addition and then explained, "When I pull out our *ethical yardstick* and use the *treat others appropriately* side of it, I think your actions leave much to be desired."

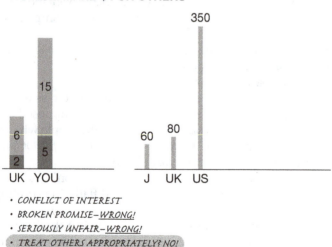

"But as I'm sure you can guess," he continued as he looked back my way, "the *serious* stuff I'm talking about is connected with the *other* side of our ethical yardstick, the one that tells how you've been doing with *do no harm*."

Before he got up a head of steam, I needed to set him straight.

"Wait a minute!" I interrupted. "Surely, you're not suggesting that people got *hurt* because of my decisions. We aren't involved in anything like manufacturing, mining, nuclear power, or oil exploration. Our employees don't work with heavy machinery or toxic substances. We're in financial services. We're a service industry. We make money by helping people with mortgages, business loans, and investments. The worst that happens in this industry is that people lose money. And while I'm not minimizing the seriousness of that, nobody dies. When you talk about 'harm,' I think you need to be more reasonable and not exaggerate things."

Socrates grimaced and, once again, wrote something in his notebook. " 'Doesn't recognize all of the consequences of her actions,' " he read off when he'd finished.

"You're kidding!"

"I wish I were," he replied somberly, "but this may be your most serious weakness. And just as serious is the fact that you're clueless about it."

"Clueless? Really!" I said with a mocking tone that Socrates didn't appreciate.

"Do me a favor," he said, after pausing to register his unhappiness about my attitude with another hard look. "Tell me about all of the *good* the lending side of your business does. Tell me about all the wide-ranging *positive* consequences."

Since Socrates had been focusing on my shortcomings for a while, I was surprised he now gave me a chance to tell him about the things I was most proud of. "All the *good*? That's easy. Mortgages let people have homes. And if we're talking a *new* home, the money makes its way into the pockets of lots of people in different parts of the economy: people who sell the materials needed for construction, the workers actually building the house, painters, stonemasons, landscape gardeners, people who work at companies that make stoves and refrigerators. I could keep going, but you see the point. It's estimated that every dollar spent in building a new home generates more than two and a half times that in positive economic impact. And that's just from the immediate spending. Then the mortgages are bundled as mortgage-backed securities. People working at the companies who put them together make money, as do the people who invest in them.

"We also do a lot of small business loans—which support family businesses, generate jobs, bring goods and services into particular communities, and generally improve the quality of life.

"Then we have a host of products that extend credit to many people for lots of different reasons: students who need money for education, people buying cars, consumers who need credit.

"Whatever you think about some of my decisions, you've got to give me credit for running this company in a way that's done a considerable amount of good for many people."

"I wouldn't argue a bit," Socrates replied, to my surprise. "You have much to feel very proud of," he said, seeming quite genuine.

"Thanks," I said suspiciously. "So, what's the other shoe?"

"Other shoe?" he asked with a pretend-innocence. "I can't imagine what you're talking about."

"Sure, sure," I laughed. "You're predictable. Get on with it."

"OK," he replied. "Do you feel *responsible* for all of the good you've just described?"

"What do you mean: 'responsible'?" I asked, sure I was being set up again.

"I'm not attempting to trick you," he replied, trying to reassure me. "Do you take any credit for the benefits you just ticked off? Do you feel that your decisions and good judgment actually led to the good you described?"

"Of course. That's why I feel proud. I'm not saying I did it single-handedly. But I feel responsible for making good things happen in the lives of many people."

"And you *should* feel that way," he added. "It may sometimes involve a long chain of events before we get from 'loan' to 'good stuff in people's lives,' but we're simply talking *cause and effect*. So, you've shown how much good your company can generate—when things go right. But things didn't exactly work out that way, did they?"

I thought back to how recently it seemed like one thing after another went wrong. "That's true, and it's very sad," I said, meaning it. "It was like Hurricane Katrina crushing New Orleans. All of a sudden we're in the middle of this maelstrom, being pummeled by forces out of our control. We're lucky we survived."

" 'Resorts to false analogies,' " he muttered, scribbling again in that note-book. "Please!" he groaned, as his mood changed again. Slamming his hand down on my desk and staring into my eyes, he said, *This was not an 'act of God!'* The meltdown was the result of decisions made by people—maybe thousands or millions of people acting independently of each other—but *people* nonetheless. This was *not* some economic version of a hurricane! The only people who say that are the people who don't have the ba- . . . sorry, who don't have the strength to accept responsibility for the consequences of their actions! Moral weaklings who are looking for a way to cover their a- . . . . This was *cause and effect*—*unintended* and *undesired* effects, to be sure, but *cause and effect*, nonetheless!"

"But you don't understand," I jumped in. "Everything was so inter-twined that there really wasn't anything we could do to stop it. It's not like we didn't try. It wasn't like seeing a train in the distance coming at you and you can jump out of the way. It really was like being hit by a hurricane."

I could tell by Socrates' expression as he listened to me that I'd hit an-other raw nerve. At least this time, he got up and paced around my office before saying something—but he was clearly fuming. After a couple of min-utes, he turned to me and said with more than a touch of frustration in his voice, "Do you really think that the rest of us are that stupid? We know that the disaster was created by people—not mysterious and uncontrollable forces. It came from foolish, risky, and greedy decisions by lots of people—none of whom will accept responsibility for what happened.

"Say what you want. Believe whatever rationalization you like. But you need to recognize the fact that you look ridiculous whenever you try to pass this off as an 'act of God' or 'market forces.' And you're insulting the intelligence of anyone you try to sell that story to." He took a deep breath and let it out.

"Look," he continued in a studied and patient way, "what I'm complaining about here applies to virtually *every* industry, not just yours. You know how much *good* your actions can do. Therefore, you should automatically be able to identify the kind of *harm* that can happen when things go wrong. That gives you the opportunity to stop it—or at least to limit it—*before it happens*. And if you don't, you're *responsible* for that harm. It's cause and effect."

"So now I'm responsible for knowing the future?" I said, scoffing. "Don't you think you're being unreasonable?"

"There was an incident in New England a number of years ago," he said in what seemed to me to be a puzzling change of topic. "Deer hunting season. Around dusk. A woman puts on a pair of white work gloves and heads into her backyard to clear out some brush. A hunter at some distance in the forest sees a flash of white and thinks it's a deer. He shoots and kills her."

"That's terrible."

"Yes," Socrates agreed. "But it gets worse. Do you know what the hunter said? 'I'm sorry, but she knew it was hunting season. She should have had on orange gloves, or she should have stayed inside.'"

"He actually said that?" I cringed. "That's horrible."

"What's your take on what happened?" Socrates asked.

"It's obvious," I said. "He had a gun. There were people and houses in the vicinity. Clearly, he didn't *know* for sure it was a deer. It was wrong for him to pull the trigger. You don't take a chance with someone's life like that. And if you do—if you choose to be that negligent—I think you should be treated as though you did it deliberately! How hard is it to exercise some caution when people can get hurt so badly?"

"Nicely put," said Socrates with an approving nod. "And that's all I'm saying."

"What do you mean?"

He was back at the whiteboard writing as he talked. "Trillions of dollars lost. Millions of people out of work. A recession. Millions of foreclosures and personal bankruptcies," he said pointedly. "Doesn't measure up particularly well against *do no harm*, does it? You didn't lie, cheat, or steal. And you didn't break any law. But your actions put too many people at risk of too much serious harm. There were warnings, but you ignored them. And when everything started to collapse, you had no way to stop it. You were negligent. You share responsibility for this catastrophe."

• *DO NO HARM*
··*$ LOST*
··*UNEMPLOYMENT*
··*FORECLOSURES*
··*RECESSION*

"Wait a minute," I said. "No one forced anyone into a mortgage they couldn't afford. That was their choice. Responsibility cuts both ways, you know."

"Let's see," he said, ticking things off on his fingers. "No verification mortgages. Bogus assessments. Reassuring words from loan officers, 'You don't have to worry. Property values never go down.' In my opinion," Socrates continued, "saying 'responsibility cuts both ways' in this situation sounds a lot like 'She should have had on orange gloves.' If I may quote a sage I know, 'How hard is it to exercise some caution when people can get hurt so badly?'"

"Hoisted on my own petard, eh?" I quipped glumly.

"Precisely. But as I said, this isn't just about you. For years there were warnings that we were like the Titanic heading for an iceberg. The only problem was that experts and executives like you labeled the people sounding the alarm 'crackpots.' It was so obvious that even college students could see it. I judged in an intercollegiate business ethics competition in Los Angeles a couple of years before the meltdown and heard one presentation on the dangers of the sub-prime phenomenon and another on the fact that General Motors was heading for bankruptcy. If 20 years olds could see it, CEOs could as well. You all just focused so much on short-term profits—or what protected your own personal interest—that you pretended everything was OK.

"In your particular case, you know very well just how important your industry is for the health of the entire economy. If things go south in banking, the harm that results is catastrophic. If you were selling fountain pens, it would be a different story. Defective pens will just leave ink on someone's hands. But your role in the economy is as important to everyone's welfare as the presence of a healthy water supply is to any human community. But you didn't run your company that way. You ran it as though the harm that could result from things going bad was minimal.

"The *job* of business is to make sure we get a decent life. You and many other corporate leaders didn't run your companies that way. Lots of people got seriously hurt—particularly as a result of decisions made in *your* industry. I know you didn't want that. But it happened. People got hurt as a result of your decisions."

He was back at the whiteboard. "How'd you do on 'do no harm'?" he asked. "Not very well," he said, answering his own question. "Didn't you tell me that the very first line in your mission statement says your primary goal is to serve your clients and stakeholders? It looks to me like both groups took a pretty big hit on your watch."

```
• DO NO HARM ──────▶ RESPONSIBILITY TO PREVENT HARM
  ··$ LOST                    FAILURE = WRONG
  ··UNEMPLOYMENT
  ··FORECLOSURES                     │
  ··RECESSION                        ▼
                            SUCCESSFUL? NO!
```

I wasn't at all happy with what Socrates was saying. But I'd be an idiot to say that people didn't get hurt. And Socrates was right that I'd ignored the warnings. At the time, I was sure I was doing the right thing. But looking back now, I had lots of regrets. And it's not just that "hindsight is 20-20." To be honest, I hadn't been entirely comfortable with some of my decisions when I made them. There was never anything specific I could put my finger on. I just had this gnawing feeling in the pit of my stomach. At the time, I thought it was because it felt like we were all being swept along by some great wave and that everything seemed out of our control—and if we tried to swim against it, we'd drown. But maybe I'd actually been uncomfortable for a different reason. Maybe my conscience bothered me at the time and I decided to ignore it.

Socrates let me sit in silence for a few minutes, since he could see I was ruminating about what he said. And when he continued our dialogue, I could tell he was trying to be reassuring.

"I'm not saying you're a bad person," he explained. "You did the best you could. You didn't intend to treat anyone inappropriately or to hurt anyone. But you are responsible for actions that have done just that."

I continued to brood about our conversation. Then I swallowed hard, opened my desk drawer, pulled out my checkbook, uncapped my fountain pen, and wrote a check for $200,000. "You win the second hand. I keep my word. But since I still don't know your real name," I said with an air of resignation. "I've left that line blank."

"I admire your honesty," he said with a gracious nod in my direction, as I slid the check toward him.

"So, that's that. Thanks for the *swell* time," I said, noticing that Socrates had left the check where I'd pushed it. "So, let's shake hands and call it a day. I still have that hearing to prepare for."

"And give up an opportunity to win it back?" he said with a wink.

7

Ethics on the Job

"Did you say, 'Win it back?'"

"Look," he explained, "while it may not have felt like this to you, I didn't come here to *blame* you. I'm here to *help* you do things differently in the future."

"Fine, I'll make sure not to have a hand in bringing on another major economic collapse," I said, trying to laugh. "More importantly, not to seem mercenary about things, how do I win my money back?"

"Easy. We finish the conversation. I'm not done."

"That's all?" I asked, with more than a little amount of skepticism. "You're going to walk away from $200,000 just because you're 'not done'?"

"That's right. I'm willing to walk away from my winnings because I'm not finished helping you. I'm not finished making sure you don't make the same mistakes again. I didn't come here for the money. The bet was just a way to get your attention.

"So, are you game?

"The first hand was about the job of business. The second hand was about whether you did anything wrong. This third hand is about what to do in the future."

"And all I have to do is to play out this 'third hand'?"

"Well, that and maybe one other small thing." He winked good-naturedly.

"One other *small* thing?" I said, making it plain that I was feeling set up.

"Trust me. You don't have anything to worry about. I'm actually giving you an easy way to get your $200,000 back. Are you in or out?"

"We'll see about the trust, but I'd be stupid to say no," I said, mostly relieved. "I'm still in."

"Good. But first, before I forget, give me my watch back. My friend would be very upset if I lost it."

"Fair enough," I said as I handed over the timepiece. "But if you're serious about helping me for the future, first you have to give me some credit. I've learned from my mistakes. We're doing many things differently now. You don't seem to recognize any of that."

"Sure, you're making important changes in products and processes," he acknowledged, "and that's great. But I'm not talking about the technical side of things. I'm talking about your company's culture. I'm talking about making sure that when you and your people are faced with decisions, you handle the *ethical* issues better.

"You know as well as I do that at far too many companies, the top three questions everybody asks when evaluating a decision is, 'Will it make money? Will it make enough money? And will it make as much money as possible?' At most companies, people add at least, 'Is it legal?' I gather that you personally add, 'Does it involve lying, cheating, or stealing?' But that's not enough."

"OK, so you represent the 'we can always do everything better' school of thought. I get that. But, again, you're not giving us enough credit. We have a company mission statement. We have a statement of corporate values. We have a corporate ethics department. We have ethics training. We have a helpline. We're doing everything we can to get ethics on the front burner."

"Everything you can?" he asked, skeptically.

"Yes, we're doing everything we can."

"No you aren't," Socrates said flatly. "You aren't even coming close."

"So you've decided to just be insulting now? That's really helpful," I added sarcastically.

"But you've had all of those things in place for years, right?"

"Yes, which we're very proud of."

"And you're not alone in that. Most of the companies in your industry have ethics programs," he acknowledged, "as did Enron and a bunch of other prominent companies that found themselves embroiled in scandals."

"Oh, that was a cheap shot, and you know it."

"Cheap shot? I admit comparing you to Enron isn't fair. *But* how well did your industry's ethics programs do at stopping all these companies from making decisions that led to enormous harm? Not any better than Enron's stopped what was going on there.

"But the problem isn't that these programs *can't* be effective. They *are* effective—up to a point. As I see it, the problem is that you don't *want* them to be more effective."

"You're crazy," I replied. "I'm our ethics program's biggest supporter. They have plenty of resources; I see to that. I appear prominently in all of their videos and printed materials saying how important ethics is to the company. I tell all of my people that, as far as I'm concerned, CEO also means 'Chief Ethics Officer.' "

"Sure, sure," he said patronizingly. "And then you go and marginalize them."

"*Marginalize*? You're not serious."

He sighed. "Let's keep this simple. I assume you'd say that doing business ethically is just as important as doing business *legally*, right?"

"Frankly, I think it's more important," I countered proudly. "I believe that if we focus on operating ethically, we're shooting for a higher standard."

"And yet the way you communicate that to your organization is to pay your Chief Ethics Officer about *half* what you pay your Chief Counsel," Socrates said sarcastically. "And don't even *try* to explain away that one by appealing to 'market forces,' " he interrupted me as I began to answer. "I didn't buy that as an explanation for your salary, so I'm certainly not going to buy it here. Besides, you know as well as I do that in business, you're only taken as seriously as what you earn. And speaking of your Chief Counsel, when you have a major discussion about corporate strategy, do you ever include him?"

"Of course. I want to make sure we're doing things appropriately, and I don't want us wasting time and money always being in and out of court."

"And at those same meetings," he continued, "do you ever have your Chief Ethics Officer at the table? I mean the *real* one, not you."

"As I just said, I have Legal there, so I figure that's all we need."

"And that's precisely my point. You don't even see how you marginalize ethics. Ethics isn't in the C-suite. Ethics isn't even at the table."

"But I didn't appoint my ethics guy because he was an expert in strategy. That's not his strong suit. So he's not going to add much to a meeting like that. That's not why I hired him."

"Hmmm," Socrates brooded. "You didn't hire your ethics guy to help you make sure that company strategy was ethically solid. Then why did you hire him?"

"To run the ethics program, of course. We have thousands of employees that the ethics program has direct contact with. And Ethics stays in close touch with Legal and HR if they uncover any problems. Believe me, my head of ethics is very busy. And that department does a great job."

"So, let me make sure I understand this right. The main job of your ethics program is to, shall we say, 'keep the help from stealing the silver.' You don't use your ethics department as a resource for the really *big* decisions."

"You know, being cynical and insulting isn't helpful," I replied. "I'm not going to apologize for how I use my ethics department. And just because my Chief Ethics Officer isn't part of strategy discussions doesn't mean that ethics isn't 'at the table.' The men and women on my team are all individuals of honesty and integrity. If there's an ethical problem with any part of what we're doing, I expect them to bring it up."

"Like they brought up the ethical issues connected with what even you now see were problematic decisions a few years ago?" Socrates remarked, underscoring our failures.

"Being snarky is no help either. You're saying we aren't ethical?" I asked, with obvious annoyance.

"No, I'm not!" he said, clearly exasperated with me. "You're still not getting what I'm saying. This has nothing to do with whether you or the people on your team are ethical individuals. My point is that you lack the *technical skills* needed to recognize and resolve the complex ethical issues that come up in business."

"So you're saying that I need to involve our Chief Ethics Officer more in critical decisions," I said.

"Maybe yes, maybe no. I don't know this person. I don't know his background. It sounds like you hired him because he was a good manager, not because he was a first-rate ethicist. Besides, even if he does have the technical skills, *you* need them as well. And so does every senior person on your team. You think of yourself as a great strategist and problem solver. Why not get to the point where you can think of yourself as a respectable *ethicist* as well?"

"You keep saying 'technical skills' and 'ethicist.' What do you mean?"

"Look, easy and obvious ethical problems are simple. When you have one of those, follow a few common-sense rules and you're fine: don't lie; don't cheat; don't steal; don't hit; share your toys; play nice with the other boys and girls. But simple honesty and integrity aren't enough for the really tough ones—because they're so complex. And you really have to dig into them—both to describe the problem and to figure out what to do. Frankly, right now, most of the time you—like most senior executives—don't even *recognize* when you have an ethical issue on your hands, never mind resolve it well. The problem is that most people—including you—don't recognize that '*ethical* analysis' is as sophisticated as '*financial* analysis.' So even if you understand the problem correctly—which is unlikely—you use a simple approach to a complex problem."

He paused for a moment and looked up at the ceiling. He was clearly trying to find a better way to explain what he meant.

"Think about it this way. Imagine you're vacationing at the ocean and, as you're relaxing on the beach, you're watching a swimmer a couple hundred yards offshore. It occurs to you that he's been in one spot for a while. Maybe he's taking a break and relaxing. But maybe he's in trouble. The problem is that your eyesight isn't good enough to see something that far away. You can't tell whether the swimmer needs assistance or not. Wouldn't it help to have a pair of high-powered binoculars?

"That's a big part of the problem with handling ethical issues. Ordinary 'ethical vision,' shall we say, isn't enough.

"And let's say you realize the swimmer needs help. A rip current came up suddenly and he's making the mistake of trying to swim against it. Wouldn't it help if you knew how to swim, so you could go out there and give him a hand? Wouldn't it also help if you knew enough about currents to tell him that all he has to do is swim parallel to the beach until he's out of the current, not directly into it? Wouldn't it help to have the skills of a professional lifeguard?

"That's another part of the problem with handling ethical issues—having the right skills to diagnose the problem and come up with a solution. The average person isn't an 'ethics lifeguard.' "

"So now it sounds like you're saying that I always need an 'ethics lifeguard with binoculars' by my side," I said. "Although, maybe having a big, hunky ethics lifeguard in red trunks follow me around wouldn't be such a bad idea," I continued with a laugh.

"Well, I wouldn't put it quite that way," Socrates smiled. "But the object of the game is for you to develop the necessary technical skills yourself."

Changing the topic, he said, "I see you're training for a CEO Challenge marathon, right?"

"I'm tempted to ask you why we're now talking about something completely different, but I'm sure *you* have some idea about what running has to do with ethics. Yes, I'm training for the marathon. What can I say? I'm a type-A overachiever. I also have a sizable bet with the CEO of one of our competitors that I can beat him by 15 minutes."

"And you have a coach who's helping you."

"As you obviously found out in your research on me."

"But why do you have one? You're smart. There are lots of books you could read. There are loads of training programs online. What can a coach give you that they can't?"

"I want the best I can get. Sure, there are books. But I've got the coach who—literally—*wrote the book* on heart rate training. Roy Benson tailors my training to my particular situation and abilities. He gives me advice about nutrition and recovery. He's an expert. He's been doing this for years. He's one of the best coaches in the country. There's no way I could learn that much that fast on my own."

"And are you learning anything that you'll apply later on your own, or are you just following directions?"

"Are you kidding? I want to understand everything that's behind his plan. I'm intensely curious about everything involved in the process."

"Great! That's exactly what I'm saying about ethics. This is an academic discipline with a 2,000 year history. So spend some time with an expert who's been studying this. There are plenty of excellent ethicists around. Find one who's been doing it for years because they have a passion for it—not someone who's gotten into the area because it's a 'growth industry.' Find an 'ethics coach' who understands both the theory and practice. Learn enough that you become good enough to do this on your own. Actually, if you've been paying attention in our conversation, you've already learned a lot. And I'll give you some more pointers shortly. But there's no reason you can't have an 'ethics coach' to refine your skills.

"And this also applies to your board. I'm sure they're good and decent people, but being honest—as opposed to having the technical skills that let you do first rate ethical analysis—are two different things. Besides, my contacts at the Federal Sentencing Commission tell me that they think that ethics *training* for board members is required. Most companies—yours included—substitute ethics *communication* and just give statistics about the ethics and compliance program. But if you're serious about making sure your directors can do their job as well as possible, you have to make sure they have all the tools they need. And technical, analytical skills of this sort are crucial in complex cases. And if you have a board member who's insulted by this—ask them to resign. If their ego is so big that they think they can't learn something new that will let them do a better job, they don't belong on a board of directors."

"An ethics coach?" I'd never thought about that. It actually wasn't a bad idea. "OK, what about you? You seem pretty competent. How'd you like the job? But first I'd want more of a taste of what you could teach us. I want to make sure you'd be worth your fee."

Again with the notebook, scrawling and mumbling, but smirking as he wrote, "*Unusually arrogant for someone who just lost $200K to me.* I'm flattered at the offer," he said when he looked up, "but my plate is full. Besides, I don't do auditions. I'll tell you what, however. I'll give you a 'freebie,' just for fun."

"What sort of freebie?"

"The sort that demonstrates what I mean when I say you lack the technical skills involved. Not a big ethical problem. But a situation you should have handled differently. Not your best moment as 'Chief Ethics Officer.' Something subtle that you completely missed. In fact, most people would probably say there are no *ethical* issues here at all."

"Subtle sounds appropriately challenging, but I can't imagine what you're talking about."

"My point precisely," he noted seriously. "Do you remember that Chief Information Officer who was here for only a few months?" he asked.

"How could I forget? What a prima donna!"

"*She* was the prima donna?" he replied skeptically.

"I take it that you don't think so."

"When we look at your statement of company values," he said, picking up his notebook again and obviously having no intention of giving me a direct answer, "we find, *We treat one another with professionalism and respect. We treat each other as we'd want to be treated ourselves.*"

"Yes, and you didn't have to look in your notebook for that. We have the mission statement and list of company values on the wall in every office and conference room."

"Yes, I noticed. But that wasn't what I was looking for," he said as he continued to flip through pages. "According to my information, here's how you handled this person. On top of doing her regular IT job, she came up with the idea for a new product she'd developed on her own time. You had only two meetings with her. You met with her when she pitched the idea, and you said you'd 'think about it.' You either completely ignored her e-mails asking for a decision or kept putting off making up your mind. At your second meeting, which she thought was to discuss the project, you complained to her about where she sat at a banquet."

"Right," I said, interrupting Socrates. "A number of us from the company attended a fund-raiser for our local hospital. It's a very important event in this community. She decided to sit at another table although I'd saved her a seat. I knew it was a deliberate snub because . . ."

"Just to be clear," Socrates interrupted, "without knowing why she sat where she did, you called her in and told her you took this as a personal insult. And then you put off talking about the project again."

"I was insulted. What kind of message does that send to everyone when one of my main people snubs me in public? She said it was a misunderstanding—that she had friends from the hospital she sat with—and she apologized."

"And what did you do?"

"I accepted her apology and told her we'd talk about the project another time because I was busy. And the next thing I know, a month later she's leaving us to work for one of our competitors in Europe. And *they're* going to be rolling out her idea as a new product. I don't know why you're suggesting I missed the ethical issue here. I was furious that she *stole* something that belonged to us and took it to another company. But Legal told me there was nothing we could do. She claimed she developed the idea on her own time and on her home computer. She didn't use any proprietary information. There was no non-competition clause in her contract that we could enforce. The least she could have done was to come and talk to me before she left. She was *too important* even to *talk* to me? That's what I said before—a real *prima donna*."

"First of all," sighed Socrates, "let me give you a hint. After your second meeting, you had no reason ever to expect her to walk back into your office. And if I have to explain this to you, your 'ethical vision' is far worse than I thought.

"So here's the short version of your free analysis. Your statement of company values says: *We treat one another with professionalism and respect. We treat each other as we'd want to be treated ourselves.* If that's supposed to be anything more than window-dressing, that's essentially a *promise* that everyone makes to one another here. And you broke that promise. You certainly didn't act professionally or treat her with appropriate respect. In not getting back to her in a reasonable amount of time, you broke your word to her. And you also broke your promise to the company to look out for the firm's financial interests. You lost a potentially profitable product to a competitor. And your egotistical behavior caused the company not only to lose a talented employee, but also to incur the costs of hiring and training a replacement. That you violated *treat people appropriately* is obvious. Does losing money count as violating *do no harm*? I suppose it depends on how much money's involved. But giving away money like this is never a good idea.

"And what about that 'personal insult' crap?" he asked sharply. "You use *company time* to indulge your ego and blow off steam? To make matters worse, *she* ends up apologizing—not *you*? And then, because you're *so* important, you're *too busy* to talk to her about business?"

I had to confess that I'd never looked at it the way Socrates saw it. "OK, when you put it that way, I guess it wasn't my proudest moment."

"An understatement—to be sure. But be certain you recognize that it wasn't your proudest moment from an *ethical* perspective. You weren't just arrogant and stupid. The way you behaved was *wrong*. I wouldn't say it was *seriously* wrong, but it was *wrong*. As I said, most people wouldn't think there were any *ethical* issues here. They'd probably just say you were rude and unprofessional. Maybe they'd say, 'Oh, that's just Queen Wendy. She gets that way.'

"But remember," Socrates continued as he went back to the whiteboard and started writing again, "ethics is about helping create situations that give *us a decent life, the kind of life we want. Ethics is about treating others appropriately* and *doing no harm.* I hope that by now you understand that acting ethically means more than just not lying, cheating, and stealing. Sometimes the issues connected with *treating others appropriately* are found in the day-to-day matter of simple *respect.* And we don't have to wait until a business has gone under or people have been put out of work before *do no harm* kicks in. That idea also implies a duty to *prevent harm before it happens.*

KIND OF LIFE WE WANT/DECENT LIFE

↓

ETHICS

↓

• *DO NO HARM/PREVENT HARM*

• *TREAT OTHERS APPROPRIATELY*

"Moreover, in a business," he added, "ethics isn't just about single actions. It's about the company's *culture.* You'll find that when you have an *ethical culture,* everyone has a much easier time doing what they know is the right thing to do. But whether or not your company has an ethical culture is up to *you* more than to anyone else. And speaking of building an ethical culture, make sure you worry about how you *reward* your people for doing the right thing.

"So, these are the kinds of issues you have to understand—*before* you make decisions or take any actions—before you get to call yourself 'Chief Ethics Officer.' And that's your freebie."

"Wait a minute. Did you say *reward*? You want me to *reward* people for being ethical? Shouldn't being honest just be part of the job? Shouldn't we simply be able to *expect* people to be honest?"

"Of course we should, just as we should be able to expect people in sales to sell as much as possible or division heads to see to it that their areas run as profitably as possible. But you don't just *expect* employees to do their best in those areas, do you? You reward them. You give them bonuses."

"Right, because people perform better when there are incentives."

"Exactly. It's human nature. And everybody knows that what's important in an organization gets rewarded and what's unimportant doesn't. Humans *are* intelligent, you know. We figure out what behaviors get rewarded pretty quickly. So, if ethics is as important to your company as you say it is, why not reward it? Or, to put it another way, if you reward one bunch of priorities and don't reward ethics, how can you reasonably expect people to take you seriously when you say how important ethics is?"

"I didn't expect such cynicism from you. You're saying that people do things only for rewards?"

"Not at all. But I am saying that when you have an organization where there's a clear system of rewards, you're telling people what you value most. And they respond appropriately."

"So you want me to start giving out bonuses for ethical behavior?" I said with some disbelief. "And just how do I do that? Figuring out a bonus for sales is easy. They get a 'piece of the action.' A share of the profits they've generated. How do I determine—or *justify*, for that matter—a bonus that has nothing to do with increasing our profits. What are you talking about? A reward for whistle-blowing?"

"First, I didn't say 'an ethics bonus' or anything about whistle-blowing," he groaned. "You still don't listen carefully. This is about your finding a way to encourage people to do good behavior, not to catch bad behavior. And I said *reward*, not *money*. Money's a good motivator, but it's not the only one. Frankly, intangible rewards are more powerful motivators than tangible ones. Look at how hard exceptionally talented people work in nonprofit organizations. They're sure not doing it for the money. So consider it part of your 'homework' from today's discussion that—if ethics is going to be as important a part of your company as you say you want it to be—you need to think about how to have incentives and rewards that will motivate people appropriately. Second, you can also spend some time thinking about whether ethical behavior actually has *nothing to do with increasing your profits*.

"And one more thing."

"Is this the one *small* thing you mentioned?" I asked.

"No," he replied, "the one small thing is still to come. This is one *more* thing," he smiled. "At least on your own set of values, add *humility*. Great leaders are humble. They know their own weaknesses better than anyone else does. They truly appreciate the talents other people have that they lack. Trust me on this. No one worth his or her salt respects anyone who insists on being told how great, successful, or special they are. Acting like you're more important than the people around you is a sign of weakness. It's a sign of any number of possible shortcomings. And in a CEO it's especially unacceptable.

"And just to make sure you understand how important this is, let me remind you that I control 30% of your stock. You pride yourself at being no-nonsense when it comes to the numbers. I respect that; so am I. But I'm just as hard-nosed about ethics. And from now on, I expect you to be as well. Keep your promises and honor your commitment to the company's values. Treat others appropriately. Do no harm. When you make a mistake—which you will—accept responsibility and fix things. Remember what the *job* of business really is. And temper that damned ego of yours with humility. The way I see it, you're not a profit center. You're *overhead*. Act like it!

"There are plenty of great CEOs out there—people who are smart, talented, focused on doing the job, and humble. If you work at it, you can be one of them. That's why we're having this conversation. You have the *potential* to be great. It may not be apparent in your most recent decisions, but I see it there. Whether you deliver on that potential is up to you."

Socrates' phone chimed to let him know he'd received a text. His taking the time to read it let me mull over what he'd just said. When he was done, he looked up expecting some sort of response.

"First," I said, "I hear you. I honestly do. Second, thanks for the vote of confidence. I mean it."

"You're welcome," he said enthusiastically. "I know I've been tough on you, and I respect how well you've handled yourself. I never would have sat down with you if I didn't think you had promise."

"So how about if I ask a question now?"

"Seems fair enough."

"How about some practical advice? Believe me, I'll think about what you've said and how I can come up with ways to strengthen the company. But I'd like something I can start using tomorrow."

"Great question, because that takes us to the *one small thing* I mentioned."

"Convenient. What's that?"

"I have an unusually astute friend who's a Chief Ethics Officer—Barney Rosenberg. He told me about a company in the chemical industry that was so serious about safety that every meeting started with someone identifying the chemical risks in that part of the facility—and what to do if there was a problem. The person running the meeting would point out the emergency exits, the location of air masks, the water fountains that let you flush your eyes, and so on. It didn't matter if everyone in the meeting had worked there for years and knew all of this. It was a way of saying, 'We have a culture of safety, we take it seriously and we take nothing for granted.' Not surprisingly, they had a great track record."

"Impressive, but our greatest danger is probably from paper cuts," I joked.

"So Barney said to me," continued Socrates, ignoring my quip, "'Wouldn't it be great if we had something like that for ethics? A simple way to make sure the ethical issues got paid attention to. What would be the equivalent of that for ethics?'"

"Interesting question," I said, my curiosity piqued. "What'd you say?"

"I said that I didn't see any reason why it couldn't be on the agenda of every meeting to ask a few key questions:

"* When we look at our mission statement and list of company values, are we keeping our promise? Do our *actions* match what our *words* say we're committed to?

"* Are we treating everyone involved in this matter *appropriately*?

"* Is there anyone who *will* get hurt or *could* get hurt by what we're doing? Are we keeping the risk of harm at a reasonable level?"

Then he got up, headed back to the whiteboard and jotted down abbreviated versions of these questions.

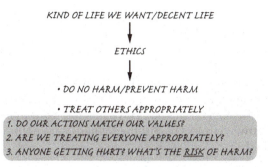

KIND OF LIFE WE WANT/DECENT LIFE

ETHICS

• DO NO HARM/PREVENT HARM

• TREAT OTHERS APPROPRIATELY

1. DO OUR ACTIONS MATCH OUR VALUES?
2. ARE WE TREATING EVERYONE APPROPRIATELY?
3. ANYONE GETTING HURT? WHAT'S THE <u>RISK</u> OF HARM?

"And let me guess," I interrupted. "The one *small* thing you want me to do is for us to do that here."

"Congratulations, you got it right on the first try. You said yourself that you have the mission statement and company values on every wall. Lots of companies have those things on the back of the ID badges everyone wears. You think of yourself as a savvy manager. Figure out a way that everyone takes it seriously. Think of a way to make it normal in your culture—so that people feel it's just part of 'how we do things here.'"

"OK, it's an interesting challenge. I accept."

"'Interesting challenge,' my ass," said Socrates laughing. "That's what lets you keep that $200,000!"

"Touché," I replied as I got up to get another cup of coffee. I figured that our conversation was done, but I was going to be working on my testimony for a while. I needed the caffeine.

"You know," I remarked as I looked out the window, "when the CEO of one of my competitors appeared before these hearings, someone asked him if he really understood the *ethical* implications of his actions. I guess I get to say there's no question that *I* understand them, because I spent the afternoon discussing ethics with a mysterious VC with the nickname 'Socrates' who can fly under the Feds' radar so well that he controls 30% of my company's stock without anyone knowing it—and, oh yes, he walks around with an $11 million pocket watch. They're going to love that."

When I turned around, he was no longer sitting in the chair by my desk.

I scanned the room and still didn't see him. He must have quietly left while I was looking out the window with my back to him. He probably thought he was teaching me a lesson by sneaking out while I was going on and on with no one in the room to hear me. But he wasn't getting off the hook that easily. I still had a few questions of my own. I stepped out of my office, expecting to find him standing there laughing at me.

Not there.

"Marie," I said to my assistant, whose desk is right by the door to my office, "Where'd he go? Is he coming back?"

"Where'd who go?"

"The guy I've been talking to."

Marie gave me a peculiar look. "Well, I heard *you* talking. But I figured you were on the phone. I didn't hear anyone else."

"No. The guy in the charcoal suit. White hair. Beard. He must have walked right past you."

"I don't know who you mean. I've been at my desk all afternoon, and you're the only one who's come or gone." Her expression went to something that looked like she wanted to ask, "Have you lost your marbles?"

I didn't know what to say. But the longer I said nothing, the more worried Marie looked.

"Are you OK?"

"Sure. I'm fine. Rough day," I stammered.

Grasping at straws, I said the first thing that came to mind. "I meant that after today's disaster, I asked Phyllis to arrange for some spin doctor to stop by to help me prepare for the hearing in Washington. He's supposed to be here by now. I forget his name. All I remember is she said, 'charcoal suit, white hair, beard.' Any sign of someone like that yet?"

"Not yet," she replied—obviously trying to pretend she bought my explanation.

I went back into my office, closed the door, and sat down at my desk.

What had happened? Was the whole conversation real or not? Marie didn't see him arrive with me. She didn't see him leave. Could I really have imagined something that long and involved? Maybe it was a dream. But it felt too real to be a dream. My quantum physicist daughter is always saying "reality's a whole lot stranger than we can imagine." Maybe this is what she means. Parallel universes, I'm willing to consider. But conversations with people who aren't there? I have a *very* hard time believing that. It had to be some sort of stunt. *This* Socrates was as annoying as his namesake!

Then, on the other side of my desk, I noticed that damned notebook. I opened it. Blank. Then I wondered whether I hadn't bought one just like that the other day. I stared out the window for a few minutes. Socrates' shenanigans were a distraction. I had work to do. I buzzed Marie.

"Yes, boss."

"Marie, do me a favor. Please get that journalist who interviewed me earlier today on the phone. I need to apologize to her."

"OK."

"And then," I continued, "see if you can track down Jane Colt, the CIO who left a couple of months ago for that British company. I need to apologize to her as well."

"Understood," she replied, "but that's about a six-hour time difference. So that may take me a couple days to set up."

"I understand," I said. "And then why don't you call it a day. I'm going to stay for a while and rewrite my testimony."

8

Socrates Returns—The Second Conversation

I was lucky it was pouring when I emerged from the building. That way, the reporters chasing me were secretly happy to have an excuse to call it a day. They could tell their editors I simply raced out of the building and jumped into my car to avoid getting drenched. "But we have calls into her office, boss, so we'll definitely follow-up," they'd all say. And I would talk to them eventually.

It *was* true that I didn't want to get soaked. But the main reason for my speedy exit was that I finally had the good sense to stop talking when cameras were running. Of course, it would have helped if that happened *before* I realized the camera was there and *before* I lectured the Senator. How did a day that started so well end up being such a disaster?

Settling into the back seat of the limousine, I simply pressed the intercom button and told my driver, "Drive."

"Ma'am? The hotel? The airport?"

I sighed in exasperation. All I wanted was to be as far away from the Senators and journalists as possible. "Just drive anywhere for now. I need to think."

"Yes, ma'am. Leave it to me." My driver's tone made me think he'd watched the hearing and understood I wanted a chance to decompress. I needed to figure out what went wrong and, more importantly, what to do next.

But first I needed a combination of quiet and something to take my mind off of my most recent public relations' gaffe. Again, my driver must have understood, because it quickly became apparent he was taking me on a tour of D.C. landmarks. I've always loved Washington. It's a great city for walking, jogging, and touristing. Anyone who isn't awestruck by the Jefferson and Lincoln Memorials, the White House, and the Washington Monument has a heart of stone. In a way, the stormy skies and rain made the buildings more impressive than usual, as their light-colored stone stood out against the background of dark clouds.

I gave myself permission to take 30 minutes, enjoy the sights and appreciate where I was. I shut off my phone.

"Driver. Please turn off your phone. I'm sure that any number of people will be calling you when they can't reach me. Let's just go off the grid and hide for a while."

"Excellent idea, ma'am. Consider it done. If it's any help, even *I* don't know where we are," he said with a chuckle.

Being lost was a lie, of course. We were going by the Kennedy Center. And both of our phones, as well as the limo, had GPS. But I appreciated that he recognized what I needed and wasn't arguing. I was sure he'd catch hell not only from his boss but from Phyllis, my head of PR, for whisking me away and 'going dark.'

When I finally felt more like myself, I reached for my phone and called Phyllis.

"Where are you?" she asked calmly. "When you left so quickly, I came back to the hotel for the reception. Are you stuck in traffic? Do you know that both your phone and your driver's phone aren't working? Have you been sitting in a tunnel?" Her tone was professional, but I could tell that she was frantic. I never simply *disappeared*.

"I needed to gather my thoughts. And while no one is going to like this, I'm not attending the reception. Please extend my apologies—especially to the three board members who said they'd show up—and make sure everyone has a good time. When it's over, thank everyone from my office for working so hard on the day's events and tell them to take the long weekend off. We'll worry about damage control back in New York. We have the suite booked through Monday. Make sure someone enjoys it. Just do me a favor and throw all of my clothes into my suitcase and take it back with you on the flight."

I knew that Phyllis would want to argue with me and convince me to attend the reception and, as she always put it, "get out in front of things." So before she could reply, I simply said, "I know I can count on you to do your best. Sorry to have thrown you another curve ball. And thanks for respecting my need to be left alone for the weekend." There was silence on the other end as she gauged whether or not she should try to get me to change my mind.

"No problem, Ms. Summers. We'll talk in New York. Try to get some rest."

"Thanks, Phyllis. You too."

Before tackling this disaster, I also needed to contact my husband and daughter. Texts from them had come in while I had my phone off. Bobbi was in Istanbul, which was seven hours ahead of D.C. It was sweet of him to have watched the hearing, but it was now the middle of the night there. I texted him that I was OK and that we'd talk in the morning. I did the same for Sasha, who was in London.

Switching my phone off again, I started trying to figure out where I could hide out for the weekend.

"Excuse me, ma'am. I don't mean to interrupt. But do you have any further instructions for me yet?" the driver asked.

I decided I needed the advice of a local.

"I assume you live in this area. Right?"

"That's correct."

"So if I wanted to spend the weekend someplace quiet—where I could think without being found—what would you recommend?"

"Actually, I know just the place. But let me find somewhere I can pull over so I can tell you about it. In the meantime, you might want to open up that envelope that came for you."

I reached for the large blue envelope with my name on it and opened it. The only thing inside was a yellow card. No note. No name. I assumed that someone had left out whatever was important. That's something else I'd worry about back in New York.

We drove for another few minutes and then pulled over.

The partition in front of me lowered. I assumed the driver was going to show me a map and tell me about some options. When I looked at him, it was the last person I expected—or probably wanted—to see. *Damn! Socrates! Not again!* At least that answered my question of whether I'd dreamed or imagined our last encounter.

*

He greeted me with a big, friendly smile. "It's nice to see you again, Wendy. Although, frankly, I didn't think it would be quite so soon," he chuckled.

"You won't be offended if I don't match your enthusiasm for another 'chat,' " I said wryly, as we shook hands. "So, before we do anything else, you need to tell me how you got Marie to pretend you never existed."

"That was easy. When you and I were talking in your office, the Vice-Chairman of the Board came by and told her that we were playing a prank on you. It was all in fun. He asked her to pretend she'd never seen me. When we learned how well she did, we sent her a gift certificate to her favorite spa. I wanted you to question as many of your assumptions as possible. I thought it would help if I could even get you to doubt your senses. Questioning your preconceived ideas about business, then, would seem trivial by comparison."

Grumbling at being so easily duped, I waved the card I found in the envelope at him. "So, let me guess, this yellow card is from you?"

"Indeed. And it means?"

The pause said that this was another one of his *let's-see-if-you-can-figure-this-out-for-yourself* moments.

"OK. You're European. Soccer. I'm sorry, *football*. So it means that after today's disaster, I'm being 'thrown out of the game.' You can pull the strings on 30% of the stock. You gave me a shot across the bow the other day. I blew my second chance. I'm fired, right?"

As he looked at me somberly, I braced myself for the confirmation and quickly tried to remember the severance package in my contract.

"For someone who likes to travel so much, you can be awfully provincial. It takes a *red* card—or *two* yellow cards—to get ejected. This is your first. It really wasn't as bad as you think."

Relieved that I still had my job, I was puzzled about why he was here.

"So if you aren't going to spend the next few hours grilling me, berating me, and verbally beating me up, why the unexpected visit?"

Feigning disbelief, he said, "I'm shocked! I thought you enjoyed our conversation as much as I did. It was supposed to make you feel *energized*—the way a good workout does."

I was so tired from everything that had happened I was in no mood for his joking around.

"It's been a long day. Would you mind just telling me what's going on?"

Finally seeing how worn out I was, he gave me a friendly smile. "OK, down to business.

"First, you're not fired. You're still my guy *girl woman* whatever you prefer.

"Second, that's not to say that you didn't screw up today. You just didn't screw up *so badly* I've lost hope in you. Your prepared testimony and the way you handled questions from the committee were, for the most part, quite good. You accepted responsibility for your company's role. More importantly, you accepted *personal* responsibility for what you now see were poor decisions that had wide-ranging consequences in the lives of many people. In fact, you did such an exemplary job of accepting responsibility that I'm sure your Chief Counsel is pulling his hair out. And you offered some intelligent suggestions for ways to avoid a similar disaster in the future.

"Yes, you did very well right up until the point where you got into it with the Senator from New Jersey and his Chief of Staff after the session was formally over. *On camera.* You know, I thought you would have learned your lesson on that one. You really need to pay attention to what's going on around you more.

"Lecturing a Nobel Prize–winning economist *about the economy! What were you thinking?* Didn't it dawn on you that an award like that plus teaching economics for years at Princeton were pretty good signs that he knew what he was talking about? Spirited disagreement is one thing. But getting so frustrated you told him he couldn't see straight because his head was up his. . . . Well, you, I, and, by now, millions of people know what you said. So there's no need rehashing that.

"And don't you do your homework? Before joining the Senator's staff, his Chief of Staff specialized in environmental law. Considering that New Jersey has more Superfund sites than any other state, you should have thought twice before telling him that the threat of global climate change has been exaggerated and the only people crying 'The sky is falling!' are tree huggers looking for a federal grant to keep them from having to get a *real* job.

"You definitely need to learn how to dial it back in situations like that.

"So, what all this amounts to is that you and I need to cover more ground. As it happens, I own a beach house on the Maryland shore. That's where we're headed. I thought it would be better if we weren't disturbed. That's why I canceled your car and showed up myself. It will take us a while to get there. So just relax in the meantime."

I was relieved he wasn't *red carding* me, but I honestly had no interest in another marathon conversation. Maybe I could talk him out of it.

"But the Senator *was* wrong, you know. I admit I could have put it better, but he has things backward. And since my disagreement with him and his Chief of Staff was about economic policy and the weather, I don't think that has anything to do with what I do as CEO. If you want to talk economics or climate science some time, I'm glad to do that. But I'd really just like to go home, regroup, and get ready for the onslaught I'll face when I get back to New York."

"This isn't about the substance of your disagreements with the Senator and his Chief of Staff, Wendy. It's about what your comments showed—how limited your perspective remains about a variety of ideas that affect your decisions and your actions as CEO. You seem blind to the *ethical* dimensions of a number of issues. For example, there's the bank's relationship with some companies whose actions merit closer scrutiny. I found some of your answers to the Committee troubling when they asked about this. I'm also concerned about how you've used your position to promote the interests of a couple of your client companies and to advance some highly questionable positions about global climate change and economic policy.

"So the bottom line is that when we get to my beach house, *business ethics school* will be back in session. In the meantime, make yourself comfortable. There's coffee, tea, soft drinks, and fruit back there. I'll put the divider back up in case you want to nap."

I sighed, surrendered, closed my eyes, and brooded. Relationships with some of our customers? Using my position in certain ways? As far as I was concerned, nothing was inappropriate or even slightly questionable about any of that.

The bank provides a variety of high quality services to our corporate clients. This makes their businesses possible. They can provide jobs for their employees, and goods and services to their customers. And we make a reasonable profit.

Any informal lobbying I do—whether local, state, or federal—is for the purpose of encouraging policies and legislation that benefit the company. The way I see it, we aren't lobbying for a *political* outcome but an *economic* one.

I groused to myself about being kidnapped and having my job held hostage by an eccentric who could indulge himself in these stunts simply because he had remarkably deep pockets. He was also able to do this because he had connections with and influence over people on my board. *Note to self. When "Socrates" is off your back, revisit board membership. Clean house.*

*

I took my captor's suggestion that I take a short nap. As I was waking up, the fresh sea air told me we were close to the ocean. When I heard the car's tires crunch over the gravel driveway, I knew we'd arrived. When I got out of the limo and looked at the beach house, I was surprised that it wasn't huge. I guess I thought that anyone who carried around a pocket watch worth millions of dollars would have something that looked like a palace. Walking inside, I was impressed with how simple, elegant—but homey—the place looked. I suspected that the furnishings, art work, and decorations showed a woman's touch. Nonetheless, as comfortable as the place seemed, I wanted to get home. Socrates had opened the glass doors leading to the deck and was admiring the ocean and listening to the waves.

I put my purse on the glass coffee table and stepped outside with him. "OK, *Teach*, let's get this over with. How shall we start? *My* suggestion is that you just tell me what I've been doing wrong and how you want me to change."

"Admirable enthusiasm," he said with a big smile. "But totally insincere! You figure that if we do things that way, it should take me no more than 20 to 30 minutes. Then you get to go home before the engine has even had a chance to cool down. I'm not that naive."

"Actually, brevity isn't your strong suit. I assumed it would take you at least an hour," I joked.

His expression said he didn't appreciate my sense of humor. *Oh well, it was worth a try*, I thought to myself.

"Besides, you know how this works. I'm not going to *tell* you anything about what you need to do. This is about making sure you see more about the ethical dimensions of issues than you currently do. In fact, if I'm successful, you won't know what *I* think about any of the areas we discuss. This is about my being reassured that you have the kind of astute perspective a really top CEO needs these days. So this is going to take a couple of days. You're welcome to change into something more comfortable than your business suit. In the closet of the bedroom at the top of the stairs, you'll find a selection of things Marie suggested. Again, we brought her into the loop. I'm changing as well. I don't normally dress like a limo driver."

As Socrates walked down the hall, I decided that as long as I was stuck there for a while, I'd put on something more relaxing. When I went upstairs and looked in the closet, I found a variety of things my size. So I pulled out jeans, T-shirt, a red Red Sox sweatshirt, and running shoes.

When I returned, Socrates was sitting out on the deck waiting for me.

"There's about anything you'd want in the refrigerator: soda, iced tea, mineral water, and fruit. Or there's coffee, hot tea, or snacks in the kitchen. But nothing alcoholic. We want to keep clear heads."

I took out an iced tea and sat down opposite him. I pointed to the printing on the front of his blue T-shirt.

"Does that slogan say what I think it does? Is that supposed to reveal your true nature?" I asked wryly.

Ignoring my editorializing, he stood up so he could show it off. *"More fun than decent people think should be legal!* Good goal in life, don't you think? I got it when I judged an international intercollegiate business ethics case competition recently. Clever for a bunch of academics. I can get one for you, if you like. In fact, speaking of that competition, a couple of students I met there will join us at some point. I thought having the perspective of young people will help us with some of what we're going to discuss."

"And speaking of what we're going to discuss," I said, indicating I thought it was time to move things along.

"Done with the formalities, then, are we? Fine."

Sitting back down, he looked squarely at me. He was back to being all business. *This* was the guy I'd tangled with in the office.

"Like I said, your prepared testimony was fine. Same with *most* of your answers to the questions. Your exchanges with the Senator and his Chief of Staff? Not even close. So we'll start this way. Let's remind ourselves what went on among the three of you. Conveniently, I have the video." He handed me a tablet with the video cued up.

It was clear I had no choice. I tapped play. First was the Senator.

"I appreciate your recognizing that the actions of your bank and your industry were more responsible for the damage I've seen than CEOs like yourself have done in the past. And I'm glad to hear that you're taking actions to make your operations less risky.

"But my concern is more than the meltdown. I think that your bank needs to take a closer look at ongoing harm to stakeholders perpetuated *today* by the way you do business. Specifically, I mean that by being the bank for certain companies, you facilitate some ethically questionable actions on their part. It seems to me that while you take credit for any of the *good* things that come from those banking relationships, you say you have nothing to do with anything negative. You kept repeating how important your bank's commitment to its stakeholders is. Frankly, I'm more than a little skeptical.

"I also have major reservations about the role you take in throwing your weight around for and against certain policies. Of course, every citizen has a right to do this. But it's your position as *CEO of a major financial institution* that gets you this access to legislators. And that position also gives you considerable credibility with legislators, the business press, and the general public when you argue that certain policies will help or hurt businesses. My objection is that many of your claims are simply false. And you must *know* they're false. So I'd like to know why you keep repeating them."

In view of the fact that I'd just been insulted, I answered with what I thought was admirable restraint:

"As you said, Senator, as far as what happened in the past is concerned, we're reviewing our policies and practices to eliminate or manage any high risk practices. So that will take care of the future.

"We truly are scrupulous in our commitment to our clients and stakeholders. If it helps them for me to use my position to do so, I see that as my job. We do business according to the law and to our own strict internal guidelines. So I have no idea what you're talking about when you say we facilitate unethical practices.

"I resent your suggestion that I go around lying. So I'm not even going to dignify that with a response.

"I don't want to be rude, but I have nothing more to say unless you can be more specific about your complaints."

They weren't satisfied and the Chief of Staff added the specifics,

"You want more detail? OK, here are just a few businesses you're the bank of record for: the company that manufactured one of the weapons used in a school massacre; a company that's very profitable and was very generous with its senior executives, but insisted its union employees take a pay freeze; a petroleum company that spent millions of dollars of its profits to derail anything we've tried to do about global warming.

"Also, at critical junctures, some of these businesses arranged meetings between you and key legislators so you could explain why you thought a particular piece of legislation was or wasn't a good idea. Doesn't any of this strike you as harming some stakeholders?"

And then, before I had a chance to say anything, the Senator jumped back in and was just plain insulting:

"As far as making statements about the economy that are false are concerned, I apologize for saying that you were lying. Apparently, you don't know that statements like 'wealth inevitably trickles down' are simply false. So, my mistake. You weren't lying; you're *stupid*."

It was downhill from there. I shot back with my unfortunate evaluation of his grasp of the economy, sparred with the Chief of Staff again, saw the camera, cursed (loudly) when I realized I'd let this happen *again*, and stormed out.

Socrates' expression said he was enjoying my embarrassment and bad luck at being caught looking stupid on camera twice within a few days. This time, they even had to bleep what I said when I noticed the film crew. "It could have been worse," he said chuckling, but obviously trying to make me feel better. "And you *did* have the good sense to leave at that point. Don't worry. By tomorrow morning, you'll be old news. Everyone will be fixating on some juicy scandal that's about to come out in the tabloids."

"And you know this, *how*?"

"Oh, just idle speculation on my part," he winked. "You know how scandals pop up all the time."

I didn't believe him—and was impressed, and unsettled, by how far-reaching his sources of information were.

"So, what *should* you have said?" he asked.

"How about this? 'Senator, I'd be glad to discuss at length any topic you'd like. But I'm afraid I can't do that right now. An eccentric billionaire, who's posing as my driver, is waiting for me in my limo. He's about to threaten to fire me again.'"

"Cute. But you aren't getting off the hook that easily. The point of our conversation is to help you expand your perspective. It will make you a better CEO. And it should also keep you from 'shooting from the hip' when you say something about *ethics*. Think of it as a do-over."

I couldn't argue that I didn't have the world's best track record for handling the press. So, a practice session wouldn't be a bad idea.

"OK, I'll play along. If you want a serious answer, here's what I should have said.

"'First, our mission statement begins by saying that our chief goal is to serve our clients and stakeholders. So, in that spirit, I want to go on record as objecting to your suggestion that part of the way we serve our clients is to encourage or allow them knowingly to engage in unethical behavior. We have strict guidelines that must be met before we take on a new business. A company must be profitable, deliver a fair return on investment to its shareholders, and scrupulously obey the law. We regularly do thorough background checks, and if any red flags come up, we immediately reserve the right to terminate the relationship. We consider ourselves to be important partners with all of our client companies. We take those relationships very seriously, and we insist on integrity at every turn.

"'Second, the examples you just gave may be controversial or debatable practices, but that doesn't make them unethical. Our mission statement—and I'm sure the mission statements of our client companies—refers to *stakeholders*, not innocent victims, future generations, or third-parties. Despite what our critics want to believe, businesses aren't responsible for most of the bad things that happen in the world. We operate according to the law. Integrity is very important to me.

"'Third, part of serving our clients and stakeholders means taking seriously my responsibility to advance their interests any way I can—even if it means getting involved in the political process. I see nothing wrong with that. If Congress wants companies to operate differently, all you have to do is to pass the laws to make that happen. Business plays by the rules that *you* make. If local, state, or federal legislators don't want to talk to me, they don't have to. I can't make anyone listen to me. And as far as how the economy works goes, if I'm wrong, why don't the two of us sit down sometime with the textbook you used when you taught economics? I'll be glad to show you where I'm right and you're wrong.'"

Socrates had been listening seriously. "OK, except for that final barb, that is closer to what you should have said. I'm not saying that it was a *good* answer. But it would have been *better* than what's running on CNN," he added with a laugh.

"Which means I get to go home now, right?"

"Irony. That's a nice touch. You might keep that in mind for the future," he said, completely ignoring my desire to cut this short. "So, let's get down to work."

9

"Ethics Is Rubbish!"

"As I said, that was a *better* answer. But it wasn't a *good* one. When it comes to ethical issues, it's like you've still got some major limitations in how you look at things. It's like you're wearing blinders that keep you from seeing the *whole* picture. For example, despite our other conversation, you still seem stuck at, 'If it isn't lying, cheating, stealing, or illegal, then it's OK.' I can also imagine that some people would say you have a pretty narrow concept of *responsibility*—whether you're talking about the *bank's* responsibility or your *clients'* responsibility. And, going hand in hand with that, you could be accused of having a very limited understanding of who a *stakeholder* is—despite the prominent mention of those people in your mission statement."

"So, what do you propose? The last time, you hooked me in with that ridiculous bet. What's it this time?"

"Ridiculous?" he said with a laugh. "Considering the fact that I could have pocketed your $200,000 instead of giving you a break, I didn't find it ridiculous at all. But this time it's actually more serious. This conversation is about my desire to give you a new opportunity. It would be a major bump up in your career."

"New opportunity?"

"I've been contacted by board members of an international company whose CEO has decided to retire. They want to bring in somebody from the outside. They asked me if I could recommend someone. I thought of you and said we'd chat about it."

"So this is a job interview? Which company?"

"Job interview? No, it's just a chat," he said smugly, making it plain he wasn't going to give me any details at this point.

I got up and stared at the ocean. I was obviously surprised that on the heels of another PR gaffe, Socrates was seriously considering recommending me for a major international position. My impression was he was the entire selection committee. Turning back toward him, I sat down and asked, "So, what will it take?"

He leaned toward me from his chair and said, "Nothing more than a good, honest debate. I want to know that you really are as smart as I think you are. I want to be reassured that those silly remarks and the tunnel vision aren't the *real* you. The way I see it, either you have the brain you need for this new job, or you don't. If you have it, you certainly haven't been using it lately. But I believe it's actually there. I just want to kick-start it so I know it's back online."

"You said 'debate.' So you want me to defend some of the comments I made earlier today?"

"On the contrary! *I'm* going to defend them. *You're* going to *attack* them. You need to show me that you don't just keep repeating some pre-packaged beliefs. You're going to show me that you can force yourself to look at evidence that challenges what you really believe. You have to show me that you truly understand perspectives you don't agree with. We don't want a CEO who's a self-serving ideologue.

"You keep saying you want to serve your clients and stakeholders. 'Ethics' and 'integrity' show up in lots of your remarks. I want to know that you truly understand what it means to put all that in practice. And we want a CEO who is willing to run this company in line with what we agreed in our last conversation was the 'job' of business.

"You've been spending too much time with people who all say the same things about business and the economy—over and over. And who say it with the certainty and sincerity of the members of a religion who are listing off their central beliefs which are heresy to doubt. You're the CEO of a major corporation, not a High Priestess. Your job is to challenge beliefs, to question 'what everybody knows.' Business—like life—is dynamic, fluid, ever changing. If you're going to make *ethical* decisions and policies, you need to show me that your brain can separate ideology from fact—and make decisions according to the latter."

Aside from the fact that I clearly had no choice, the challenge appealed to me. I did think of myself as a hard-nosed *facts and numbers* person. I'd gotten to my current job because the Board saw that in me. Socrates obviously thought it qualified me for a more important position.

"Fine. Where do you want to start?"

*

Socrates got up and paced back and forth on the deck a few times with his hands behind his back. When he smirked to himself, I assumed it meant that he'd decided where we'd begin. Then he walked over, leaned down, braced himself on the arms of my chair, and gave me a really mean look.

"Let's start with this *ethics* and *integrity* nonsense you keep spouting. I can appreciate that this is good PR. But you can't seriously expect me to believe that a grown woman actually *means* all of that baloney. I expect that anyone who sits in the big chair at a company knows that. You may have to worry about laws, but this ethics stuff? *Rubbish, rubbish, rubbish!* If there were something *real* to ethics, don't you think that 2,000 years of philosophers brooding and arguing would have produced something? Do you know the only thing philosophers agree on about ethics? That anyone who doesn't see things their way is wrong!"

I hated to admit it, but he really knew how to throw himself into a part.

"For openers . . . " I started to reply.

"And before you give me some Boy Scout, Girl Scout platitudes," he interrupted, "let me make it clear that I'm not saying just that *ethics in business* is rubbish. I mean that *ethics in anything* is rubbish. At best, *ethics* is wishful thinking. The idea that there are some overarching, universal standards of right and wrong? That's as believable as Santa Claus and the Easter Bunny. Right, wrong, Father Christmas, the Tooth Fairy, the Easter Bunny—they're all just fictions we concoct to make ourselves feel better.

"First, think about how many people say that ethics is entirely a matter of *individual conscience* or *intention*. Let's say you break an important commitment to me—which costs me money—in order to help your best friend with some emotional crisis. As long as you *sincerely believed* that you had a greater responsibility to your friend and you didn't *intend* to do me any harm, I'm supposed to accept that you didn't do anything wrong. But all you've done is to come up with the neat rationalization to keep yourself from feeling guilty. I have a lot of respect for the fact that an action can look very different to individuals in different circumstances. And I believe it when someone tells me they're acting according to deeply held beliefs. But *sincerely* doesn't guarantee that what we do is right. In fact, all that sincerity does is let me show that ethics is rubbish. If all that it takes for an action to be right is for me to *believe* it's right, then *anything* can be justified.

"The way I see it, people label their actions 'right' and 'wrong' just to feel better about doing what they simply wish to do.

"Instead of saying, 'I want to cheat on an exam because I want to, and because I think I can get away with it,' we say, 'I think it's OK to cheat on an exam because I was too sick to study as much as I wanted to, and a bad grade wouldn't really reflect what a good student I am, or because everybody else in the class is cheating and I'd get penalized for being honest.'

"We don't say, 'I'm going to lie to a customer about how good a product actually is because I'm greedy and can make more money this way.' No, we say, 'Business is aggressive and competitive. The rules of the game are that you look out for yourself. Customers understand that. If they don't, it's their own fault for being stupid and trusting.'

"That's why there's no agreement in ethics. It's all about emotions. People don't need a reason to feel the way they do about things. They just do. And we end up with so many contradictions because people *feel* differently about things. Especially when so much of what we're talking about is rationalizing how you feel so you get to do what you want to do.

"You said you aced your business ethics course. You must have heard about the 'emotive theory of ethics.'"

"Hey!" I interrupted. "Last week you said bringing in anything from philosophers—although I believe you actually called them the 'dead white guys'—was out of bounds."

"Sorry, that was then, this is now, and I still make the rules. So, as I was saying, ethics isn't like science, where we're talking about some sort of objective facts that can be verified. I think that A. J. Ayer was right in claiming that anyone who says, 'Killing is wrong' is really just saying, 'Killing, boo!' If I'm an employee complaining that it's *unfair* that your compensation is so much higher than most people who work for the bank, all I'm really saying is 'I'm *jealous* that you get that much money.'

"When you recognize that ethics is just about emotions, it at least explains why there's so much disagreement about ideas of right and wrong. We don't need a good reason—or any reason at all for that matter—for how we feel about something. We simply feel that way. We feel happy, sad, love, hate for good reasons, bad reasons, and no reason at all. That's why we're all over the place when it comes to ethics. Our judgments about right and wrong are just verbalizations of inner feelings. When people say they think some action is *wrong*, they mean that if someone does it to them, it makes them feel *angry*, *sad*, or *hurt*. Or if they do it to somebody else, they feel *ashamed* or *guilty*. It's all *emotion*!"

As Socrates walked back and forth on the deck, he got more animated. His trashing of ethics also got more passionate.

"I lie to people like crazy. I do it well. I don't feel guilty when I do it, and I think there's nothing wrong with it. The only thing I worry about is being caught in a lie. And if that happens, I just come up with a better lie to cover myself. From everything I know about you, you refuse to lie. So the difference between us is just that lying makes *you* feel guilty and makes *me* feel great. If there were any solid reason to think that lying was wrong, why would you and I feel so differently about it?

"And even if you reject the idea that ethics is just about emotions, consider the idea that right and wrong are grounded in something more substantial, like the norms and traditions of societies. But the problem is there's hardly anything everyone agrees about. And even if most societies say that something like killing is wrong, they're awfully quick to find exceptions that make it OK in certain circumstances. Cultural traditions can be notoriously self-serving—like the idea that buying and selling people of a different skin color is defensible because it's 'our peculiar institution.' Or like the idea women are inferior to men and belong in the home, rather than in the workplace, because it's 'our way.' Sure, that makes sense as long as you're free, white, and male. But ask the slaves, women, or people of color if the fact it's 'a revered cultural tradition' to treat them like inferiors makes it OK.

"Even trying to use some sort of formal procedure to establish ethical standards doesn't save us from all the disagreement, confusion, and inconsistency we find across the planet in how people use 'right' and 'wrong.'

"Let's say we use *law* as the standard and that 'ethically wrong' then just means is '*against the law*.' But 'illegal' simply means that some government can punish you for doing something. And what's legal versus illegal in the world's nations is absolutely contradictory. It's even contradictory within nations—when you look at the differences among states. In some places, discrimination is barred; in others, it's an honored way of life. Abortion is a right in one place and the equivalent of murder in another. The dignity of homosexuals is protected in some places; in others, these people are treated like pariahs. So anyone who tries to elevate 'legal' and 'illegal' to 'ethically right' and 'ethically wrong' is naive. 'Legal' and 'illegal' don't refer to any universal standard. As I said, they simply refer to the rules some group was powerful enough to impose on everyone else.

"But if law won't work as a foundation for ethics, what about *religion*? Well, it turns out this approach isn't all that different from a legal approach. From that perspective, 'right' and 'wrong' is still about getting in trouble with what some authority says you can and can't do. Only in this case, it's about what that authority says will get people punished in the hereafter.

"And do the different religions agree? Of course not! Even though they all claim there's only one God, when you step back and compare their beliefs and practices, you see they're so contradictory there are only two reasonable possibilities. Either there are many gods and not just one, or the one God has a cruel sense of humor and enjoys pitting believers against believers. Virtually all of these religions claim that they have the Truth, while all of the others are wrong. So this is a blueprint for conflict.

"And to make matters worse, some religions' ideas about what's 'wrong' are so expansive that they include not simply what people *do* to each other, they also include *blasphemy*—what people may *say* about their deity or religious figures or treat a religious object—and *heresy*—beliefs they hold privately. So in these religions, even though you treat other people in a perfectly good and decent way, if you *say* or *believe* the wrong thing, you turn out to be someone who deserves to be killed now and flame-broiled for eternity.

"And while they're often too polite or diplomatic to say so, in their hearts, many believers think people from another religion can't be trusted. People from a different faith may even be seen as a threat. However, the *real* threat—and this may be one of the few things on which all of these competing religions agree—are people who are atheists or agnostics. 'If someone isn't afraid God will punish them for doing something wrong,' the Believer says, 'what's to stop them from doing whatever they want?'

"Oh, let me translate that for you. What they're really saying is, 'I know that if *my* desires weren't held in check by fear of being caught and punished, I'd do whatever I damn well felt like—no matter what the consequences to other people. So I'm sure that's true of any atheist.'

"So, just like with 'legal' and 'illegal,' it seems to me that 'ecclesiastically acceptable' and 'ecclesiastically unacceptable' simply means what some religious authority—a sacred book, teacher, or hierarchy—*says* is the case. As some sort of universal ethical standard, it leaves us with even more confusion, conflict, inconsistency, and irrationality than if we said that 'wrong' simply meant 'illegal.'

"See, none of these gives you anything close to a universal, objective, rational, logical standard for positive and negative actions. Personal emotions, individual conscience, social and cultural norms, law, religion. They all fail. Ethics is rubbish, I tell you. *Rubbish! Rubbish! Rubbish!* Moreover, ethics is *unnatural.*"

Every now and then during his tirade, I'd tried to get a word in. But he'd worked up such momentum that he just ignored me. So I did something similar to what I do when my cats climb up the curtains. I stuck my fingers into the glass of ice tea I had in my hands and flicked him in the face with the liquid.

He was startled and then laughed as he stepped back to pick up a towel on the railing. "Unorthodox, but effective. I assume you want to say something."

His expression of approval told me I'd passed some sort of test. Apparently, he wanted to see how far I'd let him go before I *made* him stop. Now I was supposed to show him why his withering assault on ethics was wrong.

"OK, you want to say that *ethics* as some sort of intellectual enterprise is nonsense across the board. I don't agree with that. But I'm not going to argue with what you've just said about emotions, conscience, cultures, law, and religion because the flaws you point out with all of these approaches are real. So let's just say these approaches are *irrelevant* to determining a foundation for ethics. Instead of being cynical and say that the failure of these approaches shows that ethics is rubbish, let's say that when people link ethics with any of these things, they're well-intentioned, but *confused.* I say that 'ethically right' and 'ethically wrong' actually mean something. We just have to look elsewhere than emotion, conscience, circumstances, cultures, law, or religion to see what that is."

Socrates sat down and thought for a moment. His pause made me think I'd made some headway with him.

"*Irrelevant?*" he yelled with an astonished look on his face. "Do you mean to tell me that none of these has *anything* to do with ethics? The pronouncements of the world's great religions. The careful decisions of wise and learned jurists. The deepest and most sincere reflections by all of us on the ethical issues we inevitably face in life. Buddha. Confucius. The Torah. Jesus. Mohammed. Gandhi. Martin Luther King. You're saying all of these are entirely *irrelevant* and *useless* in any inquiry into ethics? None of these has anything substantial to contribute? What are you, an amoral enemy of all that is good and pious in the world?"

I should have seen this coming. First, he points out the flaws in these approaches and suckers me into agreeing with him. Then he jumps on my obvious mistake. This was going to be a long, frustrating conversation.

I got up and paced a bit so I could put this more precisely.

"Let me rephrase that. Emotions, conscience, circumstances, law, and religion aren't irrelevant to an ethical discussion. They just aren't the final word.

"The problem with those approaches is that in addition to coming up with some standard for appropriate behavior, other things—that have nothing to do with ethics—are in the mix.

"*Laws*, for example, are the result of a *political* process, so there can be lots of compromise among legislators for strictly self-serving reasons. Behaviors can be allowed or prohibited for any number of reasons other than their ethical status. And there's also the problem of enforcement. It would be impractical—not to mention crazy—to try to have a legal system that punishes every unethical act. If I lose my cool and publicly humiliate my assistant by blaming her for a mistake I actually made, the best way to handle this for me is to admit I was wrong to treat her that way and to apologize, not to have to go through a formal or legal process.

"*Religions* have to worry about all kinds of things that don't necessarily have anything to do with ethics—rituals and practices, keeping their members engaged, and the like.

"How we *feel* about something may just be a function of having had unreasonable parents. My brother has terrible eye–hand coordination, but our father made him feel like he'd committed a crime when it turned out he couldn't play baseball well. Our mother punished us more often for not getting A's than for something like lying.

"So there are lots of things that are factors in these other perspectives than ethics.

"*But* as examples of thoughtful attempts to identify how we should and shouldn't treat each other, these different outlooks provide us with 'grist for the mill,' shall we say. It's not the *judgments* per se—whether something's acceptable or not from a legal or religious perspective—that are important. It's the *reasons behind* the judgment.

"If something's illegal and it involves either harming people or treating them inappropriately, I want to know *why* it's illegal. Murder, rape, discrimination, for example, are clear violations of someone's right to life, a safe environment, and dignity.

"Similarly, if a religion tells me that part of being married means that it's wrong for me to verbally abuse my husband, I want to know *why*. And the fact that I made a solemn promise to 'love and honor' him is a good start to understand why my action is wrong.

"On the other hand, if a cultural norm says that if you're born into a 'royal' or 'noble' family, the ordinary rules of justice, fairness, and equality don't apply to you, I can see good reasons to question *family lineage* as ethically relevant."

Socrates got up and slowly paced around the deck. From the serious glances he shot my way, I got the sense he was trying to stay in character as 'aggressive skeptic' but still determine if I actually understood ethics.

"Look, the best you've done is to suggest that maybe these perspectives have *something* to contribute to what I still maintain is a fundamentally empty enterprise. The problem is you're begging the question. That is, you're assuming what you're supposed to prove.

"Even if you were magically able to find agreement on what everyone *says* is right and wrong—in all of those perspectives—that doesn't mean anything to me. Humans are remarkably facile with language. We rationalize just about anything. If you want to know what people actually believe, look at what they *do*. And human actions say that, on balance, humans promote their own, selfish interests or simply choose to live according to some totally irrational or arbitrary set of beliefs and then use 'right' and 'wrong' to make it all look proper. Slavery and murder on the basis of skin color. 'Honor killings' of women who were raped. Systematic discrimination, unfairness, and injustice on the basis of every imaginable human trait: gender, religion, sexual orientation, ethnicity, tribe, nationality, whether or not you're 'cool.'

"As far as I'm concerned, *ethics* is just a childish fantasy that humans use to tell ourselves we aren't really the selfish predators our actions reveal us to be. People don't have the stomach to recognize human nature. Or they aren't strong enough to stake their claim, get into the game, and fight for what they want. So they use *ethics* to make themselves feel better about being nothing more than *weaklings* or, and this is probably closer to the truth, ethics is something the *weak* and *fearful* make up to protect them from the *strong*.

"If you can't see this and if you can't get past thinking there's some virtue in being *nice*, I guess it's because you're such a *girl*. With so little testosterone, I'm amazed that you ever got to the point of impressing a board enough to be made a CEO."

10

"Ethics Is Rubbish!" (continued)

I knew the insult about being a 'girl' was just meant to see if I'd keep my cool. So that was easy to ignore. But I couldn't argue with Socrates' description of how 'right' and 'wrong' get used throughout the world in such contradictory and chaotic ways. This was an effective attack on ethics. And he was right when he said I'd gone in a circle. My points made sense on the surface but they didn't prove what I claimed they did.

I also hated to admit that when he said that ethics was something that the weak made up to protect themselves from the strong, part of what he said hit a sympathetic chord. I didn't agree with the way he applied the idea to ethics. However, I've been in plenty of meetings where people's insecurities made them demonize someone who was actually smarter and more perceptive about the problem we were trying to solve or simply willing to take more risks than they were. How many times had I heard a new idea—especially when offered by someone young or less experienced or female or Black—immediately dismissed? Sometimes it's by a patronizing remark: *You haven't been here long enough to know that's not how we do things here.* Sometimes it's with a chuckle or a 'knowing' look around the table. Sometimes, the idea is simply ignored until a few minutes later, when one of the 'guys' revises it slightly and floats it as *his.* Then, his cronies fall over themselves saying it's the best thing since sliced bread. So, if weakness can see strength as a threat in a business setting, isn't it reasonable to think it's a general human weakness? Shouldn't we actually *expect* that to happen when people are trying to define something as important as 'right' and 'wrong'?

All of a sudden I felt something bounce off my head. I looked up to see Socrates, rolling up another wad of paper to throw my way. "I appreciate that my words are so profound you get lost in thought. But it would be nice if you responded eventually when I ask you a question. You've been sitting looking at the waves for five minutes. Care to share?"

I had no idea what he'd asked me. I hadn't even heard it. But I wanted to think about things more before saying anything because I figured he wasn't actually finished.

"If you don't mind, I'd like to hear more of your pearls of wisdom about why ethics is rubbish. Knowing you, you're just getting started."

He laughed at the good natured barb. We both knew it was true. He could talk more than a philosopher.

"As you wish." He stood up and leaned against the railing. "Here's the way I see it. The world is made up of the strong and the weak. It doesn't matter whether you're talking about humans in the middle of New York City or lions and gazelles in some jungle. The strong survive and the weak perish. That's a basic law of nature. And that determines what's 'right.'

"That's what I was about to say before you interrupted me a while ago with your tea. Ethics is *unnatural*.

"Think of it this way. *Science* tells us something real about the world. We learn facts. We're dealing in truth. *Medicine* is real. It may not be a perfect science, but it's something that lets us understand disease and heal it. *Engineering* and *architecture* let us work with facts to solve problems. Good solutions *work* in the real world. *Mathematics* lets us uncover and describe patterns that are too complicated for our eyes to see. All of these disciplines discover something or fix something in an objective, measurable, and practical way.

"By contrast, ethics is something that's made up. It's like literature, art, and music. It's a product of our imagination. It's not based in facts—because when we look at the world, the facts tell us the strong dominate the weak.

"Among humans, the weak are always looking for a way to rein in the strong. So they make up ideas like 'wrong,' 'unfair,' and 'unjust.' This lets them make virtues out of their weaknesses—and vices out of the superior traits of the powerful. The weak say, for example, that everyone should be treated 'equally.' The strong say that's ridiculous. People should be treated according to their abilities.

"So, come to think of it, when I said that ethics is rubbish, I was wrong. Ethics is worse than rubbish. It's absolutely *harmful* because it tells people something that's completely false. Ethics says that weak is good."

Socrates walked over to the refrigerator to get another drink, sat down, and picked up his phone to check his e-mail. I could tell he was going to give me as much time as I needed to answer. But after a speech like that, he clearly wanted a strong reply. I thought for a minute, and then it dawned on me.

"Callicles!" I said.

"Callicles? No, *Socrates*," he answered, without looking up. "I thought I told you that last week," he added with a smirk.

"You know what I mean. You just gave me Callicles' speech to the *real* Socrates from Plato's *Gorgias*." I'd read that dialogue years ago in college. It stuck with me for two reasons. I found one of the ideas—unethical behavior contains its own punishment—engagingly peculiar. Also, because I had always aspired to wealth and power, if the dialogue's idea were true, it meant I had to be careful about what I wanted and how I went about getting it.

"I have no idea what you mean," he said casually, still staring at his phone. "No self-respecting VC would waste his time reading something like that and certainly not in the original Greek. Besides, it doesn't matter if I found this perspective on the back of a cereal box. It's a realistic, practical point of view that you and I both run into in business every day. All that matters is your answer. I'm still waiting for a decent reply. Shall I repeat my argument?"

I knew that *my* Socrates was lying about being ignorant of the *Gorgias*. And he was such an odd duck that I wouldn't be surprised if he had read it in Greek. The argument he just gave me was straight out of the mouth of the character Callicles—a 'man of action,' a 'man of the world' who thinks that philosophy in general and ethics in particular are worse than useless.

The *Gorgias* starts off being about rhetoric—the art of public speaking. But it gradually becomes a discussion about which way of life will make us happy and why anyone should live ethically. That is, it explores the *real* Socrates' signature idea that "vice harms the doer." The final part of the dialogue is a conversation between Socrates and Callicles—a bright, ambitious, greedy, selfish, and unscrupulous Athenian. He tells Socrates he should stop wasting his time with philosophy, give up his ridiculous ideas about ethics, and make something of his life.

The Greeks debated among themselves about what came from nature (*physis*) and what was a product of human convention (*nomos*). The weather, for example, is determined by the forces of *physis*. Law is an obvious example of *nomos*. In the *Gorgias*, Callicles claims that the law of nature (*physis*) is that the strong should rule the weak. He maintains that the strong are superior to everyone else. Therefore, they're entitled to get whatever they want—precisely because their talents allow them to. Happiness comes from letting their desires grow as much as possible and doing whatever they need to in order to get what they want. If that means stomping over other people, taking what belongs to someone else, or manipulating them to your benefit, so be it. Accordingly, it's better to be the person who does something unethical than to be the victim of it. This, very simply, is the law of nature.

Callicles dismisses traditional ideas about ethics, then, as *nomos*. They're artificial, not natural. Moreover, he thinks that ideas like justice, fairness, conventional ideas of morality, and virtues like compassion and moderation are concocted by the weak in order to protect themselves from the strong. Inferior people make virtues out of their weaknesses as a way of protecting themselves from people like Callicles.

Not surprisingly, Socrates' view is the exact opposite. He considers ethics to be a matter of *physis*. Happiness comes from a life of moral virtue, and the freedom and power that comes from controlling one's appetites—not the life of self-indulgence and maximum gratification that Callicles recommends. Moreover, in Socrates' view, behaving unethically comes with a steep price because "vice harms the doer." In fact, because of the seriously negative consequences that people who behave unethically will experience, Socrates claims they actually are harmed *more* than their victims.

Socrates was unusual as a philosopher in that he wrote nothing. Most of what we know about him comes from dialogues written by his contemporary Plato. Also, Socrates advanced relatively few philosophical tenets. He is best known for the way that he conducted conversations: question, answer, follow-up question, answer, another question, and so on forever. The 'Socratic Method' is a time-honored pedagogical method in law schools and philosophy classes. However, one of the few claims that he unambiguously made is that "vice harms the doer."

When Socrates says "harm" here, he has two very particular things in mind. He thinks that vice makes us slaves to our desires and, literally, weakens our minds. Socrates would say that while someone like Callicles may *think* he's doing what he wants and that he is getting what he desires, he's actually doing nothing but servicing a deep, irrational, and insatiable appetite for anything that feels pleasurable.

If, like Callicles, we constantly give into our desires—for money, sex, popularity, the hottest clothes, the newest 'cool' thing, power, thrills, or whatever—they will grow to be the most powerful force in our personalities. In fact, our *desires* will become so strong, they will literally be insatiable. At the same time, our *minds* will be clouded by the desperate hunger of our desires, and the objectivity and power of our *intellect* will be compromised. Getting what we want as soon as we can is all that counts. We'll rationalize our desires. We'll remind ourselves of our superiority. We'll become so arrogant that we'll ultimately become self-defeating. In short, the cost of vice is that we'll become so greedy and stupid that we'll invariably ruin our lives. We'll get caught, alienate everyone around us. We'll blow up our own lives.

Although Socrates doesn't use these words to describe the harm, in contemporary terms, we'd say he refers to a combination of *affective* and *cognitive* damage to the human personality that sets us on a path of self-destructive behavior. We become unable to feel fully satisfied. Nothing is ever 'enough.' And our brains develop tunnel vision, focusing on whatever we need to do in order to satisfy our desires. Unfortunately, we get so caught up in securing what we want that we don't realize we aren't thinking straight. Most commonly, we underestimate the risks we run in being selfish and greedy. We stupidly 'go to the well one time too often,' and we either get caught or guarantee that we'll lose the very things we're trying to get.

Because I recognized the argument, I knew that the only way to counter it—and to refute *my* Socrates' claim that ethics was 'rubbish'—was to show that I honestly believed that the *original* Socrates was right.

"First," I said. "I want to make sure you're done. That's your entire argument? Lions and gazelles? Strong and weak?"

"I think that's plenty. After all, I'd say that being a predator works perfectly well for the lion."

I thought for a minute about how to approach this. "Am I right in assuming that even if I make a good case for ethics in general as being real, substantial, and important, your next move is to say something like, 'OK, ethics is all well and good in other parts of society, but that doesn't mean that the idea of *business* ethics isn't rubbish. In fact, our best bet is to encourage *everyone else* to play by the rules and play fair while we only *say* we'll behave the same way, but actually cheat like crazy. That way, we end up with more of what we want, while the suckers hold the bag.'"

Nodding approvingly the whole time I was talking, Socrates gave me a "thumbs up" when I finished. "Impressive. That's the first time you've anticipated my next move. Well done. And your answer would be?"

"Not so fast. I just wanted to make sure I saw which traps you were laying out. So, ethics in general first. Then business ethics."

I got back up and paced for a couple of minutes as I gathered my thoughts.

"OK, *Socrates*, I assume you have no objection to playing by your namesake's rules."

"Which are?"

"I ask questions and you have to answer them. Your own answers will show that your position is untenable."

"Do you mean you're going to show that I don't really mean what I say when I claim that ethics is rubbish? Has a familiar ring doesn't it? I have to admit turning the tables on the teacher has a certain symmetry. I'm ready."

"And just so we understand one another, I don't deny that 'right' and 'wrong' get used in all sorts of contradictory ways. All I need to do in this conversation is to get you to admit that there's a way to think about ethics that's objective, meaningful, and based on facts—not empty and arbitrary and just a product of human imagination."

"Fair enough."

"So, since we both know that you were just paraphrasing Callicles' argument from the *Gorgias*, let's stay with that discussion for a while. In response, your namesake maintained that 'vice harms the doer' and that when 'the strong' dominate the weak to get what they desire, they're being harmed. In fact, the unethical actions of 'the strong' actually weaken them so much, they turn out to be their own worst enemy. They basically self-destruct. What do you say to that?"

"I'd say that the only way you can expect me to take you seriously is if you offer me some proof. Does some specific example come to mind?"

"Plenty. But for every single example I give you, you'll find some way to say it's unrepresentative. So what's more important than any single example of 'vice harming the doer' is pointing out what's in common in a number of cases. Would you agree that if I can show you a common kind of 'harm' associated with a wide range of cases of people who engaged in unethical behavior, you'd concede that we're looking at a real, fact-based phenomenon?"

"I'd say that would be a good start."

"That's good enough for now," I said. "So here's how we proceed. I want you to think about some of the most high profile scandals in the last decade. In particular, think about individuals who got caught doing something seriously wrong—sports figures, religious figures, politicians, executives. Make it a decent sized group. Maybe about 10. And be sure it includes both men and women. Odds are that you actually know some of these people personally."

"Sadly, you're right. I wouldn't call any of them 'friends,' but definitely 'acquaintances.'"

"Good. Now, looking at everyone in the group, are there any traits they all share?"

Socrates closed his eyes so he could concentrate. He mumbled to himself as he counted off on his fingers as he ran down his list.

"First," he announced, "they're all very smart people. As you probably guessed, at least a couple of people on my list were at Enron. And the title of the book on that scandal—*The Smartest Guys in the Room*—was perfectly chosen. They really were that smart.

"Second, they're all ambitious. They're absolutely *driven* to succeed. For some it was money. For others, being *the best* in their sport. Power. Sex. And that drive meant that they'd work longer and harder than anyone around them. These people didn't kid themselves about what it takes to make it. Not luck, but hard work.

"And when you pair brains with drive, you get people who are very strategic. They aren't just working *hard*, they're working *smart*. They formulate plans with specific goals and timetables. They're organized and clinical in their approach. Frankly, they're so obsessed with reaching the top they can be ruthless in their objectivity. At least on the way up, they don't kid themselves.

"At the same time, they're confident enough to change the plan and do things on the fly when necessary. So I guess I'd say that most of them also have great instincts and intuition.

"And finally, whether you call it charisma or something else, they all have a quality that sets them apart from everyone else around them. They're special."

Nodding, I agreed with Socrates. Those were exactly the same traits I'd identify. "And they recognize that, don't they—as well as all of the other qualities you just listed off?" I asked.

"Well, that's part of what gives them the nerve and drive to be such high achievers. They *believe* in themselves. They know they *deserve* the success they aspire to. They know they're *meant* to beat the odds. If they didn't have such strong self-confidence, they'd have given up before they really made it. By the way," he said pointing directly at me, "except for the bit about being involved in a major scandal, I see you as having all of these qualities—which is one of the reasons I'm impressed with you and I also worry about you."

I wasn't sure how to react to what Socrates had just said. It felt like a back-handed compliment. "You have all these admirable traits—just like the people who ended up in the middle of huge scandals."

Reading my concern, he said, "Look, that was supposed to be a compliment—but also part of the explanation for why we're talking. I don't want what happened to them to happen to you. But you had something in mind with this line of discussion. So keep going."

I decided to take him at his word but this also made me more curious about how he'd answer my next question.

"OK, now think about one or two of the things people in this group got brought down over. Put yourself in their shoes as they're in the middle of whatever mess they've made. Would you do anything differently?"

Socrates paced back and forth again. When he turned toward me, it looked like he was blushing—although it was hard to tell with his beard covering so much of his face. "I'll confess this to you in the spirit of trust. But when I read about any scandal, I have two reactions simultaneously. Half of me is disappointed at reading about yet another example of wrongdoing. And any time it's in *business*, I find it doubly depressing because so many people already think we're crooks. But . . . ," Socrates was clearly hesitating, "the other half of me is saying, 'You idiot! *I* could have gotten away with that! What were you thinking!' So, the answer to your question is, 'Yes, I definitely would do things differently. And I already know how.'"

I pretended to be skeptical and shot him a glance that said, "Prove it."

"Fine. For openers, I'd use burner phones so that my communication couldn't be tracked. I would limit knowledge about the scam to an absolute minimum number of people. I would *always* have a plausible explanation and alibi—with superbly falsified documentation—for what I was doing. I would operate as though someone was working 24/7 to try to catch me. That means that I'd take even more precautions the longer I was doing something. And I would definitely establish a limit to whatever it was I was after. I would know when I was 'going to the well one time too often.' I would know when to say 'Stop.'"

The fact that Socrates had all of this worked out made me wonder whether he'd actually done something and gotten away with it. I hoped it just meant that he enjoyed thinking about things like this as entertainment—the same way that I like puzzling out British murder mysteries.

"In other words," he continued, "I would not make the two mistakes I see over and over again in the men and women we're talking about. Despite all their impressive abilities, these people failed to assess the risks of getting caught accurately, and they didn't have a point where they knew it was time to say 'enough' and walk away. And, since I can only imagine what you're thinking, *no*, I am not speaking from experience. I'd like to think that I've learned from their experience not to be stupid enough to try something dishonest."

"Perfect answer," I said. "Thanks for your candor. So, is it fair to say that, based on your observation of these very talented people, they got greedy and stupid?"

"Greedy and stupid? Absolutely, that's the simplest way to put it. That's why they got caught."

"Were they always that way? Was it just that those traits never had a chance to surface before?" I pressed.

"I don't think so. Something about them changed. I'm thinking of the two people I know best from this group. They were always ambitious, but they weren't the crooks they became. I think what happened is they lost any real sense of perspective about themselves. They ended up thinking not just that they were different from most people because they were so talented and hardworking. They came to see themselves as rock stars who were entitled to anything they wanted. They saw themselves as bulletproof. It's like they believed the newspaper stories written about them that made them look bigger than life. They didn't think the rules applied to them.

"It's like two parts of their brain got shut off. The part that says, 'Enough!' and the part that says, 'Danger!' Looking back on this crowd, the thing I find most surprising is how badly they read the odds of getting caught. Here they are doing things that in business, at least, are plainly illegal. Scams that the Feds have teams of people looking for all the time. And yet, the longer they got away with something, the more relaxed and careless they became. In reality, from a purely statistical perspective, the odds were running *against* them. But they assumed it was *exactly the opposite*.

"And every time I see something like this, I want to yell: *How can you be so stupid!* But the thing is, I know they *aren't* stupid. So something else is going on."

I found Socrates' line of thought very interesting. Like him, I'd known exceptionally smart people who not only did some dishonest things, they also did stupid things that guaranteed they'd be caught. I'd never looked below the surface at what might cause this, so I was curious how Socrates saw it. "Want to hazard any guesses? What do you think caused these people to go from *smart and in control* to *stupid and greedy*?"

"This is going to sound strange," he replied thoughtfully, "but the more I look at it, I can't get past how much it looks like *addiction*. Now, I want it clear that I'm not saying it's the same. But it's almost as though it's in the same ballpark. Never being able to get enough of what you're hooked on. Blindness to the harm it's doing to your own life and the lives of people around you. Being so single-minded and obsessed that you take foolish risks."

"Interesting. So I guess the *real* Socrates was right after all. *Vice harms the doer*. I suspect that Callicles would feel right at home in the group of people we're talking about. He'd see them as 'the strong' whose natural superiority led them to realize that the true law of nature was that they shouldn't be held prisoner by the foolish limitations of conventional morality. But Socrates— that is, the *real* Socrates—claims it's these very unethical pursuits that lead to their undoing. Their vice harms them. And I think that going from *smart and in control* to *stupid and greedy* certainly counts as *harm*. Don't you?"

Socrates leaned forward in his chair and gave me a big smile. "I absolutely do! And, to save you the trouble, if we're identifying genuine and important capacities that get compromised by a habit of serious, unethical behavior, then I guess you have at least one plausible argument for why ethics is objective and meaningful—not empty and arbitrary."

"So," I asked, "are you willing to say I've convinced you that ethics *isn't* rubbish?"

"Well, I'd say you've made a good start. But more importantly," he winked, "I'd say *you're* willing to say that you now honestly believe that ethics isn't rubbish."

He was right. While I've always talked a good line about ethics, I'd never been able to dismiss the fact that 'right' and 'wrong' got used in so many different ways on the planet. Ethics always seemed so subjective to me. My exchange with Socrates didn't settle all of my doubts. But I could now honestly say that ethics wasn't rubbish and that there seemed to be at least some objective dimension to it. If nothing else, I had to say that the idea that 'vice harms the doer' had never seemed so plausible to me.

"You're brooding," Socrates noted.

"The first time I read Plato's dialogues," I answered, "it was fun to play with Socrates' idea that 'vice harms the doer.' But I always thought of it closer to fiction. The way we've just been talking about it, however, makes it look like a real phenomenon."

"You mean that something about the way people act changes something in them—cognitively and affectively."

"Something that weakens us *cognitively* and *affectively*? So we're going more high-brow than *stupid* and *greedy*," I joked. "But, yes. Particularly when you said how this looked to you not entirely unlike addiction, it's almost as though we're talking about some sort of syndrome in which certain behaviors cause specific personality traits to weaken."

"I think that's a fair way to put it—even though that's typically not how contemporary philosophers explain the importance of ethics. So what's bothering you?" he asked, noticing my furrowed brow and perplexed expression.

"If this is real, why does this happen? The only explanation that comes to mind—and it's completely strange in my book—is that we're talking about how humans are hardwired. If we engage in a pattern of seriously unethical behavior, we start acting in a self-destructive way."

"To be honest," he answered, "I think this is so complicated that we'd need a team of specialists from a variety of fields to get a really good, research-based answer. But frankly, I don't think that your 'hardwired' explanation is so bizarre.

"And since our conversations fall under the august category 'philosophy,' we can give ourselves permission to indulge in wild speculation. After all, only the seagulls and dolphins can overhear us, and I'm sure we can trust them not to make fun of us.

"So, do you want to speculate, or should I?" he asked.

"After being recorded—twice—saying stupid things, I'm not even going to risk it. Be my guest."

"Suit yourself." He leaned against the railing, studied the ocean, and then looked up at the sky. Every now and then, he'd mutter something. "Hardwiring, genetics, adaptation, social intelligence, language, gossip, maladaptive behavior." While he pondered, I decided to go inside and get something warmer to wear. It was getting cool on the deck, but the sunset was too beautiful to miss. When I returned, Socrates looked up. "I'm not going to say 'eureka.' But given my limited knowledge of evolutionary science—especially evolutionary psychology—I think the best I can say is that this is at least 'wildly speculative but theoretically possible.'

"I'm going to run through this very quickly. Compared to the important topics we need to discuss, this is just a lark. I'm going to overstate this like crazy. But once you floated the idea, I couldn't resist."

"I'm intrigued," I replied, sitting back down.

"Evolution 101. How well we survive, evolve, and advance depends on how well we *adapt* to the environment. Some traits increase the odds of survival. Others don't, and we call those *maladaptive*.

"Humans are social beings. We need to be able to work together to survive and prosper. In fact, one theory holds that the primary reason we ended up with these big brains was to operate effectively as part of a community. In fact, from this point of view, the primary reason we developed language is so we could gossip about each other."

"Gossip? Not make fires, build tools, and skyscrapers?"

"No. Gossip. Remember, humans are part of the Great Ape family. Primates groom each other as a way of promoting social cohesion. When human communities got too big for us to physically groom each other, talking about each other—gossiping—did the same job.

"Because we're so thoroughly social, it's obvious that any sort of anti-social behavior is *maladaptive*. That's why human evolution has, generally speaking, favored norms, rules, and procedures that let us manage our dealings with each other without violence. If force and aggression were our default way of dealing with each other, life would be, as Hobbes said, 'nasty, brutish, and short.'

"But not all anti-social behavior is obvious. And it's definitely in the interest of the species to minimize it. So, I like the idea that evolutionary pressures encouraged the development of the mechanism we're talking about. That is, from the perspective of the good of the species—the good of a community of social beings—a mechanism by which seriously unethical behavior weakens us so much that we make it more likely that we'll get caught is *adaptive*. From an evolutionary perspective, 'vice harms the doer' is good for the species."

"So you're telling me that you think that ethics, like language, somehow developed as a tool to facilitate living in a group?"

"All I'm saying is I think that's an interesting idea to ruminate over. I'm not an evolutionary psychologist, so I haven't a clue as to whether this makes sense. But, if true, it would certainly give us another reason for arguing that ethics isn't made up rubbish.

"And speaking of the idea that ethics isn't rubbish, all I've conceded is that your 'vice harms the doer' argument is a good start. You need to do more than that."

11

Is There an Objective Foundation to Ethics?

"Don't you think we've spent enough time on theory? You told me you were unhappy about my relationships with some of our customers, my support for some of the bank's clients, and my statements about public policy. If you're trying to decide whether you're going to offer me this new job, don't you think we should talk about these things rather than whether or not ethics is or isn't rubbish?"

"Those *are* important topics, and we *will* get to them. But first I need to know that you have the intellectual horsepower to be in charge of a major financial institution with international reach. I want to reassure myself that you're the person I think you are—someone whose intellectual *vision* isn't limited to numbers and traditional ways of thinking.

"Our discussions about ethics are important for three reasons.

"First, and most importantly, I have to know that the captain of the ship has a good moral compass. Even from a strictly pragmatic perspective, it's not good for *anyone* connected with the company if it gets embroiled in some scandal. Bad press. Investigations. Subpoenas. Legal bills. Damaged reputation. Do you know how much money that would cost?

"Second, especially if you want to operate on an international stage, you need to be able to think about ethics as something more than obeying the laws of the countries in which you operate. That's *compliance*, not ethics. Ethics is bigger and broader than that. At least it is if you can convince me it's something that isn't rubbish," Socrates concluded with a smile.

"And speaking of operating on an international stage, I don't suppose you could tell me more about this company."

"The most I can say is it's a major international corporation in another industry. And while I'm sure you may think that my unorthodox way of doing things—like kidnapping you—means I have no scruples, I do keep my word. And I promised the people who asked me to do this that I would tell you no more than what I have at this point."

"OK. So where do we stand?"

"It's exactly what I've told you before. You have potential. But I need reassurance that you can operate successfully on a bigger stage that includes a far wider range of values and cultures than you've had to deal with so far. I need to know that when you face the problems that invariably come up in an organization that big and diverse, you have an anchor that keeps you from being blown around by expediency, money, politics, ego, or stupidity. I also think that it's time for you to get back to work."

*

I was beginning to see why the theoretical discussions could matter in terms of day-to-day decisions. Laws, rules, policies—even mission statements and lists of corporate values—cover only so much. I'd seen too many of my colleagues blindsided by situations that blew up because they never had a good grasp on the intangible parts of a problem. "Number fixation" my business ethics prof called it, as he tried to warn us about some of the pitfalls of being in a business school.

"You're all being trained to be 'number crunchers' with a pretty short checklist when it comes to making decisions. Stock price. Quarterly profits. Return to shareholder. Legality. If you're lucky, you'll end up at companies with a longer list. But even those places can have boards comprised of number crunchers. So you're back to your short list. And while those factors may be the most important ones for many of the problems you'll solve, if issues like that are the only ones you're really good at, you'll end up in trouble. If some part of a problem is 'soft' or 'fuzzy,' you'll think it can't be important. Or, following the principle, 'if the only tool you have is a hammer, you treat every problem like a nail,' you'll try to make it into the kind of issue you're comfortable with. And yes, that is a cliché. But it's a cliché because it's *true*.

"The first thing you need, then, is the equivalent of *'ethical night vision.'*

"Think of what happens on a sunny day when you go into a movie theater or a completely dark room. You can't see much. You bump into people and furniture. The longer you're in the room, however, the more your eyes adjust. You now see things that at first were invisible to you. 'Ethical night vision' is like that—except you have to be trained to 'see in the dark.' And that's why you're in this course. We're going to spend the semester walking around the equivalent of a very dark room filled with furniture. At first, you'll think I'm crazy when I tell you what's in the room: chairs, sofas, a piano, and a couple of mirrors. All you see is darkness. Fortunately, when I tell you to try to walk around, you bump into furniture. That will tell you there's actually something there. But then I'll be running you through certain exercises that sharpen your vision. And eventually, you'll be able to see what's there on your own. Only what's in *our* room isn't furniture, it's concepts like 'right,' 'wrong,' 'conflict of interest,' 'moral responsibility,' 'stakeholders,' 'manipulation,' 'deception,' and 'rights of future generations.' "

And he was right. If you worked at it, you really could develop "ethical night vision." By the end of the semester, I was taking seriously some topics I'd initially dismissed as soft, silly, or left-wing propaganda.

"And even when you develop that, you still need *perspective*," he added. His favorite exercise to show us how stupid a roomful of very smart people could be was a discussion of truth in advertising. We all knew the legal definition of misleading and deceptive advertising, but we were challenged to come up with a definition from the perspective of ethics. Where did honesty end and deception begin? Was there any difference between "misleading" and "deceptive"? If what you say in an ad is true just not the whole truth is it lying? We came up with so many competing answers, so many good examples of "exceptions to the rule" and so many conflicting sets of criteria for ethically questionable ads that after an hour we were exactly *nowhere*.

"When the prof asked what our general conclusion was, someone in class said that if a group of intelligent, well-intentioned, business-savvy people couldn't agree, maybe the distinctions we're trying to draw are, in essence, the equivalent of *fictions*. Perhaps the difference between honesty and dishonesty in advertising is so complicated and situational that it should be seen as *arbitrary*. Maybe there isn't a hard and fast difference between the two after all. It's not like 'legal' versus 'illegal' or 'profitable' versus 'unprofitable.' Those distinctions can be based on hard evidence. They mean something substantial. We'd have an easy time getting agreement from everyone in the room on those. But since it was impossible to do that on 'honesty' versus 'dishonesty,' maybe it tells us there's nothing solid and substantial there."

"Interesting idea," our teacher replied thoughtfully. "How many of you agree?"

Every hand in the room shot up.

"Absolutely everyone. Very impressive. And very *wrong*. Think about it this way. If instead of asking you to draw the line between 'honest' and 'dishonest' advertising, I'd asked you to tell me where the 'front' of your head ended and the 'back' began, we'd have just as much disagreement and confusion. And yet, is there anyone in the room who would disagree with the statement that my nose is on the 'front' of my head and most of my hair is on the 'back'? Of course not. The difficulty in determining the criteria regarding a distinction doesn't mean that the distinction itself is meaningless. My point is that you can get so fixated on one thing—in our case, it was where 'honesty' ends and 'dishonesty' begins—that you lose any perspective. You look at minutiae rather than the big picture. And that's an easy mistake to make when you're dealing with ethical issues."

*

"Fair enough," I replied to Socrates. "So I need to do more to convince you that ethics isn't rubbish." I thought for a minute and then began. "In my undergrad ethics class, I found the ideas of Mill and Kant very illuminating. Now Mill . . . "

"Whoa there, Sparky!" Socrates shouted, laughing. "Mill and Kant? Are you kidding? When was the last time you heard any of those names during a board meeting—or at *any* business meeting, for that matter? If that's the best you can do, we can pack it in right now. You need to explain why ethics isn't rubbish as one regular person to another."

"Do I detect a double standard, here?" I asked calmly. "Wasn't it *you* who threw that argument out of Plato's *Gorgias* at me? Now you're saying I have to come up with my own explanation?"

"First, *you* said the argument came out of Plato. I told you it didn't matter if I found it on the back of a cereal box. What mattered was your response. And that's still true. I don't care whose ideas you use, but I need to hear in your own words why ethics isn't rubbish."

I grumbled because I was in no mood to come up with an elaborate defense of ethics on the spot. And while I was willing to play along because a future job was on the line, I wasn't happy that Socrates was setting all the rules of the game. Sensing my frustration, he said, "How about if I meet you half way? First, explain things in your own words as far as you can go. Then, you can shift gears. Use any thinker you want. Just translate their ideas into commonsense terms we can use in a business."

I knew that was the best I was going to get, so there was no point arguing. But I needed some time to plot this out. I took my tablet out of my bag. "Fair enough. So first you want my own explanation for how ethics has an *objective, rational, logical* foundation. But to do this properly, I'll need about 30 minutes and an internet connection."

"No problem. With the sun going down, it's getting cool out here anyway. Let's go inside and I'll start a fire. My assistant will be arriving shortly and he'll make dinner for us. It's bad enough that I shanghaied you. The least I can do is to give you a decent meal. There's Wi-Fi throughout the house. Here's the login information," he said, handing me a card with what I needed to know. "Do you need someplace else to work, or will the living room be OK?"

The overstuffed leather chairs were definitely inviting. "I'll be fine as long as I can concentrate."

By the time Socrates had a decent fire going, I'd found what I was looking for online and figured out a commonsense strategy for how to get even a stubborn skeptic (the role my host had decided to take) to agree that ethics wasn't "rubbish," that is, that ethics had an objective, rational, logical foundation. *Finally,* I thought to myself, *I get to use some of those gen ed courses I thought were a waste of time in college.*

"Before I start," I began, "I want to point out that since you conceded that 'vice harms the doer' is a genuine possibility, I'm going to view that as relevant evidence to the question we're considering. The cognitive and affective harm we regularly observe in people who have engaged in serious wrongdoing is real. Also, I think your theory that 'unethical behavior is maladaptive when looked at from the standpoint of the evolution of a social mammal' is actually an interesting—if highly speculative—explanation. I may not include this in my final defense of ethics. But let's recognize that as an important bit of evidence."

"So noted," Socrates nodded.

"Also, I'm going to give you a two-for-one. I'll show you not only that ethics isn't rubbish but that *business* ethics isn't rubbish."

"Impressive, if you can do it. And it will definitely save us time."

"Let's return, then, to the imaginary tribal village we used in our discussion last week," I said. "It will help keep things simple."

"OK."

"We started by agreeing that the point of our living together in the village was to make it possible for us to have a better life than if we were on our own. Division of labor and specialization of labor make things more efficient. We also said this would give us a specific 'kind of life' or 'quality of life.' The overall 'job' of the village is to give us a particular way of life."

"Correct."

"Or, to put a finer point on this, getting *a particular way of life* is the primary reason any of us would *agree* to form a village. This also determines the *terms* of the agreement we'd make in forming the village."

"Right. And by 'a particular way of life' we meant . . .?" Socrates asked.

"First, a life where we *get our material needs* met. Also, a life where *we're treated properly*—with fairness, equality, and respect. We said the basic principles to respect when you live in the village are 'do no harm' and 'treat others appropriately.' "

"OK."

"And that then gave us an 'ethical yardstick' we could use in evaluating the ethical character of any action in the village. One side of the yardstick measures the *tangible* good and harm connected with the action: physical harm, emotional harm, short-term harm, long-term harm, harm that can be repaired, harm that can't, and so on. The other side of the yardstick tells us whether or not that action treats others properly. Are people being treated in a way that's fair, honest, respects privacy, honors promises, and so on? These are the *intangibles*."

"Again, I recall all of that," Socrates nodded.

"And basically, that's all we said we'd mean by *ethics* in our village. We seemed to assume that 'do no harm' and 'treat others appropriately' would give us the particular 'kind of life' or 'quality of life' we were looking for."

"Agreed."

I paused to make it plain we were now getting into new territory. *"However*, this is where we need to break new ground on two fronts.

"First, 'kind of life' and 'quality of life' are actually pretty fuzzy and imprecise ideas, so we need a clearer explanation of what we're talking about with phrases like that."

"And second?"

"At some point, once we get a clear definition of the 'kind of life' we're talking about, I expect you're going to object that this is something we're just making up. That it's based on something *subjective*, not *objective*. You'll say that the elements that make this a good 'quality of life' and the specific features of the 'kind of life' we're aiming for in the village are things that we're *choosing* and that we're *agreeing* what should be there. Again, you'll object that this is a subjective process not anything firm and objective."

"I'm impressed and disappointed," Socrates replied. "I was hoping to spring that on you later. Nicely done."

"And, anticipating that you have some other traps I haven't noticed yet," I answered with a smile, "here's how I want to proceed to make sure we're grounding this in something *objective*.

"First, the simplest way to put this is that the 'kind of life' we're looking for is one where we experience at least *a rudimentary sense of satisfaction with life*."

"Sense of satisfaction. Interesting approach," he said stroking his chin. "On the surface, this doesn't seem to have anything to do with ethics. I'm intrigued."

"The feeling that life is basically OK," I answered. "There are a variety of ways to describe this: a sense of well-being; happiness (although this has more emotional connotations than I'm comfortable with); a feeling that there are no major, fundamental frustrations with getting what we need.

"Life in the village isn't perfect, but things are organized and people treat each other in such a way that everyone has a reasonable chance at a decent life. We don't necessarily get everything we *want*, but our *basic needs* are satisfied. And because *those **needs** get met in the village, we experience a **basic sense of satisfaction** with life.*

"And it's important to recognize that we're talking about *needs* here, not *wants*—because the idea that *there is a set of basic human needs* is going to be the basis of my argument that ethics—and business ethics—has an objective foundation. *Wants* are the result of any number of things—our *emotions, personal history, individual, idiosyncratic quirks of our personalities*, and the like. And not only are those things *subjective*—even *arbitrary*—we've already disqualified them as possible foundations for ethics for that very reason. But *needs* are *objective* and, as I'll explain, they're grounded in the nature of our species."

Socrates stroked his beard as he puzzled over what I'd just said. "You're claiming that ethics is somehow connected with a series of basic needs that human beings have that can be established *objectively*?"

"Yes, *objectively*," I answered with confidence.

"Hmmm," Socrates replied, arching his eyebrow. "And you're going to apply this idea to life in our village as a way of showing that ethics isn't rubbish?"

"Correct."

"And on top of that," he added, "this is going to let you show me how *business* ethics isn't rubbish—that is, that there are solid, objective reasons why business needs to abide by 'do no harm' and 'treat others appropriately.' "

Thanks to the hunch I followed when I did some quick research on the internet, I could say, "Yes. That's exactly what I'm going to do."

Socrates scratched his head and stared at me, clearly thinking about all of this. His skepticism seemed genuine. Maybe I was finally one step ahead of him in our discussion. "Ambitious. Let's hear it."

I was getting tired of sitting down, so I got up and walked over to the fireplace so I could lean against the mantle as I planned exactly how to proceed. This would have been much easier in my office where I have that massive whiteboard. Annoyed at having to keep everything straight in my head, I remarked, "You know, if you knew you were going to kidnap me for another one of your weird conversations, the least you could have done is to have a whiteboard so that I could sketch things out."

"Right! Sorry, I forgot," he pressed a button on a small box beside his chair—an intercom, I guessed.

"Yes, sir. How may I help?" came a masculine British voice.

"I'm sorry, Colin, but I forgot to ask you to turn on the technology. If you can tear yourself from preparing dinner, would you mind?"

"Of course, sir. Be right there."

"Sorry," Socrates said apologetically. "Where were my manners? It will be right here."

A tall, handsome, muscular man dressed in black slacks and black T-shirt walked into the room and stepped up to a panel on the wall. He punched a few keys, and what I'd originally thought was a huge mural turned into a white screen. He nodded at me politely, "Ma'am," and handed Socrates a stylus and a slip of paper. "Excellent menu, Colin. We're on schedule, so we'll eat when we discussed. And please call Anastasia and give her the green light on finalizing that Singapore matter. Tell her that whatever she decides as appropriate final terms are fine with me. I trust her judgment. She's closer to the situation than I am."

"Very well, sir," he replied and walked back down the hall.

"Sorry, we'll do formal introductions later. When Colin's in the middle of preparing a meal, he doesn't like being disturbed. And since cooking's not really part of his job—more of a hobby—I try to respect that. But he's better with technology than I am, so I need his help whenever I want to use the system."

"So he's your . . .?"

"Pro tem PA. Chef. Majordomo. Driver. Pilot. You know, all the usual. So, back to business. You. The whiteboard," he added, tossing the stylus at me. "It's great flat screen technology. You're going to love it."

"If I remember correctly," I said as I quickly wrote on the screen, "here's what we said last week."

Socrates got up and walked over to the screen. "Looks good to me. Close enough."

"Let's start by defining what we mean by the 'kind of life' the villagers get. They have their *basic needs* met. And by this I mean they experience *the conditions that are absolutely, positively necessary in order for any human being to grow, develop, or flourish in a healthy way.* I'm claiming that—*simply because of the nature of the cloth from which we're cut*—there is a set of necessary conditions that must be met in order for any human being to grow, develop, or flourish in a healthy way. If we get these things, we have a shot at a decent life. At least there's no major way we're hampered. So when I say 'sense of satisfaction' or 'well-being,' I'm thinking of how it feels when we have at least the bare minimum of what members of the village need in order to feel that it's doing its job."

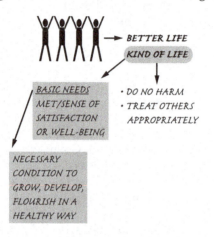

"Basic needs determined by the cloth from which we're cut," he said slowly, carefully studying the screen. Then pointing at "basic needs," he said, "You mean *physical* needs—clean air and water, healthy food, shelter that protects us from dangers in our environment."

"*Physical needs* are part of what I mean. But I'm referring to something broader than that. Here's what I think every villager needs in order to feel that life is at least satisfying in the most rudimentary way.

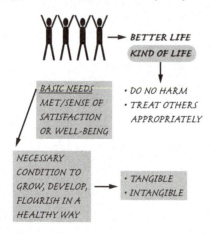

"First are *tangible* needs: life; physical health and safety; emotional health and safety; absence of pain and suffering; being cared for when you need assistance; the skills and knowledge needed to operate in the village; social interaction and access to relationships; and rest.

"Second are *intangible* needs: freedom—in our actions, thoughts, and beliefs; equality; fairness; privacy; respect for our dignity as persons; honesty, and the like."

"Wait a minute," Socrates said as he returned to his chair, "it sounds like you're describing some sort of utopia. I think you're being awfully unrealistic and impractical. You say 'physical health'; but everyone gets sick. You say 'relationships'; but falling in love and living happily ever after are more the exception than the rule. You say 'honesty'; but we run into liars every day. I thought we were talking about ethics, not speculative, utopian fiction that's no more meaningful than someone's 'I want a pony for Christmas' letter to Santa Claus." Throwing his hands up in the air for dramatic effect, he said, "*Please* tell me you aren't serious with this nonsense!"

Apparently relaxing in front of a fire gave Socrates a second wind when it comes to being annoying.

12

Is There an Objective Foundation to Ethics? (continued)

"Let's take a step back," I replied calmly, brushing off Socrates' obvious attempt to bait me. "I'm showing you that ethics isn't 'rubbish.' To be precise, I'm showing you that there is a way to evaluate the ethical character of actions that isn't *arbitrary* and *emotional* and that is distinctly different from other ways that we appraise what we do: *legal, profitable, religiously orthodox*, and the like. I'm saying I can show you a meaningful, logical, rational, and objective way to label actions *right, wrong, ethically acceptable, ethically unacceptable*—whatever terms you like to use. Are we on the same page so far?"

"Sure," he replied. "But for *that* you need an objective, universal standard. That's why emotions, laws, religious teachings, and personal convictions are disqualified because they give us so many inconsistent and contradictory judgments about what they say is right versus wrong."

"That's why I'm coming at this from a different direction. And your comment about utopias is actually helpful."

"Helpful? Hardly!" he mocked. "Utopias are meaningless fantasies! We're business people. We deal in reality and hard facts."

He wasn't seeing my point—or he did and he was being a nuisance again. Realizing the latter was more likely, I ground my teeth silently. "Let me ask you this. What do utopias promise?"

"That's easy," he answered, clearly getting warmed up to mock this line of discussion. "Perfection! Bliss! Euphoria! Universal wealth! Peace! Everyone loving each other! Sex! Drugs! Rock and roll! Happiness! Eter-"

"Stop there!" I interrupted. "I assumed that if I waited you out, you'd finally say something helpful."

He laughed in a way that told me he'd heard this before in discussions.

"Authentic utopian speculation," I continued, "isn't an exercise in mindless fantasy. It's a serious examination of two things: first, the conditions necessary for a good life—calling it *happiness* is fine with me—and, second, the things that get in the way of our getting that kind of life. And since a good utopia has to be built on a realistic understanding of human nature, it's actually relevant to our discussion. When I just referred to basic needs that are determined by 'the cloth from which we're cut,' I was talking about the first thing I want a good utopia to identify—*the conditions necessary for a decent life.* You interrupted me and started complaining about the practical issue of whether those conditions get met. If you let me finish, you'll see my point. Remember, I'm laying the foundations for a universal, objective standard for evaluating actions—an objective basis for ethics."

Socrates shifted impatiently in his chair. "I'm not sure where you're going with this detour, but go ahead. I'm not the one in a hurry to get home."

"Since you're the one who brought up utopias, let's stick with that for a minute. A good one to look at is B. F. Skinner's *Walden Two.* Skinner thinks we need only five things to live a satisfying life: health, a minimum of unpleasant labor, a chance to exercise our talents and abilities, intimate and satisfying personal contacts, and relaxation and rest. And make sure you appreciate the fact that Skinner was a *behavioral scientist.* Now I'm not going to debate with you about whether Skinner's list is accurate or complete. I just want you to understand the basic idea behind it—that human beings are all configured in a way that determines the conditions that have to be met in order for us to say that life is even rudimentarily satisfying.

"This is *exactly* the same thing I was saying in claiming that there is a set of conditions that absolutely, positively must be met in order for any human being to grow, develop, or flourish in a healthy way.

"I'm the first to admit that for billions of people on the planet, these conditions don't get met. They don't experience anything even close to that. It's also true that humans are a remarkably adaptable species and that we can put up with miserable circumstances. But just because we can find a way to tolerate them doesn't mean that we're OK with them—*or* that these conditions are letting us grow and develop in a healthy fashion.

"Let's go back to physical health. We know which conditions have to be met for a human body to be healthy. Billions of people aren't healthy—through bad luck, circumstance, or choice. But the necessary conditions for physical health are set by the body. What someone like Skinner argues is that when we put in the rest of who we are—the psychological piece of our nature—we can identify the rest of the necessary conditions that, when met, would give us a sense of what you mockingly referred to as *happiness.*

"So let me say what I mean again. In order for *all* human beings—whether they live in our imaginary village or somewhere else—to be able to grow, develop, or flourish in a healthy way, there are some *tangible* things they need as well as some *intangible* things. The *tangible* things are what we can call the practical 'stuff of life': life; physical health and safety; emotional health and safety; absence of pain and suffering; being cared for when we need assistance; the skills and knowledge needed to operate in the village; social interaction and access to relationships; and rest. The *intangible* things have to do with how we're treated by others. Do they respect our freedom—in our actions, thoughts, and beliefs? Are we treated with equality, fairness, and honesty? Do they respect our privacy and dignity as persons?"

Socrates nodded as I spoke, making it clear he was listening carefully and following me.

"OK, I understand what you're claiming. But let's get on with it. What's the connection between all of this and *ethics*?"

"Something you're going to have to wait patiently for." I wagged my finger with a laugh, getting back at him for all the times he called me impatient. "Because, first, it's important for us to talk about whether or not you *agree* with what I've just said."

"Do I agree that we *need* certain things in order to grow and develop and to experience life as at least basically satisfying? And do I accept your list as accurate?"

"That's right."

"If this is so important, let me see that whole list. Just tap twice. What you've done will be saved and you get a blank screen."

During my research on the internet, I found a decent list of 'basic tangible and intangible human needs' in connection with a site discussing human rights. I simply transferred it from my tablet to the screen.

TANGIBLE NEEDS/THE 'STUFF' OF LIFE

- *LIFE*
- *PHYSICAL HEALTH AND SAFETY*
- *EMOTIONAL HEALTH AND SAFETY*
- *ABSENCE OF PAIN AND SUFFERING*
- *BEING CARED FOR WHEN WE NEED HELP*
- *THE SKILLS AND KNOWLEDGE NEEDED TO OPERATE SUCCESSFULLY IN THE VILLAGE*
- *SOCIAL INTERACTION AND ACCESS TO MEANINGFUL RELATIONSHIPS*
- *REST*

INTANGIBLE/HOW WE'RE TREATED

- *FREEDOM IN ACTION AND THOUGHT*
- *FAIRNESS*
- *EQUALITY*
- *HONESTY*
- *PRIVACY*
- *RESPECT FOR OUR DIGNITY AS PERSONS*

Turning around after it appeared on the big screen, I explained, "I'm not saying this is either some sort of 'official' list or even that it's complete. But I believe it's a reasonable description of the conditions we human beings need in order to grow and develop in a healthy fashion. This is the 'kind of life' we're aiming for in our village."

Socrates got back up from his chair and studied the list carefully. Then he turned around.

"*Yes*—I agree we need certain conditions. But, *No*—I don't accept your list—especially your intangible needs. Human beings *do* need food, shelter, air, water, a physically safe environment. Deprive people of food and water, and the odds are that you'll see violence pretty quickly. But the fact that so many people live in societies built on discrimination, unfairness, and inequality—*and*—that they *tolerate* it tells me the *intangibles* you refer to are *wants* not *needs*. People may not like living without these things, but they find a way to cope. They don't absolutely, positively *need* everything on your list to survive."

Now it was my chance to turn the tables on my host. I reached into my pocket and pretended to take out a notebook and pen. "*Doesn't listen carefully,*" I said out loud shaking my head in mock exasperation, pretending to jot something down the note. As I looked back up at Socrates, he was smiling in appreciation of the humor. "The issue isn't whether humans can *cope* or *adapt* to poor conditions. We know we're a remarkably adaptable species. The question is whether there's a set of conditions that has to be met in order for us to experience *full, healthy growth and development* and which makes it possible for us to experience life as at least *basically satisfying*.

"Take *equality* and *liberty*, for example. For years in the United States, it was legal to treat whites and blacks differently and to restrict the liberty of Black Americans as long as there were no tangible differences in what they got in terms of food, shelter, education, transportation, and the like. The law of the land said that *separate but equal* was acceptable. African-Americans rejected the idea because the policy was based on the idea that one race was superior to the other. They asserted a need for equality and for liberty, which the courts finally recognized. But in the process, no small number of people died fighting for that need. So it isn't just food and water that people will risk their lives for."

Socrates nodded thoughtfully. "Point well taken."

"The critical point here is that I'm identifying these *needs* as the conditions necessary for full, healthy growth and development. We need these conditions in order to develop the strengths and capacities to have a reasonable chance of success in the village.

"What I'm saying about our list is that I bet that whenever you imagine life without any of these items, you'll feel you've been blocked in some fundamental way from being able to grow and strengthen. That's the difference between a *need* and a *want*. Failing to get a *basic need* met? A life stunted in some fashion. Not getting a *want*? Disappointment. But nothing critical."

I pointed to each item as I read it off, and I gave Socrates time to imagine a life without them. I could see by the expression on his face that he was taking my request seriously.

"*Life, physical health and safety,* and *emotional health and safety*? We wouldn't even have the basic conditions for becoming much of anything or accomplishing much in the village.

"Regularly experiencing *pain and suffering*? We can't develop strengths that way.

"*Not being cared for when we need help?* That would be like having a business that's always losing money. You're scrambling just to keep your head above water.

"*Being ignorant of the skills and knowledge we need to be successful in the village. . .*"

Socrates interrupted me. "I'm starting to see what you're saying. If our village is pretty simple, that would be something as basic as literacy and arithmetic. If someone's deprived of those, their prospects are going to be grim. It's like telling someone to build a house and then keeping them from getting the tools they'd need."

I nodded in reply. "Precisely. . . . *Being isolated from people?*" I continued.

"Being deprived of the opportunity to form any meaningful relationships. Serious business," Socrates said thoughtfully. "There are a variety of valuable social skills we'd never develop. And, because humans are such highly social mammals, I suppose there's a good chance that, from an emotional perspective, we'd end up seriously harmed."

Finishing the list, I read, "*Not being able to rest?* That's going to compromise our health. . . . So those are our *tangible* needs."

I pointed to the following section. "Then there are the *intangibles*—which you initially wanted to dismiss. So, how do we *need* to be treated?"

I read off the next part of the list. "Again, think of whether you'd be able to grow and develop in a healthy way without these things. How well would you be able to develop strengths and capacities? What kind of a life would you have in the village? *Freedom . . . fairness . . . equality . . . honesty . . . privacy . . . respect for our dignity as persons.*"

I waited while Socrates stared at the list.

"Reasonable argument," he finally said. "Humans are complex beings with physical, emotional, intellectual, and spiritual dimensions. It's logical to say that our basic needs would, therefore, extend beyond the physical.

"OK, let's say I accept this as an objective list of necessary conditions for healthy human growth and development. . . . But you also said something about these as conditions for a *satisfying life*. . . . You're referring to a *subjective* feeling. . . . You already gave me an *objective* basis to ethics with your list of basic needs. What's the point of backtracking to something subjective?"

"For our purposes," I answered, "I just want to use the idea of the subjective experience of being deprived of a need as another bit of evidence for why these items are needs, not wants. Let me see if I can put this differently."

A phrase my daughter regularly uses gave me an idea. "Humor me a moment," I said. He smiled again as he recognized I was using one of his annoying expressions from our last conversation. "Go back to our list and go down one by one again. This time, think about how it would feel not to get each one . . . *but*, I want you to use a specific criterion."

"And that is?"

"I want you to use my daughter's *T-J-S* criterion."

Socrates gave me a puzzled look. "*T-J-S?*"

"*That Just Sucks*. . . . It is, shall we say, a . . . *prosaic* . . . criterion. But it's surprisingly illuminative. . . . When Sasha was young, this is what she said when something *really* bothered her. I told her I wanted her to feel free to tell me how she felt about things, but that for this particular complaint, I'd prefer she just say 'T-J-S.' I'd get the point.

"The interesting thing is that I started using it myself—but it was triggered only by something very important. When I was diagnosed with cancer. When I discovered my e-mail had been hacked. Being treated unfairly. Whenever someone lies to me. . . . *TJS*.

"Faced with other things that went wrong, I'd grumble and get over them fairly quickly. But the really serious stuff produced a characteristic, deep disappointment that would settle in and eat at me for a while. *TJS*, I'd repeat over and over.

"And here's something very interesting. There have been times when the disappointment I've felt over something *intangible* was even stronger than about some *tangible* issue. When I recovered from a broken ankle, I was so grateful to be healthy again, I was able to put the illness behind me. But I still sometimes get very angry over that time I was passed over for a promotion because I'm a woman. Being treated unfairly bothers me *that* much."

Socrates turned back to the screen and looked at it for a while. Then he chuckled. "As you say, a surprisingly useful and *prosaic* way of putting things. I agree. . . . When I imagine a life without any of these, *TJS*! . . . And, you're right, when I think of not getting some *want*—even an important one—the kind of disappointment isn't the same."

"Right. So when I say 'rudimentary sense of satisfaction,' I mean a subjective sign that you aren't missing something big. You may be disappointed with parts of your life, but there's no deep sense of frustration and deprivation that makes you say '*TJS*!' "

Socrates paused again. "OK, I can live with that. . . . But now I believe you need to tell me what all of this has to do with *ethics*. How does this show that ethics isn't rubbish?"

"Here's how everything connects," I said. "Call this a 'stipulative' definition if you want to be fussy, but I'm claiming that when we say an action is *ethically negative*—wrong, bad, ethically unjustifiable, whatever language you like to use—that's shorthand for saying the action prevents or at least makes more difficult our getting one of these *basic needs* met. Conversely, to say an action is *ethically positive*—right, good, ethically defensible—*that's* shorthand for saying the action promotes or protects the satisfaction of these basic needs."

I walked back to the screen and sketched what I meant.

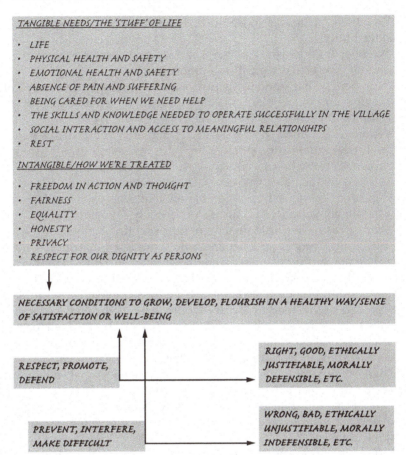

TANGIBLE NEEDS/THE 'STUFF' OF LIFE

- LIFE
- PHYSICAL HEALTH AND SAFETY
- EMOTIONAL HEALTH AND SAFETY
- ABSENCE OF PAIN AND SUFFERING
- BEING CARED FOR WHEN WE NEED HELP
- THE SKILLS AND KNOWLEDGE NEEDED TO OPERATE SUCCESSFULLY IN THE VILLAGE
- SOCIAL INTERACTION AND ACCESS TO MEANINGFUL RELATIONSHIPS
- REST

INTANGIBLE/HOW WE'RE TREATED

- FREEDOM IN ACTION AND THOUGHT
- FAIRNESS
- EQUALITY
- HONESTY
- PRIVACY
- RESPECT FOR OUR DIGNITY AS PERSONS

NECESSARY CONDITIONS TO GROW, DEVELOP, FLOURISH IN A HEALTHY WAY/SENSE OF SATISFACTION OR WELL-BEING

RESPECT, PROMOTE, DEFEND → RIGHT, GOOD, ETHICALLY JUSTIFIABLE, MORALLY DEFENSIBLE, ETC.

PREVENT, INTERFERE, MAKE DIFFICULT → WRONG, BAD, ETHICALLY UNJUSTIFIABLE, MORALLY INDEFENSIBLE, ETC.

Socrates walked up to the screen and studied it. "So, according to you, that's all ethics is—a way of evaluating actions that tells us simply whether or not they promote or interfere with the people involved getting their basic human needs met, that is, the conditions necessary for healthy growth and development and a very rudimentary sense of satisfaction."

"Correct. . . . Of course, because life is complicated and imperfect, we're regularly going to run into situations where my attempt to have *my* needs met is going to clash with your attempt to have *your* needs met. That's one way to look at a typical ethical dilemma."

Socrates studied the screen some more, then looked at his watch. "OK, as I said, I can live with that. I still have lots of questions about this. But, I'm hungry and Colin will be announcing dinner shortly. So, let's wrap this up. Now that you've walked me through all kinds of details, give me your shortest explanation for why ethics in general—and ethics in business—isn't rubbish. And to speed things along, use this."

He tossed me the stylus Colin had originally handed him.

"It's also a microphone. I forgot to tell you that the system handles voice recognition."

"OK, then," I said as I cleared the screen with a couple of taps and pressed the button.

"Number 1. Ethics isn't rubbish. That is, actions can be evaluated with a standard that is objective, logical, and rational.

"Number 2. That standard is *basic human needs*—the necessary conditions (tangible and intangible) for healthy growth, development, flourishing, and a rudimentary sense of satisfaction (no TJS).

"Number 3. 'Ethical' terms (right, wrong, etc.) and principles ('do no harm' and 'treat others appropriately') refer to the relationship between any actions under examination and the basic needs of individuals involved."

As I paused, Socrates went back to the screen and looked it over. He seemed pleased. "Very neat. . . . I don't know that everyone would agree, but at least for our conversation, I'd say it's not entirely ridiculous."

"And I even have a little something for a skeptic," I added.

"Intriguing. You mean someone who would say that there's no such thing as human nature, basic needs, and an objective basis to all of this?"

"*Precisely*. . . . I'd say, 'Even if you don't accept our list as *needs*, this is the absolute minimum that any rational, self-interested person would insist on as the specifics of the 'kind of life' we would want as the goal of the village. If we were to draw up an agreement that specified the traits of the 'particular way of life' the village would aim at, this is the least that a rational, logical, self-interested person would insist on.' What rational, self-interested person would agree to anything less than getting our basic needs met so that we can experience a fundamentally satisfying way of life?

"And if they still balked, I'd toss my copy of John Rawls' *Theory of Justice* at them and tell them to read the section on the 'veil of ignorance' you used against me last week."

I edited my on-screen presentation a bit and stepped back to admire my handiwork.

1. ETHICS ISN'T RUBBISH—ACTIONS CAN BE EVALUATED WITH A STANDARD THAT IS OBJECTIVE, LOGICAL, AND RATIONAL

2. THAT STANDARD IS BASIC HUMAN NEEDS—THE NECESSARY CONDITIONS (TANGIBLE AND INTANGIBLE) FOR HEALTHY GROWTH, DEVELOPMENT, FLOURISHING, AND A RUDIMENTARY SENSE OF SATISFACTION (NO TJS)

3. "ETHICAL" TERMS (RIGHT, WRONG, ETC.) AND PRINCIPLES ("DO NO HARM" AND "TREAT OTHERS APPROPRIATELY") REFER TO THE RELATIONSHIP BETWEEN ANY ACTIONS UNDER EXAMINATION AND THE BASIC NEEDS OF INDIVIDUALS INVOLVED

4. AND A LITTLE SOMETHING FOR THE SKEPTICS.... EVEN IF YOU DON'T ACCEPT THE LIST AS <u>NEEDS</u>. THIS IS THE ABSOLUTE MINIMUM THAT ANY RATIONAL, SELF-INTERESTED PERSON WOULD INSIST UPON AS THE SPECIFICS OF THE "KIND OF LIFE" WE WOULD AGREE WOULD BE THE GOAL OF THE VILLAGE. (RAWLS' VEIL OF IGNORANCE.)

Socrates read it over. "As I said, I can live with that."

"Dinner is ready, sir," came Colin's voice over the intercom.

I put the microphone down on the table and looked over at Socrates. "Perfect timing. I'm *done*. . . . And by *done*, I mean *exhausted*, not simply finished with my explanation. Which way to dinner?"

"Not so fast! Aren't you forgetting something?"

"No. There's everything you asked for," I said, pointing at the screen. "You even said you could live with it."

"I'm still waiting for your defense of ethics in *business*. This just shows why *ethics* isn't rubbish. You promised to show why business ethics isn't rubbish as well. Or did you bite off more than you can chew?"

Annoyed, tired, and hungry, I pointed at the screen. "Isn't it obvious?"

"It is to *me*. . . . I just want to make sure it is to *you*."

"Seriously?" I asked with a scowl. It had been a long, long day.

Socrates reached into his pocket, pulled out a yellow card, and posed as though he was thinking of using it.

"You do know that the Athenians killed your namesake for being *annoying*, don't you?" I grimaced. "I'll tell you what," I offered. "If I can give you a short answer under 90 seconds, will you agree to wait for a longer answer until tomorrow?"

"Under 90 seconds?" he asked, intrigued. "You can do that?"

"Give me a couple of minutes to gather my thoughts, and I'll show you."

By the time Socrates returned with a watch with a stopwatch function on it, I was ready.

"Whenever you want," I said, standing beside the screen.

"Go."

"When people say, '*Business ethics is rubbish*,' or '*business ethics is an oxymoron*,' they usually mean something like, *The conventional rules of right and wrong— which might be appropriate for our dealings with friends and family—don't apply in business because we have our own understanding of what counts as violations of 'do no harm' and 'treat others appropriately.'* That claim is incorrect for two reasons."

I pointed to number 3 on my list. "First, *basic needs* set the standard for evaluating how well *any* activity in the village—business, medicine, government, education, whatever—contributes to our getting the 'kind of life' the village is founded to achieve in the first place. We have a general, overarching, logical, rational, objective standard for evaluating how well actions—in business or in something else—promote or interfere with the satisfaction of the basic conditions necessary for healthy growth and development and the reasonable opportunity for having a successful life in the village."

Then I pointed to number 4. "Moreover, no rational, self-interested person would ever agree to anything less than a fair, neutral, and objective interpretation of 'do no harm' and 'treat others appropriately' in business dealings with each other."

Socrates nodded approvingly. "*Very* impressive. Just over 60 seconds. Let's eat."

13

Business, Ethics, Apple/Proview, and John Stuart Mill

Socrates apparently realized how tired I was after such a trying day. As soon as we sat down to dinner, he forbade any serious topics for conversation. We agreed to wait until the morning to take up the rest of what he wanted to talk about. Instead, because we both love to travel, we spent the meal comparing notes about our favorite big cities (him: Singapore, Venice, and Seattle; me: Boston, London, and San Francisco) and swapping "the next time you're there, you really must go to . . . " suggestions.

It was about midnight when we called it a night. I wanted to stay up so that I could chat briefly with my husband and daughter and fill them in on my day. They found my "kidnapping" amusing. They found Socrates so eccentric they made me promise to invite him to dinner at some point. "Fine, I promise," I told Sasha—*just not too soon*, I thought to myself.

Socrates' beach house was so close to the ocean that when I crawled into bed and pulled up the covers, I could hear the hypnotic sound of the waves. Within minutes, I was asleep.

*

A louder version of the same sounds that lulled me to sleep woke me up. There was a storm offshore producing waves that crashed against the sand. After preparing myself for another day's inquisition, I found Socrates out on the deck. Strolling around, he was in the middle of a conversation in Arabic. "*Masaa Al Khair*," he said he said as he ended the conversation. "Time zones. The bane of the international VC. My circadian rhythms are always off because of the various deals I'm doing in different parts of the planet." A small breakfast table was set up. As we walked toward it, Socrates pulled out my chair. "Allow me."

"I can't remember the last time someone pulled out my chair. You're a vanishing breed—a gentleman. I'm impressed."

"It's a losing battle, because—especially when there are a lot of younger men around—I feel that the barbarians are not only already inside the gates, they're starting to run things. I don't think there's anything wrong with courtesy intended to show respect. . . . And just so that you don't think there's an undercurrent of sexism in my actions, if you were a man, I'd still pull out your chair and hold your coat."

As the two of us settled in, Colin appeared. "Colin's exceptional at everything he does. Ask for whatever you want. I guarantee it will be the best breakfast you've ever had."

Once we finished eating and caffeine had jump-started my brain, I decided to get back to business. *The sooner we start; the sooner we're done*, I thought. But Socrates beat me to the punch.

"Before we begin, I want to tell you how impressed I was with you in yesterday's conversation. First, you know as well as I do that I couldn't *make* you talk to me. You could have called Phyllis and had a car come and get you. I admire your willingness to hang in there—especially after the hearing. And for all of my *yellow-card-red-card-I-control-30%-of-the-stock* theatrics, you know that booting you out of the big chair isn't quite as simple as I make it sound.

"Second, I recognize and appreciate how different you are from some of your opposite numbers at other banks. You and I both personally know at least one individual who seems to be presiding over what we'd agree is a culture of *hubris*. Bank examiners were screamed at and called 'stupid.' Executives felt it was OK to be less than forthcoming with authorities looking into massive losses. And while suggesting to the outside world that the bank was taking a prudent approach to risk, the CEO himself signed off on changes to an internal alarm system that underestimated losses. Not surprisingly, the company has been hit with huge fines.

"I have no regrets telling the company which has approached me for a recommendation that I'd chat with you to see if you're a match for this new post. I think it looks promising so far."

I hoped his compliments meant today would be a relatively easy day. "I appreciate the compliments. To be honest, on our ride over, I *did* consider calling to have a car come pick me up and drive me back to New York. But I always at least *try* to be willing to talk to anyone about anything to do with the business for as long as they want. I know I sometimes get impatient and brusque. But I'm trying to change that. For all your bluster and eccentricities, I believe you when you say you're trying to help both me and the company. And as annoying as you are, I'd rather be talking to *you* than to the press."

He chuckled in response. "Not exactly 'high praise,' but I'll take it. So, back to work. I say, 'ethics in business is rubbish.' Your reply?"

"You got the short answer before dinner last night. But since you cheated by quoting Plato and then stopped me when I wanted to use Mill and Kant, today you get the long, dull explanation."

"Fair enough. But I didn't *quote* Plato. I *allegedly* appropriated his ideas and made them eminently more interesting by applying them to our ultimately very practical discussion. So, I'll expect you to do the same with those two old, useless thinkers—or you'll have to wake me up every 2 minutes," he joked.

"Oh, you want *interesting*?" I quipped. "For that, I need your magic flat-screen."

We walked back into the living room, and I tapped on the screen to bring up my last slide. What came up was something different.

"When I looked at your final slide this morning," he said, "I decided to try to take what you said about ethics in general and adapt it to business ethics. I decided we needed to remind ourselves of the 'job of business.' So number 3 is different. And I decided to be a little more direct when it came to number 4."

I read over Socrates' edited version of the slide.

1. *BUSINESS* ETHICS ISN'T RUBBISH—*BUSINESS* ACTIONS CAN BE EVALUATED WITH A STANDARD THAT IS OBJECTIVE, LOGICAL, AND RATIONAL

2. THAT STANDARD IS *BASIC HUMAN NEEDS*—THE NECESSARY CONDITIONS (TANGIBLE AND INTANGIBLE) FOR HEALTHY GROWTH, DEVELOPMENT, FLOURISHING, AND A RUDIMENTARY SENSE OF SATISFACTION (NO TJS)

3. THE "JOB OF BUSINESS" (ITS CONTRIBUTION TO THE "KIND OF LIFE WE WANT") IS TO PROVIDE THE GOODS AND SERVICES THAT WE NEED IN A WAY THAT'S CONSISTENT WITH RESPECTING AND PROMOTING THOSE BASIC HUMAN NEEDS. *BUSINESS* ACTIONS THAT MEET THESE NEEDS ARE ETHICALLY POSITIVE; THOSE THAT DON'T, ARE ETHICALLY NEGATIVE.

4. ANYONE WHO SAYS THAT *BUSINESS* IS SOME SORT OF "SPECIAL CASE" WHEN IT COMES TO ETHICS IS A SELF-DESTRUCTIVE IDIOT.

" 'Self-destructive idiot'? You call that *direct*? Don't you think *insulting* is closer to the mark?" Once again, I pretended to take out a notebook like the one Socrates taunted me with last week and frowned. "*Leaves something to be desired when it comes to stating differences of opinion diplomatically.*"

"OK," he laughed. "It was early and I hadn't had any coffee yet."

"Let me change number 4 to something I can work with. Let's say, 'Anyone who says that business is some sort of special case when it comes to ethics needs to re-examine the facts. You can't do the *job of business* in the village if you operate unethically.' "

After I changed Socrates' sentence, I realized I needed something for the skeptic who simply says, "But that's the way business is, and everyone in business knows and agrees to it. And if you don't like that, go into something else. Don't go into business." So I added, "Why would anyone in the village agree that business—which touches the lives of absolutely everyone in the village ever day—could compromise 'do no harm' or 'treat everyone appropriately' and not respect and promote our basic needs?"

1. *BUSINESS* ETHICS ISN'T RUBBISH—*BUSINESS* ACTIONS CAN BE EVALUATED WITH A STANDARD THAT IS OBJECTIVE, LOGICAL, AND RATIONAL

2. THAT STANDARD IS *BASIC HUMAN NEEDS*—THE NECESSARY CONDITIONS (TANGIBLE AND INTANGIBLE) FOR HEALTHY GROWTH, DEVELOPMENT, FLOURISHING, AND A RUDIMENTARY SENSE OF SATISFACTION (NO TJS)

3. THE "JOB OF BUSINESS" (ITS CONTRIBUTION TO THE "KIND OF LIFE WE WANT") IS TO PROVIDE THE GOODS AND SERVICES THAT WE NEED IN A WAY THAT'S CONSISTENT WITH RESPECTING AND PROMOTING THOSE BASIC HUMAN NEEDS. *BUSINESS* ACTIONS THAT MEET THESE NEEDS ARE ETHICALLY POSITIVE; THOSE THAT DON'T, ARE ETHICALLY NEGATIVE.

4. ANYONE WHO SAYS THAT *BUSINESS* IS SOME SORT OF "SPECIAL CASE" WHEN IT COMES TO ETHICS NEEDS TO RE-EXAMINE THE FACTS. YOU CAN'T DO THE "JOB OF BUSINESS" IF YOU OPERATE UNETHICALLY. (WHY WOULD ANYONE IN THE VILLAGE AGREE THAT BUSINESS—WHICH TOUCHES THE LIVES OF ABSOLUTELY EVERYONE IN THE VILLAGE EVERY DAY—CAN COMPROMISE "DO NO HARM" OR "TREAT EVERYONE APPROPRIATELY" AND NOT RESPECT AND PROMOTE OUR BASIC NEEDS?)

"Much better and nice addition," he pointed out. "Too many of our colleagues have the attitude that business somehow operates outside the norms of village life and that those of us running businesses can agree to our own rules about how it operates. But, as you say, everyone in the village is involved in business in some way virtually every day—through buying something for themselves, working to pay their bills, or making and selling something that someone else needs. Business is the foundation—not some sort of superfluous superstructure. Business is *so* fundamentally important to our getting the 'kind of life' we want in the village that it's insane to think that ethics doesn't apply. So, now explain how this lets you take a bunch of insufferably dull, head-in-the-cloud philosophers and make me think that 'business ethics isn't rubbish.'"

"They key is in what we agreed last week was 'the job of business.' We said the way business contributes to getting us the 'kind of life' we want in our village is that it provides us with the goods and services we need, and that it does so by making money. Profits are the means to a specific end—a particular kind of life. Companies that make piles of money but don't get us the 'kind of life' we want aren't doing their 'job.'"

"Right," he chimed in. "In the same way that a for-profit hospital that achieves a high ROI by compromising the health of its patients is neither a good hospital nor a good business."

I had the feeling in last week's conversation that, given how strongly Socrates felt about the 'job of business,' he'd simply decided not to push me when I wouldn't budge from my judgment that the hospital we'd discussed was a 'bad hospital' but 'good business.' The fact that he backed off didn't mean he thought I was right. Now he apparently saw an opportunity to get me to change my mind, and he was going to try again. But given the way I'd rephrased number 4, I saw the matter somewhat differently now.

"Fine," I conceded. "If a for-profit hospital doesn't give our villagers the kind of medical care they need, or if a for-profit university doesn't teach young people the knowledge and skills necessary to operate successfully in the village—despite the fact that they're making piles of money—they aren't doing their 'job' as a business. *But,*" I continued before Socrates could interrupt me, "profit has to be a measure of the success of *any* business—even a for-profit hospital. But we're looking for *optimum* profits, not *maximum* profits."

"Interesting distinction," he remarked as he got up to refill his mug. "Would you like to elaborate?"

"It's nothing fancy. Maximum profits means, 'Let's make as much as we can, take the money, and run. Long-term risk, ethics, and the 'job' of business in the village be damned! Full speed ahead!' Optimum profits means, 'Let's make money. But let's be sure to stay in business for the long term. Let's operate efficiently. Let's do our part in giving us the 'kind of life' we want in the village.' So when I say 'business ethics isn't rubbish,' " I continued, "I mean you can't achieve optimum profits without operating ethically. And I've got one or two practical examples and a pair of 'insufferably dull philosophers' to back me up. But first, I need a refill as well."

*

As soon as I'd started using Socrates' flat-screen yesterday, I realized it was no ordinary bit of technology. So, with both of us ready to resume, I asked, "May I assume that this screen connects directly into the internet and that I can do searches and bring up Web pages?"

"Of course." Tossing me the system's pen sized microphone again, he added, "And the voice recognition works for searches as well."

"In that case, . . . " I did a quick search on a lawsuit I'd heard about that intrigued me because of the ethical issues involved. It involved Apple and a Chinese company, Proview Electronics. I brought up a copy of the complaint, a couple of articles discussing it, and I walked Socrates through it.

"In the late 1990s, Proview began developing an all-in-one internet terminal for Web browsing. They called it the 'internet personal access device'— iPAD. They trademarked the name in the European Union, Mexico, China, and a number of other Asian countries. Unfortunately, in 2008 Proview's two biggest customers—Polaroid and Circuit City—filed for bankruptcy. That meant Proview had to reorganize and was strapped for cash.

"Around this time, Apple was working on its new tablet computer, and was planning to call it the 'iPad.' However, it discovered that Proview held the trademark. The most direct way to buy the trademark, of course, was to contact Proview and negotiate the deal. However, Apple chose a different strategy, presumably one they hoped would let them purchase the rights for less money.

"At least according to what Proview alleges in its original lawsuit, Apple's lawyers created a dummy British corporation called IP Application Development Ltd. An individual who identified himself as 'Jonathan Hargreaves' contacted Proview about acquiring the trademarks. In the course of negotiations, Proview asked for detailed information about the company and why it wanted the trademark. In e-mails, Hargreaves answered that they were a British company. He also said, 'The intention is for the company to be involved in the computer field, but since we have only just incorporated, it is premature to disclose more than that. In any event we will not be competing with your company. Hargreaves explained they wanted the iPAD trademark because it 'is an abbreviation for the company name IP Application Development Limited.' Hargreaves went on to reassure Proview: 'This is a newly formed company, and I'm sure you can understand that we are not yet ready to publicize what the company's business is, since we have not yet made any public announcements. As I said in our last message, I can assure you that the company will not compete with Proview.' Hargreaves subsequently informed Proview that if they wouldn't sell, he would initiate legal action to cancel their trademarks—a move that would have cost Proview a good deal of money to keep them. A few months later, Proview agreed and sold the trademarks for £35,000 (about $50,000). A month after that, Apple announced the 'iPad' as the next big thing.

"Proview's lawsuit claimed that Apple committed fraud, that is, that it intentionally misrepresented and concealed a number of facts.

"First, 'Jonathan Hargreaves' was actually 'Graham Robinson.'

"Second, Robinson's company wasn't in the computer business. It existed only to acquire the iPAD trademark for Apple.

"Third, Apple and Proview were, in fact, competitors.

"Finally, Robinson said the reason his company wanted the trademark was because it was the abbreviation for 'IP Application Development,' when in reality he was acquiring it for Apple to use on their new tablet.

"Initially, Apple was able to get the lawsuit—which had been filed in the United States—dismissed over a jurisdictional issue. A clause in the agreement said disputes would be resolved in Hong Kong. However, before the lawsuit was filed elsewhere, Apple and Proview settled the case with Apple paying $60 million."

"Nice summary," Socrates said. "I'd heard something about that dispute, but I never knew the details."

"And I'm sure there's much more to this that only people inside Apple and Proview know—especially like what actually happened. Officially, we only know what Proview claimed happened," I cautioned.

"Except we do know that Apple ultimately paid $60 million, not $50,000, for the trademark."

"True. Keep that $60 million number in mind. And also, keep in mind that the two companies settled after the Apple iPad had been on the market for a few months and was selling like crazy."

"You mean," Socrates said, "remember that by the time Apple settled, the popularity of the iPad made it clear that Proview was now in a position to negotiate a small fortune. Apple was lucky. I would have gotten more."

I wasn't surprised that Socrates recognized the cost of having the weaker hand in negotiations—or that he thought he could have done better. "My point," I said bringing the conversation back on track, "is that this case lets me use two head-in-the-cloud philosophers to give you an *objective, practical,* and *business-based* explanation of why 'business ethics isn't rubbish.' "

"Right—your 'we don't get *optimum* profits without ethics' claim. Interesting if you can do it. But I went easy on you yesterday because you had such a tough morning and I'm such a nice guy. Let's hope you can handle a *real* debate today." Getting back into his "Annoying Guy" character, he added a scowl—which was so artificial I had trouble keeping from laughing.

*

I turned back to the screen and called up a couple of Web pages, one of which had a picture of the first philosopher I was using. "John Stuart Mill. Nineteenth-century British philosopher, political economist, and politician."

"Don't forget *businessman,*" Socrates interrupted.

"Businessman?"

"I thought you would have known that," he said, surprised. "Mill's long career with the East India Company? In fact, Mill makes one of the most interesting comments I know about the efficiency of business and government. And remember that he had direct experience with both. Given how often you rail against 'big government' and 'government waste and inefficiency,' you should think about what he says." Taking the pen/microphone from me, he spoke into it and a Web page with a passage from Mill's *Principles of Political Economy* popped up.

The third exception which I shall notice, to the doctrine that government cannot manage the affairs of individuals as well as the individuals themselves, has reference to the great class of cases in which the individuals can only manage the concern by delegated agency, and in which the so-called private management is, in point of fact, hardly better entitled to be called management by the persons interested, than administration by a public officer. Whatever, if left to spontaneous agency, can only be done by joint-stock associations, will often be as well, and sometimes better done, as far as the actual work is concerned, by the state. Government management is, indeed, proverbially jobbing, careless, and ineffective, but so likewise has generally been joint-stock management. The directors of a joint-stock company, it is true, are always shareholders; but also the members of a government are invariably taxpayers; and in the case of directors, no more than in that of governments, is their proportional share of the benefits of good management, equal to the interest they may possibly have in mismanagement, even without reckoning the interest of their case. It may be objected, that the shareholders, in their collective character, exercise a certain control over the directors, and have almost always full power to remove them from office. Practically, however, the difficulty of exercising this power is found to be so great, that it is hardly ever exercised except in cases of such flagrantly unskilful, or, at least, unsuccessful management, as would generally produce the ejection from office of managers appointed by the government. Against the very ineffectual security afforded by meetings of shareholders, and by their individual inspection and inquiries, may be placed the greater publicity and more active discussion and comment, to be expected in free countries with regard to affairs in which the general government takes part. The defects, therefore, of government management, do not seem to be necessarily much greater, if necessarily greater at all, than those of management by joint-stock.

"Think about what Mill says at some point. But for now, please continue."

"OK. Philosopher, political economist, politician, *and businessman*. Author of 'Utilitarianism' and 'On Liberty.' Advocate for women's rights. For our purposes, he's most important for showing the cost of lying."

"The cost of lying? That's interesting. I was expecting you to go into how Mill's *utilitarian* approach is what people in business use all the time when we do *cost/benefit analysis*."

"Actually, I am," I answered. "But I find Mill's comments about the negative consequences of lying a better example of just how *practical* his ideas are. They show how Mill's approach can help us get a truly comprehensive picture of the consequences of our actions. Typical cost/benefit analysis uses only a fairly unsophisticated version of his ideas, focusing on only the most obvious parts of his theory.

"Remember. Like his godfather Jeremy Bentham, the founder of utilitarianism, Mill believed that all actions are morally neutral. It's the real-life *consequences* of actions that make them *right* or *wrong*. That's why their theories are technically called *teleological*. *Telos* is the Greek work for "end." So the *end* of an action—not *the action itself*—determines whether it's right or wrong. And as far as consequences go, Bentham and Mill agreed that the only thing we look at is pleasure and pain."

I picked up the microphone, spoke a few words and read off a few sentences from Bentham.

Nature has placed mankind under the governance of two sovereign masters, pain and pleasure. It is for them alone to point out what we ought to do. . . . [T]he standard of right and wrong. . . . [is] fastened to their throne. . . . By utility is meant that property in any object whereby it tends to produce benefit, advantage, pleasure, good, or happiness (all this in the present case comes to the same thing) or (what comes again to the same thing) to prevent the happening of mischief, pain, evil, or unhappiness to the party whose interest is considered. . . .

"Or to put it more simply," Socrates said, "something is *morally good* only if it's *useful*—that is, has some *utility*. And it's *useful* only if it produces *pleasure* and prevents *pain*. Like cost/benefit analysis. A deal or project makes sense only if the benefits are greater than the costs."

"Right, *except* that Bentham and typical cost/benefit analysts make similar mistakes. Bentham said all pleasures were equal. Cost/benefit analyses usually just look at money."

"So? You said you were being practical. What's the problem?"

"There's *practical* and then there's *short-sighted*. Remember, I said that Mill gives us a way to get a *comprehensive* picture of the issue we're considering. He said that Bentham was wrong to say that all pleasures are equal." I went back to the screen, tapped it and read off a line from Mill.

[S]ome kinds of pleasure are more desirable and more valuable than others. It would be absurd that, while in estimating all other things quality is considered as well as quantity, the estimation of pleasure should be supposed to depend on quantity alone.

"So Mill recognizes that if we're going to evaluate the positive and negative consequences of what we do, we need to factor in the *type, kind*, or *quality* of good or harm produced as well as the *amount*. That's the first important way Mill improves on Bentham's ideas. So, a smaller amount of high quality good or harm outweighs a larger amount which is lower quality. The second, . . . "

"Wait a minute," Socrates interrupted, getting up and walking over to the screen. "I just want to make sure you see that you're shifting ground here. You said you were going to give me a practical, tangible explanation for why 'business ethics isn't rubbish.' If you're going to say that some benefits are simply so much better than others that they outweigh even a larger amount, you're making all of this *subjective*, not *objective*. We can weigh and measure amounts. But what you're talking about is someone's personal opinion."

I groaned because I didn't want another detour. I was also starting to feel I was in over my head. I'd had one general philosophy course and a logic course in college and one business ethics course in my MBA program. I was not an expert in any of this material. But I had come across some very specific ideas I thought could apply to business to help me make better decisions.

"First, I'm taking about *judgment*—judgment informed by experience—not personal opinion, which may have no reasonable basis whatsoever. Second, remember that just because a judgment is *subjective*, that doesn't make it *arbitrary*. . . . And before you interrupt me again, why don't we just let Mill answer the question you're dying to ask me. *Who decides which pleasures or benefits are better than others?* . . . And *then* you're going to let me get to my main point."

"Agreed."

"In a nutshell, Mill says that only people who have actually experienced the potential benefits and costs are in a position to judge which is better—that is, which pleasures or benefits are more important or satisfying, and which pains or costs are more serious. He says that most people with roughly the same experience would agree. Of course, like you, he can't just put it simply. He has to go on and on." I teased Socrates about his proclivity for dragging out our conversations. "Here's the example he gives that's supposed to convince us that a smaller amount of high quality pleasure outweighs a larger amount of lower quality pleasure."

Tapping the screen, I brought up another quotation and read it.

> Now it is an unquestionable fact that those who are equally acquainted with and equally capable of appreciating and enjoying both do give a most marked preference to the manner of existence which employs their higher faculties. Few human creatures would consent to be changed into any of the lower animals for a promise of the fullest allowance of a beast's pleasures; no intelligent human being would consent to be a fool, no instructed person would be an ignoramus, no person of feeling and conscience would be selfish and base, even though they should be persuaded that the fool, the dunce, or the rascal is better satisfied with his lot than they are with theirs. . . . It is better to be a human being dissatisfied than a pig satisfied; better to be Socrates dissatisfied than a fool satisfied. And if the fool, or the pig, are of a different opinion, it is because they only know their own side of the question. The other party to the comparison knows both sides.

"Right. The famous human being, pig, Socrates, fool line—which, by the way, I always felt was insulting to pigs. The latest research on intelligence in pigs clearly shows . . . "

Fortunately, there was glass of water nearby, and all I had to do was to hold it up and put two fingers into it. The threat was clear.

"You promised," I warned.

"I did. I won't interrupt you again," he said sheepishly and sat back down on the couch.

"Mill had an ever bigger problem than *Who decides?* It was, *What about when an action that 'everyone knows is wrong' gives us more benefits than costs? What about lying?* After all, a good lie lets us avoid the negative consequences of not treating other people honestly. A good lie produces more benefits than costs."

"Spoken like someone who's had some experience. Do you really want to admit that?" he joked.

Ignoring him, I continued. "Mill's answer is it only *looks* that way because our analysis isn't comprehensive. We aren't taking into account *all* consequences of the lie. Because if we did, we'd see it's the other way around. And the key here is to appreciate how ruthlessly practical Mill is about identifying the long term consequences of the lie."

I tapped the screen to scroll down to another part of *Utilitarianism* and read.

> [I]nasmuch as any, *even unintentional*, deviation from truth does that much toward weakening the trustworthiness of human assertion, which is not only the principal support of all present social well-being, but the insufficiency of which does more than any one thing that can be named to keep back civilization, virtue, everything on which human happiness on the largest scale depends . . . he who, for the sake of convenience to himself or to some other individual, does what depends on him to

deprive mankind of the good, and inflict upon them the evil, involved in the greater or less reliance which they can place in each other's word, *acts the part of one of their worst enemies.*

I went closer to the screen and pointed out the most striking parts. "The first time I read this I thought that Mill was exaggerating the costs of lying. Any *'even unintentional* deviation from the truth' is problematic. 'The trust-worthiness of human assertion' is central to 'civilization, virtue, everything on which human happiness' depends. . . . The deliberate liar 'acts the part of one of [our] worst enemies.' "

Socrates got up from his chair and walked back to the screen. "I've read Mill, but I never noticed that passage. I agree with some of it, but parts of it seems awfully extreme to me. Even an 'unintentional' misstatement is harmful?"

"Let's start small," I answered, "and go back to the Apple/Preview case. However the lawyers may decide things, if Proview's account of Apple's actions is accurate, they're at least the equivalent of a lie. Any average person is going to say Apple misrepresented the situation. They didn't tell 'the truth, the whole truth and nothing but the truth'—which is certainly a reasonable standard for identifying lies.

"And look at the cost. By the time the dust had settled, Apple had to pay $60 million for the iPad trademark. And that doesn't even factor in the legal fees. If they had been upfront in the first place, I'm sure they wouldn't have gotten away with paying only $50,000 for the trademark. But I have no doubt it would have been significantly less than $60 million. And then there are the other, longer-term costs that lots of other people will end up paying."

"You mean that the cost will somehow be passed along to consumers?"

"Maybe it will, but I was thinking of other people and companies that get involved in negotiations. Let me ask you this. Will anything about this episode change your behavior in the future?" I asked.

"Actually, it already has. I didn't need to look into the details of this case, because as soon as I heard the main lines of the story, I established protocols for very detailed background checks on anyone we negotiate with. The final contracts also spell things out to an insane level of detail so there's no room for anyone to trick us and get away with it. We definitely spend more money in doing 'due diligence' in any negotiation than we did before."

"And what about any future dealings with Apple?"

"First, we'll spend some time learning exactly what happened. But if Proview's account turns out to be accurate, *if* we do any business with Apple—or with a company they might be using as a front—we'll do our best to figure out exactly if it's another ruse."

"But why?" I asked. "Don't you think they've learned their lesson? $60 million is a pretty big number, even for them."

"I see two problems," Socrates said as he walked up to the screen. "First, I believe that sometimes *one* action reveals a pattern. In my opinion, any company that engages in such an elaborate bit of misrepresentation has a culture that I'd be very uncomfortable with. In what I'd consider to be an ethical culture, someone would simply have said, 'we don't do things that way here.'

"Now this doesn't mean that they had to call up Proview and say, 'Hi, this is Apple and we'd like to buy something from you that is worth tens of millions of dollars.' Among negotiators, it's considered to be perfectly acceptable to say that you can't identify the buyer. Obviously, that tells the seller there's a reason you aren't saying whom you're representing, and it will affect the price. But at least you won't be lying.

"However, since Apple didn't do that and chose to use the fictional company instead, I assume their corporate culture has a higher tolerance than I do for what I'd consider to be questionable behavior. So I'd assume I can't trust them. You know what they say about trust—hard to win, easy to lose. And in my world, trust, reputation, and credibility are more valuable than money."

"Stop!" I interrupted. "Did you mean that? Trust, reputation, and credibility are more valuable to you than money?"

"Of course," Socrates answered. "In my line of work, trust and reputation are everything. At least for me, even one instance of untrustworthy behavior has massive consequences. It would take *years* before I'd completely trust any company that did something like that."

"Which is exactly Mill's point. A violation of trust is a small amount of *high quality* harm, but has very significant, wide ranging, long-term consequences."

"True," Socrates nodded.

"And how common do you think your reaction is?"

"Anyone with an ounce of sense is doing exactly the same thing we are. Anyone who isn't deserves what they get," he snorted.

"So is it fair to say that the 'ripple effect' of something like Apple's deception will raise costs?"

"Absolutely. Once everybody decides you can't trust each other, business becomes much more expensive. The only people who benefit are the lawyers. And it seems that once everyone crosses that bridge, there's no going back."

"Which is *precisely* Mill's point," I explained. "Whether or not we can believe what we say to each other is so critical that *lying* has very powerful *wide ranging* and *long-term* negative consequences."

"OK, but how does this show that business ethics isn't rubbish?" he prodded.

"Simple. First, every variety of unethical behavior—lying, cheating, stealing trade secrets, bribery, and the like—is going to raise costs. *More importantly*, however, if unethical behavior is the norm in business, that means we'd all operate in an environment of distrust. Even if we could find a way of out-performing—or out-cheating—our competitors so that we were making plenty of money, we would spend our days regarding everyone else as a potential adversary. In Mill's mind, that's high quality dissatisfaction and frustration. And I doubt that you or I would consider that to be the 'kind of life' that business activity is supposed to be supporting in the village."

"Nicely done," said Socrates. "Bad ethics creates major, unnecessary costs and decreases the quality of life of those of us in business. That's good enough for me as another way of understanding 'business ethics isn't rubbish.'"

14

Business, Ethics, Apple/Proview, and Immanuel Kant

There was a set of e-mails to department heads that I always handled on Saturday, so I excused myself, took my tablet, and went out onto the deck to take care of them. When I returned, I saw that Socrates had summarized our previous discussion in a "Business Ethics Isn't Rubbish, Part 2" list on the screen.

BUSINESS ETHICS ISN'T RUBBISH: PART 2, MILL

1. RIGHT AND WRONG — "REAL LIFE" BENEFIT AND HARM

2. BENEFITS AND HARMS — AMOUNT *PLUS* TYPE, KIND OR QUALITY

3. BENEFIT AND HARMS — WIDE-RANGING *AND* LONG-TERM

4. "REAL LIFE" FACTORS — PROFIT/LOSS, ATTRACT AND RETAIN BEST EMPLOYEES, QUALITY OF RELATIONSHIPS (CUSTOMERS, INVESTORS, EMPLOYEES, ETC.), REPUTATION, TRUSTWORTHINESS, **GOODWILL**

5. EFFICIENCY IN DOING "JOB" OF BUSINESS

6. BOTTOM LINE: *MOST IMPORTANT* BENEFITS AND HARMS — "KIND OF LIFE" IN THE VILLAGE

7. CAVEAT ABOUT ETHICS AND PROFITS

"I took the liberty of capturing the eloquence of your last argument," he said as I walked back into the room.

"And adding a few things," I noted.

"Not really," Socrates answered, trying to cover the fact that he actually had. "I just fleshed things out a bit."

"Well, since you're the skeptic," I said, reminding Socrates of the role he'd taken on, "why don't you explain this so I can confirm that you truly understood 'my eloquence'?"

"Only if you insist," he said enthusiastically, obviously wanting to point out what he thought I'd missed. "Numbers 1 through 3 are what you said were Mill's main ideas about how we decide whether any action—in business or elsewhere—is right or wrong. If the positive consequences are greater and/ or better than the negative consequences, an action is good.

"Number 4 identifies the main real-life, 'on the ground' consequences of actions in business. Whether we make or lose money. Whether we can hire and keep the best employees. Whether the relationships we have with all the people we deal with make them want to do business with us again. All those intangibles that even accountants recognize as affecting the value of a business—*goodwill*. You made the same point with the Apple/Proview example. I just generalized it."

"OK, I see that. But I don't remember saying anything about 'efficiency,' your 'bottom line,' or that final 'caveat.' "

"As far as 'efficiency' is concerned," he said, pointing to the line on the screen, "again I'm just generalizing from the specific case. Ethically questionable or controversial actions always seem to add costs to doing business. You claimed that with Apple. The Pennzoil/Getty/Texaco mess in the 1980s is a classic example of billions of dollars being spent since then in how certain deals and lawsuits are handled. And while lots of executives complain about the costs of following the Sarbanes-Oxley Act, they conveniently forget that the only reason we have these requirements is because of the accounting scandals—which *never* had to happen. I don't consider costs that are the direct result of unethical behavior in business to be *efficient*."

"Your 'bottom line'?" I asked, joining him at the screen and pointing to number 6.

"Just putting a fine point on something we've already agreed on. If business gives us the combination of a good *amount* and *type* of positive consequences—which means operating ethically, in Mill's view—then it's doing its part in giving us the tangible features of the 'kind of life' we organized the village for in the first place. I'm sure it was just an oversight on your part not to phrase it this way."

"OK. Reasonable way of putting it. But I'm certain I never said anything about that final caveat."

"Right," he noted, turning toward me. "But you were heading in that direction and I wanted to stop you."

"Stop me? From what?" I asked as I walked over to pour myself another cup of coffee.

"I got the impression from your remarks about the costs of unethical behavior and the benefits of ethical behavior that you were on your way to making the mistake of claiming that 'doing business ethically invariably gets rewarded with profits.' It doesn't."

I jerked my head around so sharply that an audible "crack" came from my neck. My host just chuckled in response. "I *thought* that would get your attention."

"Wait a minute," I said, more than a little annoyed. "After giving me such a hard time over the course of more than two days about how important ethics is in running the business, you're now saying that we can make money without it."

"Of course we can! It would be nice if 'good ethics' meant 'good business,' but it doesn't. 'Bad ethics' can definitely lead to piles of cash—especially in the short run. Look at organized crime and corruption all around the planet. Bad ethics can even give us the goods and services we want in the village at a low price when we treat employees miserably, establish hidden sweatshops in the United States, or exploit labor markets in developing nations. And sometimes ethics is irrelevant to a company's success or failure. There's no way that the most ethical company making mechanical rotary telephones was going to thrive over the long run unless they changed with the times. The market has too many forces that have nothing to do with ethics.

"In conversations like this, it's tempting to say that the market will always reward ethical businesses. Sometimes it does, but not always. There's no guarantee. That's why it's critical to remember that our bottom line is the 'kind of life' we're looking for in the village. Doing business ethically isn't rubbish because it helps give us the 'kind of life' we want. The costs of doing business ethically are simply too high—in terms of compromising 'the kind of life' we want.

"So if I'm correctly understanding your explanation of why Mill would say that *business ethics isn't rubbish*, it's that doing business *unethically* will give us the wrong combination of benefits and costs. We'll end up, say, with lower quality benefits (profits) at the expense of forgoing higher quality benefits (for example, a longer and more satisfying life through less workplace stress) and maybe even find some high quality harm in the mix (for example, more workplace deaths and injuries) unless . . . "

I recognized the expression that Socrates had on his face. It said, "Get ready to shift gears because the other shoe is about to drop."

"Stop!" I interrupted. "At least you're predictable. You're going to describe some silly, carefully crafted hypothetical that gives us a different mix of benefits and costs—where the benefits are so spectacular that they outweigh even a fair amount of high quality harm involved in producing them. Something like exploiting workers and ending up with a cure for cancer. Then you're going to tell me that the crucial flaw in utilitarianism is that scenarios like this basically say that the ends justify the means. And you were going to ask how I'd handle that. Right?" I was sure I was one step ahead of him.

"Not bad," Socrates answered, not at all surprised at my comment. "Actually, I was thinking of something *realistic*—like the way that migrant workers can be mistreated in the production of affordable food. From a utilitarian perspective, what's a better, higher quality benefit than health?

"All of which tells me that any defense of the idea that 'business ethics isn't rubbish' that relies only on utilitarianism won't work. But you obviously knew that, because you already promised me Immanuel Kant."

As I watched Socrates walk back to his chair and sit down, I realized that his additions to our last conversation had simply been his way of moving things along. He was right. I'd been getting enamored of Mill's tangible, "no harm/no foul" approach to ethics.

"Fine, the 'hole in the deal,' as it were, with utilitarianism is that it tempts us to ignore our 'treat others appropriately' side of the 'kind of life' we want in the village. So *Kant's* perspective gives us a different point of view for why 'business ethics isn't rubbish.' "

Socrates waved his arm my way. "Right. 'Business ethics isn't rubbish, part 3.' It's your show. *But* before you get started, you need to explain how Kant is relevant to anything practical. Bentham and Mill ground their ideas about ethics in tangible human experience—*pleasure* and *pain*, *happiness* and *unhappiness*, or however you like to talk about it. But Kant's foundation is *reason*. How can a theory grounded in reason and not real life help an executive? Maybe it's interesting to mathematicians, logicians, or philosophers—that is, people who waste their time with their heads in the clouds. But business deals with the real world, not make-believe."

My host noticed my surprise that he seemed comfortable talking about one of the most difficult philosophers on the planet.

"This isn't my first encounter with Kant, you know. You can't spend any time at a German university and not end up in a 'Kant drive-by' while you're hoisting beers at the local *Kneipe*. It's like the local obsession. You're talking about the weather or sports, and then all of a sudden someone brings up Kant and what he really means. For the rest of the night, that's what everyone fights about. And the debates never have anything to do with something real."

Socrates got up, walked to the screen, tapped up a Web site and started reading.

Analytic judgments (affirmative) are therefore those in which the connection of the predicate with the subject is thought through identity; those in which this connection is thought without identity should be entitled synthetic. The former, as adding nothing through the predicate to the concept of the subject, but merely breaking it up into those constituent concepts have all along been thought in it, although confusedly, can also be entitled explicative. The latter, on the other hand, add to the concept of the subject a predicate which has not been in any wise thought in it, and which no analysis could possibly extract from it; and they may therefore be entitled ampliative.

"That was a little something from the *Critique of Pure Reason*, Kant's first masterpiece. And you know what he's describing? Not some amazing discovery about the nature of reality. No, he's describing the difference between two sorts of sentences. Something like, 'Herbert the bachelor is unmarried' and 'Herbert the bachelor is wearing a red cap.'"

He turned and gave me a mystified look. "Are you really telling me that someone who makes such a fuss about this nonsense has anything to say to people in business?"

I now regretted ever bringing up Kant. To be honest, when I first rattled off Mill and Kant, I was showing off. It's not that I didn't know what I was talking about. I just didn't have much depth when it came to someone as theoretical as Kant. Mill was more practical. But I *did* have a point to make about Kant. It had to do with the proper way to treat people.

"I'll be the first to admit that I'm much less comfortable with Kant than with Mill because utilitarianism is so practical. And I've read only one piece of Kant's writings—his short discussion about ethics—*Grounding for the Metaphysics of Morals*. But I think there *is* something practical and helpful there. So I'm just going to give you, let's call it, 'a busy executive's version of the surprisingly practical application to business of Immanuel Kant's ethics.' If you want something more academic, you're on your own."

He settled back into his role as skeptic. "Understood. Let's see if you're up to the challenge of moving Kant from the classroom to the boardroom."

I called up a couple of Web sites on the screen, checked out a few details and took a deep breath.

"OK. Immanuel Kant. Early modern German philosopher. Lived before Mill. A giant in his field. Wrote about every branch of philosophy, not just ethics. He supposedly lived a life so regular people could set their clocks by his daily walk. But he reportedly had a rich social life. So it's not as though he was some rigid, purely cerebral, philosophical automaton.

"For our purposes, Kant and Mill disagree in *one* critical way. Remember that in utilitarianism, all actions are morally neutral. Actions' *consequences* determine whether they're right or wrong. For Kant, however, actions are *intrinsically* right or wrong. Consequences are irrelevant. It's all about which actions treat others *appropriately* in the village. Philosophers label his theory as *deontological*. *Deontos* means 'duty' in Greek. The idea is that if an action is the right thing to do, we have a duty to do it. If it's wrong, we have a duty not to do it, no matter what the benefits."

"So," Socrates interjected, "there's no temptation to say 'the ends justify the means' because we never even look at the ends. If an action is in and of itself unacceptable, we can't do it, no matter what?"

"Correct. So let me give you a classic example of how Kant explains what he means. Then we'll look at the Apple/Proview case again."

"And then," he interrupted, "you can explain the *other* major difference in how Mill and Kant go at things."

"The *other* difference?" I asked, puzzled and having no idea what he was referring to.

"Don't worry. We'll get to that. Go ahead with what you were about to say."

"It's really pretty simple. It's Kant's standard for how we know we're treating others appropriately in the village. No matter what tangible benefits we can get from an action, we must treat others with respect. We don't treat them as though they are objects. People are special and deserve to be treated as such. We're autonomous beings who deserve to freely decide what we do."

I tapped up one of the Web sites. "Kant says, 'everything has either a price or dignity. Whatever has a price can be replaced by something else which is equivalent; whatever, on the other hand, is above all price, and therefore admits of no equivalent, has a dignity.' We have a dignity. And that means . . . " I brought up another passage, " 'Act so as to treat humanity, whether in your own person or in that of any other, in every case as an end, never simply as a means.' So this is a great reminder that we need to treat our customers, employees, investors, and all of our stakeholders with appropriate respect. We don't try to trick them into something or put something past them.

"Kant even has a good example that shows why lying is wrong. He's talking about someone who needs money, but knows the only way he'll get it is to promise to repay it, even though he knows he never will. Kant writes, 'The individual who is thinking of making a false promise to others will see at once that he would be using another man merely as a means. . . . For whomever I propose to use for my own purposes by such a promise cannot possibly agree to my way of acting towards him. . . .' "

I added a slide of Kant's main points.

BUSINESS ETHICS ISN'T RUBBISH: PART 3, KANT

1. RIGHT AND WRONG—TREAT OTHERS APPROPRIATELY

2. RESPECT PEOPLE'S FREEDOM, AUTONOMY AND *DIGNITY*

3. DON'T TREAT THEM AS A MEANS TO AN END

"And that's what the Apple/Proview case shows. Apple was trying to get Proview to do something they wouldn't have freely chosen to do if they knew all the facts. Apple was using the people they were dealing with at Proview as a means to an end.

"Capitalism is an economic system that's supposed to be based on *freedom* and *free choice*. That's why we call it *free* market capitalism. So any business transaction that isn't based on everyone's full and free consent doesn't pass muster."

"Let's say that in theory I agree with you," interrupted Socrates. "What does this have to do with *doing* business?"

"I was just getting to that. If you found out that a business manipulated you or treated you disrespectfully, would you do business with them again?"

"Of course not."

"Me neither." I then added another line to the slide.

BUSINESS ETHICS ISN'T RUBBISH: PART 3, KANT

1. RIGHT AND WRONG—TREAT OTHERS APPROPRIATELY

2. RESPECT PEOPLE'S FREEDOM, AUTONOMY AND *DIGNITY*

3. DON'T TREAT THEM AS A MEANS TO AN END

4. TREATING PEOPLE IMPROPERLY CAN COST YOU

"So Kant shows that 'business ethics isn't rubbish' because he reminds us how crucial it is to treat everyone properly. By directing our attention away from consequences and making us focus just on how we're treating people, Kant reminds us how important it is for us to be treated properly. Even if being treated without proper respect doesn't have any practical impact on our lives, we're very sensitive to this. Think of how upset people get over privacy concerns, even when it has no tangible, negative impact on their lives. Look at how often people fuss about that with social media sites, ad tracking, e-mail scanning, and the like. Remember that people often get more upset about the *intangible* issues related to how they want to be treated—with fairness, justice, respect, equality—than about some tangible harm like losing money. Kant reminds us not to kid ourselves and say, 'It's no big deal. They'll forget it, get over it, or figure that's just how things are done in business. If they think about it, they'll even thank us for reminding them to be less trusting.'

"*Kant* may not be talking about consequences, but we all know how quickly you can lose money by failing to treat customers, employees, and other stakeholders with proper respect. Treating people poorly can *cost* you."

I stepped back to check the slide. "You know, everyone says how hard Kant is. But I think the idea 'don't treat people as objects' is pretty simple."

Socrates shook his head and looked at me with a sigh. "Well, I'm not going to challenge anything you've just said. And it does add to your explanation of why 'business ethics isn't rubbish.' "

"Then why do I hear a *but* coming?"

He pulled out that damned notebook from our earlier meeting.

"Not that thing again! I'd hoped I'd imagined it. Don't you think it's time to burn it?"

"And add CO_2 to the atmosphere? That would just be *wrong*. It was a simple sleight of hand the other day. Your back was turned, so I left a blank one. I promise I'll leave this with you this time. I just want to check whether I wrote down *Cocky* as one of the traits you need to work on."

"*Cocky?* Where'd that come from?"

"Immanuel Kant is one of the great minds of Western philosophy, yet you say with surprise in your voice, 'everyone says how hard Kant is.' You don't read very closely, do you? Don't you think you might have missed something?"

I went back to the screen, looked at the passages I'd called up, and my summary slide. "I don't think so."

Socrates walked up beside me and highlighted the word "simply" in "Act so as to treat humanity, whether in your own person or in that of any other, in every case as an end, never *simply* as a means."

"Do you want to explain that?" he asked.

I looked closely and re-read the sentence. "To be honest, I never noticed it before. But it's just one word. What difference can it make? The idea is still to respect the dignity and autonomy of the people you're dealing with."

"What difference can it make? How about this. It seems to me that the sentence recognizes that dealings between people are more complicated than you think. Kant doesn't say *'never* as a means,' but 'never *simply* as a means.' That suggests to me that it's possible to treat someone as an end and as a means at the same time. The challenge is, as you suggest, to do so while respecting their dignity.

"In my opinion, treating someone *simply* as a means is something like coercing them. Giving them no choice in the matter. But what if they formally agree or don't object and just go along with being treated as a means to your end—compromising their own interests in the process? Or what if their actions suggest they don't care that much? Can't we say we're then treating someone 'as an end'?"

I still thought he was just being picky. "Why don't you give me an example."

"I'll give you three. First, a simple one. Imagine I want to hire a gardener for as little money as possible. If I hire someone who's undocumented, I can pay less than minimum wage and less than market rates. He could refuse. Or he could threaten a stand-off where we each say we'll blow the whistle on the other. But he accepts what I offer. Setting aside any legal issues, it seems to me that I'm both treating him as a means to my end—by taking advantage of him— and treating him as an end—by recognizing that he ultimately has to agree.

"Second, a little more involved. What if I said that anyone who complains about how Facebook, Google, or any other company that tends to be insensitive to issues of privacy has no leg to stand on? These are businesses, after all, not charitable services. Their products aren't free. The cost to people using them is giving the companies their personal information. It's all spelled out in the terms and conditions. Most people never read them. But by clicking through, we freely agree to all of this. If I'm Facebook, maybe I can be accused of taking advantage of people's ignorance or laziness—so maybe I'm treating them as a means. *But*, no one forces anyone to use my product. They have to click that box that says they consent to the conditions. They can leave at any time. Isn't that respecting them as ends?"

I wasn't sure whether I agreed with Socrates or not. He was making things more confusing. "Let me think about that. Go on to your last example."

"Let's go back to Apple and Proview. Someone from Apple could point out that no one ever forced Proview to sell the trademark. It's true that the deception and the threat of a lawsuit were designed to push them along. But they still acted freely, didn't they? Furthermore, wasn't it the job of executives at

Proview to protect the interests of their company? They certainly could have negotiated more aggressively with 'IP Application Development' and at least gotten more facts on the record. If they took the time to do some research, maybe they could have uncovered the whole scam. None of the negotiation was done face-to-face, right? Couldn't they have had a friend in England check out 'IP Application Development'? But they chose not to do that. Don't their actions show that, at the very least, they didn't really care as much as they should have? You claim they ended up as a means to Apple's end. But if they were willing to go along with things, weren't they also being treated as an end?"

I understood what he was saying, but I needed more time to think about looking at things this way. "Let's just say I agree that '*simply*' in that sentence is more meaningful than I'd first recognized."

"Excellent—which means, I'm sure, that you'll be glad to explain the other part of the sentence you skipped over." This time, he highlighted "in your own person."

"'Act so as to treat humanity, whether *in your own person* or in that of any other, in every case as an end, never simply as a means.'"

Keeping his finger pointed to the phrase, he continued, "Kant is saying something here about how we should treat ourselves, not just how we treat others. You've been applying his ideas only to our 'treat others appropriately' rule in the village. Where does treating humanity 'in our own person' come in?"

That was something else I'd never noticed. "I suppose that if Kant thinks he's discovered some universal rule, it would have to apply equally to everyone involved. Right? But as long as we freely choose what to do—no matter what it is—what's the problem? Wouldn't that fit what you just explained as treating people both as means and as ends?"

Socrates got more animated as though moving his arms would make the point clearer to me. "First, it isn't just whether we *freely choose* our actions. It's also whether they're *appropriate* to the dignity of the human person." Then he paused. "Let me suggest a different way of looking at this. Think of a free choice as a case of telling ourselves to do something. But now imagine that we're telling someone else to do the same thing. Would we be comfortable doing that?

"Let's take a specific example. *You.*"

"Me?" I asked, surprised—but definitely wondering what Socrates had up his sleeve.

"Too close to home?" he replied, as he flipped through that damn notebook again.

"Go ahead. In for a penny; in for a pound." This felt like another one of his challenges.

"You, like many people in business—especially senior executives, experience great stress."

"It's part of the job. Everyone knows it," I said, minimizing the point. "Besides, as you've pointed out, I get rewarded very generously."

"But the reward doesn't change the effects of the stress.

"There's the physical impact of chronic stress: a compromised immune system, susceptibility to infections, high blood pressure, greater risk of cardiovascular disease, stroke, diabetes, the list goes on.

"Then there's the emotional cost. That temper of yours. Being so fixated on the job that you neglect other relationships."

He paused and made a point of picking up the coffee pot and refilling my cup. I immediately understood the meaning of the serious look he gave me. It told me he knew my first marriage had failed because I was obsessed with succeeding. He also apparently knew I was trying to do better with my current marriage, but that I still struggled. I appreciate the fact that he had the decency not to state this directly.

"Would you even *ask*—never mind *tell*—anyone who works for you to live their life the way you choose to live yours?"

"No. Of course not. And if I had a friend living that way, I'd certainly try to talk some sense into her," I admitted.

"Then you see my point. I think you have a bad habit of treating yourself inappropriately—like a means to an end. And *choosing* to do so doesn't change the fact."

I got back up and read over again the statements Socrates had highlighted. "So you're saying that, according to Kant, there's nothing wrong with your hiring the undocumented gardener, Facebook failing to respect members' privacy scrupulously, or Apple allegedly tricking Proview. But there *is* something wrong with my working so hard? That just seems crazy."

Socrates replied forcefully. "No. That's *not* what I'm saying. I'm just trying to show you that Kant points to *a number of* factors that need to be considered when we try to decide whether or not an action treats people—including ourselves—appropriately. It's more complicated than the means/ends formula."

He went back to the screen and added to our Kant slide.

BUSINESS ETHICS ISN'T RUBBISH: PART 3, KANT

1. RIGHT AND WRONG—TREAT OTHERS APPROPRIATELY

2. RESPECT PEOPLE'S FREEDOM, AUTONOMY AND *DIGNITY*

3. DON'T TREAT THEM AS A MEANS TO AN END

3 (REVISED). DON'T TREAT THEM—OR *YOURSELF—SIMPLY* AS A MEANS TO AN END

4. TREATING PEOPLE IMPROPERLY CAN COST YOU

"And finally, we can now look at the *other* major difference between Mill and Kant. The most basic one that comes from the fact that Kant builds his ethics on reason alone. And I'm sure you can't wait to explain this to me."

I looked back blankly. I had maxed out my knowledge of Kant and honestly didn't know what he was referring to.

15

Business, Ethics, Apple/Proview, and Immanuel Kant (continued)

When I hesitated, Socrates scrolled around in a couple of Web sites. As he turned around and looked at me, I could tell he was debating with himself about how hard to push me. "OK, you say that Kant is practical for business people. I agree. You said you'd connect his ideas with the Apple/Proview case, as you did with Mill's. You did so, but you used Kant's means/end formulation.

"Now, let's see why Kant has a problem with lying for another reason—because he bases his ethics on *reason alone*."

I was curious about what he had in mind, but was lost.

"What is Kant's most formal, technical, rational explanation for why lying is wrong?"

I didn't have a clue, and there was no point pretending otherwise.

"You're simply going to have to tell me," I said, shrugging my shoulders.

"Sorry, you have to discover it for yourself." He paused and thought. "Tell me this. What's a lie?"

I sighed, realizing I had no choice but to be led down whatever path Socrates had in mind.

"A lie? A statement that's not true, dishonest, manipulative, deceptive."

"Good start. What do you mean *not true*?"

I stared back blankly. "*Not true* means *not true*. *False*. I can't put it any more simply than that."

Socrates thought for a moment. "Humor me. Give me $100 from your wallet. I'll give it right back."

I fished my wallet out of my bag and handed him the bill.

"Great," he said, as he put it into his pants' pocket. "Thanks. I lied. You'll never see it again."

"As I said before, you're getting predictable. Why don't you just tell me the point you're trying to make with this stunt?"

Ignoring my suggestion, he asked, "What was the lie I told you?"

I grumbled. "You said, 'I'll give it right back.' "

"And why was it a lie?"

"Because your intention all along was to keep it."

"Excellent. And what's the relationship between *my statement* and *my intention*? Take your time. There's no rush. I want the most formal, technical, logical way to describe what's problematic about my lie to you. Figure that out and you'll understand a big part of what it means to say that Kant bases his ethics on *reason alone*. Actually, you'll figure it out if you can do these two things. First, rephrase the problem so it's about *two sentences* that differ by only *one word*. Second, tell me why—at least in theory—Vulcans don't lie. I need to make a phone call. I'll be back in a couple of minutes."

"Vulcans? Are you serious?" I called after him as he walked down the hall toward his office.

This was beginning to feel like an odd, but interesting puzzle.

Hmmm. I didn't know a lot about science fiction, but I did know more about Star Trek than I was willing to admit publicly from overhearing my now-physicist daughter argue with her friends all through high school about every conceivable aspect of those movies and television shows. OK. Vulcans . . . Spock . . . logic. . . . Logic! That must be it. Logic. Rules of reason. Reason alone. . . . That must be the angle. Vulcans don't lie because it's illogical? I'm still missing something. Maybe, the other part. The lie was 'I'll give it back.' The intention was 'I'm keeping your money.' But they aren't two sentences with only one different word. The lie, 'I will give it back'; the intention, 'I will not give it back.' That's the one word difference. It's like a negative sign. Like a math thing where they cancel each other out. No. Not a math thing but a logic thing. The rules of reason. That's it!

"A lie is a *contradiction*," I announced proudly as Socrates returned. "The lie and the intention contradict each other."

"Quicker than I thought. Well done. And our Vulcan friends?" he asked with a smile.

"Vulcans are logical. Contradictions are illogical. Lies represent contradictions between what I *say* and what I *know* or *intend to be* the case," I explained, wondering whether I'd actually admit to my daughter how much I benefitted from her youthful obsession.

"Top marks. Now do you see it?"

I looked back blankly again.

"Ethics and *reason*," he prodded.

"Kant thinks a lie is morally wrong because it's illogical?" The idea made hardly any sense when I thought it. It sounded weirder when I said it out loud. "At least for *humans*, that sounds like apples and oranges—ethics and logic. You're going to have to help me see the connection."

"Fair enough." Socrates went back up to the screen. He obviously thought this was important, or he wouldn't keep pestering me like this. But frankly, in terms of my responsibilities as a CEO, it seemed ridiculous to spend so much time and energy on something so abstract.

"Let's back up a bit," he said. "The reason you're getting lost is because I haven't shown you the big picture and explained why something so thoroughly theoretical can help you as a CEO. This is about knowing what kind of evidence to trust when you make decisions. I'm insisting that we talk about this because—as you admitted in our first conversation—you've been making some bad calls. I'm trying to give you a different way to approach problems. Trust me. This will make sense when I finish. Just hang in there for now.

"The most fundamental disagreement between Kant and thinkers like Mill has to do with what's the best kind of evidence for saying that you *know* something."

"Right. Empiricism versus rationalism. I remember," I said, surprising myself. "I guess all that trivia was buried somewhere in my brain."

"Then you should know where this is going." Socrates walked back to the screen and made another chart.

TRUTH/KNOWLEDGE

EMPIRICISM	PHYSICAL EVIDENCE SOLID PROOF, UNQUESTIONABLY TRUE	"THE FRAME ON THE FLAT SCREEN IS BLACK"
RATIONALISM	REASON UNIVERSALLY TRUE	"A SQUARE HAS FOUR SIDES"

"Empiricists," he continued, "argue that in order to say that you *know* something, you need hard, physical—empirical—evidence. We know that 'This frame on the flat screen is black' is true because we can look at it and verify it. The fact that this is true is unshakable.

"Rationalists, however, aren't impressed. They argue that empirical statements are changeable. For example, if I paint the frame a different color, it isn't black anymore. And anything I say about the screen—its size, shape, condition—will be true only as long as that piece of equipment exists. However, the truths of mathematics, logic, and philosophy will never change. And we discover and understand these truths using reason alone.

"A square will always have four sides.

"The sum of the interior angles of a triangle will always be 180 degrees.

"If I start with any statement of the form 'if P, then Q' (if I was born in Athens, then I was born in Greece), I know it will never be true to say 'if not-P, then not-Q' (if I wasn't born in Athens, then I wasn't born in Greece). After all, there are plenty of other cities in Greece. A claim like that would violate a rule of logic.

"And, since we're talking about contradictions, we know that any statement of the form 'P and not-P' will also always be false.

"Empiricists would concede all of this, but they'd point out that the only things about which you can say 'this will always be true' have nothing to do with the real world.

"So rationalists think that empirical claims are limited; empiricists think that the examples rationalists hold up are trivial. With me so far?"

"Yes," I nodded. "But what does this have to do with helping me as a CEO?" I asked, as he added to his TRUTH/KNOWLEDGE slide.

<u>TRUTH/KNOWLEDGE</u>

EMPIRICISM	PHYSICAL EVIDENCE SOLID PROOF, UNQUESTIONABLY TRUE	"THE FRAME ON THE FLAT SCREEN IS BLACK"

RATIONALISM'S EXAMPLES OF KNOWLEDGE ARE TRIVIAL AND IRRELEVANT TO THE REAL WORLD.

RATIONALISM	REASON UNIVERSALLY TRUE	"A SQUARE HAS FOUR SIDES"

EXPIRICISM'S EXAMPLES OF KNOWLEDGE ARE CHANGEABLE AND EPHEMERAL.

"Didn't we talk about your impatience the other day?" Socrates chided. "Just relax. It's a beautiful day at the beach, and I'm still protecting you from the press. I told you I'd make the connection. Take a deep breath and relax.

"Remember that Kant's a rationalist. He's trying to uncover truths by reason alone. When it comes to ethics, Kant believes he has discovered a fundamental moral principle that lets us determine the ethical character of our actions. He calls it the *categorical imperative*—a command (imperative) that we must always (categorically) follow. You forgot to mention that his 'treat people as ends in themselves' idea is one version of the categorical imperative. He explains it in a variety of ways—each explanation capturing what we might call a different facet of the concept. We've already looked at one. Now we're going to look at another.

"But first you need to know that Kant's model for how we act is that we make a conscious decision, engage our *will*, and *voila*! Moreover, we can always describe the general principle the general principle for any specific action. For example, . . ." Socrates walked over to the small refrigerator in the corner, removed a water bottle, and opened it, "when I twisted off the top, I applied the following general principle to this situation—'whenever I want to remove the cap of a threaded water bottle, I will turn it counter-clockwise.' Kant calls that kind of general principle a *maxim*. And his *categorical imperative* tells us what kind of *maxims* are appropriate—*ethically* appropriate."

Socrates tapped the screen, highlighted a passage and read it out loud.

"'Act as if the *maxim* of your action were to become by your will a *universal law of nature*.'"

I got back up and walked over to the screen still not sure where this was going. "Kant is a rationalist. So any *maxim* or general principle which is true has to be *universally* true?"

"Close enough. But before you ask anything else," he said as he punched up another screen, "here's one of the specific examples Kant uses to illustrate this. Obviously, because we're talking about ethics, the maxims we're going to worry about involve people, not inanimate objects like water bottles. In this case, Kant is saying that acceptable maxims can't be self-contradictory. *Contradictions* don't work as acceptable principles for our actions."

Socrates read the passage.

Another man finds himself forced by necessity to borrow money. He knows that he will not be able to repay it, but sees also that nothing will be lent to him unless he firmly promises to repay it in a definite time. He wants to make this promise, but he has still so much conscience as to ask himself: "Is it not unlawful and inconsistent with duty to get out of a difficulty in this way?" Suppose, however, that he resolves to do so: then *the maxim of his action* would be expressed thus: "*When I think myself in want of money, I will borrow money and promise to repay it, although I know that I never can do so.*" Now this principle of self-love or of one's own advantage may perhaps be consistent with my whole future welfare; but the question now is, "Is it right?" I change then the suggestion of self-love into a universal law, and state the question thus: "*How would it be if my maxim were a universal law?*" Then I see at once that it could never hold as a universal law of nature, but would necessarily *contradict itself*. For supposing it to be a universal law that everyone when he thinks himself in a difficulty should be able to promise whatever he pleases, with the purpose of not keeping his promise, the promise itself would become impossible, as well as the end that one might have in view in it, since no one would consider that anything was promised to him, but would ridicule all such statements as vain pretenses.'

"Now," he said, turning to me, "explain this to me as simply as you can." I studied the passage for a minute, isolating the maxim.

> WHEN I BELIEVE MYSELF TO BE IN NEED OF MONEY, I WILL BORROW MONEY AND PROMISE TO PAY IT BACK, ALTHOUGH I KNOW I CAN NEVER DO SO.

"Lying would get me out of a jam. *But,* if we're being absolutely technical about this, my statement and my intention would be *contradictory*. 'I *will* pay you back.' 'I *will not* pay you back.' So, strictly speaking, my lying would be *illogical*?" Socrates nodded, and I added this to the slide. "Which reminds me, this is the same as your stealing my 100 dollar bill a few minutes ago."

WHEN I BELIEVE MYSELF TO BE IN NEED OF MONEY, I WILL BORROW MONEY
AND PROMISE TO PAY IT BACK, ALTHOUGH I KNOW I CAN NEVER DO SO.

MY STATEMENT: "I WILL PAY YOU BACK"
MY INTENTION: "I WILL NOT PAY YOU BACK."
CONTRADICTION

"Very good, and thanks for the reminder." Socrates was genuinely impressed and handed back my money. "But you look puzzled. What's the problem?"

"I understand the point about the maxim of my action involving a contradiction. However, because lying can get me out of a jam, there's a way in which it's *absolutely* the *logical* thing to do."

"That's the problem with using the same word to mean various things," he explained. "If by 'logical,' you mean 'a course of action that will make life easier for me,' you're right. Lying would be 'logical.' But we're using 'logical' to mean 'follows the rules of reason.' Of course, since humans aren't Vulcans, we have no problem acting according to maxims that don't follow the rules of reason—especially when each of us decides we're a special case and should be able to do things other people shouldn't.

"But let's get back on track. Your explanation stopped before the '*universal law*' part of Kant's statement."

Pointing to the spot in the passage where I got stumped, I explained, "Which is because I honestly don't know what a maxim that 'contradicts itself' has do to with making 'the promise itself impossible.' Why didn't Kant just stop after 'contradict itself' and say, 'so don't act illogically'?"

Socrates laughed. "That obviously wouldn't say a lot to you about how you should act now, would it? The way I like to look at this is that Kant actually goes easy on us and cheats a bit to give us a simple way to test whether a particular maxim is appropriate. He has us try to imagine a world in which the maxim of our action has the force of a law of nature. The maxim, then, describes exactly how everyone in that situation acts. Can that 'work'? What are the *practical consequences* of everyone acting that way?"

I went back to the screen, studied the passage some more and thought out loud.

"Gravity's a law of nature. When everyone drops a hammer, it falls. I can picture that. In our world, *lying's* a law of nature. When anyone's in a bind, they promise whatever they need to in order to get out of trouble. Can I imagine a world in which that's a fixed rule for how everyone behaves?"

I needed to isolate the maxim again.

UNIVERSAL LAW OF NATURE: WHENEVER ANYONE WANTS SOMETHING THEY
CAN'T GET OTHERWISE, THEY WILL PROMISE WHATEVER THEY THINK WILL LET
THEM GET IT, BUT THEY'LL HAVE NO INTENTION OF KEEPING THE PROMISE.
DOESN'T WORK

"No. This doesn't work. Not when *everyone* behaves that way. That's the key. Lying works only when most people tell the truth and keep their promises. As soon as *everybody* lies and makes false promises, it doesn't work. In this world, the concept of a promise as we know it doesn't even exist.

"In *our* world, a promise says that my statement—*I will pay you back*—and my future action—*I pay you back*—will be consistent. In the world we're imagining, they're guaranteed to be *inconsistent*.

"In the world we're imagining, if I say, 'I promise,' everyone would hear, 'I'm about to describe to you something I will never do, and you'd believe me only if you're remarkably stupid or gullible.' That's why Kant says people would *laugh*. In this world, a statement that starts 'I promise' would sound like, 'two guys walk into a bar . . . ' in our world. The only way it would mean anything is as a joke."

"Very good!" Socrates said. "*Now* do the same thing with a genuine promise, that is, when we intend to keep our word."

I added to the slide.

> UNIVERSAL LAW OF NATURE: WHENEVER ANYONE WANTS SOMETHING THEY CAN'T GET OTHERWISE, THEY WILL PROMISE WHATEVER THEY THINK WILL LET THEM GET IT, BUT THEY'LL HAVE NO INTENTION OF KEEPING THE PROMISE.
>
> **DOESN'T WORK**

> UNIVERSAL LAW OF NATURE: WHENEVER ANYONE WANTS SOMETHING THEY CAN'T GET OTHERWISE, THEY WILL PROMISE WHATEVER THEY THINK WILL LET THEM GET IT, AND THEIR ACTIONS WILL MATCH THEIR PROMISE PRECISELY.
>
> **WORKS**

"A *real* promise? The maxim of my action would be something like, 'Whenever I make a promise, I will keep it.' I think of a world in which this is a 'law of nature.' Everyone acts this way. Can it work? Yes. So that must mean 'keeping your promises' with people counts as treating them appropriately."

"Very good. Now apply this approach to the Apple/Proview case."

I thought about the case, figured out the maxim, and added to our list of "universal laws of nature."

> UNIVERSAL LAW OF NATURE: WHENEVER ANYONE WANTS SOMETHING THEY CAN'T GET OTHERWISE, THEY WILL PROMISE WHATEVER THEY THINK WILL LET THEM GET IT, BUT THEY'LL HAVE NO INTENTION OF KEEPING THE PROMISE.
>
> **DOESN'T WORK**

> UNIVERSAL LAW OF NATURE: WHENEVER ANYONE WANTS SOMETHING THEY CAN'T GET OTHERWISE, THEY WILL PROMISE WHATEVER THEY THINK WILL LET THEM GET IT, AND THEIR ACTIONS WILL MATCH THEIR PROMISE PRECISELY.
>
> **WORKS**

> UNIVERSAL LAW OF NATURE: WHENEVER ANYONE WANTS SOMETHING THAT BELONGS TO SOMEONE ELSE, THEY WILL USE STRATEGEMS THAT INCLUDE DECEPTION AND DISHONESTY TO ACHIEVE THEIR GOAL.
>
> **DOESN'T WORK**

"It's a variation on the false promise," I explained. "If deception and dishonesty are the norm, it's impossible to believe anything anyone says.

When I try to picture what it would be like to do business in such a world, all I can think of is chaos. Everything is unpredictable. Everyone is so undependable and inconsistent, it just doesn't work."

"Excellent! You've got it!" Socrates said with enthusiasm.

"Got it? Got what?" I asked, puzzled and frustrated. "Identifying the maxims of actions and imagining fictional worlds with these as 'universal laws of nature' may be an interesting intellectual exercise, but I don't see what it has to do with ethics. Why does that make the false promise, deception, or dishonesty *wrong* rather than just technical examples of inconsistency? I understand why making a false promise or trying to trick someone is wrong because actions like this treat someone as a means to an end. But what's the *ethical* significance of the inconsistency in all of this?"

Socrates sat back down and motioned that I should do the same.

"I appreciate your frustration, but this is simpler than you realize. Let's take it one step at a time.

"Imagine that two people on your staff work as a team to solve a major problem. You reward one. You absolutely ignore the other. All things being equal, what do you think of what you just did?"

"That's easy. It was *unfair*."

"Why?"

"They did the same job. They should get the same reward." I thought for a moment. "I'm *inconsistent* in the way I'm treating them."

"Brilliant! And when we started talking yesterday about finding some foundation for ethics, why did we rule out laws, religions, customs, and personal emotions?"

I thought back to where we'd begun and ran through our conversation in my head. Then I saw what Socrates was referring to. "Because none of them were *universal*. We had *inconsistencies* all over the place. That's why we ended up grounding ethics in the necessary conditions for a satisfying life."

"So?" Socrates prompted.

"So if we can find some universal principles we can apply consistently, ethics has some sort of solid foundation."

"Putting it simply," Socrates added, "principles like that let us say that *ethics isn't rubbish*."

"Agreed."

"Do you remember I said that I regard the different versions of the categorical imperative as describing different facets of Kant's standard for right and wrong? The *means/end* version of the categorical imperative shows us one feature of a good ethical standard—respecting the dignity of everyone involved. The *universal law of nature* version shows us another—making sure our judgments are rational, logical, consistent."

"Right. Got it."

"OK. Keep that thought in mind while I ask you two final questions."

Two final questions. At last.

"Number one. Do you ever make decisions based on 'gut feeling,' 'instinct,' 'intuition,' the 'seat of your pants,' or some other such thing?"

"Of course. I think that intuition is an important tool in decision making. The whole is sometimes more than the sum of its parts. Intuition lets me see that. I don't know a senior executive who doesn't rely on intuition or gut feeling at some point."

"Excellent. Number two. When you do that, do you ever worry about consistency—or some other technically rational or logical part of the issue?"

"Of course not. When I rely on intuition, it's more about 'feeling' or having some intangible insight. Consistency would be an awfully narrow and limiting factor."

"I understand," Socrates nodded. "But, what's your track record lately? Considering how bad a job your 'intuition'—or the 'gut' of your compatriots—did in the run-up to the meltdown, I'd say it's time to rethink the value of *your* or *anyone else's* 'gut.'

"Let me tell you a story I ran across in an interesting book that talks about the value of introverts in an organization. Given how many extroverts and narcissists you and I know who call the shots in so many companies, it's fair to say that it's heresy to suggest that maybe we should have been listening to the quiet, thoughtful, and cautious people. In fact, . . . " He spoke into the microphone and a passage from the book appeared on the screen.

"The person telling this story was an associate at a Wall Street law firm representing a bank considering buying a portfolio of subprime mortgage loans made by other lenders.

I heard a story circulating on Wall Street about a competition among investment banks for a prestigious piece of business. Each of the major banks sent a squad of their top employees to pitch the client. Each team deployed the usual tools: spread sheets, "pitch books," and PowerPoint presentations. But the winning team added its own piece of theatrics: they ran into the room wearing matching baseball caps and T-shirts emblazoned with the letters FUD, an acronym for *Fear, Uncertainty, and Doubt*. In this case FUD had been crossed out with an emphatic red X; FUD was an unholy trinity. That team, the vanquishers of FUD, won the contest.

You and I have been in this business long enough to know that the attitude represented by that team and the people who chose them is what put us over the edge. And we also know that anyone who asked whether a certain amount of calm, logical rationality should be part of the decision making process would be laughed to scorn."

As Socrates paused and let me take in what he'd just said, I couldn't argue with him. In fact, I'd told plenty of people who worked for me that they needed more nerve.

"As I said before, I'm fixating on this aspect of Kant because I want you to think about what kind of evidence to consider—and to *trust*—when you make decisions. Given what we just said about the need for consistency and universality in assuring that ethics isn't rubbish, maybe you should start seeing factors like consistency, logic, and cold rationality as a backstop or a safety net. Maybe you shouldn't be so enamored of instinct and gut feeling. In the world of business, worrying about whether or not the maxim of your action can be universalized as a law of nature isn't sexy. But your job is to make the best possible decisions, even if you feel like a geek doing it.

"Or think about it this way, if it makes you feel more 'businesslike.' All Kant is asking you to do is to identify the *principle* underlying your action. You talk about *acting according to principle* all the time. This is a specific way to help you make sure the principle you're acting according to is a good one. In the Apple/Proview matter, let's give 'Jonathan Hargreaves' the benefit of the doubt. Let's say he saw himself as acting according to a principle like, 'In negotiations, get the best deal for your client possible without *technically* lying.' And on the surface, that probably would sound acceptable to any executive. But once we subject it to stricter analysis of the sort Kant's perspective suggests it looks more like a *rationalization*.

"And that's one of Kant's most important contributions to you as a CEO. He can help you separate a rationalization—something that sounds like a reasonable argument, but is just a smokescreen for what we *feel* like doing—from a solid analysis. That's why Kant's 'Can your maxim work as a universal law of nature?' test is so important. This approach can help keep you from kidding yourself. Remember, I'm just trying to give you a way to approach problems that's different from what you used in the past."

Socrates stepped back to the screen and finished off the "business ethics isn't rubbish" slide we'd been working on.

BUSINESS ETHICS ISN'T RUBBISH: PART 3, KANT

1. RIGHT AND WRONG—TREAT OTHERS APPROPRIATELY

2. RESPECT PEOPLE'S FREEDOM, AUTONOMY, AND *DIGNITY*

3. DON'T TREAT THEM AS A MEANS TO AN END

3 (REVISED). DON'T TREAT THEM—OR *YOURSELF—SIMPLY* AS A MEANS TO AN END

4. TREATING PEOPLE IMPROPERLY CAN COST YOU

5. RIGHT AND WRONG—THINK ABOUT THE PRINCIPLE UNDERLYING YOUR ACTION

6. THINK ABOUT WHETHER OR NOT THAT PRINCIPLE CAN <u>WORK</u> UNIVERSALLY

7. ARE YOU ANALYZING LOGICALLY AND OBJECTIVELY, OR ARE YOU <u>RATIONALIZING?</u>

"What do you think?" he asked as he finished. "This is what you meant when you said Kant also supported your argument that 'business ethics isn't rubbish,' isn't it?"

"Absolutely," I laughed, "it's as though you read my mind."

"Great, because I'm famished. We'll finish off our little project after lunch."

16

Corporate Responsibility—The Gun Company

"OK, you've made it over the first hurdle," Socrates said when we came back from lunch and sat back down on the deck. "You've successfully convinced me that 'ethics isn't rubbish' and that 'business ethics isn't rubbish.' Congratulations."

"Thanks," I responded with no small amount of dread. I could tell that he was just getting warmed up. I was sure the really important, practical issues were now about to be rolled out. When Socrates picked me up in D.C., he said he had reservations about the bank's relationships to some of our customers and with my lobbying. Our discussions of ethical theory were obviously just the preliminaries. My fears were immediately confirmed.

"And now," he said seriously, "we get to the more central part of our conversation. We're going to look at some things you've said or done that concern me. And we're going to look at them *very* closely. In fairness, I should warn you that you'll probably find this much more difficult than our conversations the other day.

"But I want to make a couple of things clear. First, I'm not doing this out of gratuitous meanness. I want to see how well—in this case, how *deeply*—you can think about ethics. Second, I'm not saying I have a preconceived idea of some 'right' answer to these issues that I'm looking to badger you into agreeing with me on. This is about exploring how sophisticated and how clearly you can think about complicated ethical issues. My goal is to push you to look at perspectives you typically don't consider. This is more about having you spend some time out of your comfort zone than convincing you of a particular position."

It was clear that nothing I said would stop Socrates from doing what he wanted, so I just nodded my head.

"Let's talk about *responsibility*. A few years ago, about 30 people—mostly children—were massacred in an elementary school in Connecticut. One of the weapons used was made by a company which is a client of your bank. I'm told that in the spirit of being sensitive to the needs of your clients, you have participated in a series of meetings between the CEO of the company and the staff of Senators and Representatives. The CEO is aggressively lobbying against any gun control. He obviously thinks your presence in the meetings can help. My information is that you say very little during the sessions. You don't take a position on the issue of gun control, but you do support his claims about the effect of strict regulations on his company's financial position and the like. To your credit, you've been discrete about your involvement. You're apparently aware how sensitive a matter this is."

I'd tried to keep my presence at the meetings out of the press and off anyone's radar. But I was no longer surprised at the kind of information Socrates could get about me.

"I felt caught in the middle," I explained. "We've been the gun company's bank for years. The CEO was feeling beleaguered by all of the lobbying for stricter gun control. He made it clear that if I didn't show *some* support, he'd consider moving his business. Frankly, I doubt he'd have asked me if I were a man. I suspect he thought that having someone who was both a bank CEO and a mother sit in on the meetings would help him. At the same time, we have a significant retail presence in Connecticut, and I did not want to risk having our branch customers think we were insensitive to the tragedy. So I agreed to the meetings if we could keep my involvement quiet."

"Yes, I understood those were the terms of your participation. And I'm glad you recognize that your involvement was a direct result of your position and your gender. If you weren't the CEO of a major financial services institution, you wouldn't have been there.

"My question, however, is whether you think you bear any responsibility for the deaths of those children?" he asked clinically.

I was stunned and *insulted*. "*Responsibility?* Of course not! How could I be responsible for the actions of someone who was so emotionally disturbed that he was a ticking time bomb? It was a terrible tragedy, and I can only pray that this remains a horrible aberration."

"Aberration? In *America*?" he shot back. "Apparently, you haven't been paying attention. Let's see," he flipped open his notebook, "I want to make sure I get the numbers right. Every year about 30,000 people die from guns; almost 20,000 of those are suicides. Here's just a sampling. Six people killed at a Sikh temple in Wisconsin; 12 people in the movie theater in Colorado; 6 killed in Arizona—that's the attack that wounded Representative Giffords. Here's another—32 students at Virginia Tech.

"It's true that your guy's products weren't involved in all of these episodes. But a major reason the body count was so high is because of the semi-automatic weapons used in these massacres. And the gun company is lobbying Congress to continue letting them sell these kinds of weapons.

"So let me ask you again. Since you're part of a process that provides the financial support for manufacturing these guns and that continues to make them legal, do you share any responsibility for the deaths?"

At other points in our conversations, Socrates took a hard line just to bait me or to see how I'd respond. This time felt different. I suspected something personal behind his words.

"Look, I understand why you might want to talk about my taking part in those meetings on Capitol Hill. It could alienate some of our retail customers in Connecticut. But we're just the bank. *We don't make guns.* I think the ethical issues connected with being the *manufacturer* are very different from being their *bank*. It's not like I'm a member of the board of that company and can legitimately have some influence over their policies. We're just their *bank*. We help facilitate cash flow, offer loans, lines of credit, and the like.

"Besides, you're overlooking the most important fact. We have plenty of competitors. If *we* weren't their bank, someone else would be. It wouldn't change anything. It doesn't matter that we're the bank. We have a duty to our stakeholders. And I think having this company as a client and helping them when we can squares with that duty."

I appreciated the seriousness of innocent people being murdered, but I thought it was unfair to lump the bank and the manufacturer together.

"Hmmm," Socrates said thoughtfully. "If you weren't their bank, someone else would be. I never thought of that."

I was sure he was being sarcastic, but he looked quite serious. Checking his watch, he said, "Oh, I have to make a quick call." As he got up, he said, "In the meantime, why don't you check out the view from the top of that sand dune by that telephone pole over there? We can often see a pod of dolphins at this time of day. I'll be right back."

I walked down the sandy path and then up the dune. Socrates was right. There was a spectacular view of the bay. And, in the distance, I could see a few dolphins making their way toward our part of the beach. And then, *Splat!* I felt something drop onto my shoulder. I looked up and saw a seagull perched on the top of the telephone pole. *Damn!* I'd already come to the conclusion that nothing that happened while I was with Socrates was an accident. He'd deliberately had me stand under the spot where the local gulls relieved themselves. I walked back to the house. Socrates was still on the phone, but smirked as I walked past him to go to my room and put on a clean blouse.

"In some cultures, that's considered good luck," he said smugly as I came back out onto the deck. I wasn't amused. "Besides, if it weren't *that* seagull, it would have been another. It wouldn't have changed anything. You still would have ended up with seagull droppings on your shoulder no matter what."

"I assume that was supposed to be some sort of 'object lesson.'" I was getting increasingly annoyed with his stunts. "You don't really think this is relevant to our conversation, do you?"

"I can't think of anything *more* relevant. I took your position to be, 'Things that we don't like happen. That's life. Nothing we do is going to stop it. But someone's going to benefit. It may as well be us. And as long as the bank doesn't directly cause it, we're not responsible.' Unfortunately, in this instance, you were in the wrong place at the wrong time. Something you didn't like happened on your shoulder. You have no reason to complain."

I wasn't taking his bait. "We *aren't* responsible," I said forcefully.

"So you *aren't* part of the 'causal chain' of actions in which the manufacture of a certain sort of weapon could lead to a child being killed."

I paused and thought a minute, looking for Socrates' traps. "Sure, *technically*, we're part of a long, complicated series of events that could end in tragedy. But you can say that about virtually any event. For all we know, somewhere along the way you fired some unstable person who might decide to exact revenge against you or one of your people. Your action is part of the causal chain. But I'm not going to say you'd then be *responsible* for what some crazy person does as the last link."

"Artful dodge. But we're talking about probability and predictability here. It's virtually impossible to predict whether or not the crazy person I fire will go after me. But it's quite clear that the ongoing manufacture of certain kinds of weapons and their ready availability—both of which you facilitate— lead to a predictable number of deaths each year."

"Which is *exaggerated*," I interrupted. "Assault rifles always get a lot of attention after a tragedy, but they're responsible for a tiny percentage of the gun deaths in the United States each year." No matter where I personally stand on gun control, I had learned that many well-meaning people fixate on a couple of big gun death numbers without drilling down to see exactly how they break down.

"Considering that I haven't said anything about 'assault weapons,' I think you need to pay more attention to exactly what we're talking about. I referred to semi-automatic weapons and 'a certain sort of weapon.' Your client may make assault rifles, but his company's primary sales are in semi-automatic handguns. And I'm well aware of the statistics—homicides, suicides, handguns, rifles, and the like. Let's keep it simple. We aren't going to debate numbers. Dead means dead. In the United States, about 30,000 people die each year from guns. In countries like Australia and England, that number is almost negligible by comparison. Mass shootings—which are made far more deadly because of semi-automatic weapons—are much more common in the United States.

"Moreover, there's widespread public support in the U. S. for stricter gun control—even among gun owners. Only about a third of the households own guns, and that figure has been going down, not up. Yet you end up supporting a position which the overwhelming majority of Americans thinks is bad for the 'village.'"

"And if those Americans want to exercise their Constitutional rights," I replied firmly, if defensively, "they can contact their Senators and Representatives and make their positions known. That's the way the system works. That's how you get your voice heard in this country. That's how you make change. That's exactly the process I was a part of in that meeting. It's open to everyone."

Socrates shook his head in a way that I couldn't tell whether he was amused or disgusted. Once he started talking, however, it was clear it was the latter. "I thought I made it clear at the outset that we were having this conversation in the first place because I respect you, I think you're made for better things, and I want to help you. But if you're going to respond with simple-minded pap which you know is false, we should call it quits now." He paused, looked out at the ocean, then back at me, and thought for a moment. "I think I misjudged you. I'm sorry I wasted your time. I'm even more sorry I wasted *my* time. We're done. I'll have Colin drive you back to New York. If you'll excuse me." He got up and started to head inside.

At first, I thought this was like his seagull stunt. But his expression suggested he had in fact turned the page on me. After all he'd put me through, however, I wasn't going to let him just brush me off like this.

"Hold it!" I barked at him. "That's it? No explanation. Just a parting insult?"

He stopped and turned. "Tit for tat seemed appropriate. Was I supposed to take your fourth grade characterization of American democracy as a serious comment? Especially when you were part of a process that derailed a proposal that more than 90% of the country supported? One of the things that first caught my eye about you was your practical, fact-based approach to making decisions. So I know you understand the power of money in the way modern government works. But if you're just going to skip over that part and tell me that all people need to do is to contact their Representatives in Congress and 'the will of the people' will prevail, you're being either disingenuous or dishonest."

Socrates gave me a hard stare, and then he asked, "And how were you planning to characterize the extortion? A friendly suggestion?"

"Extortion! Are you crazy?" I was furious at the suggestion that I was involved in something so seriously illegal. But as Socrates took a step closer to me, it was clear he wasn't backing down.

"Then you tell me what you call it when the head of a gun company suggests that an attempt to protect the lives of children will lead to jobs being pulled from the state."

Again, I wasn't surprised that Socrates knew every detail of the conversation I was involved in with the CEO in the Senator's office. And I wasn't entirely comfortable when the CEO made it plain that if the Senator voted for stricter gun control legislation, the company would move at least some of its operations out of the state. But again, I felt that Socrates was oversimplifying things. Stricter regulations could affect profits and jobs.

"I call it 'economic reality,'" I shot back.

"No. 'Economic reality' is when you talk about wage rates, the cost of public utilities, taxes," he answered firmly. "'Economic reality' is when you go to someone local and say, 'Let me show you the math, Governor. Here are our costs. Here are our profits. If we can't get some help, we'll either have to lay people off or move somewhere our costs can be lower. We don't want to do that. What can you do to help us?'

"You don't want to call a barefaced threat 'extortion'? Fine. What *shall* we call it?"

"It's using whatever leverage you have. It's a CEO trying to get the best deal he can for his company, shareholders, and employees. Don't forget that jobs and profits are on the line here."

"*Leverage?* Oh, that's a nice, neutral way to describe threatening and bullying. 'Nice little factory town you have there, Governor. It would be a shame if someone pulled the plug on it and all of those people were out of work. Of course, if we could put a stop to that gun legislation, maybe we'll keep the plant there . . . for now.'

"And as far as 'getting the best deal' for the company goes, you make it sound as though moving operations from one state to another has no costs. Is that CEO so limited in his abilities that he can't manage the company in a way that it can adapt to changing circumstances and still be profitable? Are the shareholders supposed to subsidize unnecessary expenses just so that your guy can ignore the rest of the company's 'job' in the village?"

"*Ignore* it? I see it just the opposite," I pushed back. "He's doing his best to create conditions that will keep more people in the village employed."

"Perhaps," Socrates conceded, surprising me. "But at the same time he's fostering conditions that eat away at the 'kind of life'—*safe*, for openers—that we want.

"You may think I'm oversimplifying things," he continued, "but you're missing the big picture. The gun lobby is one of the most serious examples of the impact of money in undermining the overall 'job' of the 'village'—and this includes *corporate* money, in case I need to spell it out.

"I had wanted to talk to you about the appropriate use of corporate resources when we got to some of your public statements on economic policy. I thought you were smart enough to be up to the challenge. I thought you were open minded and interested in other perspectives. You *do* realize that the wealth that can undermine the 'kind of life' we want in the village is generated through business, don't you? In my mind, that puts a special responsibility on those of us in business to make sure we don't misuse corporate wealth. Don't you think that's important for us to discuss? Or did I misread you? Is it going to turn out that your mind can't handle anything more sophisticated than a press release?

"*This* discussion was supposed to be about the admittedly complex issue of how much responsibility we have for the results of actions we *facilitate*, but don't actually *do*. Is that too difficult as well?" he added sarcastically.

As Socrates paused and looked at me, I saw he was giving me one last chance. He was right. I hadn't intended my answer to be insulting, but it was. I was already feeling defensive about my involvement in the meeting with the gun company CEO, so I had said the first thing that came to mind. And while I didn't appreciate his barbs, I could tell he wanted to see if I could control my temper. I made an "I surrender" gesture to make it clear I wanted to continue our conversation.

"You're right. We should talk about corporate wealth," I said seriously.

He nodded my way, indicating he knew I'd just apologized and wasn't going to make me say it.

"But first you need to tell me why you say you share no *responsibility* for the harm that comes from a product for which you provide financial support.

"And don't even think of offering some parallel to deaths in car crashes and tell me that, like automobile deaths, gun deaths are caused by a person, not the product. Automobiles are machines designed to transport people from point A to B. Accidents and crashes happen, but cars are designed to help protect passengers in such circumstances. Ideally, they get safer and more efficient. It's true that the number of deaths each year is predictable and that the auto industry has historically lobbied against strict safety regulation. Guns, on the other hand, are designed to kill someone. To the extent that they get more efficient, it means that they can inflict more damage."

Clearly, we were settling in for another long discussion. I got up to get something else to drink and sat back down.

"Number one. I've checked that out with our lawyers," I said thoughtfully. "Their explanation was . . ."

Socrates couldn't keep himself from laughing. "I'm sorry, I can see you're trying. But we had an understanding last week that we are talking about ethics, not law. You definitely spend too much time talking to attorneys. Fine. They told you that you weren't *liable*. If someone sues the gun manufacturer—even if they win against the company—the bank is protected. And I understand why the rules of the game are set up that way. After all, legally, the point of incorporating is to make sure that everyone in business isn't held *personally* liable for everything. But we're discussing *moral* responsibility, not legal responsibility."

Socrates was right. Those were the terms of our conversation. Part of the problem with running a business is that I worry so much about the financial issues that my perspective gets skewed. And most *legal* issues in business turn out to be *financial* ones because I'm looking at whether we're doing something that's going to cost us money, not worrying about whether anyone might go to jail. Moral responsibility, of course, is a completely different domain. And I usually didn't think about it separately. But because no one had ever complained to me that we bore some responsibility for what people did with the guns our client sold, I wasn't sure how to respond.

Sensing that I was stuck, Socrates continued.

"Frankly—forgive me for the tangent, because this isn't a business example—but I am baffled why even in absolutely clear-cut cases, people can somehow think that the *legal* should trump the *ethical*. I recently read about the case of a Jewish family who discovered that a work of art stolen from one of their ancestors by the Nazis was on display at a museum in another country. Because the evidence is clear, the museum didn't dispute the facts. But their first response was that the laws of their country said they now owned it. The museum had purchased it in good faith and, at the time, didn't know the painting's history. Furthermore, the artwork is one of the museum's most prized possessions. The last I heard, the family and the museum were in discussion.

"But however the matter gets resolved, why wasn't the museum's first response 'Of course, we will return the painting'? We're talking about the

17

Corporate Responsibility— The Gun Company (continued)

Apparently convinced I'd stay within the terms we'd agreed to, Socrates relaxed and sat back down. "So, having kicked the lawyers out of our discussion of responsibility, let me make this simpler for you.

"I see myself as a commonsense, practical individual. I have a simple understanding of when I'm *morally responsible* for something. Did I know what I was doing? Did I freely choose what I did? And did I know—or could I reasonably be expected to know—the likely consequences of my action? If I can answer 'yes' to all three, then I'm responsible—at least to some extent—for the consequences of my action."

He was out of his seat again and right back at the screen.

WHEN AM I MORALLY RESPONSIBLE?

1. I KNOW WHAT I AM DOING.

2. I FREELY CHOOSE THE ACTION.

3. I KNOW WHAT THE LIKELY CONSEQUENCES MY ACTION ARE. (IF I DON'T KNOW OR IF THE CONSEQUENCES ARE UNCERTAIN, IT'S REASONABLE TO EXPECT THAT I'LL FIND OUT AS MUCH AS I CAN ABOUT THE CONSEQUENCES.)

"Obviously, there are a variety of fine points that deserve attention," he said as he turned back toward me.

"If I don't know what I'm doing because I'm drunk, for example, that's no excuse. I *chose* to get drunk. If I don't know what

I'm doing because I have a seizure, however, that was out of my control. So that's different.

"If I get so angry I can't control myself, I can't say, 'I have anger control issues,' and think that mitigates responsibility. Aristotle makes the great point that there was surely a time in my life when I could have worked on this enough to stop myself. So I'm still responsible for any harm I do because I chose to let myself keep losing my temper.

"If something unforeseeable or out of my control happens, that would limit my responsibility. But if I act without doing everything I can to identify the likely consequences of my actions, then I'm not only still responsible. I'm *negligent* to boot.

"And certainly in business, other people do many things that affect the outcome. So I'm not *completely* in control of the result. But because my action is part of the mix, I share some of the responsibility."

I could see where he was going. My expression must have made it clear I thought Socrates was setting me up.

"I'm not trying to trick you here," he said. "But you have to appreciate the fact that since the very essence of a corporation—as a legal entity—is to minimize personal responsibility, I think many of us in business develop some bad habits. I think we assume we have less moral responsibility for our actions than we actually do. That's why I prefer to use a simple, commonsense way of looking at things. So, does this seem reasonable to you?"

I thought again for a minute. "Sure, if all three conditions apply, then—*in a certain, limited sense*—I can see where I *might* share some amount of *moral* responsibility," I said carefully. But I didn't want to be caught in another of Socrates' snares. "However, tell me *exactly* what you're claiming and *why* before I say more than that."

"Fair enough," he replied, although he obviously wasn't pleased I was hedging so much. "Simply put, I think the bank bears at least *some* responsibility for the deaths and injuries that result from the guns made by the company which is your customer."

I tried not to show how insulting and simple-minded I thought his comment was, but he saw it anyway.

"And before you get your back up, notice that I said *some* responsibility. I don't see this as an all or nothing proposition. People at your bank aren't pulling triggers, and they aren't making or selling guns. But they are facilitating those actions. What happens at the bank is part of the causal chain that begins with approving a credit line and too often ends with the death of an innocent person. What I want you to think about is whether it's possible that, without intending it, you're actually facilitating ethically questionable actions.

"I'm looking at this as simply and as practically as I can. Action A leads to B, which leads to C, which leads to D, and so on. It's the same connection as with the benefits that you explain come from a single home mortgage that your bank issues. I clearly remember that last week you were very proud of all of the downstream benefits that a single home loan produces. You took some credit for that. As you explained, approving a mortgage for a newly constructed home (action A) leads to (B) the purchase of the requisite materials and appliances, (C) the hiring of carpenters, electricians, plumbers, painters, and gardeners, and (D) all sorts of other purchases. If you want to claim some responsibility for the *good* the bank's help leads to, don't you have to accept responsibility for the other side as well? I'm just identifying links in a causal chain."

I was ready to jump down Socrates' throat until he quoted back to me what I'd said last week. I *do* regularly tout the downstream benefits of what, to the outside world, looks like paper shuffling. But those benefits are all planned for. That's the way the industry is structured. We *know* that's how the money will flow. We never authorize a loan that doesn't have positive results virtually guaranteed.

For Socrates to apply the same argument to the gun business felt like comparing apples to oranges. If everyone else did their job—the police, the ATF, the courts, politicians, psychologists, parents, teachers—we wouldn't have these tragedies. Unlike the housing market, the consequences Socrates was referring to were the result of random factors that were only tangentially related to the gun industry.

"I understand your logic," I said. "And I can appreciate your desire to keep things simple. But you're looking at things *too* simply. There are many other people than those at the bank making decisions that have a more direct bearing on the outcome. We provide financial support. We don't make any production or marketing decisions. We probably have less power to determine the outcome than anyone. Also, as I said before, if we weren't their bank, someone else would be. So while we may be part of the 'causal chain,' it's irrelevant that it's *us*. If we stepped out, someone would take our place, and nothing would be any different. No, that's not entirely true. What would be different is that we wouldn't be making the profit that would go to our shareholders and employees. So what's the good in that?

"We were just talking about Mill. The *consequences* determine whether the action is ethically acceptable. The way this looks to me, the only change in the mix of positive and negative results if we aren't the gun company's bank is that the stakeholders of some other bank benefit. That can't be right."

"First," Socrates answered, "Mill does have a significant contribution to make to this discussion. Only that's not it—but we'll get to it shortly. Second, if you can replace the business with another customer, your shareholders and employees are taken care of. Is that your only defense?"

I went back and looked at his criteria for being morally responsible for something. "No. I still say the bank isn't responsible because our involvement doesn't change the final outcome. Doesn't it make sense to say that in order for me to be responsible for something, my action needs to be powerful enough to make a practical difference? Aren't you leaving something out of your 'responsibility' list? Shouldn't there also be a line that says that my action actually has to have the power to bring about the outcome? Why is it OK to say I'm responsible for something that will happen no matter what I do?

The way I see it, I'll agree I share some of the responsibility if you can say, 'If I do A, then B will happen, but that if I *don't* do A, then B *won't* happen.'"

Socrates walked over to the coffee table, picked up a folder and looked in it for a minute. Glancing my way, he smirked. Then he went back to the screen, opened a new window, and wrote what looked like a mathematical formula.

1. [(L&H)->R]
2. H
Therefore, [(~L&H)->~R]

I got up and looked at it more closely. "You're either being deliberately obtuse, or you're just showing off."

"It should look at least vaguely familiar. You took a logic course in college." He waved a sheet from the folder at me. *My transcript.* I looked at the screen again.

I recognized it as a symbolic representation of an argument. "OK. *Vaguely* familiar. You wouldn't want to give me a hint about what this means, would you?"

He walked back to the screen and added something.

L = THE BANK LENDS MONEY TO THE GUN COMPANY
H = PEOPLE GET HURT
R = THE BANK SHARES RESPONSIBILITY

I started remembering what the different symbols meant. It was supposed to be my argument. I slowly read off the main statements.

"IF L (the bank lends money to the gun company) AND H (people get hurt), THEN R (the bank shares responsibility). THEREFORE, IF NOT-L (the bank does not lend money to the gun company) AND P (people get hurt), THEN NOT-R (the bank does not share responsibility)."

It seemed right, but this felt like one of Socrates' traps. "You're saying that this is the logical structure of my saying, 'If we lend the money and are part of the causal chain that ends up with people being hurt, then we share some responsibility. *But*, if we don't lend the money and people still end up getting hurt, then we have no responsibility.'"

"Yes. And stop looking at me so suspiciously." He pointed to the three lines of symbols. "This is a symbolic representation of your argument. Lines 1 and 2 are your premises. Line 3 is your *'But'* conclusion. If you want to change it, we can. I'm not trying to trick you. Your argument *sounds* logical, but this is a way of checking whether it actually is."

I studied the screen some more and finally decided that what Socrates had come up with actually did represent the skeleton of my argument. "OK, what next?"

"Next, we test for validity. Give me a few minutes." He pulled an old red book out of the bookcase and paged through it until he found what he was looking for. He rested the open book on the coffee table and kept checking back with it as he drew an elaborate table on the screen.[1]

	A	B	C	D	E	F	G	H	I	J	K	L
1	L	H	R	{[(L&H)	→	R]	&	H}	→	[(~L&H)	→	~R]
2	T	T	T	T	T	T	T	T	T	F	T	F
3	T	T	F	T	F	F	F	T	T	F	T	T
4	T	F	T	F	T	T	F	F	T	F	T	F
5	T	F	F	F	T	F	F	F	T	F	T	T
6	F	T	T	F	T	T	T	T	F	T	F	F
7	F	T	F	F	T	F	T	T	T	T	T	T
8	F	F	T	F	T	F	F	F	T	F	T	F
9	F	F	F	F	T	F	F	F	T	F	T	T

When he was finished, he said, "There's probably a more elegant way to do this, but we're pressed for time. This at least confirms what I suspected. Your argument is *invalid*—sounds logical, but isn't. It's a variation on a classical logical fallacy—denying the antecedent. It's like if I said, 'if someone was born in Boston, then that person was born in Massachusetts' but then said, 'so if someone wasn't born in Boston, then they weren't born in Massachusetts.' Doesn't follow, does it?"

"Of course not. They could have been born in some other city or town in the state. But that's not the sort of argument I made."

"It's not *precisely* the same argument, but, like I said, it's a slightly more complex version of the same thing. The point is, however, it's still invalid. There's probably a way to do this using the rules of logic, but I'm too rusty for that. But this truth table shows that the structure of the argument is invalid. It's illogical. It doesn't matter what subject you're talking about. The conclusion doesn't logically follow—even though when we think about things using everyday language, it sounds like it ought to.

"But because you're still giving me that 'you're putting something over on me' look, let's shift gears. If you really have doubts about my analysis, look at it again after you get back home. If you find a problem, let me know.

"The whole point of doing this in the first place was to see whether an argument that *seemed* logical *actually is* logical. Remember, part of the point of my having us look at Kant was to show you a way to figure out if you were rationalizing something. As you know, I find Kant's 'can the maxim of my action work as a universal law' question a useful exercise for keeping me honest. In fact, that's what I want us to use next with this issue."

As far as determining the validity of my argument using symbolic logic goes, I was in over my head. If I took some time, I could probably remember much of what I'd forgotten from that course. But I did know that Socrates' basic claim was true. Simply put, some arguments sound logical, but aren't.

---

[1] It's beyond the scope of a business ethics book to go into the kind of detail needed to give a full explanation of what Socrates is doing to someone who has never had a logic course or a college math course that worked with truth tables. The short version, however, is that one way to determine whether an argument is valid is to convert it into symbolic form and then to test it with truth tables or the rules of logic. In this case, the fact that the value of I6 is false shows that the argument is invalid. There are plenty of internet sites that explain truth tables.

If Socrates said my argument was like that, I wasn't going to insist he was wrong until I knew more about what I was talking about. And I agreed there was something about Kant's "maxim" approach that made sense. Now that Socrates had explained it, the idea of studying the "maxim" of an action struck me as a neutral, technical—yet practical—way of evaluating actions. It at least would give me a different perspective to consider. And, as anyone on my staff will tell you, I exhaust them asking the question, "Is there still another way we can look at this problem?"

"As long as we agree that I haven't said I'm changing my position yet, I think that would be a good way to go."

"That's fine. I'm *not* trying to push you around or force you to take a position. My overall goal of our conversations is to encourage you to look at things differently. I thought my good faith was established right at the start of our first meeting when I let *you* decide whether you lost our bet."

Feeling guilty now that I kept getting so suspicious, I said. "You're right." But I couldn't resist adding, "Why would I question your sincerity when all you've done is to compile a dossier on me that probably covers every detail of my life, threaten to fire me, take me for $200,000, and then kidnap me? Moving on. Kant?"

"At least you haven't lost your sense of humor. And don't forget that I did let you keep the money," he said good-naturedly. "OK, given how you've described your position, it sounds to me like the maxim of your action would be, 'If I have the opportunity to benefit from facilitating an enterprise the actions of which will likely—even if indirectly—lead to people being seriously harmed *and* I know that if I don't, then someone else will, then I will take that opportunity.' " He wrote this out on the screen.

> MAXIM
>
> If I have the opportunity to benefit from facilitating an enterprise the actions of which will likely—even if indirectly—lead to people being seriously harmed *and* I know that if I don't, then someone else will, then I will take that opportunity.

"I think that's OK. For me, the critical word there is '*indirectly*.'"
"Understood." He nodded, adding some more to the screen.

> MAXIM
>
> If I have the opportunity to benefit from facilitating an enterprise the actions of which will likely—even if indirectly—lead to people being seriously harmed *and* I know that if I don't, then someone else will, then I will take that opportunity.
>
> IMAGINE THIS DESCRIBES HOW EVERYONE BEHAVES (UNIVERSAL LAW OF NATURE).
>
> CAN THIS "WORK"?

"So the exercise is to imagine a world in which this is the norm. In fact, it's so much the norm it describes how everyone behaves—absolutely and without exception—when presented with such an opportunity.

"First, any logical problems? Any internal contradictions?"

I got up, paced around, and thought.

"Let me know what you're thinking," Socrates recommended. "Talk me through your train of thought."

"OK. I'm doing this to benefit myself. But someone will probably get hurt and that 'someone' could even be me or someone close to me. For openers, then, there's some tension between 'advancing my own interest' and 'compromising my own interest'—helping myself by possibly hurting myself. It may not be a logical contradiction like Kant's false promise example, but there's certainly a serious conflict. *However*, while the profit I'd make is *certain*, the harm is only *possible*. Does that matter? Probably not. Because *everyone* behaves this way whenever there's an opportunity of that sort, the odds are high that I'd somehow eventually be harmed in some way.

"So, when I close my eyes and try to picture what it would be like, all I can say is that it looks like Hobbes' 'war of all against all.' So, from a practical perspective, no, I don't think that maxim can 'work' as a universal law of nature."

"Nice analysis," Socrates said sincerely. "So I assume we can say that even if you haven't changed your mind, you see there's reason to question your claim that you share no *responsibility* for the harm that comes from a product you provide financial support for."

I nodded in agreement. "If you were sincere in saying that your goal was to get me to consider alternative perspectives, then you've succeeded. I agree that there are facets of the issue of responsibility that I hadn't considered. And before you bring it up, I imagine you'd say that Kant's idea that we should 'treat people as ends in themselves' makes it even harder to defend having a gun company as a client. I'll mull things over from that point of view as well."

"That's good enough for now," he said as he sat down—which I took as a signal that I should settle in for the next question. "Nice job for someone who isn't that comfortable with Kant.

"Now let's approach this from a different, more practical direction. You like Mill more than Kant, so let's consider the relationship between the real-life benefits and harms."

"Practical always works for me."

Socrates took a deep breath. "I need to warn you ahead of time about what I'm going to ask you to do, because you definitely are *not* going to like it. But I want us to use a very specific part of Mill's approach—his point about the *quality* of the benefits and harms. In this case, we want to know whether we have a situation where a small amount of high quality harm can outweigh a larger amount of lower quality good."

"OK." His grim expression made me apprehensive about what he was going to ask.

"Let's turn back the clock to when your daughter was seven. You drop her off at school, and when you get to the office, the CEO of that smaller bank you were working at calls you into his office and offers you the CFO slot you were hoping for. He says, 'Wendy, I know you're young, but we believe you can do this job. I see a great future ahead for you. I know you have to discuss this with your husband, but we'd like an answer in a couple of days.' Of course, you're thrilled. And he was right. It turns out that position was critical to your ending up where you are now. 'Wendy the Wunderkind' everyone called you.

"You go back to your office and call your husband. He's just as happy as you are, and the two of you agree to discuss it that night. But there's no question what you'll do. As soon as you put down the phone, however, your assistant rushes into your office, tears streaming down her face. 'Wendy! There's been a shooting at Sasha's school. I just heard it on the radio.' Tell me what happens next."

My heart sank at even thinking about this. "Now you're just being cruel," I said, refusing to play along.

"No, I'm being practical. I appreciate how difficult this exercise is, but it's important. We're identifying consequences, and we need to be thorough. This is non-negotiable. Besides, I told you we were now entering the toughest part of our conversation."

Figuring out how I'd feel actually wouldn't be difficult at all. Every time I'd heard about any kind of shooting that involved a child, I put myself in the shoes of his or her mother. But it felt *so* bad it would be difficult describing my feelings out loud. I took a deep breath.

"I feel terror and absolute panic. I grab my bag and run out of my office. I don't wait for the elevator. I run down the stairs while I call my husband. He says he'll meet me at the school. Sasha's school is only 10 blocks from my office, so I feel that it will be faster for me to run there, rather than wait for a cab. The entire time I tell myself that Sasha is OK. My assistant said 'shooting.' That doesn't necessarily mean any of the children are dead. But I feel dread, knowing I may be wrong.

"As I get close to the school, I hear sirens. I see an ambulance tear by. My heart sinks. When I get to the school, I have to fight my way through the crowd up to the police tape. As I go under it, a police officer runs over to me. 'Parent?' she asks. She must know from the crazed look in my eye. I simply nod my head. She rushes me up the front stairs into the main lobby and down the hall into the auditorium. She hands me off to another officer who takes my name.

" 'We're asking all of the parents to wait her, ma'am. We're bringing the children down in an orderly way. Then you can leave out the side exit away from the press.'

" 'What can you tell me?' She knows what I'm really asking.

" 'I'm sorry ma'am. I don't know any of the specifics. Please wait here.'

"I know she's lying to me. But I'm sure she's been told not to say anything. Not knowing is agony. My husband arrives shortly and we wait."

I'm not sure what Socrates wants. I can guess. But I decide to hand it back to him. "Why don't you tell me what happens next?"

He swallowed hard. This was no easier for him than it was for me, which made me wonder something.

"After about an hour of watching children being reunited with their parents," he said, "you and your husband are called into a separate room where you're given the worst news imaginable. Your daughter is one of the children killed."

Even though this was only fiction, I felt as though someone punched me in the stomach. I slumped down into my chair, finding it difficult to breathe.

"Just tell me what would happen next," he said quietly.

I thought for a couple of minutes. "Everything would be a blur. I wouldn't want to believe something so terrible had happened. It feels like someone ripped out my heart. I would be in so much pain the only way I could function would be to retreat into myself. It would be like I was sleepwalking—at the hospital, through the funeral, the memorial service at the school. I tell my boss I need to take some time off to let me regroup. It goes without saying I turn down the promotion.

"At that point in our marriage, my husband and I were already feeling some strain. All of this hits him as hard as it does me. Emotionally, we're both empty. Nothing dramatic happens. We spend time in therapy. We try. But life has become too difficult for each of us. My husband wants to move to the other side of the country and start fresh. He says that living in the neighborhood of her death reminds him daily of the tragedy. I can't bear the thought of living in a different city. It's impossible for me to consider living in a place where I can't visit her grave whenever I want. We just gradually drift apart, eventually formalizing the divorce.

"You never heal from something like this. One day you just decide whether or not you want to continue with life. I get back to work. But not with the enthusiasm or ambition I had before.

"For the rest of my life, every time I see a child, a teenager, a young woman who would be the same age Sasha would be, I try to imagine what she'd be like at this point in her life. And I'd regularly grieve over what was stolen from her by some maniac."

The pain I felt from just imagining such a terrible loss was as much as I could take. I was about to chide Socrates again for being cruel when I noticed him staring down at the floor with a look of unbearable sadness on his face. He knew something firsthand about tragedy. He glanced up at me, embarrassed at my having caught him in such a private moment. His expression quickly changed, and he was all business.

"I'm sure the point of this exercise was clear. You've just described a lifetime of very severe, high quality pain. It is a real, predictable consequence of gun death. Multiply that by the parents, brothers, sisters, friends of people—especially children and young adults—killed by the guns made by your manufacturer and facilitated by your participating in lobbying. Is there enough good in the mix to offset that? Without question," he continued, "there are jobs and profits, and I'm not dismissing that. There's also whatever pleasure gun enthusiasts feel at being able to own firearms with minimal restrictions. And although I hear claims about people using their guns to protect themselves or people they love, that's actually not that common.

"So, is the quality of the benefits as high as the quality of the harm? Does the mix of *amount* and *type* of benefit offset the pain and loss?

"I'm not asking for an answer. I'm just asking you to think about it in a hard-nosed, *practical* way."

Socrates got back up, went to the screen, and magnified a page from one of the Web sites we'd been working with. "Let me just leave you with this to think about." He brought up a passage from Kant we'd talked about earlier and read it out loud slowly.

> In the kingdom of ends everything has either a price or dignity. Whatever has a price can be replaced by something else which is equivalent; whatever, on the other hand, is above all price, and therefore admits of no equivalent, has a dignity.

"There's absolutely no debate," he said thoughtfully, "about how unique, special, and priceless each human being is. When all of us in business—and I include myself in this—sit around the table in some board room fixating on numbers, do we do as good a job as we should at factoring in the things that never show up on a balance sheet?

"And one last point. The next time you're part of a meeting about guns in D.C., I'll trust you'll make sure that more than 'Second Amendment rights' and 'the impact on the local economy' get discussed."

18

Corporate Responsibility and "Return on Infrastructure"— Caterpillar

Our gun conversation had put Socrates in a somber mood. And it was clear both of us needed a break. Fortunately, he said he wanted to make a call and take care of some e-mails before we continued. Maybe he did. Maybe our conversation had stirred up some painful memories, and he just wanted to be alone in his office. I decided to go back outside onto the deck.

I noted that the adversarial tone Socrates had taken with me first in my office and then yesterday (during our "ethics is rubbish" conversation) had changed. Our gun conversation was, as he warned me, difficult and uncomfortable. But I felt that, as he said, he was trying to get me to examine points of view I typically overlooked, not that he was trying to push me to a particular conclusion. I was beginning to appreciate better the complexities of the ethical issues he had us exploring.

I was also beginning to feel a tad ashamed at how glib I— and most other people on my team—typically were about ethical issues. We'd scrutinize spreadsheets, forecasts, and any numerical data we got our hands on like Sherlock Holmes with his magnifying glass. But when "soft" issues like ethics came up, we'd pretty much all immediately agree we were OK. We were people of integrity. We weren't lying, cheating, or stealing. We were obeying the law. We were good and decent men and women.

All that was true. But the fact that we were good and decent people didn't necessarily mean our actions were also good and decent. I now saw that our approach to ethical issues was regularly simplistic and superficial. We considered any suggestion that the bank's policies or practices were anything less than ethical as a personal insult. Instead, we should have seen such comments as an opportunity to look at problems differently and to identify risks to the business we'd overlooked. Our knee-jerk reaction to criticism was usually to dismiss it and follow it up with self-congratulation.

The dust-up over that guy who left Goldman Sachs came to mind. In an op-ed piece in the *New York Times*, Greg Smith said that during his 12 years with the company, Goldman's culture went from being about "teamwork, integrity, a spirit of humility, and always doing right by our clients" to making money— even at the expense of the clients. I remembered a particularly striking line from the column. "You don't have to be a rocket scientist to figure out that the junior analyst sitting quietly in the corner of the room hearing about 'muppets,' 'ripping eyeballs out' and 'getting paid' doesn't exactly turn into a model citizen." Goldman's CEO and COO replied by calling Smith "disgruntled." They admitted that the company was "far from perfect," but said that "where the firm has seen a problem, we've responded to it seriously and substantively."

My sympathies usually fall with the CEO, especially if it involves an issue in my own industry. In this instance, however, I was disappointed that Goldman didn't take this as an opportunity to admit that our industry has a culture problem. Anyone who had spent any time on Wall Street knows we're an aggressive, big ego, high testosterone, "take no prisoners," "greed is good" industry. We think we're special and act accordingly. If we display excellence in one aspect of our business—making money through very technical instruments—we think that means we're experts across the board. Our worst error is to think this means we're as savvy ethically as we are financially.

Our industry doesn't have the best reputation. Even before this op-ed came out, Goldman had already paid $550 million for misleading investors in a subprime mortgage product. A Senator accused the company of not being entirely upfront with a Congressional investigation. A Senate report reamed JPMorgan Chase for taking excessive risks; the company's CEO admitted that "we made a terrible, egregious mistake." And then there were the billions of dollars in fines the company paid. On the eve of the 2013 tax increases, Goldman granted $65 million in stock to 10 executives a month early so that they'd have a smaller tax bill—this on the heels of the CEO endorsing the idea that wealthy Americans should pay more to reduce the deficit. One survey showed that nearly a quarter of financial service professionals felt that it was at least sometimes necessary to do illegal or unethical things to be successful. And the popular press in New York seems to delight in running stories about substance abuse in our industry. I remember watching a Congressional hearing in which some of my colleagues didn't seem to understand the question when asked, "Didn't it occur to you that misleading your clients was *wrong*?" I had a better understanding of why Socrates hammered me last week about "humility."

When my host returned and joined me on the deck, his mood had improved. I, too, was feeling more relaxed the more time that elapsed since my televised misadventures. I very much appreciated the fact that Socrates was hiding me from the press and from my board and that there was the prospect of a new position.

He walked up to me and surprised me by putting his hand on my shoulder. "I apologize if you felt that our last conversation was unfair to you.

I truly appreciate the difficult situation you find yourself in. And I don't want to make it sound as though complicated issues that truly involve competing rights, responsibilities, and interests are simple. As you gather, I feel very passionately about gun violence, and I feel that too many discussions among executives fail to remember that we're talking about the risk of horrific pain and suffering that no one should ever have to experience."

"Believe me, there's no need for apologies," I said. "I struggle with more parts of the business than I'm comfortable admitting to many people. Besides, if you aren't willing to get pushed around and justify everything you're doing, you don't deserve to sit in the big chair. In the end, I'm an employee as much as anyone else is working with *other people's* money to advance *their* interests, not mine. I confess that, like most CEOs, I can forget that because everyone around me treats me like royalty. So I don't mind at all being reminded that I'm accountable to other people for my actions."

Socrates' look back conveyed a sense of mutual respect. When he sat back down opposite me, I could see that we were shifting gears again.

"You can never overemphasize the fundamentals," he said good-naturedly, sounding like my college volleyball coach. "*So* let's go back to the village. Remind me why we've organized things as we have?"

Taking the conversation in this direction surprised me. I didn't know where this was supposed to take us next, and it felt like we were going backward. But since "the village" was comfortable territory, I didn't mind. "So we get to have a life of a certain sort," I replied.

"Details! Details! Young lady," he joked, wagging his finger at me.

"Fine," I answered. "At a minimum, our basic needs—tangible and intangible—are met, and we want everyone in the village to operate in a way that respects principles like 'do no harm' and 'treat others appropriately.' That's the 'kind of life' you and I keep referring to."

"And that makes the 'job of business' . . . ?"

"Providing *its* part of what we need in a way consistent with how we expect villagers to treat each other."

"Excellent. And those are the 'rules of the game,' 'organizing principles,' or whatever you call them which you'd *freely agree* to about the relationship between business and the village?"

"Absolutely."

"And those are principles that *any* rational, self-interested person would freely agree to?"

"True," I answered suspiciously—suspecting that Socrates was setting another snare. "But since we established all of that last week, you don't mind my asking why we're backtracking all of a sudden."

"Oh, no reason," he said disingenuously. "As I said, it's just good to review the fundamentals sometimes. And speaking of fundamentals, let's look at another couple of your clients and see whether or not they're doing their 'job.'"

"You mean whether they're fulfilling their *responsibility*? Didn't we just get through talking about that? I really don't have any more to say about that. You're probably going to ID another company with a product line you don't like and tell me I'm responsible. Or—and this is more likely—you're going to point to one you think pollutes the environment. Don't think I've forgotten that you reminded me about my 'tree hugger' comment to the Senator and his Chief of Staff. I admit I spoke too quickly. Why don't we move on to something else. I'm sure you've got a long list. A long list of *really* annoying topics," I joked.

"I guess I didn't make myself clear. We *are* moving on. And while we will get to your 'tree hugger' comment, it's farther down on my list. Again, you need to listen better. I said I wanted to talk about whether or not these clients were doing their 'job' or not—not what the bank's share of responsibility for their actions are. You're right. We finished that discussion. And we agreed that you and I see things differently.

"What I want to do now is talk to you about two particular companies that have been in the news for the issue of who deserves a share of the profits. The fact that these companies are your clients is just a nice coincidence. I want your opinion of these companies independent of the fact that they're your clients. Don't forget the main point of this conversation. Maybe the company that's interested in you has some similar issues on the horizon and wants a sense of how you'd handle them."

"So, who do you have in mind?" I asked. "Let me see. A significant client. Doing well. Record profits. Controversy over who is and isn't getting a piece of the pie."

I mentally ran down a list of our clients who had been in the press and had been the subject of not entirely complimentary stories. "Caterpillar?"

"Good job. Got it on your first try." Socrates picked up his tablet and called up some charts, graphs, and spreadsheets.

"Let's start with the big points. Caterpillar. In the last 15 years, stock price has gone up nearly 500%. In the last decade, profits have been in the $2–4 billion range every year. Senior management was rewarded for record profits. At the same time, however, the company insisted that workers accept a multi-year wage freeze, pension freeze, and contribute more to health insurance. Some employees were even told they needed to accept a significant pay *cut*.

"So, here's my question. If the 'job of business' isn't *to make money*, but *to do its share in supporting the 'kind of life' we want in the village*, do practices like this do so?"

I knew where he was going with all of this. I was going to get a lecture on "the social responsibility of business" of the sort I yawned through in business school. I wanted to go home, but he expected a serious reply, so I'd accommodate him.

"First, you and I have already agreed that part of the 'job of business' is to support a particular 'kind of life' in the village. So you don't have to keep harping on that. Where you and I disagree, however, is that I think you need to expand your view of the village. We live in a *global* village now. So when Caterpillar moves jobs from the north to the south or from the United States to Brazil, India, and China, they're just moving them to a different part of the village. You know that everyone agrees that the BRIC countries—Brazil, Russia, India, and China—are where the action is. Why shouldn't people in those countries have the opportunity to get good jobs as their countries' educational systems and infrastructure become able to support them? So, if the social responsibility of business is to promote prosperity throughout the village, it seems to me this is *exactly* what Caterpillar is doing."

Socrates gave me a puzzled look. "*Social responsibility of business? Where'd that come from?*"

"But that's what you were about to complain about. It was obvious."

"Obvious to *you*, maybe. But we talked about responsibility in connection with the gun company. I want us to move past that. Now we're talking about a combination of fair agreements and reasonable ROI."

"ROI? If that's what we're talking about, we're done. When you look at the last 15 years for example, the company has done extremely well."

"Yes, that's one way to look at things. However, now you're doing exactly what you accused me of doing—using too narrow a perspective. But instead of expanding the boundaries of the 'village,' as you were just suggesting, I want us to broaden our perspective in a different way."

"Different way?"

"Let me explain it like this. Both of us like to think of ourselves as 'hard facts,' 'numbers' people. That's one of the things I admire about you. However, I also know you do an excellent job of telling your people always to look beyond the numbers in order to understand the 'full costs' connected with a decision. These are factors they may be overlooking that will have a negative impact on how their decision works once it 'hits the ground,' as you put it. What is it that you say? *'Just because a cell on your spreadsheet looks empty doesn't mean something's not going to appear there later as a negative number.'* You're fond of telling your subordinates that the fact that the numbers work is no guarantee that a decision is a good one. I believe your favorite example is that 100% of mergers and acquisitions look good on paper, but only 50% succeed."

"That's true. When the bank is putting real money into something, I hate to be caught from behind by factors we could have anticipated if we carefully studied all the ways a deal could go south. I do my best to look at a situation from a perspective no one would usually take—but that reveals a downside that won't be obvious until it's too late."

"Excellent," he said. "And *my* pet peeve in this regard is when someone I'm putting a deal together with tries to shift costs to me. I'm unquestionably old school. If you're going to be in business and want to keep all the profits, pay all your costs. If you get someone else to pay them, you aren't smart, you're a thief. Like you, I tell my people to look for invisible ways that someone may be trying to tilt the deal in their favor.

"So we're going to do something like that now. We're going to take a different perspective on ROI and look for ways that investors are being taken advantage of. In general, we're going to look at what constitutes a good 'return on investment.' But we're going to re-define ROI for now as 'return on infrastructure.'"

"*Return on infrastructure?* I've never heard that before."

"That's the idea. Think of it as an empty spreadsheet cell that should have a *whopping* big number in it but is currently empty," he explained. "And as long we're talking about spreadsheets, we need to go back inside so that I can illustrate what I mean."

We got up and returned to the living room. Socrates tapped the screen so that it lit up again, turned to me, and said, "OK, we're back in the village, and . . . "

"Which village?" I interrupted. "Small village? Global village? Don't think I didn't notice you never responded to my BRIC comment."

"You're right. I didn't. Remind me and we'll get back to that. But for now, let's start with our small village. But the time is now."

"Fine," I said, walking over to the sideboard to get another cup of coffee, "we're back in the village, one more time. What next?"

"You want to start a business in the village. Tell me what you need."

"A business? What sort of business?"

"Let's make it your fantasy business. Something you dream about doing, but you know you never will. Let's make this a fun exercise."

I don't know about other CEOs, but I regularly get frustrated by the fact that I'm insulated from our retail customers. And while I repeatedly toy with the idea of spending a couple of days a month at one of our local branches, it never happens. Socrates was right. I did have a fantasy about what I'd do when I decided it was time to cash out. I dreamed about moving to Boston and opening a small upscale shoe store on Newbury Street—a mecca of designer shops, salons, boutiques, and restaurants. Between what we had in the store and what we stocked in our warehouse, we could make any woman's wish come true. Shoes for the office. Shoes for parties. Shoes for ordinary life. Sandals. Low heels. Dangerously high stilettos. Practical shoes. Fun shoes.

"Wendy's Shoe Fetish," I announced. "The name may sound a little shocking—but, hey, we need to get everyone's attention. A specialty shoe store that carries . . . "

"*Any* shoe that any woman might imagine that she'd want. No surprise there," Socrates chuckled. "That's what Bobbi thought. He said I should see your bedroom closet. He said it's like a shoe museum. I think that's a great idea. Every village needs a shoe store."

I'd stopped being surprised by how nosy Socrates had gotten about me and how much information he was able to gather. "When did you talk to my husband?"

"Oh, we've been chatting off and on. I'd never let you be considered for the kind of job at issue without bringing your family into the loop. I simply asked them to keep things quiet for now. Your husband and daughter seem like very interesting people. I look forward to meeting them. But we're getting off track. I'm sorry I interrupted you. So, Wendy's Shoe Fetish. What do you need to get it off the ground? Just free associate about everything you need. I'll jot things down."

"OK, I'll need a store in a good location in the village. Next, I'll need to hire some people to design and make the shoes. Just a few employees at the start. A bank. Lawyer. Accountant." As Socrates added to the list, I asked. "How ambitious can I be? Are we staying small and rustic?"

"I said a *small* village. But it doesn't have to be rustic. Remember, we're talking about the present day."

"OK. We'll start small and local to test the waters. However, if my instincts are right, we can be huge! I have big plans. The storefront will simply be our original anchor. But once we take off, I'm not going to want us to be headquartered in a small village. I'll want to be in a major city with a reputation for fashion."

As I paced around the room, I ticked off the elements of the "big picture" I had in my head and how we'd expand. "We'll quickly want an online presence. I'll want to work closely with the designers, but doing the kind of volume I imagine, we'll move production offshore to where labor is cheaper as soon as we can. Because I want us to have a big inventory, I'd like to avoid the expense of a huge warehouse. So I'll try to make arrangements with the plants we're using in other countries to ship directly to the customers. Many of the shoes I have in mind typically have a hefty mark-up, so we'll promote service. Great service in our stores—we'll have just a few in major cities. Better online service than anyone has done yet. We'll be very aggressive about using online video technology. We won't use some annoying 'chat' box. We'll connect online customers with one of our salespeople who really knows shoes. Someone who can show what they look like in real life, not just as a JPEG. To ensure satisfaction and to encourage repeat business, we'll do our best to connect customers with the same online salesperson every time. We'll want to have a sales force that takes pride in personal service and developing relationships with their customers. Of course, we'll have a generous return policy.

"Did you get all that?" I asked as I walked back to where Socrates was making my list. As I read what he had on the screen, I was puzzled and *annoyed*. "Wait! That's nothing like what I said. What are you up to?"

"I asked you to tell me what you would need. In a way, you did that. But there's a deeper level that you ignored. There are a number of things you'd need first in order to get what you listed off. Think of it this way. Imagine you told me what you'd like in a house. What I did was to jot down the kind of foundation you need before you can build the house. I've listed what you need in an *infrastructure* in order to build a business of the sort you want."

ESSENTIAL INFRASTRUCTURE

SAFETY AND HEALTH: POLICE, MILITARY, FIRE, MEDICAL/HEALTH

PUBLIC UTILITIES: ELECTRICITY, WATER, INTERNET

COMMUNICATION: TELEPHONE, E-MAIL, FAX, VIDEO CHAT

TRANSPORTATION: LOCAL, REGIONAL, NATIONAL, INTERNATIONAL; ROADS, BRIDGES, RAIL, AIRPORTS, SEAPORTS.

STABILITY/PREDICTABILITY: LAWS, REGULATIONS, TREATIES; GOVERNMENT

EDUCATION: SCHOOLS (ELEMENTARY THROUGH HIGHER EDUCATION)

I read over Socrates' list and understood why he saw these things as the "foundation" under the "house." But this was irrelevant to our current topic. Feeling sandbagged yet one more time, I decided to let him do the work, take the lead and explain himself. I sat back down on the couch, put my feet up on the leather ottoman and waved my hand at the screen. "OK, Professor," I said grumpily. "This is your show. Enlighten me."

Ignoring my mood, he simply launched into his explanation.

"Before you'd be willing to open the doors of your shoe shop, the village would need to provide you with certain guarantees. There has to be some mechanism for ensuring it won't be robbed daily—and also that the village is, overall, safe enough for people to go to your store. *Police*," he said, pointing to the screen. "Assuming that our village is part of a bigger community—like a country—with some unfriendly neighbors, you need protection from them. *Military*.

"Next, just as important as being protected from one another, is protection from other kinds of threats. If your store catches fire, we need people to put it out. *Firefighters*. The water needs to be clean. The environment, disease free. The food, safe. In case of disease, illness, or injury, there have to be people dealing with those things. So, *medical and health professionals*.

"In addition to a safe environment, however, you're going to need electricity, the internet, running water, *public utilities*, and a variety of communication technologies—*telephone, e-mail, fax, video chat*. You said that, ultimately, your inventory won't be produced locally, so you need a way for it to be shipped to stores. And since you're planning to sell on the Web, you need a way to ship purchases to customers. *Transportation*. To make sure your business has a reasonable chance of succeeding, the legal and social environment have to be stable—and you need guarantees that competition will be fair. *Appropriate laws and regulations*. And because you're operating internationally, your business will be possible only if there are *treaties and a way of adjudicating disputes*.

"Finally, you'll need all sorts of talented people—shoe designers, shoe makers, a sales force of committed individuals with superior people skills, a sophisticated team to manage your Web business. Those people will have to be educated in certain ways for *years* before they'll have the skills you need. So, *schools!*" He said, ending with a flourish.

"I take it I'm supposed to be impressed, surprised, or both. But that's all obvious. *Of course*, I'd need all of those things. I'm not stupid," I grumbled. "Virtually every business needs those things."

"And am I correct in assuming," he continued, ignoring my obvious unhappiness with this irrelevant tangent "that virtually every business also needs *someone else* to pay for those things. You couldn't afford to pay for all of this before you opened your original store."

"That's why the most practical and efficient way to handle this is for the village to pay for it," I explained. "It's also the fairest way. Everyone uses the roads and bridges, for example, so everyone in the village should pay for them. That's why we have *taxes*. Public goods get paid for by public money."

"Excellent point." Nodding in my direction, he added it to his list.

ESSENTIAL INFRASTRUCTURE

PAID FOR BY PUBLIC MONEY (TAXES)

SAFETY AND HEALTH: POLICE, MILITARY, FIRE, MEDICAL/HEALTH

PUBLIC UTILITIES: ELECTRICITY, WATER, INTERNET

COMMUNICATION: TELEPHONE, E-MAIL, FAX, VIDEO CHAT

TRANSPORTATION: LOCAL, REGIONAL, NATIONAL, INTERNATIONAL; ROADS, BRIDGES, RAIL, AIRPORTS, SEAPORTS.

STABILITY/PREDICTABILITY: LAWS, REGULATIONS, TREATIES; GOVERNMENT

EDUCATION: SCHOOLS (ELEMENTARY THROUGH HIGHER EDUCATION)

"Obviously, in our contemporary economy," I added, "some of these functions get done by businesses or non-profits: shipping, communication, private schools, and the like. But if our village wants me to be able to sell shoes and for other villagers to operate whatever businesses they want, the village has to provide a minimum level of infrastructure. After all, *businesses* make it possible for all the villagers to have jobs and to get what they need. So can't we reasonably expect that part of the overall 'job' of the village is to make sure we get the infrastructure we need to do business?"

"Again, a terrific point," he said with a knowing smile, as he added that to his slide. I felt like I'd stepped into a trap he'd carefully set.

"JOB" OF THE VILLAGE

PROVIDE ESSENTIAL INFRASTRUCTURE

PAID FOR BY PUBLIC MONEY (TAXES)

SAFETY AND HEALTH: POLICE, MILITARY, FIRE, MEDICAL/HEALTH

PUBLIC UTILITIES: ELECTRICITY, WATER, INTERNET

COMMUNICATION: TELEPHONE, E-MAIL, FAX, VIDEO CHAT

TRANSPORTATION: LOCAL, REGIONAL, NATIONAL, INTERNATIONAL; ROADS, BRIDGES, RAIL, AIRPORTS, SEAPORTS.

STABILITY/PREDICTABILITY: LAWS, REGULATIONS, TREATIES; GOVERNMENT

EDUCATION: SCHOOLS (ELEMENTARY THROUGH HIGHER EDUCATION)

"And what do all of the villagers want from you in return for putting up all of this money?" he asked.

"That's easy. Great shoes."

He waited for me to say more. There wasn't anything to add. After standing still for a bit, Socrates tapped his foot impatiently. "Now give me a *real* answer. What do they want in return?"

"I told you. The other members of the village expect that I'm going to be offering the kind of shoes they'd like to buy. If I don't, I'll be out of business fast."

He sighed as though I was missing something incredibly obvious. "Maybe I'm asking this wrong. You're the CEO of a bank. When you make a loan, what do you expect?"

"Obviously, I expect the loan to be repaid plus interest. We don't lend money unless we have guarantees that we'll get it back and make a fair return on the deal. But that's *not* what's going on here. The village isn't lending me any money. They're spending it on an infrastructure that will benefit everyone in the village."

"True. But just because it's not a loan doesn't mean they don't expect something in return. As you so eloquently put it, 'They're spending it on an infrastructure that will benefit everyone in the village.' They're willing to spend this money so they can have the 'kind of life' they want in the village." He repeated my comment as he added something to his slide.

"JOB" OF THE VILLAGE
PROVIDE ESSENTIAL INFRASTRUCTURE
PAID FOR BY PUBLIC MONEY (TAXES) **TO BENEFIT EVERYONE IN THE VILLAGE AND PROVIDE THE "KIND OF LIFE" WE WANT**

SAFETY AND HEALTH: POLICE, MILITARY, FIRE, MEDICAL/HEALTH
PUBLIC UTILITIES: ELECTRICITY, WATER, INTERNET
COMMUNICATION: TELEPHONE, E-MAIL, FAX, VIDEO CHAT
TRANSPORTATION: LOCAL, REGIONAL, NATIONAL, INTERNATIONAL; ROADS, BRIDGES, RAIL, AIRPORTS, SEAPORTS.
STABILITY/PREDICTABILITY: LAWS, REGULATIONS, TREATIES; GOVERNMENT
EDUCATION: SCHOOLS (ELEMENTARY THROUGH HIGHER EDUCATION)

"Right. And they *will* get something in return. Shoes. Jobs, as I hire people. Taxes, when I turn a profit. *Those things* will help them get the 'kind of life' they have in mind."

"And you think the villagers will see that as enough?"

"What do you mean?"

"You're a banker. Would you agree to a deal that has you spending money with no guarantees you'll get a significant return?"

"Of course not. That's why we insist on collateral. But, again, this is different. You're mixing apples and oranges. The system we have is that the public provides an infrastructure that lets businesses thrive—providing jobs, goods, and services to everyone. That's the benefit the society gets. We've been saying the 'job of business' is to do its part in providing the village with an appropriate 'kind of life.' That's how we do our part."

Socrates exhaled impatiently. "You keep changing the topic. Just focus on *the deal*. The village is putting up the money for the infrastructure for all of the businesses in the community. It *does* expect the benefits you identify. But don't you think they'd also want some protection against the downside?"

"You mean my doing such a bad job that I go out of business?"

"Not *that* downside. The *other* one. That you become fabulously successful."

"Success as a downside? Are you crazy? That's what everyone wants. Everybody would be thrilled."

"Really?" he asked, crooking his eyebrow skeptically. "Let's assume Wendy's Shoe Fetish becomes the overnight sensation you anticipate. It has that magic 'x-factor' that makes millions of women on the planet want to buy your shoes. What was one of the first things you said you'd do once you hit it big?"

I thought for a moment as I ran the steps in my plan through my mind. "I'd expand."

"More importantly, you'd *move*," he said. "You'd move production off-shore. You'd move your headquarters somewhere with a better reputation for fashion than our small village."

"Of course I would. How else am I going to grow the way I want to? I have to take advantage of international labor rates, the benefits of doing production on a big scale, and the like. That's how a business grows."

"True," he nodded. "That's how businesses have been growing. But how do you think the villagers will feel about your strategy? Or more to the point, do you think they would have agreed to pay for the infrastructure if you were going to use it to put yourself in the position to leave the village. They pay a steep price for your success. Lost jobs. Lost tax revenue. The long-term costs of the infrastructure."

"But if they're savvy, they'll find a way to attract someone else to the village. Or one of the other businesses in the village will fill the void."

Socrates paused before replying. "I *could* say, 'You mean like the way that lots of American cities and towns were able to continue thriving as the global auto industry changed?'" He paused again and looked at me to make sure I understood his point. "I *won't*, however, because that would take us away from our discussion of what the villagers would want from you—or from any other business benefitting from the infrastructure *they* paid for. But because you're clearly getting impatient, let me give you a hint."

He turned back to the screen and pointed to the top part of the slide.

"JOB" OF THE VILLAGE

PROVIDE ESSENTIAL INFRASTRUCTURE

PAID FOR BY PUBLIC MONEY (TAXES) **TO BENEFIT EVERYONE IN THE VILLAGE AND PROVIDE THE "KIND OF LIFE" WE WANT**

"I seem to recall a brilliant businesswoman telling me recently that one of the central 'jobs' of the village is to use public money to provide the essential infrastructure that would benefit *everyone in the village*.

"So let me ask you this. Would any rational, self-interested villager freely *agree* to spend the community's money on something that will benefit their village only until you've made enough money to shift the benefits to other villages, and leave them in the dust while you personally end up with great wealth over the long term? Villages spend public money as an *investment in their future*. Do you really think they'd agree to invest in your business when the terms of the deal are essentially that they'll help you get started until you decide to take the money and run? Is that the 'kind of life' they're trying to support? One in which villagers get to use public money to benefit themselves personally while they undermine the village and make life worse for the people they leave behind?

"And don't tell me that I need to expand my view of what counts as 'the village' the way you did when you reframed Caterpillar's international expansion. That's a nice, theoretical rationalization. I'm asking you if your neighbors in the village would *freely agree* to spend their money on an infrastructure that you may very well use against them. I doubt they'd think there's enough in it for them."

I continued to be exasperated by how Socrates ignored the way we both knew modern business operated. I was also tired of sitting down. I got up and walked up to him by the screen. "But you *know* that's how it works. Business is dynamic. We live in a global village now. We want to encourage entrepreneurialism and reward risk-taking. We rely on the workings of the market. The benefits trickle down. It ultimately all works out to everyone's benefit. Besides, this is public infrastructure, not working capital from private investors. Infrastructure isn't the sort of investment that requires anything more than that I support it through my taxes."

He replied with a silent look that said he was trying to decide how to proceed. Finally, he reached into his pocket and pulled out a pack of cards. He fanned the deck and held it with both hands.

"Pick a card."

19

Corporate Responsibility and "Return on Infrastructure"— Caterpillar (continued)

"Pick a card," he repeated.

"What?"

"It's a simple enough request," he smiled innocuously. "Pick a card."

I did as instructed.

"Now read it."

I flipped it over. I should have guessed this was another of Socrates' stunts. "It says *'You're lying.'*" I looked his way, feeling insulted and manipulated. "*Lying* about what?"

"Didn't you just say, 'We rely on the workings of the market. The benefits trickle down. It ultimately all works out to everyone's benefit'?"

"So?"

"Well, because what you just said *simply isn't true*, the cards apparently think you're lying. Are you?"

"Am I what?"

"Are you lying?" he asked with a pleasant, but, I was sure, insincere smile.

"Of course not," I answered, confused by this latest, odd turn in the conversation. "And what do you mean, 'It simply isn't true'?"

Ignoring my question, he examined the cards closely. "Hmmm. If you aren't lying, then I must have made a mistake. Let's try this again." He fanned out the deck a second time. "Pick another card."

I pulled one, turned it over, and grimaced. " 'You're stupid.' So we've moved back to insults?"

"Me? No. *The cards.* That's odd. They're usually very polite." The expression on his face said he was genuinely mystified. "Something must have made them moody." He handed me the deck, with a look I didn't trust. "Here. Just go through them and find an appropriate one."

I wasn't surprised when I flipped through the deck and found the cards said only two things, *"You're lying"* and *"You're stupid."* "Fine. And what are the *moody* cards trying to tell us?"

"Apparently, to remind me that you may not be where I hoped you were, and that you and I still have a few more topics to discuss after this one."

Once more, I was tempted simply to storm out. I was tired of his games. The only thing that kept me from leaving was I was sure Socrates' "you're lying/you're stupid" cards were just another one of his tests. If for no other reason than pride, I wasn't going to give him the satisfaction of quitting. I also did not want to close the door on the new job. I sat back down on the couch, crossed my arms across my chest, glared at him, and waited.

"Your move," I finally said impatiently. "Let's get on with it."

"Let's do some history," he said abruptly. Shifting gears, he tapped the screen to bring up a Web site he already had ready to go.

"At the end of the 19th century, Benjamin Holt, Caterpillar's founder solved the problem of large, steam tractors sinking into soft ground in California. In 1910, Holt opened a plant in Illinois. In 1925, the Caterpillar Tractor Company was formed, and a few years later, all production was moved to Illinois. Midcentury, the company established its first international operations—in Great Britain, then Brazil. A little more than 10 years after that, it formed a joint venture in Japan with Mitsubishi. At the end of the century and for the next decade, it continued its international expansion, generally through acquisitions in Russia, Germany, Northern Ireland, India, Australia, Italy, Switzerland, France, China, Canada, and South Korea.

"The company has evolved over time to have three principal lines of business: machinery, engines, and financial products. It currently has about 125,000 employees. About half are outside the United States.

"The company has done quite well overall. In the last 10 years, it's made billions in profits. It's high on the Fortune 500 list."

"That's right," I interrupted. "They're a great example of a company that started domestic and has become a multinational giant."

"Which is one of the things that's given them the leverage to keep their costs down," he added. "Now let's look at the management—say, the top 36 people in the company. CEO, group presidents, executive and senior vice presidents, and vice presidents. Twenty-nine are men, one of whom is African-American; only seven women. Its Board is also almost exclusively White and male."

Socrates looked at me and shook his head. "You know what I think of such a lack of diversity. We've talked about that before as well as the fact that I don't consider it to be following 'best practices' when the CEO is also the Chairman of the Board. I see it as an inherent conflict of interest.

"The company does have a strong reputation in terms of sustainability, which I'm glad to see. And now let's take a quick detour from corporate history to my family history," he said pleasantly. "I want to show you a picture of my great-grandfather."

"Wait a minute!" I interrupted. "What could your great-grandfather have to do with anything we're talking about."

He crooked his eyebrow at me and tried to sound enigmatic. "All in good time. All in good time."

I was more than a little frustrated. "You know, this would go a lot faster if you just moved things along for us. We started with your saying you wanted to talk about a couple of the bank's client companies that, in your opinion, weren't doing their 'job.' First, the gun company; now, Caterpillar. Then you brought up 'return on infrastructure.' Next we moved to my shoe store, the necessary infrastructure to support it, Caterpillar, and now something about your great-grandfather. I don't have a clue about what I'm supposed to see from this."

He looked at me sympathetically. "Sorry, I forgot. Bobbi told me that while *he* loves assembling puzzles, *you* hate it. So I take it you aren't finding it fun to figure out what our different 'pieces' will show when they all snap together."

"Believe me, fun is the *last* word I'd use to describe what we're doing. *Please* give me the final picture."

"OK, if you insist. I'll try to keep it as simple as possible. But you're going to have to promise not to interrupt me until I'm finished. Agreed?"

"Agreed" I nodded.

"For starters, remember what we're talking about. We're looking at whether or not some of your client companies are operating in a way that's consistent with the 'job of business' to support the 'kind of life' we want in the village.

"We've already agreed that, at a minimum, this means that a business's actions help meet the villagers' *basic needs*—tangible and intangible. Part of the 'job of business' is also to respect principles like 'do no harm' and 'treat others appropriately.' That's how business supports the 'kind of life' you and I keep referring to.

"Next, one of the most important ways we test what counts as *appropriate treatment* is whether people would *freely agree* to how they're being treated. That is, would they—as rational, self-interested people—freely agree to a particular situation?"

He paused. "Before I go on, have I said anything we didn't already agree to? I'm not trying to trick you. We did agree to all of this as part of our 'why business ethics isn't rubbish' conversation, right? And when you brought in Mill and Kant and sharpened the analysis, we said that when a company does its 'job' in the village, it produces high-quality benefits, treats people as ends-in-themselves, and, if we take the time, we'd see that we could universalize the maxims of the company's actions."

"Agreed," I replied.

"So in *this* part of our discussion, I'm asking you to consider the idea that the infrastructure which is publicly built and maintained should be seen as an *investment*. Investment deserves returns. I'm sure you remember from our discussion in your office that I think employees should be seen as having invested the irreplaceable commodity of *time*. Now I'm saying that the people who paid for the infrastructure should be treated as investors as well. With that in mind, think about the following.

"First, Caterpillar started in the United States, primarily in the Midwest. It operated there for 50 years before it began to morph into a multinational. During that initial period, its success was a direct result of the local, state, and national infrastructure provided for by public money—taxes. Remember, I see infrastructure as the *foundation* on which the *house* is built. And that success allowed Caterpillar not only to expand offshore, but also to move domestic operations from the Midwest to other parts of the country.

"Second, despite the company's success, it could be argued that the taxpayers in the region that originally provided the critical infrastructure are not getting a fair return on their investment or a reasonable share of the wealth they helped to create. In fact, the way I read a story I saw in the *Wall Street Journal* during the recession, Caterpillar didn't seem to have much interest in shouldering the financial burdens of its 'home' region so that the 'kind of life' people have had there could continue."

Socrates opened another window on the screen and read from the article.

> Illinois, struggling to control pension and other costs, raised personal and corporate taxes—drawing a public rebuke from Caterpillar. In early February, Caterpillar sent an email to officials in Peoria County, Ill., where the company has its headquarters, telling them it had decided not to build a new construction-equipment plant there, partly because of what the company called "concerns about the business climate and fiscal health" of Illinois.

"Moreover, because Caterpillar is your client, you're obviously aware of the occasional controversies about whether—even if their tax returns are all perfectly legal—the company is paying a *fair* share of local, state, and federal taxes.

"And one of the reasons this concerns me is because, in my opinion, their success depends to a significant degree on the very strong and very *expensive* American *military*. So, with that as such a big infrastructure cost, I'm not happy to see a company pay anything less than the highest rate that the wealthiest members of the society are subject to. I think those who *benefit* the most from the kind of life a country provides *owe* the most in return. In my opinion, without the U.S. military, they wouldn't have all of those international profits."

I was stunned that Socrates was saying something so ridiculous that I couldn't keep my "no interruptions" promise. "*The military?* What are you talking about? Caterpillar makes tractors! They do have some military clients. But it's not the core of their business. It's tractors, trucks, machines used in *construction!*"

"Precisely. Machines with engines that run on *petroleum*. For at least the last 30 years, the United States has spent billions, if not trillions of dollars trying to bring some stability to oil producing regions so there would be a dependable supply of petroleum to the Western industrialized nations. Do you really think Caterpillar would have been so successful if the U.S. military had stayed on the sidelines all of those years? As far as I'm concerned, companies like that have even *more* responsibility to pay for the infrastructure than businesses in other industries. And before you read anything into my point, I'm not talking politics here. I'm asking whether Caterpillar is providing a *fair return on infrastructure*. Are they doing the 'job' of business and supporting the 'kind of life' the community exists for in the first place?"

Socrates paused to let his odd and "unique" point of view sink in. I had to admit that he had a different way of looking at things from what I was used to. How much do U.S. based multinationals benefit from the fact that America has the strongest military on the planet at a cost of more than $500 billion each year? What would international business be like without that—especially for a company that relied on petroleum? I didn't know whether I agreed or disagreed with him. But I'd file the idea away to think about later.

"Critics of the company," he continued, "would obviously say that the company isn't doing its 'job.' They'd say that Illinois and the United States paid for the infrastructure that let Caterpillar prosper—everything from police, fire, hospitals, and schools to the military. And when the company had enough money, it moved many jobs out of Illinois and out of the United States to places where the costs are lower. That sure looks a lot like 'you pay for the infrastructure, and I'll take the money and run' to me. I can't imagine any rational, self-interested village *freely agreeing* to terms like that.

"And then there's the company's aggressive anti-union stance, which takes me back to my great-grandfather," he said, without giving me a chance to jump in and object.

Socrates walked over to a bookcase, retrieved a framed, old, black-and-white photo, and handed it to me. It was a formal photograph of a handsome young man. He wore a bowler. "This was taken shortly after he arrived in this country. A few years later he was working for the Pinkerton Detective Agency and was at that disaster in 1892 at Homestead, Pennsylvania."

I gave Socrates a blank look. History wasn't my strong suit.

"Andrew Carnegie? Henry Clay Frick? Steel? Strikes? Lockouts? Guns on both sides? The Pinkertons? People killed and wounded? The state militia? Does any of that ring any bells?"

No neurons were firing. The only "bell" that rang was the Frick Collection on Fifth Avenue in New York City. It's a beautiful assortment of art in the mansion Henry Frick built for himself. "Henry Frick of the Frick Collection? Where the Hans Holbein portraits of Thomas More and Thomas Cromwell hang?"

"The very same," Socrates answered. "Only I'm referring to Henry Frick *the union buster*. My great-grandfather was there when things got crazy in Homestead. Something like 10 people dead and 60 wounded, including my great-grandfather. He would never talk about what happened. He just said, 'There was plenty of wrong on both sides. But when you have to bury people who got killed in a gunfight over how to put a roof over their families' heads, it doesn't matter who was right in the first place. We should be ashamed that people have to *fight* for that.' And the Homestead disaster was nothing in comparison to what happened in West Virginia 30 years later, which left about 100 people dead in the coal industry's attempt to block unionization.

"Any time I get into a discussion that involves unions, I remember what my great-grandfather said. It reminds me that unions didn't just spring full-blown from the head of Zeus as a way to make life hard for companies. They were a response to the fact that companies were treating workers like commodities. We business owners and executives fired the first shot—metaphorically speaking. We shouldn't forget that."

"I confess that I'm woefully ignorant of American labor history," I admitted, handing the photo back to my host. "But I do know that we don't do that sort of thing anymore. Companies and unions alike engage in hard bargaining. There are no guns or knives at the bargaining table."

"Right," Socrates said with a hint of cynicism. "We're more *civilized* than that," he added in a way that suggested I was supposed to draw some meaningful conclusion from his brief historical foray.

"And while you're right that we usually don't see guns and physical assault or intimidation anymore—at least in the United States—it's no secret that Caterpillar has pursued an aggressive anti-union strategy to drive costs down. They've moved some operations to Southern 'right to work' states—so the company would be less vulnerable to labor unions. They've taken long strikes. They've adopted a very hard line in negotiations. They've asked unions to freeze wages or even take significant pay cuts at the same time they're rewarding senior executives with seven and eight figure compensation packages. And while that may make the company more profitable, is that an appropriate *return on infrastructure*?"

I had already broken my "no interruptions" promise once, so I was going to force myself to wait until Socrates finished. But his one-sided characterization of one of the bank's best customers had me steaming.

Socrates couldn't help but notice my frustration. "I told you I wasn't trying to trick or coerce you into anything. So you should have assumed I'd let you have your say when I was done. But you're squirming so badly in your seat I can tell you've stopped listening. OK. You get two minutes *if and only if* you say stay on topic and after that, absolutely no more interruptions," he added with a look of warning.

"Agreed. But you're way off base here. I admit I don't have any direct experience with unions because the financial services industry is largely non-union. But in the United States, we respect collective bargaining. It's protected by law and even overseen by a federal agency—the National Labor Relations Board. If unions don't think the resulting contracts are *fair*, they . . . "

Socrates sighed deeply, reached into his jacket pocket, and pulled out a yellow water pistol. I found myself interrupted by a squirt in the face.

"Your flicking me with your iced tea yesterday gave me the idea. Thanks. I guess it works. I told you that you needed to stay on topic," Socrates said with an odd mix of patience and frustration as he tossed me a towel. "I did *not* say 'unfair contracts' or 'unfair treatment of workers.' Many people would see that as the central issue. In fact, I find it interesting that's what *you* automatically thought this was about. And I'm not saying there aren't issues of fairness involved. When a contract freezes the most that a machinist in one of their plants can make at about $55,000 while the company CEO makes more than 300 times that at $17 million, some people would probably say this simply isn't fair.

"However, we're talking about appropriate '*return on infrastructure.*' When a company reduces wages and moves jobs elsewhere, it reduces their costs. But it also decreases the tax base in the towns, cities, and states it has been operating in. A smaller tax base means less money for the infrastructure everyone has come to depend on, and a decrease in that region's quality of life. And while you're going to tell me that the location the jobs move to will have their tax base increased, its 'bump' will be smaller than the 'hit' of the area the company's departing. That's the whole point of the move, after all. The company wouldn't make the move if it was going to be *more* expensive.

"The Midwestern towns, cities, and states in which Caterpillar first developed, for example, invested millions, if not *billions* of dollars over the decades to educate a workforce that the company could rely on and to provide a variety of conditions that would let the company thrive. Do you really think those states would have *freely agreed* to make that sort of investment if 'the terms of the deal' were that the company could use its leverage to move those jobs elsewhere or to lower salaries in a way that decreased the tax base and quality of living of the area?

"Keep it simple. Look at it from the standpoint of shareholders. If the company is doing well, don't they expect a 'piece of the action' in return for their investment? The taxpayers of Joliet, Illinois certainly made a significant investment over the years in the infrastructure supporting Caterpillar's operations there. How are they getting a piece of the action when—at a time of record profits of $4.9 billion for the company—the workers at that plant end up with a six year wage freeze? How is that going to help the tax base when the costs of sustaining existing infrastructure and building new infrastructure are only going to increase in the future?

"Or look at this like a banker. Each loan you make is an *investment* on which you plan to make a *profit*. I'm sure you do your best to cover any downside. You don't just *trust* a borrower or *hope* you'll make money. Why should we expect a village to do that when we're talking about something like the long-term, very expensive process of educating its citizens to be the sort of workers companies can hire to make a profit?"

I had to admit that I'd never looked at things this way. I have always had such faith in the system—business success will invariably lift everyone—that I was deeply skeptical of what Socrates was suggesting. But while I didn't know if I was convinced, he was right to suggest I'd never accept a deal like this at the bank. Even as an individual investor, I'd never buy stock in a company that piled up enormous cash reserves and never distributed what I considered to be a fair share of the profits to the shareholders.

As Socrates was about to continue, Colin stepped in the room. "You asked me to remind you when it was 15 minutes before that call, sir."

"Thank you, Colin," he said as he looked at his watch. "Damn time zones. I can never keep them straight. Fortunately, Colin can. I have to take this, but it will be a short call. So let me quickly wrap this up, and you can brood about my *return on infrastructure* argument while I'm on the phone. Then we'll have dinner and call it a night."

"Wrap things up—you mean you're finally going to explain how all of this ties together? And you can do that 'quickly'? "

He smiled good naturedly at the jibe. "I am prepared to be called simple-minded and naive by you or anyone. But I do not believe that the municipalities that Caterpillar left would think the company gave them a reasonable *return on infrastructure*, contributed appropriately to the 'kind of life' we all would like, and treated everyone involved—especially employees—with fairness and respect for their dignity. I'm sure the company's actions were all legal, but—given the perspective we've been taking—I think there are too many ways the company is not doing its 'job.' And, in my opinion, that means it's not operating according to the highest ethical standards.

"I've got to get ready for the call. We can talk about this more some other time, if you want. But you've worked very hard today, so I suggest that we just have dinner and spend more time comparing notes about foreign cities. Let me tell you about some of my favorite haunts in London. You might find that information useful at some point," he said with a wink.

20

Business, Ethics, and the Rights of Future Generations— Climate Change

At dinner, Socrates again showed that he was much more than an annoying remora I couldn't get rid of. When he decided it was the end of the work day, he could close the book on business. He was far better read than I was and an interesting conversationalist. As he suggested ahead of time, most of the meal was spent by his telling me about London. "They do Christmas better than any other city I've been in—lights, concerts, Christmas fairs, the works. You and your family must spend the holidays there at some point," he kept saying.

After we finished, I tried to call Bobbi and Sasha. I was surprised to get voicemail for both of them. But it was too late for me to stay up to keep trying. Socrates wanted us to get an early start in the morning. He'd promised it would be our last day. I knew it would be a long, tough slog.

*

Colin made us another excellent breakfast. Socrates had him join us because he lives in London and knew about even more hidden treasures than Socrates did.

As we finished over coffee, Socrates looked at his watch. "Our other guests should be arriving shortly. Colin, will you please get the door and make them comfortable. I need to make a couple of calls."

"Guests?"

"Right. Some students I know. Considering that our last topics have a great deal to do with the future—that is, the 'kind of life' *they'll* be living—I thought it would be interesting to bring them into the conversation. Among other things, I told them I'd ask you to explain to them why you, other wealthy individuals, and at least one of your client companies are—let's hope unwittingly— undermining the 'kind of life' I'm sure these students would want in their village. I hate to see businesses picking sides in a 'culture war'—which is why I hope this is unintentional."

"Culture war?" I asked, puzzled.

"Well, strictly speaking, I suppose I should say 'class warfare' or 'class struggle.' But every time I do, people take two steps back as though I'm a Marxist provocateur. 'Culture war' and 'power struggle' are at least more acceptable terms in the United States."

I was nonplussed to hear an international venture capitalist talk this way. I thought he was smarter and more sophisticated than that. "Culture war? Class struggle?"

"Or maybe it's just *a really good con*," he added with a wink.

"Are you serious?"

"Does it matter?" he asked with a provocative glint in his eye. "Maybe I am. Maybe I'm not. All in good time. All in good time."

I found it difficult to believe Socrates was serious when he said there was a "class struggle" or "culture war" going on *and* that I was involved in it. I was also offended at the suggestion I was part of a *con*. But my host had already trotted out a variety of odd ideas—his *return on infrastructure* notion just being the latest. I decided not to be surprised at anything he'd throw at me.

He was definitely the oddest venture capitalist I'd ever met, and he pulled enough stunts to make me suspicious of everything he said. He'd also warned me that because this was essentially a job interview, I couldn't assume he actually believed the positions he argued for. He wanted to see how I'd react to any number of things that could come up in this new job. So I was sure he'd continue rolling out odd points of view that were supposed to challenge me—and then he'd study my responses.

He'd already said the company interested in me was international. Since mainstream political views in Europe range over more of the political spectrum than they do in the United States, maybe he wanted to see how I'd do when faced with a *very* left-wing critique of business.

And what did he mean about some students joining us?

I decided to take advantage of the break and sit back outside in the sun. Just a few more topics, then I could go home. I closed my eyes and waited for Colin's announcement that we had company.

*

"Excuse me, Ms. Summers," said the deep British accent behind me, "I'd like to introduce you to our guests, Miss Natalie Middleton and Mr. Sergio Montoya. Miss Middleton. Mr. Montoya. This is Ms. Summers."

As I got out of the chair on the deck, the young lady immediately stepped forward and stuck out her hand. "I can't tell you how thrilled I am to meet you, Ms. Summers," she said nervously as we shook hands. "I'm a big fan. I'm an international business major at the same college you went to. You're a hero to all the women there. Wow, you really are as tall as everyone says you are, aren't you. I'm sorry, I shouldn't have said that. I'm just so excited to meet you."

"It's fine. I'm delighted to meet you, Natalie. I couldn't have gone to such a good school without that volleyball scholarship. So I'm grateful my family has 'tall genes.'"

"And this is my boyfriend Sergio," she said before her male companion could introduce himself.

"How do you do, ma'am," he said as we shook hands. "This is a real honor."

"Sergio's a double major—philosophy and environmental science. But he's OK. I'm teaching him about the 'real world.' He's making progress," she said with a laugh as Sergio smirked. The couple exchanged a knowing look that told me they probably regularly disagreed about lots of things—and that they were evenly matched debaters.

"Natalie's right. I'm definitely making progress in helping her see how things *really* are." He smiled as she punched him in the arm.

"Fisticuffs already? I can't leave you people alone for a second, can I," Socrates said with a friendly laugh as he stepped out onto the deck with us. "Natalie. Sergio. Good to see you again." He gave the couple a joint hug.

"Thanks for the invite, Mr. Stra . . . " the young man began before our host cut him off.

"What did we say about names, Sergio. Today, just call me *Socrates*. Let's keep things informal."

"Yes, sir. Sorry."

The exchange reminded me that I still didn't know "Socrates" real name.

"No problem. Everybody grab something to drink and take a seat inside because we're going to need the screen. Wendy is a busy executive. I've already kept her captive too long. And we want to get her home to her family. So let's get right to work."

As we settled into the circle of chairs Colin had set up, I took the lead in the conversation. "You all have me at a disadvantage. You know who I am. But I know nothing about the two of you."

"Wendy is right," Socrates said, looking at Natalie and Sergio. "But as both of you are here at my behest, I should explain." Then he turned my way. "Every year I judge in an international intercollegiate business ethics case competition. I believe I mentioned this before. In fact, my company underwrites the travel of some teams whose schools can't afford it. Last year, Natalie and Sergio were on one of those teams. I typically don't reveal myself to the team as the donor. But when I saw how smart our two young friends were, I introduced myself. And when I realized that their families live only about 50 miles from here—despite the fact that they go to school on the other side of the country—I invited them to visit me. So, whenever the three of us are in the same part of the world, we sit down for a chat. The topic their team worked on was unusually perceptive. It told me they had a good eye for the future. I'm sure you'll agree that having a good feel for the future is invaluable for a VC."

"Their topic. What was it?" I asked.

The couple looked at each other and tacitly agreed that Natalie should take the lead.

"It was about the financial, legal, and ethical issues connected with the impact of global warming on the worldwide market for petroleum and a variety of minerals. Specifically, the business implications of the impact of climate change on the Arctic. Melting ice will open new shipping lanes, and it will also make possible mineral exploration that couldn't be done before. The part of our presentation that got Mr. St- . . . *Socrates'* attention was our discussion of the military implications."

"*Military* implications?" I asked, surprised and concerned. While I thought of myself as an active and knowledgeable participant in the global climate change debate, I hadn't heard about this aspect of the issue.

"Our two young friends here predicted military conflicts at the North Pole over oil and minerals and looked at the problem from a business ethics perspective," Socrates commented. "As I said, perceptive and farsighted. I'm sure I don't have to spell out the huge number of business implications—positive and negative—and what this says about opportunities to make or lose money. So let's jump right in.

"Wendy, what do you recall from your exchange with the Senator and his Chief of Staff the day before yesterday?" he asked, in what seemed like an abrupt change of topic.

"I recall being waylaid one more time by a video camera I didn't know was there. As you know," I joked, "I can't seem to stop myself from being caught saying things I'll regret."

"At least you can laugh at it today. Besides, it's old news now. But what I meant, which you know, was what do you remember about their specific complaints related to climate change?"

"I believe the Senator's Chief of Staff objected to my support of one of the bank's client companies that donated money to organizations that were debating the scientific evidence about global climate change."

"And?" Socrates prompted.

"And he objected to my characterization of individuals who claimed the theory was true."

"And what was that characterization?" He pushed again.

I hesitated, since I preferred not to be embarrassed one more time by my bad habit of speaking too quickly.

"Just go ahead and say it. Everybody—including Natalie and Sergio—has seen the clip on the Web. I can even play it for you again, if you want."

I gritted my teeth. "I said something to the effect that the only people who think global warming poses a long-term threat are tree huggers looking for a federal grant to keep them from having to get a *real* job. As you know, I regretted the comment as soon as I said it."

"I know that, and I appreciate that you're trying to be more restrained in what you say about certain topics. Still, you're on record for having made a number of statements that echoed the positions of one of your client companies—ExxonMobil—when they were spending a good deal of money supporting individuals and organizations that denied there was an urgent need to take action. And unlike the gun issue, where you were something of a silent participant, you've been very public in your denial of climate change. And that makes it a significantly different matter, from my perspective.

"So what we're talking about is that it could be argued that your actions and those of your client company concealed the truth about a serious threat to all of us and thereby slowed the pace at which the evidence for global warming was seen as legitimate by the American public. Some might say you're not only participating in a process that keeps the truth from people in the present, but falling short on your duty to respect the rights of future generations. We're bequeathing to them a more dangerous future and leaving them to solve the problem—despite the fact they had no hand in creating it.

"So we're back to a few basic questions. In light of the fact that the evidence of the threat was clear and scientifically established, was it wrong for you and your client to try to get people to think the issue was still debatable? And because these actions contributed to delaying appropriate action being taken to deal with the danger, are you responsible for the resulting increase in the harm experienced by future generations? Are your actions and ExxonMobil's ethically defensible?"

When Socrates started describing the problem, I thought it was going to be a rehash of the gun issue. But he made it clear he saw this as a different matter. Also, "the rights of future generations" were not part of our gun conversation. If he was basing his complaint on such a silly idea, this would be a mercifully short discussion.

"You can't be serious," I mocked. "The rights of future generations? So now 'stakeholders' includes people who don't yet exist? Don't you think that's stretching the concept too far? I don't mind understanding 'stakeholders' in a broad way to include people who have a legitimate interest in a company's operations—when seen from an ethical, as opposed to a strictly legal perspective. But lumping in people who *might* exist strikes me as ridiculous."

Socrates looked me with a perplexed and concerned expression. "Wendy, are you having a stroke, seizure, brief psychotic episode, or something else that's disabling your hearing and eyesight? Should I call a doctor?"

My patience for what Socrates thought were witty, clever remarks was getting thin. "Why don't you just tell me what you think I missed?"

"First, I never said anything about 'stakeholders.' Remember, I like to look at things in an uncomplicated and practical way. This is about two simple things—whether the actions we're looking at were intrinsically questionable, and whether they'll have real-life negative consequences. If I'm thinking of having one of my companies distort the truth or do something that might *hurt* someone, I believe it would be silly and irresponsible for me to think that it matters whether or not they fall into a specific category I call 'stakeholder.'

"Second, Natalie and Sergio are sitting right here. There's no 'might' about *their* existence."

"Of course," I said dismissively, "but climate change won't affect them. *If* it's real, it will have an impact on the lives of future generations."

Socrates sighed disappointedly in that annoying way of his and walked up to the screen. He brought up a photo. "Wendy, can you tell me what this is a photograph of and when it was taken?"

Living in New York when Hurricane Sandy hit, I had no trouble recognizing it. I'd seen lots of similar pictures. "It's a picture of one of the homes devastated by Hurricane Sandy in 2012."

"And this?"

Palmer Z Index
Short-Term Conditions
June 2012

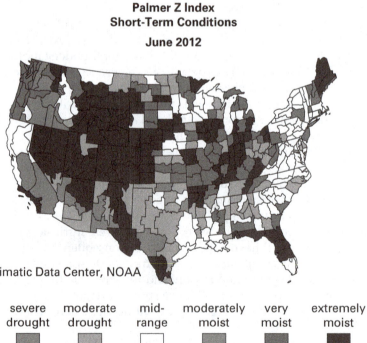

National Climatic Data Center, NOAA

extreme drought	severe drought	moderate drought	mid-range	moderately moist	very moist	extremely moist
-2.75 and below	-2.00 to -2.74	-1.25 to -1.99	-1.24 to +0.99	+1.00 to +2.49	+2.50 to +3.49	+3.50 to above

It took a minute for me to read the legends, but then it was clear. "A NOAA map that apparently has something to do with the 2012 drought."

"Yes, the worst drought in 50 years. I could also show you images of fires in California, tornadoes in Tornado Alley, a collapsing ice shelf. This is the world *you and I* live in *now*. Because Natalie and Sergio are younger than us, what they'll experience will be worse. If they have longevity genes, they'll live for another 70 years. And even if we did the impossible and stopped putting any more carbon in the atmosphere tomorrow, the inertia from the current carbon levels will continue for at least another 100 years. So our young friends here will be dealing with this long after you and I are gone. Shall I go on, or have I made my point?"

I'd heard this before. "So, you're rolling out the 'Chicken Little' argument. I take it that what I'm supposed to do is to panic, and scream out, 'Global warming is here! Run for higher ground! It's the end of everything we hold dear!' "

"For the record, your attempts at sarcasm are no more successful than mine," he grumbled. "But seriously, my point is actually *more* grim than you think. It isn't that 'Climate change is here!' It's that *it's been here for a while* and, as a prominent CEO, you've acted in a way that has kept people from seeing that. And your actions have helped delay the country's response to a critical threat. I consider that to be a serious matter from an ethical point of view."

"You mean a *theoretical* threat. I'm obviously not going to dispute the fact that we've had bad storms and droughts. But there's no conclusive proof that humans are cooking the planet and causing all of these natural disasters. And when a country—like a business—has only finite resources, it shouldn't go wasting them on what might be statistical flukes or events brought on by ordinary cycles of nature. That would be irresponsible. And I see *wasting money* as a serious ethical matter."

"Unless," Socrates replied seriously, "the consequences of following your recommendations and *not* preparing for the threat would be not only potentially catastrophic—but get increasingly expensive the longer we wait."

"*Catastrophic* consequences? I doubt it. The occasional superstorm? Sure. But hardly more than that."

"No, *much* more than that," he said somberly. "Which is exactly why Sergio and Natalie are here. I told you that what brought them to my attention was a presentation on the business implications of the *military* consequences of global warming. So I think it's time you heard a little about that."

My host turned to the young man.

"Sergio? You're on. Keep it relatively simple. But that doesn't mean you can't say a little something about the ice core data, for example."

Sergio stepped to the screen and brought up a few graphs.

"To get to the military implications, we need to start with the most general facts about global warming for which there is a scientific consensus. Let's start with one of the most famous diagrams in the climate change discussion—the 'hockey stick.'

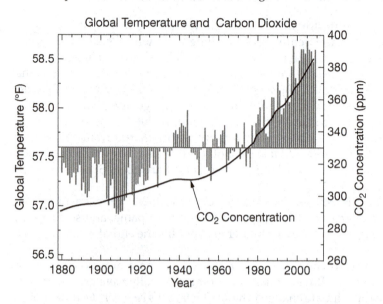

"This shows both the increase in global temperature and atmospheric carbon dioxide, CO_2, over the last couple hundred years. While CO_2 isn't the only greenhouse gas or even the most potent, I'm going to keep things simple by focusing just on that.

"You can see a close relationship between CO_2 and temperature, because increased CO_2 in the atmosphere produces a hotter planet. The scientific explanation is fairly simple. The sun's radiation hits the Earth. Some of it is reflected back by the atmosphere, some of it penetrates the atmosphere, and some of it is reflected by the Earth. Most of the radiation, however, is absorbed by the Earth and warms us. While some of the heat is released into space, CO_2 and other greenhouse gases trap the heat. In this respect, our atmosphere is like a 'greenhouse,' which is why we call CO_2 and other substances 'greenhouse gases.' As long as there's a proper level of greenhouse gases, all is well. However, the higher the concentration of CO_2, the less heat can escape to space, and the higher the earth's temperature.

"Our problem started in the mid-19th century. The industrial revolution. That's when we began running the planet's economy by burning fossil fuels—coal, oil, and gas.

"One of the most important and incontrovertible pieces of evidence is this chart that shows the CO_2 levels measured at the Mauna Loa Observatory in Hawaii. This is the longest direct measurement of CO_2 in the atmosphere, and it shows the ongoing increase in CO_2 concentration in the atmosphere since 1958. Being more than 11,000 feet high and in the middle of the Pacific Ocean, the observatory is perfect for this kind of monitoring."

He traced the significant slope of the curve.

"As you see, we've had a consistent increase in CO_2 in the atmosphere since the measurements began.

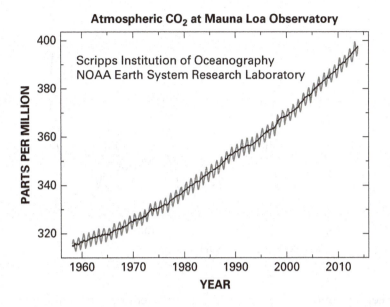

"And when we look at the ice core data, the findings are even clearer."

He stepped up to the screen and used the stylus to draw a chart freehand.

Socrates chuckled at the young man. "You'll have to excuse Sergio, Wendy. He's just showing off. He's so enamored of the ice core data that he can draw the chart from memory. But I never get tired of seeing him do it."

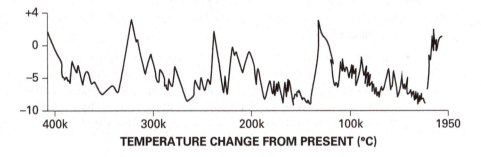

TEMPERATURE CHANGE FROM PRESENT (°C)

When he finished, he said, "This chart shows temperature fluctuations from 400,000 years ago to the present."

Then he drew a second chart.

"And this shows data about CO_2 levels over the same period."

Putting them side by side, he used his left hand to trace the one curve and his right to trace the other. "Notice the close relationship between these two lines. Higher CO_2, higher temperature. Lower CO_2, lower temperature. And the chemistry involved means that the former is driving the latter; not the other way around. The part I've circled here is what's happened just since 1950. That kind of increase is unprecedented.

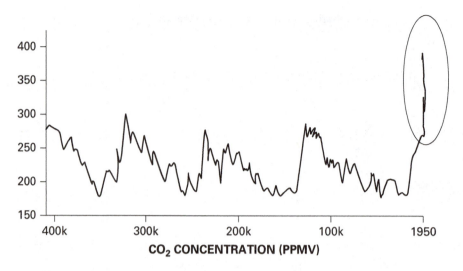

CO$_2$ CONCENTRATION (PPMV)

"And keep in mind that the most important scientific group working on this is the IPCC—the Intergovernmental Panel on Climate Change. It was formed in 1988 and issues reports every five years. The IPCC reports are about as conservative as you can get. The panel is made up of 2,500 reviewers selected by the 130 countries involved. Four hundred fifty main authors and 800 assistant authors write the reports. The reports are done by consensus. In my opinion, this means that, if anything, you're going to get *under*statement.

"Here's what they said in their first report in 1990."

We are certain of the following:

- Emissions resulting from human activities are substantially increasing the atmospheric concentrations of the greenhouse gases carbon dioxide, methane, chlorofluorocarbons (CFCs) and nitrous oxide. These increases will enhance the greenhouse effect, resulting on average in an additional warming of the Earth's surface.

We calculate with confidence that:

- Some gases are potentially more effective than others at changing climate, and their relative effectiveness can be estimated. Carbon dioxide has been responsible for over half the enhanced greenhouse effect in the past, and is likely to remain so in the future.
- Atmospheric concentrations of the long-lived gases (carbon dioxide, nitrous oxide and the CFCs) adjust only slowly to changes in emissions. Continued emissions of these gases at present rates would commit us to increased concentrations for centuries ahead. The longer emissions continue to increase at present day rates, the greater reductions would have to be for concentrations to stabilise at a given level.

- The long-lived gases would require immediate reductions in emissions from human activities of over 60% to stabilise their concentrations at today's levels, methane would require a 15–20% reduction.

"From my perspective, that's a pretty grim report—and that was *1990*! Not surprisingly, the news in the subsequent reports got worse. Here's a quick example."

- Warming of the climate system is unequivocal, as is now evident from observations of increases in global average air and ocean temperatures, widespread melting of snow and ice and rising global average sea level.
- Projected changes in the frequency and severity of extreme climate events will have more serious consequences for food and forestry production, and food insecurity.
- Climate change increases the number of people at risk of hunger.

"The more recent reports present even more evidence for the planet's warming and for the role of humans in causing it, and they make sobering predictions about the future if appropriate actions aren't taken.

"The predicted consequences—some of which we've already seen—include rising ocean levels, extreme weather, droughts, flooding, massive migration of displaced populations, an increase in certain kinds of diseases, shortages of food and water, increased extinction of species."

"I don't mean to interrupt you, Sergio," I said, "but please go back for a minute. Doesn't one of your ice core charts show that the planet's temperature has been fluctuating throughout this entire time period of hundreds of thousands of years? Isn't this evidence that it's simply a *natural* cycle—and not caused by humans burning fossil fuels?"

"No one denies that the planet goes through cycles, Ms. Summers. And while the scientific consensus is that humans are the primary cause, it doesn't matter."

"Doesn't matter? How can it *not* matter given the billions of dollars the global warming alarmists want us to spend?"

"It matters like this," Socrates interrupted, apparently assuming that Sergio wouldn't push back hard enough. "Imagine we're back in our village. We discover that—about 10 miles beyond our boundary—there's a huge forest fire. It's slowly making its way in our direction. What do you recommend we do?"

"Put it out, of course, before it gets any closer."

"And what would you say to any villagers who wanted to debate how the fire started or wait until it got closer to see if it was really going to hit us?"

"If I wanted to get my neighbors to take action, I'd talk to them directly. I'd say that the longer we waited, the harder it will be to put it out. I'd explain that the prudent thing to do would be to take action now. Privately, I'd say that anyone who was willing to take that big a risk with the destruction of their own home was an idiot. And before you give me that self-satisfied smirk, I think this is another one of your apples and oranges analogies."

"That's where we see things differently, of course," Socrates answered, "although we would agree that anyone ignoring a threat to the village is an idiot. My point is that when you know you have a threat, you don't waste time discussing the cause. You focus on a solution. That's why whether or not humans were the main driver of climate change is irrelevant. The scientific evidence certainly supports the idea that we are. But even if we aren't, the planet is warming. And we have to deal with that. The only questions are 'what can we do?' and 'how soon can we start?'

"And we can discuss whether this is 'apples and oranges' another time. But I pulled Sergio off topic before he finished with the basic science. Serg? Please continue."

Tracing the ups and downs of the two lines with his fingers, Sergio conceded, "As far as natural temperature fluctuations go, Ms. Summers, you're right. *But*," he emphasized, pointing to the last part of the top line, "natural variations have never been anything like the CO_2 levels we've seen since industrialization. And that means that humans are most likely the cause of that. There's more CO_2 in the atmosphere than at any time in the last 800,000 years. As you see," he pointed to the peaks of the top curve, "natural cycles have never taken us more than 280 parts per million. In 2013, that number reached 400.

"And here's something I'm sure is going to surprise you," he said drawing our attention back to the bottom line. "These valleys are ice ages. We see them about every 100,000 years. Notice there's only a 10 degree difference between the middle of the last ice age and the average global temperature today. The conditions that humans have been living in for the last 1,000 years haven't varied by much more than a couple of degrees. In other words, modern human civilizations have flourished in a pretty narrow range. We haven't had to deal with that much temperature variability. Contemporary humans have enjoyed a pretty stable environment.

"So while a couple of degrees of warming might not sound like something that could produce a big problem, it actually *is*. Since industrialization in the mid-1800s, the average global temperature has gone up about 1.5 degrees. And the increase will continue because CO_2 doesn't dissipate quickly. The CO_2 we put in the atmosphere today will have effects for another 100 years. We already have enough in the atmosphere to produce another increase of a degree and a half. After that, things get even more serious. So unless we keep the CO_2 levels from going higher than 450 ppm, the worst case scenario is that we could ultimately hit 10 degrees higher than when industrialization began. And that could be devastating for life on the planet.

"So, those are the basic facts. The planet is warming. It's going to get worse. Our generation didn't make the problem. Yours doesn't want to do anything about it. So we're going to be stuck with dealing with the consequences."

Because it was clear how much work Sergio had done, I didn't want to discourage him. But I wouldn't be doing him any favors if I simply nodded and said, "Well done." Like Socrates, he was simplifying a complex issue. And because he hadn't said anything related to business, I didn't understand the relevance of his remarks to my discussion with Socrates.

"I'm sure that you believe that all of your evidence is solid, Sergio, but you have to admit that you're describing only one side of things. Setting aside for now the fact that the reality of global warming is highly debatable, a warmer planet isn't necessarily a bad thing—especially if the increase is moderate. Longer growing seasons mean more food. Certain areas are more habitable. The Arctic can be explored for valuable and necessary resources. Those of us in business see lots of possible benefits for millions of people."

"True," Sergio answered. "But the disadvantages of even a small, but significant increase outweigh the advantages. The availability of clean water and food will be jeopardized. Rising ocean levels will cause population displacement. The spread of certain diseases will increase. Weather patterns will become more extreme and storms stronger. While the richer nations will have the resources to deal with many of these factors, the poorer won't. All of this will increase social and political tensions so much that military experts think that violence and military conflict will be more likely."

"The military implications. You said that before. And because I understand that's why Socrates invited you, why don't you get into that."

Sergio looked over to our host. "I still have a good deal more scientific data. Should I just skip over that and move on?"

"Just one last thing," Socrates replied. "Wendy's hinted at this, but she's too polite to ask you how much agreement there is among scientists that the data mean what you say they do. I've read some of her public statements in which she says climate change is as debatable among scientists as how many dimensions to reality string theory suggests or if the idea in quantum physics that there are multiple—if not infinite—parallel universes makes sense. Wendy keeps referring to this as a *theory* not fact. I'm sure she'd say that if the scientific community said unequivocally that global warming is a fact that deserved the kind of attention the alarmists say it does, every CEO on the planet would get behind them. She'd explain that they're the *first* group of people to know that the longer you wait to fix a problem, the more expensive it is."

"Thanks for saving me the trouble," I said, surprised that Socrates was being so supportive. "He's right, Sergio. CEOs deal in hard facts, numbers, and evidence. Move climate change from theory to fact, and I'm your number one ally."

The young man glanced at Socrates again. He was hesitating.

"Wendy would be insulted if you held back, Serg," Socrates said. "Whatever you're thinking, *say*."

"He's right, Sergio. You won't hurt my feelings. And it's not as though I'm scientifically illiterate. My daughter does theoretical physics and regularly tries to explain her research to me."

"The point of creating a group like the IPCC was to make sure the evidence was being studied by specialists. That's why the conclusions of their reports are so important. They represent a consensus among the world's best climate scientists."

"But it *is* true that some scientists disagree, isn't it? I regularly read about this in the *Wall Street Journal*," I noted.

"Yes, some scientists disagree. But most *climate* scientists are on the same page. With all respect to your daughter, I don't find the fact that a couple of prominent physicists are deniers to be as persuasive as the massive reports put out by the IPCC. When you have a marketing problem, Ms. Summers, do you care about what your head of accounting thinks? No. You listen to a specialist.

"And as for the *Wall Street Journal*—and other business publications—there's a big difference between their news pages and their opinion pages. If I want to know what scientific research says, I read science journals and scientific reports—not an op-ed page with a known prejudice on this topic."

"By the way, Wendy," Socrates interjected pointedly, "which of the IPCC's reports have you read? And where did you think they were mistaken? Data collection? Interpretation? I'll save you the trouble of embarrassing yourself. Like virtually every other executive I know who is goring this particular ox, you don't read the scientific literature. Do you?"

"Of course not. My job is CEO of a *bank*," I replied. "I spend my time promoting the interests of our stakeholders. But that doesn't mean I can't have an opinion about climate change based on what I consider to be credible sources."

"Yes. You are entitled to any *personal* opinion you want on any topic whatsoever. But when you broadcast that view from a platform you get by virtue of your position, it stops being a strictly personal matter. And when that opinion can have dangerous consequences—like keeping villagers from stopping the fire—then your actions *as a CEO* are ethically questionable."

"*Ethically* questionable? Don't you think that's exaggerating?"

"Not at all. The 'job' of business is to support the 'kind of life' we want in the village in a way that respects our basic ethical principles of 'do no harm' and 'treat others appropriately.' I think that if your actions as a CEO compromise those principles, then you've crossed a line.

"And it's bad enough you aren't familiar with the scientific literature at issue," Socrates continued. "Your insistence on absolute certainty shows that you don't have even a basic appreciation of how science works. And that lets you say all sorts of dangerous things. Sergio, please explain what I mean. You do it better than I can."

"Science is typically about *probability*," he said, "not determining what we absolutely, positively know about what's 'true' versus 'false.' Science is a conservative enterprise that moves v-e-r-y slowly. This is especially true when studying an unprecedented phenomenon—which this amount of global warming is. We want to see piles of data before we draw conclusions, and we never want to overstate them. We know there may always be exceptions and new data that will cause us to refine our findings.

"This drives nonscientists crazy. They want the answers to scientific questions to be definite. And they consider anything less than that to be a sign that the issue at hand is 'unsettled' or 'debatable.' So when it comes to global warming, this means that people have regularly either misunderstood—or been able to deliberately misrepresent—the conclusions of the IPCC. That's why it's misleading, Ms. Summers, when you dismiss climate change as 'just an unproven theory.'

"There's also the problem—which even scientists who aren't environmental scientists fail to appreciate—that the planet's like an aircraft carrier. It doesn't turn on a dime. Even if we completely stop putting greenhouse gases into the atmosphere today, we're still going to have a warmer planet. The only question is 'How much warmer?' Greenhouse gases stay in the atmosphere for decades, if not centuries.

"Also, too many nonscientists think the planet is like a machine. If we've got a wonky part, we can replace it. If a system is broken, we can repair it. But the proper way to think about the planet is that it's more like a living organism with lots of interactions we still don't understand. What we do know, however, is that as big and powerful as the planet is, it's possible for us to push parts of it past the point of repair. You can push an environmental system past its tolerance margins. If you're lucky, and can wait centuries, maybe it will regenerate. But there's no guarantee. The planet is more like an organism than a machine."

Socrates jumped into the conversation again. "And so that you don't feel as though this is all about beating you up, anyone with an ounce of sense should ignore what you or any CEO says when you're talking outside your specialty. CEOs pontificate all the time about topics they know nothing about—like when your food industry compatriot said that climate change isn't necessarily bad. *Right*," Socrates added sarcastically. "Tell that to the island nations that will no longer exist as the ocean levels rise, or to the millions of Bangladeshi who will be trying to find a new home, or to the families of people who die in extreme weather. People should just say, 'Since when does the CEO of a bank or a grocery chain know anything about climate science?'

"But as big a problem as I have with *you* from an ethical perspective, I have a bigger problem with one of your client companies. In the face of the IPCC's findings and warnings—at least one of your clients spent millions of dollars to challenge the science and muddy the waters."

I knew immediately who Socrates was referring to. "You mean ExxonMobil. But you have to concede," I interjected, "that it's the most natural thing in the world for a company to aggressively protect its interests. It has a *duty* to do that. Any initiative to reduce or tax carbon emissions would certainly have hurt the petroleum industry."

"That true," Socrates conceded. "But there's a point when 'legitimate aggressive defense' can violate our 'do no harm' and 'treat others appropriately' principles.

"As the fire's been approaching the village, we've seen companies first tell the villagers, 'It's not true.' Then they said, 'It's not as bad as the fire-alarmists say' and 'Fire's not necessarily a bad thing.' *However, the fire's still approaching.* How does protecting one industry's profits by encouraging people to ignore the fire do anything but increase the risk of harm?

"Let me be more specific.

"Dr. Lee Raymond was the ExxonMobil CEO known from his aggressive denial of the idea that burning fossil fuels contributed to global warming. Dr. Raymond was trained as a chemical engineer, not a climate scientist, and any scientist on the company's payroll would hardly qualify as a neutral observer when billions of dollars of profits were on the line. Following the 1995 IPCC report that found that most of the global warming since 1950 was caused by human activity, Raymond said the idea 'defied common sense and lacks foundation in our current understanding of the climate system.' But on the face of it, that's a ridiculous statement because the IPCC's research in fact reflected *the current understanding of the climate system.*

"The Union of Concerned Scientists claims that between 1998 and 2005—a stretch where the scientific data continued to mount—ExxonMobil gave $16 million to organizations promoting skepticism about the IPCC's findings. And that doesn't count the other millions given by other companies and organizations connected with the petroleum industry. ExxonMobil didn't officially stop this practice until 2008, and at least one report claims it continued for another year or two.

"Does a company have a duty to foster skepticism about a verified danger to future generations and encourage people to delay taking actions that would help their children, grandchildren, and great-grandchildren?

"After ExxonMobil got a new CEO, they at least moderated their position, although he framed the problem mainly as an 'engineering problem.' And if you paid attention to Sergio's explanation earlier, I'm sure you see that this approach is still faulty because it looks at the planet as though it's a machine with a glitch that can be fixed with an 'engineering solution.'

"But however we characterize the problem, the delay has *raised the cost* of the solution. In 2006, a British economist forecast that reducing carbon emissions enough to prevent catastrophic consequences would cost 1–2% of global GDP. Failing to act, however, would make that 5 to 25 times higher.

"From an ethical perspective, both of our principles got trashed.

"'Treat others appropriately' got violated when CEOs like you and petroleum companies acted in ways that worked to slow down public acceptance of the problem—*despite* what mainstream science had discovered. At some point, doesn't everyone's right to know the truth—so that they can make free and fully informed decisions about things that affect them and their children—get compromised if someone tries to sow confusion and uncertainty? Shouldn't a company in that situation stay on the sidelines and let the scientific community handle things? And in your case personally, if you were going to speak out about climate change, didn't you have a responsibility to study the science?

"Also, what about fairness? The longer the delay, the greater the likelihood that we'll pass along virtually all of the costs to Natalie and Sergio's generation. They get stuck with a problem they didn't create.

"And as far as 'do no harm' goes, there are two issues. First, there's the higher costs that Natalie, Sergio, their children, and grandchildren will have to pay because of our delay. More serious, however, are the military implications I've been hinting at, which we can now finally get to."

21

Business, Ethics, and the Rights of Future Generations— Climate Change (continued)

Sergio walked up to the screen and brought up a PDF of a report with the surprising title, "National Security and the Threat of Climate Change."

"This isn't the only evaluation of the military implications of global warming. But it's my favorite," he explained. "It's short, clear, straightforward, and persuasive. Everyone involved was a former senior military officer—General, Lieutenant General, Admiral, or Vice Admiral. And they're all heavy hitters—former Army Chief of Staff, former Commander-in-Chief of the U.S. Central Command, former Commander of the Naval Space Command, former Chief of Naval Research. It's a *very* impressive list.

"I have to say that when our team for the competition started working on the case, this was the last topic anyone had in mind. We all wanted to work on climate change, and we already knew there were lots of business implications that had ethical dimensions. Carbon taxes. Emissions from energy production sites. The fact that raising meat has such a big carbon footprint. But we wanted something different.

"I just happened across this report. I brought it to the group's attention, and we worked up the topic. We narrowed in on the impact of global warming on the Arctic. Melting ice will make it possible to mine for minerals and petroleum in a way that was impossible before. Less ice also means new shipping lanes.

"We wanted to come up with a question no one was asking in the global warming discussion. We settled on something like, 'One of the consequences of a warmer Arctic region is that corporations from a variety of industries—and from various nations—will be competing for the new resources. Given the strong likelihood of military conflict, what ethical responsibility do these companies have for preventing any possible harm?'"

"I found their question intriguing," interjected Socrates. "I hadn't heard any executive ask something like this. As I said, I thought it was farsighted that a bunch of undergrads brought it up. I also realized that it provided me with more evidence for my complaint against those of you who—deliberately or through your negligence in not studying the science—downplayed the seriousness of climate change. You failed to make sure that business did its 'job.' You increased the likelihood and the seriousness of the harm that people like Natalie, Sergio, their children, and grandchildren will experience."

"So here's the bad news," Sergio continued. "The military analysis concluded that climate change will produce specific consequences with military implications: changes in the habitats in which people live, patterns of precipitation, extreme weather events, ice cover, and sea level. The military will be involved in a few different ways: direct military action (one nation against another), military support to keep civil order (the sort of thing the National Guard does in the United States), humanitarian assistance (providing food, water, and shelter after a natural disaster), and military involvement as a result of civil unrest, political extremism, or terrorism."

"*Terrorism?*" I scoffed. "That's crazy. Terrorism as a result of global warming? Now *there's* a group of retired Generals and Admirals looking for any way to increase the defense budget. And you're telling me this is all somehow related to *business*? Ridiculous!"

Socrates sighed loudly and shot his water pistol in my general direction. He apparently thought I should be spared another soaking. "You know, you have a bad habit of jumping to conclusions before you look at evidence. I really *want* to think you can handle this new position, but you desperately need to stop yourself from saying stupid things.

"Probably the *last* people who could ever be called 'tree hugging global warming alarmists' are senior military officers. These are professionals who have spent their lives learning how to assess risk. Risk of the 'life or death' sort. Do you really think they're going to put themselves on the line for the sort of ridicule you just shot their way if they weren't serious? Are you honestly willing to say this is a Pentagon boondoggle without looking at any evidence?"

The disappointed reaction of not only Socrates but also Natalie and Sergio underscored how inappropriate my flip reaction had been. *Note to self: Bite tongue before saying something you may regret.* "My apologies. It's no excuse, but I think our marathon conversations have rattled my brain. I guess I was just trying to express how stunned I was to hear someone offer a connection between climate change and terrorism."

"You *should* be stunned," Socrates chided, "because the connection is real and serious. But you should also be angry that the deniers conveniently overlook it while they paint 'global warming' as a conspiracy meant to enrich scientists or impose some left-wing agenda on the country. You'd think that since conservatives typically rally around the military, they would pay attention to such a group of senior officers. Whatever deniers think about the IPCC, you'd expect them to listen to a team of retired Admirals and Generals. But that's the blinding power of ideology. Sorry, I'm pulling us off topic. But we'll get to that.

"Serg. Take a step back and make sure Wendy knows you aren't exaggerating the threat of terrorism. Aren't there a couple of passages in the report that make it clear?"

Scrolling through the document on the screen, Sergio brought up the page.

Socrates read the passage out loud.

Climate change acts as a threat multiplier for instability in some of the most volatile regions of the world. Projected climate change will seriously exacerbate already marginal living standards in many Asian, African, and Middle Eastern nations, causing widespread political instability and the likelihood of failed states.

Unlike most conventional security threats that involve a single entity acting in specific ways and points in time, climate change has the potential to result in multiple chronic conditions, occurring globally within the same time frame. Economic and environmental conditions in already fragile areas will further erode as food productions decline, diseases increase, clean water becomes increasingly scarce, and large populations move in search of resources. Weakened and failing governments, with an already thin margin for survival, foster the conditions for internal conflicts, extremism, and movement toward increased authoritarianism and radical ideologies.

Greater potential for failed states and the growth of terrorism. Many developing nations do not have the government and social infrastructures in place to cope with the types of stressors that could be brought on by global climate change.

When a government can no longer deliver services to its people, ensure domestic order, and protect the nation's borders from invasion, conditions are ripe for turmoil, extremism and terrorism to fill the vacuum. Lebanon's experience with the terrorist group Hezbollah and the Brazilian government's attempt to reign in the slum gang First Capital Command are both examples of how the central governments' inability to provide basic services has led to strengthening of these extra-governmental entities.

"And before your knee-jerk skepticism makes you say, 'Sad as that might be, that would be terrorism in *developing* nations, not in the United States or EU,' ask yourself how likely it would be that a terrorist organization wouldn't take aim at a rich, Western nation. Think about 9/11 and the Boston Marathon bombing, for starters. And as far as a connection with *business*, it was no accident that the 9/11 terrorists hijacked *American Airlines* and *United Airlines* jets.

You need to start thinking *globally*, Wendy. The job you're up for is a global company with a presence in almost every corner of the planet."

Considering what Socrates had just said, I had to admit that if I were the CEO of a global company, I would regularly worry about whether we'd be seen as a target for terrorism—especially if the report was correct that climate change would destabilize weak governments.

"OK, let's say I shelve my skepticism for the time being. Sergio, would you walk us through the main points of the report?"

Sergio had been waiting patiently by the screen while Socrates and I fenced. As we turned to him, he was clearly enthusiastic about continuing.

"I already have some slides that should get us through the main points pretty quickly. The report identifies the relevant consequences of the primary effects of global warming and then spells out how the military might be involved. Let me build them step-by-step."

GLOBAL WARMING WILL LEAD TO:	THIS WILL PRODUCE:	AND THE MILITARY WILL BE INVOLVED:

"The four main effects are: a rise in the sea level; increased melting of glaciers and the Arctic ice cap; changes in precipitation patterns and droughts; extreme weather, and warmer surface temperatures."

GLOBAL WARMING WILL LEAD TO:	THIS WILL PRODUCE:	AND THE MILITARY WILL BE INVOLVED:
SEA LEVEL RISE		
ICE MELTING		
PRECIPITATION DROUGHT		
EXTREME WEATHER AND HIGHER TEMPS		

"And before I show you what will happen, here are a few abbreviations I'll use for the way the military might be involved. 'MA' for direct military action. 'MS' for military support to keep civil order. 'H' for humanitarian assistance. And 'CET' for dealing with civil unrest, political extremism, or terrorism.

"Here's how it will play out.

"First, rising sea levels. Water expands when heated, so a hotter planet means the oceans will get warmer and sea levels will rise. That will be disastrous for any country like Bangladesh, where so much of the country is barely above sea level. Millions of people will want to migrate to another country. But, even now, that's a source of tension with India, which has built a 2,000 kilometer fence to stem Bangladeshi illegal immigrants. India enforces that now with a 'shoot to kill' policy. There have been more than 1,000 fatalities. It's likely that global warming will make things worse.

"Rising sea levels also means less fresh water and less food production in some parts of the world.

"In a worst case scenario, these factors can produce civil war—where one part of the country tries to protect its benefits from its neighbors—or one country attacking another. Less serious scenarios involve the military only in humanitarian or civil support. Extremism and terrorism are also realistic threats. When food, water, and a safe place to live are in short supply, the conditions are perfect for extremist ideologies that can foster terrorism."

GLOBAL WARMING WILL LEAD TO:	THIS WILL PRODUCE:	AND THE MILITARY WILL BE INVOLVED:
SEA LEVEL RISE ──▶	MIGRATIONS ────────▶ H_2O/FOOD	MA/MS/H/CET
ICE MELTING		
PRECIPITATION DROUGHT		
EXTREME WEATHER AND HIGHER TEMPS		

"Second, melting ice. At present, 40% of the world's population gets at least half of its drinking waters from the summer melt of mountain glaciers. Hundreds of millions of Asians rely on water from the glaciers on the Tibetan plateau. In India, a quarter of a billion people depend on a single glacier-fed river. Melting glaciers, ice caps, and snow pack will lead to shortages of drinking water and possible conflicts over exploring for resources like oil and minerals. So, as glaciers and ice sheets melt, drinking water will be in short supply.

"Then, there's the issue of who owns the Arctic resources that will now be able to be mined. Eight nations already have various claims about who owns what. In 2007, Russia had one of its submarines plant their flag on the ocean floor, staking their claim to all the Arctic resources. And then there's the rest of the planet that may claim a share. Resource wars are as old as humans, so there's certainly the possibility of some skirmishes before the question of who's entitled to what gets settled.

"Therefore, the military will have a role in humanitarian support, direct military action, and response to extremism or terrorism."

GLOBAL WARMING WILL LEAD TO:	**THIS WILL PRODUCE:**	**AND THE MILITARY WILL BE INVOLVED:**
SEA LEVEL RISE ⟶	MIGRATIONS ⟶ H_2O/FOOD	MA/MS/H/CET
ICE MELTING ⟶	H_2O/RESOURCES ⟶	H/MA/CET
PRECIPITATION DROUGHT		
EXTREME WEATHER AND HIGHER TEMPS		

"Third, drought and changes in precipitation will affect the production and availability of food and water. In less developed countries with fewer resources to deal with major problems, there's a significant risk of social disorder. There's also the possibility of extremists who would take advantage of people's unhappiness for their own agenda. Again, the military would assist in humanitarian efforts, supporting local governments, and, in some cases, responding to extremism."

GLOBAL WARMING WILL LEAD TO:	**THIS WILL PRODUCE:**	**AND THE MILITARY WILL BE INVOLVED:**
SEA LEVEL RISE ⟶	MIGRATIONS ⟶ H_2O/FOOD	MA/MS/H/CET
ICE MELTING ⟶	H_2O/RESOURCES ⟶	H/MA/CET
PRECIPITATION ⟶ DROUGHT	H_2O/FOOD ⟶	H/MS/CET
EXTREME WEATHER AND HIGHER TEMPS		

"Finally, extreme weather and higher temperatures. These will increase the incidence of some diseases, damage infrastructure, and lead to social disruption. Temperature and flooding affect things like where insects live, how big their populations are, and whether or not the water gets contaminated, so we'll see more malaria, dengue fever, and cholera. Extreme weather similar to Hurricanes Katrina and Sandy means huge damage to the infrastructure and all kinds of social disruption. Unless a government can respond quickly and appropriately, we again see breeding grounds for extremism. Once more, the military would be called on to assist in humanitarian efforts, supporting local governments, and responding to extremism."

GLOBAL WARMING WILL LEAD TO:	THIS WILL PRODUCE:	AND THE MILITARY WILL BE INVOLVED:
SEA LEVEL RISE ⟶	MIGRATIONS ⟶ H_2O/FOOD	MA/MS/H/CET
ICE MELTING ⟶	H_2O/RESOURCES ⟶	H/MA/CET
PRECIPITATION ⟶ DROUGHT	H_2O/FOOD ⟶	H/MS/CET
EXTREME ⟶ WEATHER AND HIGHER TEMPS	DISEASE/DAMAGE TO ⟶ INFRASTRUCTURE/SOCIAL DISRUPTION	H/MS/CET

Sergio handed the remote back to Socrates. "Admirably brief, Serg."

"And scary," I added, "on a number of fronts. If what you say is true, there's hardly an industry that won't be seriously affected. Doing business is going to be much more complicated. It's like every aspect of business could get more expensive: the cost of resources, production, labor, transportation, insurance. Maybe the defense industry and companies that sell emergency supplies will do well. But I think that, on balance, the costs will outweigh the benefits. And in the sort of climate you describe, anything could happen. For example, executives of major companies from developed nations would be prime targets for kidnapping or worse."

"Depressing, but excellent observations, Wendy," said Socrates, somberly. "You're right. Climate change is going to make doing business very different. There's hardly any industry that this won't have an impact on in one way or another.

"But I asked Natalie and Sergio to join us for a few different reasons. One was to take advantage of their expertise. You've just seen what Sergio can do, and we'll put Natalie on display shortly. As you gather, I wanted to put you on the spot with representatives of a generation who will be saddled with the consequences of what we do and don't do about some serious issues. But I also wanted to show them what a first-rate mind"—he gestured my way—"is capable of when she isn't saying stupid things."

I grimaced, but didn't want to seem petty. In light of the evidence Sergio had presented, I realized I would have to reconsider some of my earlier statements about climate change. "I guess I should say 'thank you,' because I'm sure there's a compliment hidden there somewhere."

"I'm serious. I have conversations like this only with people I respect. I told you during our last talk that, despite your rough edges, I think you have genuine promise. And we wouldn't be having this little chat unless I regarded you as a serious candidate for that new post.

"But getting back to what I was saying, I want to show Natalie and Sergio what it means to be fully committed to drawing conclusions from hard evidence, what it looks like to be intellectually honest, and to ruthlessly challenge your own beliefs—and, if you think the evidence merits it, to have the courage to modify them, even admit you were wrong. That's an ability you have, Wendy, even if it's something you don't use often enough.

"So here's the final step in this exercise.

"Over the last couple of days, you and I have covered a great deal of ground. In particular, we went much deeper into ethical theory than we did in your office. I want to see what sunk in. We all know what you've said about climate change over the years and how strongly you've supported companies and organizations that have minimized the significance of global warming. But your job now is to put yourself in the shoes of *an objective observer* and give us a proper ethical analysis of your actions and ExxonMobil's.

"So I have three questions for you. What makes the issues we're talking about qualify as *ethical* issues? Did the actions in question produce more good than harm? What's the intrinsic ethical character of the actions?

"And since, in an earlier conversation, I led our two young friends here through the same introduction to ethics I took you through, you can assume they're up to speed on the basics."

Socrates tossed me the remote. "And so that you don't feel put on the spot and can take your time, Natalie, Sergio, and I are going to move to the deck for a snack and to catch up. Just let us know when you're ready for us."

I recognized what Socrates was doing as a compliment. He was giving me the final word on the topic, and he was also letting me demonstrate to Natalie and Sergio how it's possible to set aside what may feel like cherished beliefs and force yourself to question them. I walked to the screen and started jotting down pieces of my answers to the first three questions all at once. I'd neaten the analysis up at the end, but I always start in a fairly messy way, noting whatever comes into my mind. After about 45 minutes, I called in Socrates and the students.

As everyone was getting settled in front of the screen, I explained, "I don't pretend that this is an exhaustive analysis. I also want to make it clear that I haven't decided how much I *personally* agree with every part of it. But I did exactly what Socrates asked me to do. I set aside my own point of view and looked at this through someone else's eyes. Before I decide what I do or don't accept, I'd need to take some time and look more closely at the data. I was unaware of some important claims you made, Sergio, and I would want to think about them."

"Excellent first step," Socrates chimed in. "A nice change from that bad habit of shooting from the hip. I mean it. Kudos. Also, Natalie, Serg, notice that even though Wendy's done her best at laying out a neutral and objective picture of the different elements of an ethical analysis, she doesn't feel that she has to commit to anything other than that as a first step. I asked her to describe all the pieces to the puzzle. I did not ask her to decide what sort of picture they made when assembled. I deliberately did *not* ask her to give us some ultimate judgment about whether what's going on is ethically defensible. She can decide later about whether this amounts to a convincing argument. If you try to do a neutral analysis and decide on an argument for your final position at the same time, you'll do a bad job of both."

I appreciated the fact that Socrates wasn't going to railroad me on this. I'd seen some new facts, and I wanted to think about them. I'd learned already that no matter what stunts Socrates pulls during our conversations, he respects me enough to leave me to make my own decisions.

"So, here are the pieces," I announced, bringing up my five slides. "Slide 1 answers the first question: How is it that we have *ethical* issues here? Slides 2 and 3 identify the tangible positive and negative consequences. Slides 4 and 5 focus on the actions themselves. I'll give you a quick overview. Then, while I go for a run on the beach, you can argue among yourselves how good a job I've done and what it all shows. All of this sitting is making me stir-crazy."

I pointed to the first slide.

Actions at issue: Individual/corporate challenges to claims about climate change and calls to action.
Why "ethical" issue? Basic needs: "whose" and "which"?

Whose?	Which?
Corporations (as legal person)	Need for freedom to control private resources and chart strategies that promote the interest of the corporation
Employees/Vendors (variety of industries)	Need to make a living
Shareholders (variety of industries)	Need to have agreement honored (return on investment) Need for financial security
Customers (variety of industries)	Need for necessary goods and services

(Continued)

(Continued from previous page)

Individuals who receive support from petroleum industry	Need to make a living
Public officials	Need for accurate information on important issues so that they can make informed choices
Citizens	Need for public officials to honor their duty to make decisions for the public good
Interested individuals	Need for freedom of expression
Victims of coastal flooding from sea level rise	Need for life, health, and safety
Victims of extreme weather	Need for life, health, and safety
Victims of water and food shortages	Need for life, health, and safety
Members of armed forces involved in any military action	Need for life, health, and safety
Friends and families of military	Emotional and financial needs

"As our lord and master has instructed us," I said to Natalie and Sergio, who definitely appreciated the barb I'd tossed Socrates' way, "to say that something is an ethical issue simply means that any number of people's 'basic needs' are involved. Anyone whose *job* is affected by the actions we're looking at gets on our list because of their *need to earn a living*. That's also true for investors, but they also count because the company has *agreed* to provide them with some return on their investment. There are some issues of *freedom* of expression, freedom of action, and the *need to be able to make free and fully informed decisions*."

"Nice point regarding public officials," Socrates noted, "and the promise they make when they take office to make decisions based on the public good. With politics having become a 'winner take all' blood sport, it's refreshing to see that you haven't gone over to the dark side."

"Well, one of the things we both agree on is that a free society should be based on free, rational agreements. And what rational, self-interested individual would ever agree to anything but that a public official should make decisions for the public good?

"Then there are the final set of needs—life, health, and safety of people who may be affected in any number of ways. This, of course, is taken directly from Sergio's description of the military implications.

"Oh, one final point. This is one of those things that I have no idea whether I agree with or not. *Legally*, corporations are persons. Ethically, I don't know if that's relevant and if an artificial person can have 'basic needs' that count in an ethical analysis. But I decided to list it for future consideration.

"Next, . . . " I brought up my second slide.

Actions at issue: Individual/corporate challenges to claims about climate change and calls to action.
Tangible positive consequences: short, medium, long term (st, mt, lt); quality (l, m, h)

Who	What
Petroleum industry	
Corporation (as legal person)	Financial/LT/H
Employees/Vendors	Financial/ST-LT/H
Shareholders	Financial/SL-LT/M
Customers	Necessary goods and services/ST-LT/L-H
Individuals receiving support from petroleum industry	Financial/ST/H

Industries that will benefit from warmer temperatures in certain areas (e.g., shipping, food, forestry, recreation, construction, mineral exploration, real estate), from natural disasters and disease (e.g., medical supplies, rescue equipment, construction), and from increased risk of military activity (e.g., defense, aerospace)

Who	What
Employees/Vendors	Financial/LT/H
Shareholders	Financial/LT/H
Customers	Necessary goods and services/LT/L-H
Researchers who will eventually work on solutions	Financial/MT-LT/H

"Given Sergio's presentation, there are no surprises in the tangible positive and negative consequences. Following the utilitarians, I tried to make some judgment about whether the result would be short term or long term. But in most cases, I'd have to say 'it depends.' I'd need more information. I felt more comfortable using Mill's idea about differences in *quality*. Jobs are definitely a high quality benefit. I labeled the benefits to investors as medium, because those typically don't determine whether shareholders can pay the rent and buy food.

"You'll notice that, whether you like it or not, climate change actually could bring considerable benefits to industries other than petroleum. Warmer temperatures could boost: shipping, food, forestry, recreation, construction, mineral exploration, and real estate. Natural disasters and disease would lead to increased demand for medical supplies, rescue, and construction equipment and services. And someone will make money from the increased risk of military activity: defense and aerospace.

"Of course, there's also a significant downside, which this next slide shows."

Actions at issue: Individual/corporate challenges to claims about climate change and calls to action.
Tangible negative consequences: short, medium, long term (st, mt, lt);
quality (l, m, h)

Negative

Who	What
Employees/Vendors (petroleum, industries that will not benefit from warmer temperatures)	Financial/ST-LT/H
Shareholders	Financial/ST-LT/M
Customers	Necessary goods and services/ST-LT/L-H
Victims of coastal flooding from sea level rise	Death, injury, loss of home, loss of property, trauma, grief/LT/H
Victims of extreme weather	Death, injury, loss of home, loss of property, trauma, grief/LT/H
Victims of water and food shortages	Death, illness, trauma, grief/LT/H
Members of armed forces involved in any military action and their families and friends	Death, injury, trauma, grief/LT/H

"You just have to look at big hurricanes and tornadoes to appreciate how much financial devastation extreme weather can bring. And you'd have to have a heart of stone not to see that the quality of the pain and suffering we're talking about is high. *If*—and that's the big *if* I need to think about—Sergio's account of the military consequences is accurate, there's going to be a substantial body count, especially in developing nations.

"Next, I decided to approach my analysis of the actions in two separate ways. I have to confess that I've developed a weird fascination with 'maxims' and whether or not a maxim could be 'universalized' after Socrates explained what Kant meant by this. Slide 4 is a rough attempt at formulating maxims that could apply to what I was doing in my personal campaign against the idea of climate change and in ExxonMobil's. I don't know how solid the distinction is between 'individual' and 'corporate' *actions*—or the implied 'individual' and 'corporate' *maxims*. But we so regularly attribute actions to *corporations* that I thought I should spell it out this way."

Actions at issue: Individual/corporate challenges to claims about climate change and calls to action.
Intrinsic ethical character of actions: categorical imperative and maxims

Individual Maxims

Whenever I am confronted with a perspective that challenges a favorite preconceived belief of mine, I will assess that challenge by using second-hand interpretations rather than evaluate the data myself—even if those interpretations are done by individuals with ulterior motives.

Corporate Maxims

Whenever the company is confronted with objective scientific evidence that challenges our strategy of maximizing profits, we will seek out ways to increase skepticism about the science and delay any pressure or requirement to change our strategy.

Individual and Corporate Maxims

Whenever I am confronted with a truly debatable issue for which the evidence is currently inconclusive, even if my current actions may increase the likelihood of serious harm to others, I will continue with these actions and strenuously resist any opposition.

Whenever I am able to pass along the work and the cost of solving a serious problem I had a hand in creating to people who were not responsible for creating it, I will do so.

Despite the sworn duty of public officials to formulate policy that promotes the public good, we will use corporate resources to do our best to ensure that public policy favors our industry instead.

Despite the need for all citizens in a democracy for accurate, unbiased information, we will use corporate resources to promote skepticism about any information that could make it more difficult for the company to maximize profits.

"Finally, slide 5 summarizes what I got in thinking about Kant's idea of respecting the *dignity* of people. What does it mean to 'treat others appropriately' in the village? This is where issues of freedom, fairness, and keeping agreements come in. Also, I think that respecting people as 'ends in themselves' means we have a duty to prevent harm when we can."

I tossed the remote/microphone to Socrates.

"Nicely done," he said with an approving nod. "Just one more thing before you go for your run. The most diplomatic way of summarizing the most important public comments you've made about climate change in the past is to say, first, *climate change is not a scientifically verifiable phenomenon.* I think that's a more appropriate statement than your comment that it's a 'hoax'; second, *even if it turns out to be real, the threat of global warming is exaggerated by its proponents;* and, third, *the actions called for to combat climate change will*

Actions at issue: Individual/corporate challenges to claims about climate change and calls to action.
Intrinsic ethical character of actions: respecting dignity of persons; categorical imperative and treating others always as ends in themselves.

Freedom of action: corporations

Freedom of speech: executives

Keep agreements: corporations to investors; companies to "village" (the "job of business"); public officials to citizenry

Duty to prevent harm: to people in the present and in the future.

Fairness to people in the future

cost billions of dollars and will significantly harm the world's economy. Is that a fair summary? I'm not trying to distort your words. I'm just trying to boil things down to your simplest positions. And I'm not asking you to change anything based on the evidence we're just looked at."

"You aren't distorting. That's what I've been saying. And I promise I will think about Sergio's slides before I make any more public statements. But it's pretty clear what an objective analysis shows—both in terms of the benefits and harms and how everyone should be treated."

"Fair enough. But as I said before, the reason I invited Natalie and Sergio is because they represent the next generation. You've spent no small amount of energy arguing for policies that you say will make things better for our children and grandchildren. Because I think you're often wrong on that score, I thought you needed to face directly the people whose interests you claim to be protecting.

"So, Sergio, you may ask Wendy one question that represents the perspective of your generation. She doesn't have to answer it today. But because Wendy is someone who operates in good faith, I have no doubt that she will ultimately answer it."

When Socrates looked my way, I nodded. Sergio walked back to the screen and flipped through the slides.

"Here's what I don't understand," he began. "Natalie and I plan to have a family someday. Even now we talk about what kind of parents we want to be. We disagree about many things, but the one thing we see the same is that we want things to be *easier* for our children than it was for us.

"Don't get me wrong. We've both been really lucky. We come from loving families, and we ended up at a good school. But both of us have also had to work very hard to afford college. And that meant there were things that we both couldn't do because we needed to work so much. So one of our goals as parents will be to do what we can to let our kids have it easier."

Then he pulled up the charts containing the ice core data and the parallel increase in CO_2 and temperature.

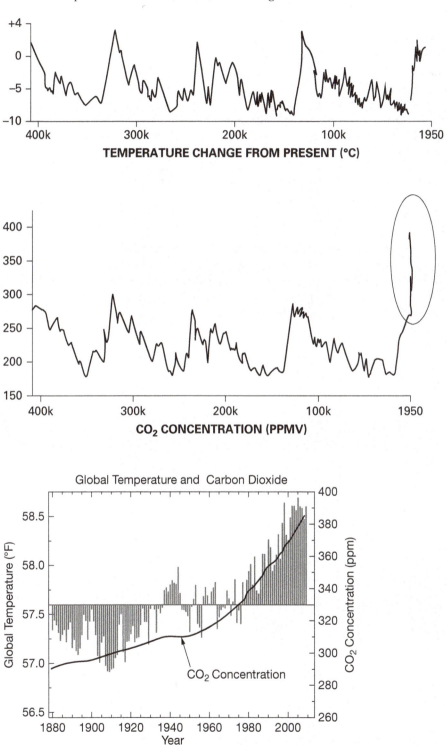

TEMPERATURE CHANGE FROM PRESENT (°C)

CO₂ CONCENTRATION (PPMV)

Global Temperature and Carbon Dioxide

"When I look at these charts, when I read the first IPCC reports from the 1990s and the subsequent grim military predictions, and when I keep hearing that the most recent decades are the hottest on record, it seems pretty clear to me that our parents' generation knew there was a good chance something bad was going on.

"So here's my question.

"With evidence so compelling and with so much at stake, why didn't people of your generation care enough about your kids and grandkids to consider that you might be wrong?"

Sergio wasn't being confrontational. He was genuinely curious and sincerely puzzled. It was a good question.

"Thank you, Serg," Socrates said. "You've given us all a great deal to think about. Wendy, go log some miles. The three of us will stay here and brood about this.

"When you come back, we'll turn it over to Natalie, and you can defend what you said to the Senator. Let me see if I remember this right. You told a Nobel Prize–winning economist who taught at Princeton for a number of years that he was so wrong about the economy he must have his head up his. . . . Well, let's not corrupt Natalie and Sergio. You can redeem yourself when you return."

22

Business, Ethics, and the Rights of Future Generations—The Economy

As I started jogging down the road from Socrates' beach house, I was so tired it felt like I was in the last few miles of a marathon. I hoped my host would keep his word that we were almost done. After a couple of miles, however, my head started to clear and I decided that I looked forward to the next challenge. Again, I hadn't been as diplomatic as I could have been in criticizing the Senator's perspective on the economy. And Socrates did have a point that the Senator had won a Nobel Prize. But economics can get so technical that I regularly think economists lose sight of the most obvious things. If a highly sophisticated, technical approach doesn't ultimately square with the day-to-day, practical workings of an economy, I prefer a common sense perspective.

Four or five miles were all I needed to get geared up for the next conversation. After a quick shower, I joined Socrates, Natalie, and Sergio back in the living room. The charts and graphs already up on the screen told me they were all set. I grabbed something to drink. "I'm ready whenever you are."

"You've become known in the popular press as something of a representative of what you call *the business perspective on the economy*," Socrates noted accurately. "You've championed an agenda of a freer global market, lower taxes, smaller government, and fewer regulations on business. And I'm convinced that you sincerely believe this is the path to prosperity for Natalie and Sergio's generation."

"True, but for *the present* as much as the future," I clarified.

"This takes us to your exchange with the Senator who has a very different point of view. What was the gist of the disagreement?"

I thought for a moment trying to picture my exchange with the Senator and his Chief of Staff. "They—like you—expressed some concern about the actions of some of the bank's client companies on stakeholders. They had a *very* broad idea of who should be considered a stakeholder. They—like you—suggested that the bank facilitates some ethically questionable actions by the way we support our clients. They were most passionate—and insulting—when they, like you, objected to the public role I take in speaking for and against certain pieces of legislation, especially when it concerns economic policy. They not only said that some of my claims were flat-out false, but that I should have known that. They pretty much accused me of either lying or being stupid. I assume they were friends of yours. Why didn't you have *them* do the card trick you pulled on me earlier?"

"Good summary. And do you remember the central claim they, like me, said was false—despite your frequent assertion to the contrary?"

"That's easy. From an economic perspective, *a rising tide floats all boats*. When you let wealth get created from business activity, it will inevitably spread through the rest of society. Profits create jobs, spur innovation, and raise the quality of living. If we want to have a certain 'kind of life' in our village, the best thing we can do is to let business try to generate as much wealth as possible.

"From the point of view of *ethics*, this is one of the most powerful, positive features of contemporary capitalism. Frankly, given your concern with ethics, I'm shocked you question something so obvious."

Socrates replied with an expression I didn't trust. "Apparently, I didn't make myself clear. I'm sorry about that. I don't *question* it. I didn't say that I *believe* that perspective is false. I said *the facts absolutely, positively don't support it*. It's simply not true. This is an *empirical* issue, not a theoretical or ideological one. Frankly, given your concern with *evidence*, I'm shocked you fail to recognize something so obvious."

He spoke that last sentence with a mocking, condescending tone. No doubt it was to see if, as tired as I was, I could still keep my cool and not respond to his insult with one of my own.

"You keep talking about evidence," I replied calmly. "Why don't you do the three of us a favor and show us what you mean. I'm sure you already have a set of slides ready to go."

Socrates shot an approving smile my way as he stepped beside the screen. "Excellent response, Wendy. And you're right. I'm ready to go.

"But first, Sergio, what was Wendy's mistake?"

The young man hesitated. He obviously felt put on the spot.

"Come on, Serg," Socrates said as he walked over to the young man's chair. "Wendy's a big girl. She can take it. She'll thank you for pointing it out."

Sergio looked at me. I was curious about what he was thinking. "Socrates is right. If I made a mistake, believe me, I want to know."

"*Inevitably*," Sergio said politely.

"You aren't doing her any favors with one word, Serg," Socrates quickly replied. "You have a gift. Show her what you can do."

Sergio closed his eyes. "From an economic perspective, a rising tide floats all boats. When you let wealth get created from business activity, it will *inevitably* spread through the rest of society. Profits create jobs, spur innovation, and raise the quality of living." Then he opened them and looked at me.

Like a kid who never tires of playing with his favorite toys, Socrates had held his stylus/microphone by Sergio as he spoke. My words were now on the screen. Socrates couldn't contain his enthusiasm. "He has an eidetic memory. Cool, huh? He just closes his eyes and plays it all back. Impressive, no?"

I *was* impressed—and envious. I'd love to be able to recall things like that.

"Your mistake," Socrates said, "is simple to identify. You think that wealth *inevitably* produces benefits throughout the economy. It *can* produce benefits. It *can* raise quality of life. But it doesn't *inevitably* do so. The error in your thinking is also apparent in the false analogy you used."

"False analogy?" I asked.

"A rising tide floats all boats. It suggests that the economy is a much simpler entity than it is."

"I don't mean to be fussy," I interrupted, "but aren't you splitting hairs, focusing on a single word, and a single implied comparison about economic forces? It sounds like you're just worrying about terminology and phrasing."

"Not at all," Socrates answered confidently. "Given the *facts*, we know not only that it's *not inevitable* that wealth 'trickles down,' but, more importantly, that it *hasn't done so*. And if we wanted to use the 'rising tide and boats' image to represent the facts, it should be more like, 'The rising tide floats the yachts, causes everyday fishing boats to take on water at an accelerating pace, and capsizes rowboats.' That's what the *facts* show."

That wasn't my understanding of "what the facts show." But I prided myself in always being willing to re-examine things if someone could make a good case for it. "OK. I'm listening. If that's what the facts show, let's see them."

Socrates tossed the remote to Natalie.

"You're up, Natalie," Socrates said. "The homework I gave Natalie in preparation for today was to see whether the economy is doing its 'job.' You can assume that in earlier conversations I've had with our two young friends, we discussed the village, *its* job, the job of *business*, and the like. The four of us have the same frame of reference in that regard, then. So, is the economy making it possible for the village to have the 'kind of life' we founded the village for in the first place? And do all the 'boats' rise and fall together? I left it up to Natalie to dig out whatever evidence she thought was relevant."

The young woman stepped confidently to the screen. I was curious how someone who, as a business major, should have a similar perspective as mine—but who hadn't had much experience in business yet—would look at the data.

"Let's start with the good news. Here's the U.S. GDP since 1950.

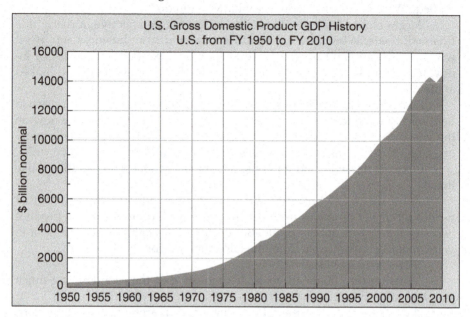

"And here's the Dow Jones.

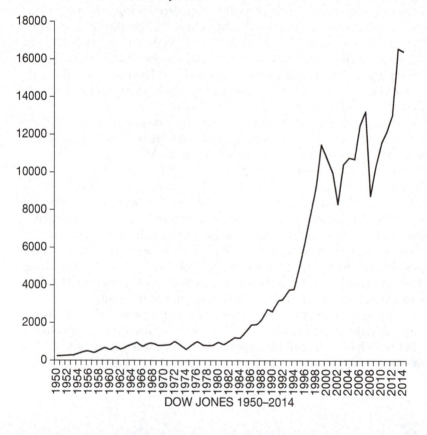

"Corporate profits.

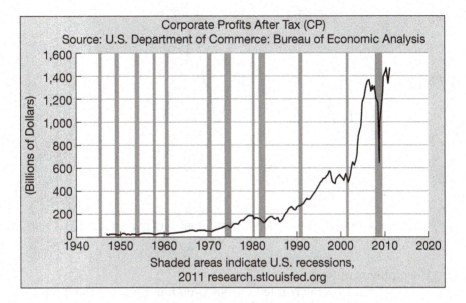

"Except for the occasional dips, notice that we have consistent growth. A rising tide. Which leads to the obvious question, did it 'float all boats'?

"Sergio?" she said, putting her boyfriend on the spot. "What's one of the first markers you want to look at to see whether an overall increase in wealth gives the villagers the 'kind of life' they want? What are *you* personally most worried about when you look at life after you graduate?"

"Me? That's easy. Whether I'm going to be able to get a job. And not just any job. A job in the area I've been studying. A job that lets me pay off my school loans. And unlike you, Nat, philosophers and environmentalists aren't at the top of any corporate recruiters' list of 'majors we must hire.' I'm really worried about that." The way Sergio wrung his hands told me he had more debt than he was comfortable with. I was aware of how big a worry this was for this generation of young people from conversations I'd been involved in with my daughter's friends when she was in school. We were lucky in being able to pay the steep costs of her education. But most of her friends had to borrow. The average debt they graduated with was about $30,000, although it could go a good deal higher.

"A job. Good. A source of income. That's the number one thing ordinary villagers need in order to have food, shelter, and the necessities of life. So, if the economy is doing what it's supposed to, we should see a strong record of jobs to match our strong GDP performance."

Natalie pulled up her next slide.

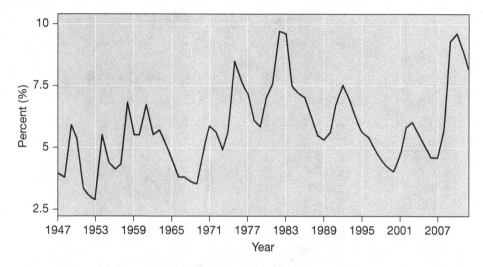

Unemployment

"Wendy," Socrates interrupted, "would you mind reading this chart for us and telling Natalie what it means?"

"I'd say the chart speaks for itself. It shows the normal, cyclical ebb and flow of job creation and job loss that go with a huge economy like ours."

The look on Natalie's face told me she'd expected a different answer. When she paused, I got the feeling she didn't want to be confrontational. "You obviously disagree, Natalie. Just spit it out. I'm interested in how you see it."

She twirled the stylus in her hand nervously as she moved two charts side by side.

"OK. During the time when the economy is growing, we see unemployment range from about 3% to nearly 10%. If a rising tide floated all boats, wouldn't the most elementary thing we could expect be that everyone who wanted a job had one? Shouldn't the unemployment graph be flatter?

"And while you refer to the 'cyclical ebb and flow of job creation and job loss,' isn't the consensus among economists that when everything's working the way it's supposed to, unemployment will be closer to 4–6%? So don't those periods where unemployment is in the 6–9% range suggest something's not working? Oh, and before I forget, some experts said that the 'official' numbers can be low because of the protocols used for who gets counted as 'unemployed.' For example, I found some research that said that, following the 2008 meltdown, the real number for unemployment was closer to 20%."

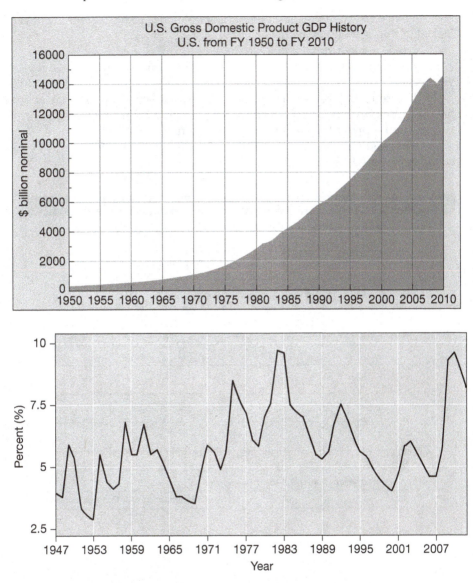

No one had ever put jobs and GDP side by side like that for me before. And while I felt there were more factors that needed to be looked at—overall population growth in the United States, total job creation, inflation rates, markers for the economy other than GDP, and so on—I was impressed with the simplicity of Natalie's comparison. Sometimes, the best question to ask is the most basic—and apparently unsophisticated—one.

And this was a good one. Shouldn't there be a close relationship between a strong economy and the ability of people to find work?

I didn't want to discourage Natalie, and I certainly didn't want to jump to any conclusions based on incomplete data.

"That's a very interesting comparison, Natalie. To be honest, I'd never looked at things that way before."

Natalie relaxed and smiled.

"But before I say anything," I added, "why don't you tell me what else you found."

"You're right," Natalie continued. "I also looked at other signs about how the economy was doing—income, wages, and wealth.

"And I'd prefer to take this one chart at a time.

"This first one suggests that from 1950 through about 1980, gains in income were shared fairly equally. Not so, since then.

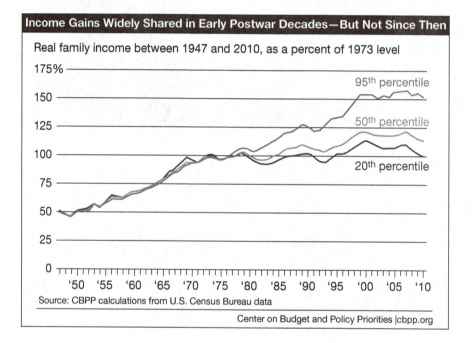

Income Gains Widely Shared in Early Postwar Decades—But Not Since Then

Real family income between 1947 and 2010, as a percent of 1973 level

Source: CBPP calculations from U.S. Census Bureau data

Center on Budget and Policy Priorities |cbpp.org

"This shows that the income gains the top 1% made have dramatically outstripped everyone else's.

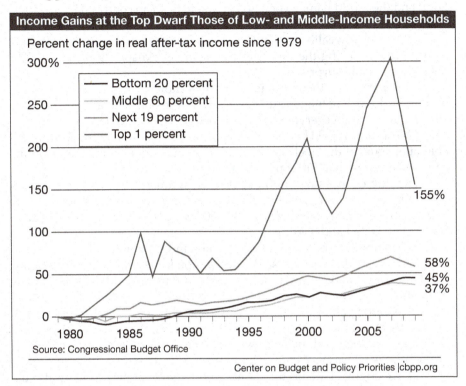

Income Gains at the Top Dwarf Those of Low- and Middle-Income Households

Percent change in real after-tax income since 1979

- Bottom 20 percent
- Middle 60 percent
- Next 19 percent
- Top 1 percent

155%

58%
45%
37%

Source: Congressional Budget Office

Center on Budget and Policy Priorities |cbpp.org

"In fact, throughout the recovery after the meltdown, while the stock market and corporate profits were up over the last few years, wages have been flat. Actually, in terms of the big picture, they've been worse than flat. They've been dropping as a percentage of the economy.

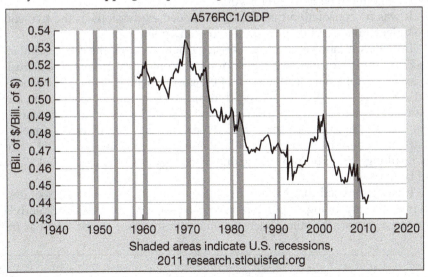

A576RC1/GDP

(Bil. of $/Bill. of $)

Shaded areas indicate U.S. recessions,
2011 research.stlouisfed.org

"And just so that everyone appreciates the practical significance of this increasing inequality, mainstream institutions like the International Monetary Fund and the World Bank recognize that inequality can contribute to a variety of negative consequences in a society.

"I looked at wealth next and, not surprisingly, saw the same pattern of inequality. Paralleling the disparity of income is a disparity of wealth. The details aren't at all surprising.

"Ten percent of the population controls more than 70% of the nation's wealth. And much of that wealth gets passed from one generation to the next. So it's not as though everyone on the Forbes 400 is 'self-made.'

"Most stock is held by a small percentage of the population. The top 10% hold about 80% of the stock and mutual funds. Less than a third of the population owns more than $10,000 in stock.

"So, there's nothing subtle about the numbers. The trends are clear. According to standard markers—GDP, Dow Jones, corporate profits—we've had a strong economy over the last 50 to 60 years. However, the benefits have been concentrated at the very top."

She handed the remote back to Socrates and sat down.

"Excellent job," Socrates said. "But, as you know, this is just our starting point. The facts you've given us are accurate. But from Wendy's point of view, inequality of wealth is not necessarily a bad thing," Socrates replied, surprising me by anticipating exactly what I was about to say. "She's told us that wealth 'trickles down.' If you don't have wealth being invested, the economy will stagnate. There will be no new jobs. Wealthy people need incentives to invest. We keep hearing Wendy refer to them as *job creators*."

"That's right," I interjected. "And don't forget that the economy also has to support a hugely expensive government. A government that has put us all deeply in the red." Turning in my chair toward Natalie and Sergio, I added, "a deficit that your generation will be saddled with all because my generation couldn't exercise a basic level of discipline and good sense. I'm really sorry things are going to be so tough for you."

It was no consolation that the disheartened expressions of the two college students made it clear they understood my point.

But I was stunned at Socrates' derisive laugh. "Ah yes, the *deficit. Fiscal responsibility.* The ox you just love to gore. You've become quite prominent as a business leader championing fiscal reform of the government. Haven't you, Wendy? What's that tag line you use? 'We need to run the government like we run our homes and businesses.' It has a nice ring to it. So tell me, do you enjoy scaring young people? Or do you just enjoy a good *con* so much, you can't help yourself?"

Before I could say anything, Natalie jumped in. "Socrates! That's not only insulting, it's rude. You accuse one of your guests of being a crook? You can't be serious."

I was impressed that Natalie had the confidence to challenge Socrates. And from the approving expression on his face, so was he. "Actually, Wendy's more like a *prisoner*, Natalie," Socrates said with the same smirk. "And as far as whether or not I'm serious, Wendy knows that it doesn't matter. Our time together is to see how she responds to a variety of challenges I'm putting her through. Don't worry. She's tough. She runs marathons."

"Even so," Natalie continued, "you're distorting things. I think she has a point. Income versus expenses. It's not rocket science. You can't run a home or a business if the numbers on the left side are always lower than those on the right."

Socrates looked my way and nodded approvingly. "Wendy, you have not only a fan, but a defender. Well done."

"Left? Right?" interrupted Sergio.

"Assets versus liabilities, sweetie. Standard accounting practice. Haven't you read anything I've given you?" Turning back to Socrates, she said sternly, "I think you owe Ms. Summers an apology."

"Maybe I do. Maybe I don't. That depends on some facts we still haven't looked at that will complete our picture. So, if you will allow me. . . . " He took Natalie's place at the screen and brought up some more slides.

"Because virtually all wealth comes from business, it should come as no surprise that corporate profits have been record-breaking.

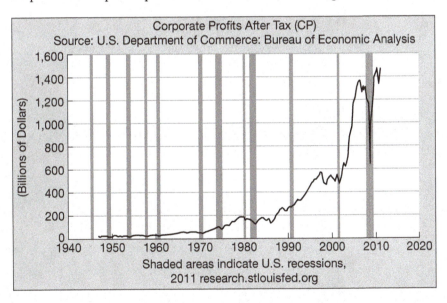

"We've already seen, however, that corporate profits haven't been directed in a way that has increased wages. But maybe there are other ways that the benefits are 'trickling down' and 'floating some boats.' Let's look at 'quality of life.' After all, we've agreed that the 'job' of business is to do its share in supporting the 'kind of life' we want in the village."

As he walked over to the dining room table to grab an apple, Socrates said, "Natalie, how do you think the United States rates in terms of 'quality of life'?"

"I have no doubt that we're at the very top," she replied. "Everything I hear says that we're the richest country on the planet. Who *doesn't* think we're the best country on Earth? That's why so many people want to live here."

"Wendy, do you agree?" he asked me.

"Absolutely. Like any country, we have our problems. We aren't a utopia. But there's nowhere else I'd prefer to live. I agree with Natalie. We're the best country on Earth."

Socrates' self-satisfied expression said I'd just stepped into one of his traps.

23

Business, Ethics, and the Rights of Future Generations—The Economy (continued)

"Best . . . country . . . on . . . Earth," Socrates repeated slowly, as he went back to the screen and brought up another series of windows, one at a time. "We certainly hear Americans say that over and over. Surely, hundreds of millions of people can't be wrong," he said with a studied, flat tone.

He brought up the first slide. "So if we're talking about the best country on Earth, I'm sure that, at the very least, this means that the wealth Natalie has shown us has decreased poverty."

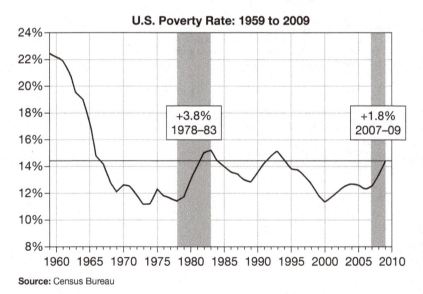

U.S. Poverty Rate: 1959 to 2009

+3.8%
1978–83

+1.8%
2007–09

Source: Census Bureau

Putting his nose millimeters from the screen, he screwed up his face in mock astonishment. "That can't be right. This shows that poverty has *increased* since 2000.

237

"Surely in *the best country on Earth*, poverty would go down, not up," he said in a voice thick with irony. "So I'm sure this chart is wrong. Maybe if we break out the numbers, we'll see what the problem is."

He brought up another one.

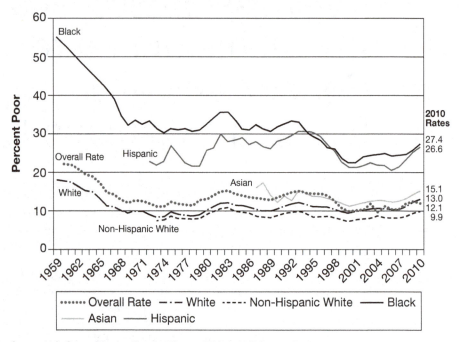

Source: U.S. Census Bureau, Historical Poverty Table 2; 2010 Census Report.
Note: Black poverty rate data from 1960 to 1965 not available. The line shown connects the 1959 rate of 55.1 percent to the 1966 rate of 41.8 percent and is included to represent the trend but not to imply specific numerical data.

"Hmmm. This doesn't help. This chart shows that while poverty among all ethnic groups has gone up, it's risen dramatically among races that have historically been discriminated against. So prosperity isn't cancelling out racial bias.

"And this next one shows that women are more likely to be poor than men.

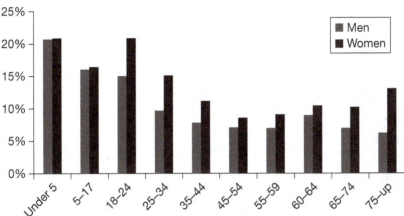

Poverty rates by sex and age

Source: U.S. Census Bureau, *Current Population Survey, 2008 Annual Social and Economic Supplement.*

"So, when wealth at the top goes up, so does poverty, and it's worse in groups who have been discriminated against in the past. That doesn't sound like what should be happening in 'the best country on Earth.' Doesn't make sense, does it?" he asked turning our way.

"Let's look at something else. How about 'quality of life'? We should do well there, shouldn't we?

"Every now and then, *The Economist* generates a 'quality of life index.' Here it is. OK, number one is Switzerland, number two is Australia, then Norway, Sweden, Denmark, Singapore, New Zealand, Netherlands, Canada, Hong Kong, Finland, Ireland, Austria, Taiwan, Belgium, Germany, and tied with Germany for 16th is the United States. *Sixteenth?* Really? Behind all of those quasi-socialistic Scandinavian countries? That also can't be right," he said facetiously.

"Maybe we'll do better on the OECD's 'Better Life Index.' That's about the same as 'quality of life.' If we look at their 'Life Satisfaction' scale, the United States is 14th out of the 36 countries they list. And about the same countries best us there. I always thought the OECD used good data. Apparently, there's a mistake somewhere in there too," he said disingenuously.

"Perhaps we'll do better on the Legatum Prosperity Index. After all, we know we can crank out real *prosperity* in America. OK, that's better. We *are* in the 'high ranking' countries. But we're only 12th."

As Socrates turned around and looked at all of us, it was clear he'd made his point. So he dropped the pretend astonishment. "I trust it's clear that, at least in terms of 'quality of life,' the United States is *not* the best country any more. However, we all have the impression that, for a long time, it used to be. Maybe we can figure out what happened.

"And for that, the first thing we need to do is to see why these other countries rank so much higher. Look at how America compares to the countries higher on the list in terms of tax revenue as percentage of GDP.

NORWAY	42.2
DENMARK	48
SWEDEN	44.3
AUSTRALIA	26.5
NEW ZEALAND	32.9
CANADA	30.7
FINLAND	44.1
NETHERLANDS	38.6
SWITZERLAND	28.2
IRELAND	28.3
LUXEMBOURG	37.8
UNITED STATES	24.3
OECD AVERAGE	34.1

"Every one of them directs more revenue toward taxes. In fact, the United States spends even less than the average of all OECD countries. So that suggests that, at least in those countries, a higher percentage of GDP going to government translates into higher prosperity, satisfaction, and 'quality of life.'

"And that takes us back to Wendy's point about the deficit—because she would probably suggest that the United States has slid from its peak because we've been so fiscally irresponsible. And while I actually agree with that—it doesn't mean what Wendy thinks it does."

Socrates was clearly taunting me, but I decided to wait him out. He brought up his next slide.

"Here we have the cost of government—local, state, and federal—in the United States, which is to say, the infrastructure connected with our village since the Depression. You can see spikes and increases connected with World War Two, Medicare, Iraq, Afghanistan, and the Wall Street bailout. You'll also see that revenues haven't kept pace with expenditures. Maybe Wendy's right. We've spent and borrowed our way into being a second class nation.

Federal, State and Local Government Current Receipts and Expenditures as a Percentage of GDP: 1929–2013

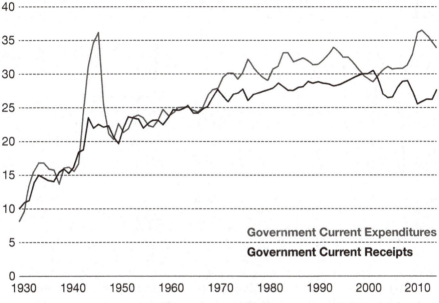

Source: Bureau of Economic Analysis, National Income and Product Accounts Tables. Table 3.1: Government Current Receipts and Expenditures; and Table 1.1.5: Gross Domestic Product.

"But why the shortfall? As Natalie said, it's just about credits and debits. You need to make sure you take in enough to cover your expenses. Why didn't we take in enough?

"Natalie has shown us that the nation's wealth has been concentrating at the top. Maybe we should look, then, at the tax rates for the top tier. The top 20% pay more than 60% of the taxes collected. Is it possible that their tax burden has been steadily increased so much that it's making the economy sluggish and reducing tax revenues overall? No, that's not it—because this next slide shows that the top rate is significantly *lower* than it was 50 years ago.

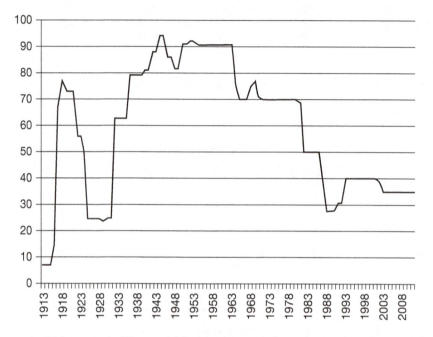

"Also, as we all know, individuals aren't the only taxpayers. Corporations pay too. And this slide shows that another reason for the deficit is that business's contribution as percent of GDP has been going down.

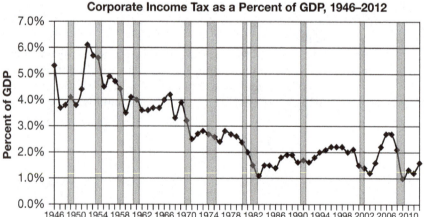

Corporate Income Tax as a Percent of GDP, 1946–2012

Source: Budget of the United States Government, Historical Tables, Table 2.3 Based on Adam Carasso, "The Corporate Income Tax In the Post-War Era," Tax Facts Column, *Tax Notes* Magazine, March 03, 2003.

Notes: Shaded areas represent recessionary periods as recorded by the National Bureau of Economic Research. Miscellaneous taxes such as estate and gift taxes are omitted for the sake of clarity, and comprise a very small fraction of total revenues in any case.

"It looks to me, then, that the best explanation for the shortfall between government expenditures and revenues is exactly what Wendy would suggest—fiscal irresponsibility. But by that *I mean* not taking in enough money from the people and companies that have it while you let them keep more for themselves.

"And in light of the numbers we looked at in connection with the Legatum Prosperity Index, it's no wonder 'quality of life' in the United States has dropped. We're putting a smaller percentage of the wealth generated by the economy into programs designed for the *public* good.

"So, Sergio, I notice that you've been studying these charts carefully and looking serious as Natalie and I have been talking. Any preliminary conclusions? You're the least financially sophisticated person in the room—and I mean that as a compliment because it means you have the fewest ideological biases. From a practical, every day, commonsense perspective, can you draw any conclusions?"

Sergio walked up to the screen and tapped up a few of the charts to review. After a few minutes, he said, "I don't know if I'd say they're definite conclusions without studying things more, but I'm struck by a few things.

"*First.* I can't figure out why, but the economy isn't 'doing its job.' It looks like it produces plenty of wealth, but this doesn't translate into a dependable source of employment and income—or the 'quality of life' such a wealthy 'village' should be providing its members.

"*Next.* I can't believe I'm saying this, but the data are clear. With people who live in so many other countries enjoying a higher 'quality of life,' I would not agree that the United States is 'the best country on Earth.'

"*Third.* Even *I* know it's bad to run in the red. I think the programs the government put in place were all good additions to life in the village. Most of the wars weren't our choice. But you pay your bills. Revenue comes from taxes. So, at least to a simple-minded philosopher like me, it looks like the government didn't hand all of us a big enough bill for 'goods and services provided.' Ms. Summers is right. You should run the government like a business. You pay your bills. Why didn't that happen?

"*Fourth.* It looks like a higher 'quality of life' requires higher tax revenues than we see in the United States.

"*Finally.* If there's so much wealth in the country, and if it's supposed to be 'trickling down,' why isn't it? Where is it going? It doesn't do any good to stuff it under a mattress. I can't tell you how many times I've heard the wealthy referred to as *job creators* or *the makers* and how important it is for the *job creators* not to be overtaxed so they can invest and create jobs. I see plenty of wealth being created. But where are the jobs?"

"Excellent questions," Socrates replied. "We'll get to why we didn't pay our bills shortly. But as to your question of where the money is, lots of it gets moved out of the village—as we see in these headlines. And as Natalie and Wendy will tell you, business is now fundamentally international. Jobs are being created. Just not in our village."

Socrates tapped up a few news stories.

Apple's Web of Tax Shelters Saved It Billions, Panel Finds
G.E.'s Strategies Let It Avoid Taxes Altogether
Biggest Public Firms Paid Little U.S. Tax, Study Says
Facebook Paid No Income Taxes in 2012: A Report
Overseas Cash and the Tax Games Multinationals Play

"Natalie. Why don't you take over again? Serg apparently thinks that business is failing to do its 'job.' But even he admits he's a 'simple-minded philosopher.' You're an international business major. Why don't you explain what he's missing in the way he's reading the 'quality of life' scores?"

Natalie went back to the screen and brought the 'quality of life' slides back up. "I understand some of this. A number of these countries are democracies like us, and maybe they're more progressive in some areas. But I don't understand *this*." She then pointed to the highest ranking countries, "These are all high-tax, semi-socialistic countries. Why are people happier there than here, Ms. Summers?"

I was glad finally to have a chance to add a different perspective. "First, Natalie, be certain that you understand what these numbers mean. Socrates has given us single 'quality of life' scores that take statistics from various aspects of life, combine them, weight them, and give us a final number. Before we can draw any conclusions, we'd need to know much more about how those indices are constructed. In a situation like this, our host isn't exactly our most trustworthy source of information."

Socrates smiled, obviously approving of my warning to Natalie that she needs to be suspect of any data until she analyzed it—even if it came from him.

"Second, let's ask what those lists probably *don't* take into account. Take a look at those countries again, and tell me what new industries they've created lately. What inventions have changed our lives? Unless I'm missing something, you don't hit a truly innovative, powerhouse economy until you get to the United States. I'm not saying that the rest of the world are free-riders, but it's the United States that has invented most of the goods, services, and technologies that make their lives so comfortable. With less of our GDP going to taxes, U.S. entrepreneurs and corporations have been able to afford to take risks. We enjoy greater freedom that ultimately benefits everyone else on the planet through the creativity that this enables.

"In a word, what these scales don't measure is the *freedom* that capitalism in America gives us."

"If you've started down that road, it feels decidedly unpatriotic of me to interrupt you," Socrates said, "but don't you mean *increased economic opportunities for people with capital*, and not *freedom*?"

"Now you're splitting hairs again. It's economic opportunities that *produce* freedom."

"You're getting ahead of yourself," Socrates cautioned. "Economic opportunities *can* produce freedom. It's not inevitable. This is the same mistake you made before."

I was about to reply when Socrates held up his hand signaling he wanted me to wait. Then he walked over to the bookcase and pulled out an old, green paperback version of Milton Friedman's *Capitalism and Freedom*.

He tossed me the book. "Let's see what The Bible says." Then he walked to the screen and called up some slides he'd already prepared. They were quotations from Friedman. He read them off.

> Our minds tell us, and history confirms, that the great threat to freedom is concentration of power. Government is necessary to preserve our freedom, it is an instrument through which we can exercise our freedom; yet by concentrating power in political hands, it is also a threat to freedom. . . . How can we benefit from the promise of government while avoiding the threat of freedom? . . . First, the scope of government must be limited. . . . [Second,] government power must be dispersed.
>
> . . .
>
> Viewed as a means to the end of political freedom, economic arrangements are important because of their effect on the concentration or dispersion of power. The kind of economic organization that provides economic freedom directly, namely, competitive capitalism, also promotes political freedom because it separates economic power from political power and in this way enables the one to offset the other.

"The book isn't called *Capitalism and Freedom* for nothing. Friedman argues that by separating economic from political power, we promote total freedom overall. He doesn't say, 'capitalism is good because it gives us *stuff*.' He says it's good because it protects and fosters *freedom*."

I was puzzled why Socrates thought this contradicted me. "Exactly. That's what I just said. That's why we need to keep political power restrained. That's why we need a small government and a robust economy. That's why you want a smaller percentage of the GDP going to taxes. Otherwise, the government will get so big, it will dictate the terms of our lives to us and ignore the will of the villagers. Friedman was right. That's why we need a counterweight to political power."

"I agree," Socrates said to my surprise. "Concentrations of power are dangerous. A free economy is an excellent way to offset political power. *However*, we also need a counterweight to concentrations of *economic* power—the kind of concentrations that get used to shape laws and policies in the interest of people with that power. You don't spend time on the Hill to help the villagers get the 'kind of life' they want. You do it to accumulate wealth—which, in our society, means power—for your industry and clients.

"Any free market capitalist who is a true champion of freedom in all of its forms should be the sworn enemy of *any* concentration of power—political or economic. Anyone who embraces economic freedom as a vehicle for amassing wealth but turns a blind eye when the resulting economic power is used to suppress the freedom of other people in the village is a hypocrite at best—and a traitor to the cause of freedom, at worst."

I was sure that Socrates' use of *traitor* was deliberate overstatement. How could free market capitalism and the pursuit of profit foster anything *but* freedom?

"But that's why we have anti-trust laws," I responded. "That's why we have the Federal Trade Commission, the Securities and Exchange Commission, and the Department of Justice. They're supposed to take action against monopolies and anti-competitive practices. That's how we keep the market free and fair."

"True. But, once again, you aren't looking at enough of the picture," Socrates argued. "What about protecting the freedom of the average person? Frankly, you've been on the wrong side of that cause more than once. You'll go to the mat to protect wealth; less so for a villager."

"For a comment that serious, I hope you're prepared to back it up," I said with a glare.

"You surprise me, Wendy. Didn't we just spend a significant amount of time talking about your support of your client the gun manufacturer? In your conversations on The Hill, didn't you weigh in *against* gun legislation that more than 90% of the American public was in favor of? That didn't strike you as an abuse of power by the industry in a *democracy*? Haven't you regularly argued for lower budgets for the very federal agencies you just praised? So if you got your way, there'd be even less strict enforcement of laws meant to protect everyone. Even now, you oppose every attempt to rein in the abuses in your own industry—despite the harm that came from such little regulation.

"Some people might argue that by ensuring a higher percentage of the GDP going to taxes, a country is going to be in a better position to foster the *public good—the good of the village* and the good of the vast majority of villagers. Maybe that's why the 'quality of life' is perceived to be higher in other countries."

"But Ms. Summers made a good point that you're overlooking, Socrates," Natalie said, coming to my defense. "Business is international. We need to look at the big picture. Maybe we need to look at the planet as one big village."

"Excellent point, Natalie" praised Socrates. "So let's ask Wendy to explain it to us. After all, I'm still waiting to be told why I should believe 'a rising tide floats all boats' and 'wealth trickles down and creates jobs' when all the evidence I see says something very different."

"Very well. It's actually pretty simple," I explained. "When a corporation can operate across nations, it's able to take advantage of lower costs for labor and materials, and to sell products to more markets. Everyone benefits.

"People who before had no job or a very low paying job now have a decent wage. They can spend that money to have a better 'quality of life.' Their local economy strengthens and expands, and the benefits flow throughout that country. Business is doing its 'job' by letting people get the 'kind of life' they want."

"But what about the villagers whose jobs got shipped to these new areas?" Socrates asked. "They aren't benefitting."

"Maybe not in the short term. But they'll have to adapt. No one ever said that everyone deserves a cushy life. You have to work for it. Local and national economies will change over time. The United States, for example, started mainly as an agricultural economy; it grew into manufacturing; now it's very much a service and a knowledge economy. We have new opportunities developing all the time. People who lose a job in one part of the economy will have to learn the skills needed to get a new one in a developing sector."

"In theory, that makes sense," Socrates replied. "*However*, Natalie, tell Wendy about your grandmother's career."

I could see from Natalie's face—and from the fact that she wasn't looking up from the floor—that this was not going to be happy story.

"Gran was always a pioneer. She was one of the few women in her engineering school. Then she worked for a NASA contractor on the space program. When money dried up for space exploration, she was let go. She had a tough couple of years, but was able to find her way into an entry level IT job—for a lot less money. Things went really well until the work was moved offshore. Finally, she was able to get another IT job at a company that specialized in work for banks. As soon as the meltdown hit, she was let go. She can't even get any interviews now. The real reason is that people think she's too old and too expensive. What they say is, 'It's just not a good fit.' She has a Ph.D., helped put people on the moon, and now she's a barista to supplement her pension and social security." Natalie looked at me and said seriously, "It's not supposed to work that way. Gran never asked for a handout. She always worked really hard. She paved the way for lots of women engineers and put up with tons of crap from the guys. She sacrificed like crazy so that my mother and uncle could go to college. And this is the reward she gets? It's just not right."

Socrates apparently was feeling generous and got me off the hook. "We'd all agree it's not right, Natalie. That's why we're having this discussion. We're all hoping that Wendy will help us change things in the future."

However, his generosity was short-lived.

"But let's remember that we're asking whether taking a broader view will let us see more of the benefits. So let's look more closely at the advantages the developing countries get.

"People there get jobs but at wages which are, by international standards, low.

"Companies set up shop in countries with labor and environmental regulations which aren't especially strict, which means there may be some health consequences down the road for those who live there.

"Major corporations decide to outsource to local vendors, which stimulates the local economy but protects the company from liability.

"Countries are willing to set up repositories for e-waste to handle the toxic trash from the developed countries, so more health concerns.

"Oh, and let's not forget that many of the countries we're talking about don't score well on Transparency International's Corruption Perception

Index—China, India, Bangladesh, Vietnam, Mexico—which means that the 'rule of law' isn't what it should be.

"How is this anything else but a 'race to the bottom'?

"Take the collapse of that clothing factory in Bangladesh that killed more than 1,000 people. Now here's an interesting coincidence, Wendy," he said sarcastically. "One of your client companies was one of their customers. And what did the CEO say? 'Our hearts go out to the families, and we will do everything we can do to see that nothing like this ever happens again. But our lawyers tell us that taking too aggressive a stand will create an unacceptable risk of litigation.' And then the company refused to join with an initiative launched by a consortium of EU garment industry companies to take concrete action.

"There had been accidents before that killed people there. But the economic power of the industry had been used only to increase profitability—even though it was obvious that workers' lives were at risk. The economic power of the industry certainly wasn't used to protect the *freedom* of the workers who were forced to go back into that building and die."

Socrates paused and turned to Sergio. "Serg, let's use that great memory of yours again. I've lost my train of thought. Where are we?" Sergio closed his eyes and thought for a minute.

"First, Natalie and you challenged Ms. Summers' claim that wealth benefits everyone else in the economy. 'A rising tide floats all boats.' Natalie's graphs and charts showed that when we look at the last 50 or 60 years, we see a strong economy with the benefits going mainly to the top. If you weren't part of the top tier, employment was dicey, and wages were flat at best. Inequality has grown in the United States. Ten percent of the population controls 70% of the nation's wealth.

"At this point," Sergio chuckled, "the issue of the cost of the government and the deficit came up, so we paused while you accused your guest of participating in a con. Natalie took you to task for being rude.

"When we got back on track, you pointed out that the increase in corporate profits was matched by an increase in poverty. You also showed that, in terms of 'quality of life,' the United States is *much* lower in world ranking than most Americans probably think. Your snarky comment about corporate profits going up while corporate taxes have been dropping suggests that you think companies aren't paying their share of the costs of a better 'quality of life.'

"When you finally gave Ms. Summers a chance to say something, she talked about how your 'quality of life' numbers didn't take into account the freedom the U.S. economy fosters. You replied by trotting out Milton Friedman to say that the current state of affairs constitutes a dangerous concentration of power—economic power—that threatens freedom. And even though developing countries do get lots of benefits from multinationals setting up operations there, you suggested that the companies are getting a much better deal than the countries are because 'the village' and 'the villagers' don't get the type of protections you typically find in developed nations. You definitely intimated that they're taking advantage of the fact that these countries have a significant level of corruption."

Sergio opened his eyes. "How'd I do?"

"Perfect!" Socrates said.

"Ms. Summers. Did I miss anything?" Sergio asked.

"Only that—as we all know—the Grand Inquisitor very likely has at least one more insult up his sleeve."

"See, I told you she was sharp. Wendy may be wrong a lot," Socrates winked and laughed, "but she doesn't miss much."

He looked at his watch and then texted something into his phone.

"It's time to wrap this up, since we still have one more topic to cover. You're right, Wendy, I do have something else up my sleeve. But it's not an *insult*, it's a *question* for you to ponder. With climate change, Sergio got to ask it. This time, it's Natalie's turn. Actually, because Natalie was so thrilled to meet you, I told her she could leave you with two questions. Natalie?"

"When Socrates told me about this, Ms. Summers, he said you liked challenging questions. He also said that you're probably going to end up as the CEO of a major multinational corporation, and so I should come up with, as he put it, *'really big questions.'*"

"Socrates is right, Natalie. I like 'off the wall,' *big* questions. Fire away."

"The first one is the simpler of the two. To be blunt, if we look at just the U.S. economy over the last 50 years or so, I honestly don't think that average people in the village are benefitting. Wealth is being concentrated at the top and we're becoming a more unequal society. My first question is: If you still think 'wealth trickles down,' what's your evidence?

"My second question is going to take a bit for me to work up to. So please bear with me.

"As an international business major, I'm a strong proponent of globalization and helping developing countries get a chance at the kind of life we've been lucky enough to have. But at the same time, I see that for lots of multinationals, the decision about where to locate operations is nothing more than the way Socrates put it—a 'race to the bottom.' Which country has the lowest wages? Who has the least strict environmental laws? Who has laws that look good but doesn't enforce them? Who has weak rules for workplace safety? I'm sure no one puts things this way. They probably ask, 'Which country is most business-friendly?' But it amounts to the same thing. It seems to me that as soon as countries get to the point where they want to put in stricter labor or environmental laws, multinationals threaten to move operations. And sometimes they actually do, because it's more profitable elsewhere. It's the same thing that happens in the United States when a company threatens to move from one state to another to avoid some new regulation.

"At the same time, it should come as no surprise that I'm also a strong believer in what Socrates keeps referring to as the 'job of business.' I think that business should make it possible for people to get a good life—and that means things like health, safety, justice, fairness, being treated with respect, and people being willing to take care of each other. And if a company is compromising those things for profit, then I think it's a bad business because it's not doing its job.

"When I look at multinationals, I see entities that have now become, in many ways, more powerful than individual countries. Many multinationals are wealthier than lots of nations, and they use that wealth to play one country off against another to get a better deal. So it looks to me that since so many multinationals operate as though they have only one goal—profit—they're turning out to be a huge threat to anything that can get in the way of that. I mean compassion, fairness, freedom, respect, equality, and the like—everything connected with what it means to me to treat people ethically. Sergio and I want to feel that our children will live in a world that will get better. Multinationals may champion *profits* and *stuff*. But, frankly, I don't see them as champions of ethics.

"So here's my question. If you end up as the CEO of a major multinational, are you willing to make a solemn promise that you won't do that? Will you refuse to participate in anything that looks like a race to the bottom?"

"Are you sure about that, Natalie?" Socrates asked. "Because if Wendy says 'yes,' she'll risk ending up with an astonishingly short tenure if her board decides she's too radical and boots her out."

"You said I could ask her anything. She can always say 'no.'"

"Those are appropriately big and fair questions, Natalie. I promise that I will give you thoughtful answers. And I truly appreciate the challenge." I responded.

"*And . . . ,*" Socrates added as we were all about to get out of our chairs to stretch, "I've decided that I'd like to add yet another question for you to consider. For the sake of argument, let's say that the wealth that has been accumulating in the hands of a small percentage of villagers ultimately goes to create jobs and a better way of life elsewhere on the planet. You'd probably defend this by invoking Mill and saying that this produces such high quality good in the lives of people in developing countries that it outweighs any inconvenience—even harm—felt by people in a country like America, even when they go through hard economic times. However, you've made it clear that you're a champion of free market capitalism. Your strongest allegiance is to *freedom*.

"So here's *my* question. In our original conversation back in your office, we agreed that if we were truly going to respect the freedom of everyone involved, the 'rules of the game' in how the village operated are that everyone would have to agree to the 'terms of the deal.' Remember that we even worked with John Rawls' 'veil of ignorance' exercise. Do you honestly think that any villager would freely agree to a system that created astonishing amounts of wealth and economic power for a small percentage of the villagers as long as some of it was used to create benefits for *other* villages, but that the price would be paid in terms of the 'kind of life' *our* village was organized for in the first place? Wouldn't that simply be crazy?"

24

Business, Ethics, and Ideology

"We've all been sitting in one place for too long," Socrates announced. "So we'll cover our last topic while we're moving. Wendy went for a run earlier today, but the rest of us haven't come close to the 5,000 to 10,000 steps we should take each day. Colin," Socrates said into the intercom, "we're going for a walk on the beach. Please have everything ready when we return."

"Understood, sir."

I appreciated the change of location for our last chat. I'm not one of those CEOs who sequesters herself in her office all day. I like to be visible, and I try to make contact with different employees each day. So being cooped up wasn't my style. It was also a beautiful day. Blue sky. Light wind. Azure ocean. A pod of dolphins was even slowly cruising our way.

I wanted to make sure Socrates didn't take the initiative, so as soon as we all got into a rhythm along the beach, I turned to him and said, "If this is our final chat, I assume you're going to explain those bizarre bombshells you've been lobbing into the conversation. Culture war. Class struggle. Con?"

"Yes and no."

"You're going to remain as annoying as ever up until the bitter end, aren't you?"

"I certainly hope so," he replied smugly. "But seriously, I promise we'll get to the other ethical issues I want us to look at. First, however, we need to discuss intellectual perspectives."

"Perspectives?"

"Well, there are lots of ways we could talk about this. Intellectual frameworks. Perspectives. Points of view. Fundamental assumptions. Intellectual contexts. Filters. Ideologies. But they all amount to the same thing—some sort of system of beliefs or assumptions that give significance to facts. Facts get their significance from the perspective through which they are viewed. Facts are *not* necessarily neutral. If you change the perspective, a 'fact' can mean something very different," he said. "So we need to talk about how the *economic* facts we've been looking at can mean different things depending on the perspective we take."

I groaned and shook my head wearily. For a final topic, I was hoping for something lighter.

"I don't suppose you'd care to enlighten us with a simple example?" I asked.

"Sergio," Socrates said, "you're a philosophy major. How about it? Something we can see right now would be ideal."

Sergio stopped and looked around. Then, he pointed at the dolphins leaping in the waves. "I want each of you to tell me what you see. In fact, I want the three of you to see if you can agree on the facts, so that you have unanimity."

Natalie immediately said, "I see happy, playful dolphins. I just love the way they're always smiling. I bet they're having the best time."

As one of the dolphins leapt high, we all went "Ooo . . . ahh" in admiration.

"I agree," I said. "They're playing." Another dolphin did a similar leap. "Maybe they're seeing who can jump the highest."

"Far be it for me to add a cynical note," Socrates chimed in. "I agree. Happy, playful dolphins."

We all turned to a smiling Sergio and waited for him to tell us how observant we'd been.

"Exactly what I expected. Exactly what I wanted to hear because you're all completely *wrong*."

"Wrong? No!" Socrates said. "I see this pod of dolphins all the time. It always makes me feel so optimistic to see them having so much fun. It reminds me not to take things too seriously. How can you say we're wrong?"

Now it was Sergio's turn to be smug.

"First, you didn't give me *facts*; you gave me *inferences*. The *facts* are that you saw a few dolphins leaping about 2 meters in the air. And they're bottle-nose dolphins—*Tursiops truncatus*." He glanced at Natalie. "The species will matter, Nat, so don't give me that 'you're always being so picky' look.

"You all *inferred* they were *happy* and *playing*. Why did you draw that conclusion?"

Sergio had made an interesting observation about what the three of us had done, so I wanted to hear more. "For me, at least, I said *happy* because of the expression on their faces. The way they're always smiling. Why *playful*? Probably because I've heard for years that dolphins like to play and surf for fun. You know, Flipper, SeaWorld, and all of that. That's certainly the image of them I've gotten over the years. Dolphins are happy, playful, and love to do tricks for us. And I don't hear any snarling or growling or any other sounds that contradict the impression that they're having a good time."

"Thank you, Ms. Summers." Sergio turned toward Natalie and Socrates. "Same reasons for the two of you? You watched the dolphins. 'The facts just spoke for themselves'? And you saw *happy* and *playful?*"

Socrates nodded as Natalie said, "Right. The facts spoke for themselves."

"But what actually happened was you processed your observations of the dolphins through certain assumptions—*largely false* assumptions. That dolphins are happy, playful mammals. That they have 'faces' that convey their emotional states. That the 'expression' on their face means the same thing it does on humans. That seeing individual dolphins jump up out of the water for no apparent reason probably means the same thing it would if a human child did the same thing . . . *playing.*"

I was more than a little surprised at being told the three of us had mis-read the situation. I'd always loved watching dolphins play in the ocean. I loved watching them at SeaWorld. I loved the image I had of dolphins so much, I hesitated to ask why we were wrong. But I really wanted to know. "OK, Sergio," I conceded, "we were all wrong. Tell us what we *are* looking at. And then explain how we missed it."

"First, without being able to see beneath the surface, I can't know for cer-tain what's going on. And that's very important to realize, because when you watch dolphins from the surface, you can't tell much. However, my educated guess would be they're probably having sex. Dolphins are . . . "

"Wait!" I interrupted. "You think they're having *sex? Dolphins?*"

I could tell from the look on Sergio's face this was exactly the reaction he was expecting. "Most people don't know, Ms. Summers, that dolphins are sig-nificantly more sexual than humans. They're naturally bisexual. Sex appears to play a major role in affirming relationships of all sorts. But some sexual contact is decidedly aggressive. The average dolphin probably has a number of sexual encounters of one sort or another every day. And it can look like this from the surface. I doubt they told you that at SeaWorld," he added with a laugh.

"Because these dolphins are *Tursiops*," he continued, "it's also possible this may just be some sort of aggressive interaction. A leap like that could mean one dolphin is trying to get away from another, and *Tursiops* are defi-nitely more aggressive than some other species of dolphin. That's *also* some-thing you probably were never told.

"So, whatever these dolphins are doing, it definitely doesn't look like lighthearted *play* to me.

"And as far as the *happy* goes, their 'facial expression' means nothing. They don't have 'faces' like primates do—with all of those muscles that we manipulate in a way that signals our emotional state. Dolphins aren't *smiling.* Their heads look that way from millions of years of evolution. It's strictly hydrodynamics and efficiency in feeding."

"So everything you're telling us is known and documented by marine scientists?" I asked.

"Absolutely. This is old news. Dolphins are complex beings. Their 'public image'—which is promoted mainly by businesses, by the way—is only partially true. But let's face it, if you want to use dolphins to make money, 'happy and playful' sells better than 'randy bullies.' "

"I knew you did work on environmental studies," Socrates said, "but I didn't know that included marine mammals. Very impressive, Serg, and a perfect example for the phenomenon we're exploring. Why don't you continue and complete the explanation for us? You told us *what* we're actually looking at. But Wendy also asked *how* we got it so wrong."

"Once you distinguish facts from presuppositions, something like this is easy to see. To draw the correct conclusions from your observations, you need to make sure that your presuppositions are true, or at least likely. The three of you, however, used false presuppositions. For example, if we had the time and I led you step by step, I could get you to see that you made the following assumptions: 'a dolphin has a face equivalent to that of a human and signals emotions in the same way'; 'the expression on a dolphin's face signals happiness'; 'apparently purposeless activity is play'; 'dolphins frequently engage in play.'

"When you viewed the facts before your eyes—dolphins leaping, the dolphins' facial expression—it seemed logical to conclude as you did. You conclusion was valid. But because your premises were false, your argument was unsound.

"And those are simply the assumptions you made about *dolphins*. Then there are the ones you made about *humans and nonhuman animals* without even knowing it. 'Humans are unique and special.' 'Humans are more intelligent than any other being on the planet.' 'The world is divided into humans and animals.' 'There's nothing wrong with owning animals.' 'Humans get to say how animals should be treated.' 'Humans own and run the planet.' If I asked you, for example, whether it would be OK for us to capture those dolphins and do research on them, those—also largely false assumptions—would have come into play."

Getting the feeling that all my former ideas about dolphins were probably wrong, I asked Sergio to continue. "Just out of curiosity, how do you know so much about dolphins, and what presuppositions should we have made about the ones in front of us?"

"I had the good fortune of spending last summer on a research boat in the Bahamas, observing the work of a scientist who has been studying a community of spotted dolphins for decades. We observed dolphin social behavior while we were in the water with them, so I got to see what went on beneath the surface. And because there are bottlenose dolphins in the area, I could see the contrast between the species. I also spent a lot of time on the boat reading the research on dolphins' emotional and intellectual abilities, as well as a book and some articles about the philosophical implications of the empirical research. I was stunned to discover that there's been scientific evidence for decades showing that dolphins have an *individual* consciousness of the same sort we do. Given their emotional and intellectual sophistication, their rich social life, and strong relationships with each other, I don't think there's any way that treating them as property—never mind killing or harming them—is ethically defensible. For years, there's been a great deal of data that supports the idea that dolphins qualify as *nonhuman persons*. They are self-aware, have personalities, solve problems, think abstractly, communicate with each other, have complex social lives, treat others appropriately. They're not human, but they are *persons*. And it's wrong to treat a *person*—no matter what their race, sex, or species—like an object and as a piece of property.

"The ideas most people have about dolphins are either only partially true or simply false. Even many marine mammal scientists don't fully appreciate the philosophical significance of dolphins' intellectual, emotional, and social sophistication. Science progresses by inches, not in leaps and bounds, so it will be a while before even all of the scientific community recognizes how dolphins should be treated. Look at how long it took even scientists to stop defending racial and gender superiority.

"And, meaning no disrespect Ms. Summers, but if companies making millions of dollars from dolphins can keep the general public thinking that dolphins are the equivalent of the Lassies of the sea and love doing tricks for us, don't you think they will? If the companies involved wanted to make their decisions based on the most progressive science, they'd realize that they needed to end captivity. What does it tell you that they don't tell the public everything known about the dolphins in their facilities?"

Socrates apparently saw that Sergio was just getting going on a favorite topic of his, so he stepped in to redirect the conversation.

"I'm sure, Serg, that Wendy would be happy to talk about this with you sometime later. But remember that I just asked you for an example about 'perspectives' or 'frameworks' that we could use as a point of departure for further discussion of the economy."

"Right. Sorry about that."

As we left the dolphins and headed down the beach, Socrates redirected the conversation.

"So, facts don't take on any significance until they're viewed from a particular perspective. And my point about cons, culture wars, and class struggles is that the apparently neutral economic data we gather can tell very different stories, depending on which framework, perspective, or ideology we use.

"You, Wendy, have been looking at the economy through only one lens—and a lens that makes it look like things are working well. Correct?"

"Yes. We've had our ups and downs. That's the nature of a market economy. But we have a high standard of living. A good, albeit not perfect, track record on jobs. People who work hard get rewarded with wealth. When they invest that money, it creates jobs. The more freedom we give people and companies in the economy, the more *makers* and *job creators* we get. I believe that it really does work out well for everyone in the long run. And the more we can stimulate developing economies, the better people in those countries will do. What's wrong with freedom and prosperity?"

"Ah, spoken like a true believer," Socrates said with sardonic smile. "It's a *religion* for you, Wendy—and for people like you. And it's based on a *creed*—a series of beliefs—not statements of fact. You all think you're pragmatists, hard-nosed empiricists—when in reality you're fervent disciples of the Church of the Free Market who look at the world through the equivalent of a theology. And before you get insulted, realize that I'm trying to help you see something that you very much need to see if you're going to step into this next job. You will be dealing with people from countries with very different ideologies about business. So you have to understand that you're bringing one of your own to the table."

Socrates was right to ask me to wait until I reacted. I was tired of his repeated, condescending remarks. But if his observations could actually help me in this next job, I at least wanted to hear him out. I was also painfully aware that whether or not I got the job was entirely in his hands.

When I looked in his direction to respond, I saw him give a quick wink to Natalie. He must have told her he was going to try to provoke me now and then. I was glad I hadn't taken the bait.

"I see you have no shortage of metaphors to annoy people with—business as part of a con, class war, now religion. I'll give you this. You aren't dull or predictable. So, if I'm a true believer, what's the *creed*?"

"That was actually another part of Natalie's homework," Socrates replied, motioning to the young woman that she should move to the front of our pack. "As you gather, Sergio has a talent with epistemology. Natalie understands business. I asked her to see what she could learn from him in identifying unstated assumptions. You've already ticked off a number of core beliefs for us. Let's see how that compares with Natalie's list. Nat?"

The young woman took out a small blue notebook from her pocket like the one Socrates always seemed to have at the ready.

"I should confess that I wrote up a list of core beliefs before I did the research Socrates asked me to do about the economy. I thought they were so obvious, it would be faster to do things this way. I didn't even see any reason to talk to Serg at that point. But after looking at the data, I was so disappointed with what I found that I talked to Serg about uncovering assumptions, went back, and made up a new list. Maybe I got carried away, Ms. Summers. I want to make sure you don't feel insulted."

"Natalie, Socrates asked you to do something perfectly reasonable. And I'm the last person who wants to make decisions based on false beliefs. So, please, tell me what you came up with. And I think it's time for you to call me 'Wendy.' You too, Serg. Stop calling me 'Ms. Summers.' "

Seeming more confident with my encouragement, Natalie explained, "I simply call this the 'Business Creed.' " She handed me the notebook, and I read down her list.

- Above all else, wealth is sacred.
- Wealth is a sign of superior intelligence, talent, good character, integrity, and hard work. If you're rich, you deserve it.
- The wealthy are the job creators, the makers. They're responsible for virtually everything good in society.
- If you work hard, you'll succeed. Everyone has the same chance for success.

- You earn what you deserve. If you end up poor, you're lazy, untalented, stupid, or a freeloader.
- Selfishness, greed, and envy are virtues. The 'invisible hand' will manage things so it all works out for the good of all.
- Capitalism is morally superior to every other economic system. Socialism and communism are evil.
- Capitalism and private wealth are the bulwark against government tyranny. Capitalism promotes freedom.
- Private ownership of property is sacred. It is always wrong to tell someone what to do with something they own.
- Competition is better than cooperation.
- Prosperity at the top of the economy will inevitably produce prosperity throughout the society. Prosperity trickles down. A rising tide floats all boats. When businesses do well, people do well.
- Business is intrinsically good; government is intrinsically bad. Business is always more efficient than government. Government's most important role is to make it easier to do business because this will benefit everyone.
- The sole goal of a business is to make money.
- In a business, nothing is more important than maximizing shareholder return.
- As long as businesses obey the laws of the host country and maximize shareholder return, all will be well.
- Newer products are always better. There's nothing wrong with buying a new product and throwing away an older one that still works.
- It is better to borrow money for something you want and have it now than to wait until you can afford it.
- It is good to want more. There is no such thing as "enough."
- You are what you have.
- "Bettering yourself" means making more money.
- We have a sacred duty to bring the free market and the opportunity to have the same material comforts we have to developing nations because this will dramatically improve their lives.
- The person who dies with the most stuff wins."

When I finished, I handed the notebook to Socrates. He read through the list a couple of times. "Interesting and provocative. A shade more cynical than I would have expected, but interesting nonetheless."

"I'm curious, Natalie," I asked. "Why did you think this would insult me? It's true that you're a little extreme here and there. But, on balance, I don't have a lot of problems with this."

Natalie hesitated.

"Natalie, friends give friends bad news."

"OK. Before I began looking at the data, I believed what I've heard from my business school professors. Capitalism. The free market. The 'invisible hand.' Wealth trickles down. Self-interest. Wanting more, more, more. All of this is *good*, because this is the path to freedom and prosperity. Government, regulation, and taxes, on the other hand, are all *bad*—or at least suspect. My teachers do talk a lot about 'stakeholders.' But in the end that sounds like PR fluff, because it's always ROI, quarterly profits, and 'maximizing share-holder value' that trump everything else.

"When I looked at the data, the facts spoke for themselves. The problem with the Business Creed is that, in my opinion, the beliefs in the Business Creed are simply false."

Counting things off on her fingers, she ticked off what she meant.

"Wealth doesn't trickle down. It's collecting at the top.

"Worse than that, at the same time, the average American family is getting *poorer*. In the last 10 years, the average American family's net worth dropped by more than a third!

"The *job creators* aren't creating jobs—at least not here.

"The individuals and corporations who benefit the most aren't paying their fair share.

"We tell ourselves we live in the best country on the planet, but the data don't bear that out.

"It's crazy to think that greed and selfishness are good. That's what motivates criminals.

"As far as the idea of our doing developing countries a favor by exporting our way of life is concerned, I think the skyrocketing rates of diabetes, obesity, and heart disease that came with their Westernized version of 'prosperity' suggest something different. Look at India and China. We've gotten them so convinced that development is the way to go that New Delhi and Beijing have terrible air quality—and they aren't even the worst on the planet. How can it make any sense to say that *wealth* is more important than *health*?

"By the time I got to the end of my research, this just looked like a giant con to me."

"Wait," I interrupted, astonished. "*You* came up with the idea it's a con? Not Socrates?" I looked back and forth between the two of them. "*Him*, I could understand. He'll say anything to get a rise out of people. But, Natalie, how could you come to a ridiculous conclusion like that? The system isn't perfect, but a *con*?"

Socrates was clearly enjoying how stunned I was that *Natalie* came up with the con metaphor.

"To be fair to Natalie, I should explain something," he said. "When she told me that she found the conclusions of her research so disenchanting, I told her that—simply as an exercise in understanding how facts can suggest very different conclusions depending on the framework or perspective we view them through—she should try out a radically different perspective. I told her the more outrageous the better. So I nudged her in that direction."

"Just *nudged*?" I asked, skeptically.

"The point is that it's a surprisingly good fit," Socrates chuckled.

"So are you serious in saying that you—a very successful VC—and I—a CEO of a major financial services company—are part of some sort of elaborate con and we don't even realize it? Or are you just saying something outrageous to test my reaction?"

"That's a fair question," he replied. "But what I actually think is irrelevant. For now, I'm just claiming that *when looked at through a particular filter*, the facts support the idea that we're involved in a con. Remember, the point of this exercise is to help you to be more objective about economic policy and recognize the ethical implications of some of your business decisions."

Seeing me bristle at the insult, Socrates looked at me seriously.

"The saddest thing, however, is that you don't even realize you're running a con. You and your colleagues are blinded by an ideology that has you convinced you're part of a system that truly benefits everyone in the village. That was the point of asking Natalie to identify the central beliefs of the 'religion.' You're so convinced they're true that your 'faith' blinds you to what the facts really show."

Socrates stopped walking and turned to the rest of us. "Everybody find a comfortable spot in the sand and let me explain how this particular con operates."

25

Business, Ethics, and Ideology (continued)

Socrates sat down on the beach and crossed his legs. It was no surprise that the way he was settling in told me that, as usual, his explanation wasn't going to be a short one.

" 'Con' is short for 'confidence game.' The way a 'con' works is that a 'mark' is manipulated so that the 'con artist' or 'grifter' wins their confidence. The con typically gets going when the grifter acts in a way that shows he or she *trusts the mark*. When the mark reciprocates that trust, the grifter wins. The most complicated cons are 'long cons'—they take a while to set up but have large rewards. They are often legal. The best ones are like a work of art," Socrates said enthusiastically.

As I looked over at Sergio and Natalie, I saw we all had the same expression—more than a little surprise at the admiration Socrates apparently had for this type of crime.

"Oh, come on!" he said. "I construct deals all the time. How can I *not* admire a good con. Admit it, Wendy. Sometimes what we do is awfully close to conning people—if not definitely on the other side of the line, from an ethical perspective. But since I don't want you to self-incriminate in front of our young friends here, let me continue.

"The mechanics of a long con are surprisingly straightforward, given how complicated the setup can be.

"You need a 'hook' to draw in 'the mark.' Let's say it's a phony investment scam where you promise big returns fast.

"You draw a mark in deeper by giving them 'a convincer' in which they get something from you. They make a small investment and it pays off handsomely. This makes them feel they can trust you, the deal is legitimate, and they're winning. And they *are* winning, because at this point, they're actually ahead in the game.

"But the 'sting' comes when they come back for more. You persuade them to make a big investment. But this time they lose. If a grifter is smart, he can even think of ways to keep the mark on the hook for more than one score. 'There was a last minute glitch.' 'In a fluke, the deal lost money, but next time will be different. I swear.' In fact, the con I'm talking about is so impressive because it has an amazingly long life.

"Every con has a name. Some of the most famous: the fiddle game, the Spanish prisoner, three-card monte, the Thai gem scam, the wire. So, what shall we call this one?" Socrates leaned back and closed his eyes in thought. "I think '*The Sheriff of Nottingham*'!," he said with a glint in his eye. "After all, this con is all about stealing from the poor and giving to the rich. Actually, it's about stealing from almost *everyone* and giving to the rich, but let's not split hairs. What's important is that when our marks are being fleeced, they're being told that 'prosperity is just around the corner.'"

I groaned at Socrates' enthusiasm for portraying me and my colleagues as criminals.

"So, everyone, we go back to the village, where Wendy is opening her shoe store, and other enterprising villagers are launching their businesses.

"As we all know, it takes a combination of the business owners' own money and the village's money to get these companies off the ground. So the 'hook' is that we promise the villagers prosperity in return for their investment in the infrastructure we talked about before.

"At first, everything works the way it's supposed to. The businesses provide jobs, goods, and services. They boost the village's economy, give everyone a more comfortable quality of life, and provide the tax revenue that pays for the infrastructure we've created. That's the 'convincer.' The village actually is getting something for its money.

"But Wendy's already told us that when she can, she'll expand and move. Labor is cheaper elsewhere, she needs a more fashionable location for her headquarters, and so on. However, she explains that in order to keep some of her operation in the village, she'll need some tax concessions—even though she's making plenty of money. This will ultimately *benefit* the village, she says, because it protects jobs in the village and lays the foundation for 'more prosperity around the corner.'

"That's the first 'sting.' The villagers go along and provide Wendy with tax benefits that allow her to keep more of her profits.

"It doesn't *feel* like a sting to the villagers, however, because 'smart and very serious people' like Wendy tell them that 'prosperity is just around the corner.' That's the way the system works, villagers are told. And it must be true. After all, the business owners are becoming wonderfully successful. They're building new, magnificent homes in a new part of the village. And the business owners *are* keeping some jobs in the village—which is another 'convincer' that makes the villagers think they're getting something for their money. The villagers aren't happy they're now paying for virtually all the infrastructure and that their wages are stagnant. But, 'prosperity is just around the corner,' so they bite the bullet. Besides, Wendy's doing her part in raising private capital to expand. Because of the scale of her business, she has welcomed investors. The other business owners who have also been prospering with their own ventures buy stock in her company.

"Now it's time for the next sting. Remember that I said this con can have a very long life. Wendy tells the villagers that although she'd like to keep as many jobs in the village as possible, another village has offered to do the same work for less. Unfortunately, because she's now responsible to *stockholders*— the real owners of her company—she has no choice but to ask the people working for her to take a pay cut. Of course, it's irrelevant that the stockholders are in reality the small number of the village business owners who are now wealthy enough to own stock. Wendy explains that her fiduciary duty is to 'maximize shareholder wealth.' 'But don't worry,' she explains, 'it all trickles down. This is how we produce new jobs. Prosperity is still just around the corner.'

"However, she's also going to need something more than the original tax incentives. In order for Wendy and the other business owners to be successful on a big playing field, the village tax laws need to be reformed. They need to be more 'business friendly.' They need to 'liberate capital' and let investors do what they do best. The tax laws need to take account of the *international* character of business. They need to accommodate the special problems that companies face in trying to be competitive *on a global scale*. Therefore, village businesses need to pay much less of the cost of the village infrastructure. In fact, it should be possible for them to pay nothing at all for it.

"The bottom line is that the villagers (the marks) keep giving Wendy and her friends (the grifters) what they want as they keep raking in the money.

"Yet the villagers *still* don't realize it's a con. 'We know times are tough,' Wendy tells them, 'but no one should worry. Trust us. This will ultimately benefit the village, because prosperity is just around the corner.' What choice do the villagers have? They still benefit—in the sense that a lower paying job is better than no job at all. And the 'smart, very serious people' still say that the benefits will ultimately trickle down.

"At the same time, Wendy and her friends are running the same con on the other villages they've expanded to. First, in other parts of the country. Then, in other parts of the world. They are careful to provide enough 'convincers' along the way to keep things going. But they make sure they're always ahead in the game. As some of the villages they operate in put strict laws of one sort or another in place, the businesses move to other villages that are happy to accommodate them with laxer rules. That way, profit margins remain high.

"And here's where the con takes a nasty turn. Wendy and her friends now start pointing out how irresponsible the villagers have been because the village now has a serious *deficit*. As a way of paying for the infrastructure and for the 'kind of life' they wanted—roads, schools, healthcare, protection against dying in poverty when they were too old to work—the villagers started borrowing money from Wendy and her wealthy colleagues after they started giving the businesses substantial tax breaks. Then in order to pay for the wars the villagers had to fight, they borrowed more money. Any time the villagers tried to raise taxes to pay for these expenses, Wendy and her friends went on the attack and used their influence to keep that from happening—although they were always happy to *lend* the village more money.

" 'You villagers wanted too much,' Wendy and her friends now lecture sternly. 'You wanted more than you could afford. You now have to accept the consequences of your irresponsibility. You need to make do with less so you can pay off that deficit.' "

Socrates turned to Natalie.

"Natalie, do you want to finish your confession about how you got so disenchanted so fast?"

"You mean the interview I came across with the CEO of Goldman Sachs?"

"Right. It wasn't as heavy handed as the way I just put it, but the message was, 'the villagers have to do with less.' Natalie, I know you have the interview in your notebook. Will you paraphrase it for the rest of us, please?"

I handed the notebook back to her. She flipped through it until she found the right page.

"During an interview in 2012," she said, "Lloyd Blankfein was asked how to reduce the federal budget deficit. He said that people had to reduce their expectations about things like Social Security, Medicare, and Medicaid because the country can't afford them."

"But that sounds like a reasonable and balanced approach, Natalie," I said. "We're overextended. As a society, we can't afford everything we'd love to have. We have to cut back somewhere. It's like the way everybody has to run their household. It's the way you have to run a business. If we don't have enough money to pay our bills, we have to cut back."

"I don't mean to be rude, Wendy, but you mean *we* have to cut back. Your compensation has made you independently wealthy. Mr. Blankfein was receiving tens of millions of dollars from his bank each year and was worth about $450 million when he made that statement. *You* won't have to cut back. *He* won't have to cut back. If Mr. Blankfein has his way, *my grandmother*—who has worked for nearly 50 years—will have to cut back. *My parents* will have to cut back, after sacrificing to put me through college. And then *Serg, I, and our generation* will have to cut back.

"So now it feels like our generation is being stiffed with *two* problems we had no hand in creating—first, global warming, and now underfunded programs that are supposed to allow people dignity at the end of their lives."

I was about to reply, but Socrates waved me off.

"As you can see, Wendy, Natalie's perspective is powerfully shaped by her grandmother's experience. One more thing, Nat. Tell Wendy about the grocery guy."

The way that Natalie huffed, I could tell this was another sore point.

"So there's this billionaire CEO who was running for mayor of New York City. One of his favorite slogans was, 'When businesses do well, people do well.' Except I think what this really means is that 'when businesses do well, the people *who own the businesses* do well.' Customers of one of his supermarkets in Brooklyn, near where a lot of seniors live, regularly complain that the prices are higher than at other markets. The only problem is that the next closest market can be hard for someone old to get to. How is his prosperity trickling down to these seniors living on a fixed income?"

"I never said we had a perfect system, Natalie," I answered. "And we all have to take responsibility for fixing it, especially those of us with more money. Everyone knows we need more revenue. The wealthy have to do more, and we will. But everyone will need to make sacrifices. We have a crushing deficit."

"Thank you, Wendy. Excellent addition to the conversation," Socrates said, to my surprise. Then he looked at Natalie and Sergio and said, "So, without realizing it, Wendy has conveniently taken us back to the way the con works by showing us the next *convincer*. The rich *will* ultimately agree to pay more to the village, just not a lot more. *However*, they'll insist that, in exchange, the villagers settle for a lower quality of life in the future.

"And here's one of my favorite parts. In the interview you're referring to, Blankfein was portrayed as a highly credible expert on how to deal with the deficit. But the interviewer never calls attention to the fact that Blankfein might not be the most objective individual to discuss this. He's a CEO from the industry that caused the meltdown in the first place by putting its own interests ahead of the nation's. *Of course*, he's going to say that the villagers should expect less. Otherwise, corporations and the wealthy will be pressured to pay more in taxes.

"See, it's a *brilliant* con. They can keep it going forever, *and* the grifters are even treated as experts for their opinion about what to do.

"In fact, it's even more pernicious than you think because Wendy and her gang of grifters do such a stellar job of convincing their marks that the scam is a good thing. For example, one study I know of shows that employees at firms with high executive compensation are more likely to see their company as one of the best places to work at than are employees at companies who pay their executives less. I might be completely wrong in this. But it's certainly tempting to think that the employees have been conned to think that having a highly paid superstar is the mark of a really good company—despite the fact that this means their superstar is making hundreds of times more than the average employee.

"Oh, and Wendy's remark about the deficit shows one more piece of the con—although this move is more characteristic of a short con like three-card monte. It's all about misdirection and distraction. First, you get people to focus so much on the deficit that they don't remember that it was created *artificially*—by the insistence that the villagers let businesses and the people in the top tier keep most of their wealth. Second, you scare the pants off everyone in the village by giving them a false dilemma—cut spending or face economic disaster. Wendy, humor me for a minute, when you look at a balance sheet at the bank and you see that your revenues aren't keeping up with your costs, what do you do?"

I didn't understand this abrupt shift in gears from the government deficit to business, but I was anxious to get to the end of the day. "I'll either cut costs, raise revenues, or do some combination of the two. It all depends on what we're talking about."

"Terrific answer. Please explain to Sergio and Natalie why you just wouldn't automatically cut costs."

"If I cut costs indiscriminately, I'll hurt our product lines. This will drive customers away, lower revenues, and, ultimately, drive us out of business. In that situation, we'll raise our prices to get the revenues we need."

"So why," Socrates asked, "don't you look at government services the same way? Why cut services rather than raise revenues?"

"Because it's *not* a false dilemma. Raising taxes *will* hurt the economy."

"But that's simply not true, Wendy," Natalie interjected forcefully. "That's the problem. The data I looked at make it very clear. The economy overall and the middle class did fine with higher tax rates for decades. There wasn't so much inequality. The economy distributed wealth more equitably. We had a healthier middle class. It's not that there's not enough wealth in the country to pay for these programs. It's that it's being accumulated by a small percentage of the population who aren't even responsible for the wealth being produced."

I was astonished at Natalie's naiveté. "Natalie, surely as a business major you know that without investment capital, economies dry up. That's Business 101. That's why the people with the resources are the ones who drive the economy."

"Right. They *get things going*. But they don't *produce the profits*," Natalie pushed back.

Before I could reply, Socrates stepped in again. "And here we have yet another example of how when you look at the facts from yet another perspective, you can draw a very different set of conclusions. When Wendy looks at the facts through the eyes of a true believer of the Church of the Free Market, she sees 'the ordinary workings of the free market.' When Natalie and I applied different presuppositions, we could see the facts showing 'a brilliant long con.' But as I've hinted off and on, yet another ideology would say that the facts show 'class warfare of the rich against everyone else.'"

"Now you're just being ridiculous," I interrupted. "This is pure Marxism!"

Socrates shot me a disappointed frown. "Wendy, it doesn't matter what kind of ideology—what kind of -*ism*—this may or may not be. This may sound like heresy to someone from your Church, but there are other 'economic religions' out there that would label *you* a heretic. And in this new job, you will have to be able to deal effectively and respectfully with them."

I was frustrated that while I had politely tolerated Socrates' disparaging characterization of my economic outlook as a religion, rather than a realistic perspective grounded in years in business, he still hadn't extended me the courtesy of allowing me to reply in any sort of length. But I now better understood his point about facts painting different pictures depending on the perspective one viewed them through. So I decided to give him more latitude.

"OK. Class conflict. Culture war. Whatever you want to call it," I replied calmly. "Through what perspective do the facts support *that* conclusion?"

Socrates seemed impressed that I was backing off so quickly.

"I gave our young friends here one more assignment. After they came up with the Business Creed, and then after I had them play with the idea of a con, I told them to come up with an alternative Creed with a set of beliefs that would, in their mind, guarantee that the economy of the village would 'do its job' in securing the 'kind of life' we say we want. It didn't have to be elaborate. In fact, I told them the shorter the better. Just big ideas. What you'll see is that when you look at the facts about the economy through this perspective, the idea that a culture war or class conflict is going on isn't so farfetched. Sergio, please tell Wendy what you came up with."

Natalie handed Sergio the blue notebook she'd read out of earlier.

"I should probably explain," Sergio began, "that a big influence on us was that discussion about John Rawls' 'veil of ignorance' the three of us had the last time we got together here. Nat and I felt it was crucial that we came up with something that *everyone* in the village could *freely agree to* as being in their interest. When we looked at the Business Creed, we decided the only people who would ever freely agree to that as the 'terms of the deal' would be people at the top of the economy. One of the reasons Natalie got so disenchanted so quickly is that 'the free market protects freedom' is virtually a mantra to her. After looking at the data she discovered, she came to the conclusion that the average person would *never* freely agree to the current 'rules of the game' as they're evidenced by the Business Creed. She feels that most people are, for all practical purposes, being strong-armed to live with an economy that no rational, self-interested person would ever agree to as *fair*. So, we kept asking each other, 'if you didn't know where you were going to end up, would you freely sign on?'

"We had more, but we decided we were getting carried away. It's still probably too long, but here's what we ended up with. We called it the Village Creed."

He handed me the notebook.

- Above all else, achieving the 'kind of life' we want in the village for all villagers is sacred.
- Villagers have a responsibility to care for each other. All villagers are entitled to a life of dignity from birth to death. We have a special responsibility to care for villagers who are young, weak, sick, poor, or elderly.
- The primary source of wealth for the village is its population. Major priorities should be the health, safety, and education of all villagers.
- Cooperation is better than competition.
- Selfishness, greed, and envy are moral weaknesses.
- There are 'makers' and 'takers,' and the former deserve a bigger share of the wealth. The 'makers'—the 'profit-producers'—are the people who actually *produce* the goods and services that are bought and sold. The latter is anyone who makes money off of these transactions but isn't directly involved in the process.

- Profit-producers deserve a major share of the wealth they produce.
- Differences in wealth are allowable to the extent that they benefit the poorest members of the village.
- The 'job' of business is to do its share in supporting the 'kind of life' we want in the village. That means providing jobs, dependable products, and quality services.
- All concentrations of power threaten freedom.
- The rights and interests of future generations and other species must be respected.

I passed the notebook along to Socrates, who nodded and mumbled as he made his way down the list. "Thank you, Sergio. Natalie. Again, interesting and provocative," he noted. "So, Wendy, you now get to close out our little exercise. Tell me what someone who believes in the Village Creed would conclude from the facts about the economy that Natalie originally showed us. In particular, what would they say about any *ethical* issues? I'm not asking you whether you believe what they've concluded. Just what things look like when you use that particular lens. In fact, to show that I'm a man of my word, let's head back. When we reach the beach house, we're done."

I crooked an eyebrow at him suspiciously. I needed to make sure this wasn't another one of Socrates' ploys.

"Let me get this clear. *Done* as in you'll finally stop kidnapping, harassing, annoying, insulting, irritating, exasperating, frustrating, and torturing me? *Done* as in you'll stop being rude, impertinent, condescending, arrogant, maddening, abusive, tiresome, and impolite?"

Socrates laughed. "I believe *rude* and *impolite* are synonyms. And you forgot *patronizing* and *snarky*. But otherwise, yes, *done* as in you get to go home."

As we all changed direction, I took the notebook back from Socrates. I wanted to press Sergio on a specific point.

"One question before I do this. Sergio, what do you mean by *profit-producers*? I take it you don't mean investors."

"Socrates said that we should try to stand things on their head. For example, he said that we should think about switching around the meaning of 'makers' and 'takers.' So when Natalie and I looked at the Business Creed and saw how it made everything at the top of the economy so important, we decided to flip things around."

Socrates could see I wasn't entirely satisfied with Sergio's answer. "Sergio's finessing his language because he's trying to avoid being insulting, Wendy. But, since I don't have to stop being rude until we make it back, let me add the details. The Village Creed says that *making decisions* doesn't count as much as *making clothing, food, cars, or anything else that gets produced and then sold*. The world you and I operate in, Wendy—financial services and venture capital—is a bizarre, almost *virtual* part of business given how much we can do with smoke and mirrors. But the tangible part of economy is made up of the people who put up the capital and the people who produce something.

And as important as the accountants, HR, middle, and senior management are—and I'm not saying they aren't critical—companies wouldn't have anything to sell without what happens on the shop floor, front counter, sales floor, or whatever. And an investment is going to be lost unless the product it's financing can be sold at a profit."

"Right," Sergio said. "So we think that ultimate responsibility for a company's profits come from what hourly workers do in a factory or when they're in direct contact with customers. And, to be fair, Nat and I thought that with the discussion about the economy being filled with so many slogans—*wealth trickles down*—and tilted terms—*job-creators*—we thought that *profit-producers* would be a good addition."

Socrates chimed in. "From a strategic perspective, I thought *profit-producer* was a brilliant idea and wondered why no one had coined it before and used it in the debate about wealth."

We walked along for a couple of minutes as I studied the list. Again, it was a matter of pride that, no matter what the issue, I could put any personal beliefs aside and look at a situation in a ruthlessly objective way.

As I shelved my allegiance to the way the global economy currently operated, I decided that Sergio and Natalie were right in making Rawls' approach their foundation. My loyalty to contemporary, free market capitalism was the same as Natalie's or at least the way it apparently *used to be* for Natalie. I too saw the free market as the most important way to protect freedom and to promote it on a global scale. But my commitment to freedom was more radical than many of my executive colleagues. Theirs was more practical. Freedom was the absence of someone—like the government—telling you what you can and cannot do. Mine was more ideological—so Socrates was right when he said this was like a religion to me. For me, freedom was about *freely consenting* to something. That's why I was interested when Socrates explained Rawls' approach when we talked in my office. What's a more radical commitment to freedom than a process that removes any material incentives or disincentives? *Not knowing how things are going to turn out for you personally, would you freely agree to the process?* In my mind, *that's* a radical allegiance to freedom.

As I ruminated over the Village Creed, I was troubled at two things. How much it sounded like Marxism, or at least warmed-over Socialism. And how appealing I found it. But I reminded myself that I wasn't making a decision about whether I would become a convert. I just needed to complete Socrates' assignment.

"For our purposes," I began, "I want to make this as simple an analysis as I can. To do this properly, we would need to go into things much more deeply. But for now, I see a few big ethical points.

"First, Natalie and Serg, I agree with you that this is something I would freely sign on to in Rawls' 'original position.' So, from an ethical perspective, I think it does a good job of respecting freedom. And I definitely agree with the point—which Socrates made when he brought up Friedman—that *any* concentration of power threatens freedom.

"Second, from a Kantian perspective, I find the way it respects the dignity of people very appealing. You're probably going to find this surprising, but I think that one of the most important points you make—from an ethical perspective—is the priority you give to education. I have always been struck by how much human brainpower gets wasted by our failure to educate people as much as possible. How many discoveries have *not* been made because people with potential never got the opportunity to get educated to the level they should have been? And while I'm referring to this on a planetary scale, it always struck me as astonishingly short-sighted and self-defeating to the country when I heard governors saying with pride how many teachers they were able to fire to balance their budgets after the meltdown. And *I* think of myself as a deficit hawk. You may as well say, 'We were able to reduce our food bill this season by eating our seed corn.' In my more cynical moments, the pride with which various people talked about how deeply they cut the school, police, and fire budgets made me wonder whether our species will fall into the 'too stupid to live' category.

"Third, I'd have to be an idiot to say that greed, envy, and selfishness are strengths. We're an absolutely schizophrenic society in this regard. When we're raising our children, we tell them to treat others properly, to share, to cooperate, and not to be greedy. When they graduate into the world of work, we tell them it's now a virtue to beat out their neighbor, play rough, and—under a veneer of civility and professionalism—to be selfish and greedy bastards. From a practical standpoint, however, selfishness, greed, and envy drive the economy. So I find myself with a classic utilitarian dilemma. Will the good outweigh the harm?

"I have a similar reaction to your maker/taker reversal and your labeling front line workers 'profit-producers.' Rhetorically and strategically, it's very clever. And I do appreciate why this looks like a more *fair* way to think about things than what we do now. My only problem is that I honestly don't know if this can work on a big scale to give us the material 'kind of life' we want in the village. At the same time, Natalie makes a solid, prima facie case that the Church of the Free Market isn't delivering on its promise.

"The bottom line of my analysis? As Socrates said, it's an interesting and provocative creed with some very strong ethical points. And if I look at Natalie's data through the eyes of a true believer of the Village Creed and that's a very big *if*, because remember, Socrates said this isn't about whether I'm converting to *your* church, I actually do see something that could be called a class struggle and a culture war. The wealthy against everyone else. The present against future generations. And, because you mentioned other species, humans against everyone else.

"The profits that your 'profit-producers' generate are being concentrated at the top—which makes for greater power by a smaller number of people. This makes a minority of the village fabulously wealthy while the vast majority of the villagers are told they'll need to do with less—especially when they're sick, weak, poor, or old. That certainly looks like aggression—even cruelty—to me.

"The wealthy villagers are deliberately using their wealth to make the village more unequal in terms of wealth and strength.

"They're using the theology of the Church of the Free Market to make it sound like they're engaged in a moral crusade. And they're not above using their wealth and power to distort the truth in a way that will compromise the welfare of future generations—as Sergio made clear with the evidence about global warming.

"Good enough?" I asked, turning to Socrates.

"Very nice. Very nice, indeed. Natalie. Sergio. That's what you should aspire to—being able to suspend your own allegiance to deeply held beliefs so that you can try on a radically different point of view. I know Wendy well enough that I'm confident she'll think about all of this for months—if not years—to come. Maybe she'll change her mind; maybe she won't. Maybe she'll make different decisions as CEO; maybe not. However, I have no doubt she *will* stop making stupid public statements in front of a camera," he joked. "But whatever she does or doesn't do, it will be from a position of strength and the ability to understand the world from dramatically different perspectives," he said seriously. "Hopefully, she'll accept this new job I've offered her, and she'll start applying her talents on a bigger, more international stage."

"Offered?" I asked. "Don't you mean, 'a job that this company might offer'?"

"Oh, did I make a mistake in how I explained things?" he said with that smug, totally disingenuous look again. "They definitely want you. My job was just to convey the offer. You know, sometimes I can get details confused. Did I make you think the offer was up in the air? I am truly sorry."

I grimaced in reply. "You know, do I have to remind you that I've heard it said that your namesake was executed by the ancient Athenians primarily for being annoying. That really is an apt nickname. So I'd be careful the next time someone hands you something to drink."

26

Epilogue

The rest of the walk back to Socrates' beach house was mercifully uneventful. Socrates finally told me the name of the company, and the location—London. Despite all of the nonsense he'd pulled, he couldn't have been more sincere in saying that he genuinely hoped I would accept the post and that he thought I'd do a great job. He said he knew I'd have to talk to my husband and daughter first. But he hoped we could make a decision fairly quickly.

As we got closer to the house, we saw the dolphins again. This gave Sergio a chance to give us his *dolphins-are-nonhuman-persons-and-if-you-don't-understand-that-you-either-don't-know-the-scientific-literature-or-you-don't-understand-its-philosophical-significance* speech. He finished up with his favorite quotation about them.

"It's from Douglas Adams' fantasy novel, *The Hitchhiker's Guide to the Galaxy*," he said.

> It is an important and popular fact that things are not always what they seem. For instance, on the planet Earth, man had always assumed that he was more intelligent than dolphins because he had achieved so much—the wheel, New York, wars and so on—while all that dolphins had ever done was muck about in the water having a good time. But conversely, the dolphins had always believed that they were far more intelligent than man—for precisely the same reason.

We concluded our walk listening to Socrates drag out of Sergio every conceivable reason why we should think that dolphins really were more intelligent than humans. Socrates remained the most unusual VC I'd ever met.

I'm sure Socrates assumed I'd be stunned when we walked onto the deck of his beach house and I found my husband and daughter waiting for me. But by then there wasn't much he could have done that would have surprised me.

"So, Dad and I have decided you're taking the job. It'll be great for the three of us to be in the same city again!" Sasha exclaimed, giving me a big hug. After kissing Bobbi, I turned to Socrates and said, "I guess it's all decided. You just should have asked them in the first place and saved both of us the trouble of our three days of conversations."

Socrates shook hands with Bobbi and Sasha and then introduced them to Natalie and Sergio. "After all of our phone calls, it's nice to finally meet you," he said. "Sasha, I appreciate your enthusiasm, but I think your mother should have at least *some* say in the decision," he added with a smile. "And as Bobbi and Sasha already know, Wendy, the three of you have the use of my beach house for the next couple of days so you can discuss this. The company would like an answer fairly quickly, but they understand that this is an important, family decision.

"Colin will drive me to the airport and then Natalie and Sergio back to their homes. He's already loaded our bags into the car. When he comes back, he'll take care of anything you want as long as you're here. I should explain, by the way, that Colin's 'day job' is president of one of the divisions of the company we hope you'll be joining. He's mainly here to answer any questions you might have. He agreed to take on a variety of roles so that we could manage the charade. If you join the company, Colin will be your main contact during the transition. When you make a decision, please let Colin know. He'll inform me.

"I hate to rush, but I'm running late. We'll talk soon."

Socrates gave me a big hug before I could say anything. Then he was out the door.

*

I'm finishing up this journal from my office in London, drinking in the spectacular view—the Thames River, the Tower of London, the top of St. Paul's Cathedral. The decision to move was an easy one. Bobbi, my husband, is a writer and can work from anywhere. Sasha was already here. And thanks to Socrates, I was ready for a new challenge.

When I went back to New York after the weekend with Socrates, I contacted my Board immediately. They were very supportive about my screw-up in Washington with the Senator. As Socrates had somehow known, a major scandal broke the following day, so my video was stale, by comparison. They asked me to stay at the bank, but they realized this was too big an opportunity to turn down. Also, a couple of them knew I was being considered for this position. Socrates had already contacted them as part of his background check and asked them to keep the matter confidential. It turns out that my first conversation with Socrates in my office was my "first interview." If Socrates was satisfied with that, he was asked to conduct a second, more extensive interview. If he felt that I was the right candidate, he was authorized to offer me the job whenever he wanted to.

We worked out a two month transition. Fortunately, one of the things I'd taken seriously was succession planning. So we had a couple of internal candidates who were clearly capable of taking over. That time frame worked well for the English company. Their CEO had told his Board he'd be willing to start his retirement whenever it was best for the company. He and Colin were a great help in the move.

Once things settled down, I wanted to capture what I could recall of my extended job interview with "Socrates." Lacking Sergio's eidetic memory, I had to struggle to reconstruct the conversations. Since Bobbi's a writer, he took my original notes and what I described to him in a number of conversations, and he turned it into something that I can use to refresh my memory when I need to.

I'd like to be able to say I could put everything I learned from the conversations into some short, brilliant sentence. But so many *different* parts of my conversations with Socrates come up from time to time that they just remind me how complex business is—and how much more complex it is to try to do business *ethically*. Nonetheless, Socrates obviously wanted to find a way to keep me focused on what he apparently thought was central, because when I sat down at my new desk, I saw a nameplate in front of me that said, "Lady Wendy Summers, Duchess of the Village."

CHAPTER SUMMARIES

Chapter 1

After a disastrous interview that has gone viral on the internet, the CEO of a major Wall Street financial services company meets a distinguished looking gentleman. The CEO assumes he is the 'spin doctor' the executive has requested, but he's actually a venture capitalist who controls 30% of the bank's stock and has reservations about how the company has been run lately. As a way of coaxing the CEO to hear him out, he proposes a wager around what the executive just said in an interview: "Business is about making money. We didn't break any laws! We didn't lie, cheat, or steal! We didn't do anything wrong!" The man claims he can get the CEO to recognize that the executive doesn't really believe this. The terms of the bet are established. They will play two 'hands.' The first will address "Business is about making money"; the second, "We didn't do anything wrong." The stakes: $400,000. The man says that the CEO may call him Socrates.

Chapter 2

What is the 'job' of business? The CEO says, "Making money." Socrates leads the executive through a dialogue about why human societies are organized the way they are. The function of the primary elements of human society is to provide the members of a community with a certain kind of life. Socrates and the CEO debate whether a privately-owned hospital which is extremely profitable because it skimps on patient care is 'doing its job' as a business. Socrates argues that the 'job' of business is to provide the inhabitants of the community with the goods and services necessary for a decent way of life. He claims that profits are simply the means to that end, not an end in itself.

Chapter 3

The CEO objects to Socrates' position about profits, and the two discuss the relationship between profits and the 'job' of business further. The first part of the wager ends in a draw. Socrates returns to the CEO's earlier comments about the importance of individual freedom. The executive argues for the importance of fostering individual rights in a modern society. Socrates introduces John Rawls' concept of the 'veil of ignorance,' relates it to individual freedom, and proposes it as a test for whether something is *fair* or *reasonable*. He applies the 'veil of ignorance' to the question of the distribution of wealth and then to the 'job' of business. He revisits the 'bad hospital but good business' example. They discuss the application of 'veil of ignorance' to the question of reasonable limits on individual freedom.

Chapter 4

The second part of the wager begins: Has the CEO done anything 'wrong'? Socrates leads the CEO through a dialogue that starts with their earlier agreement about some key features of the 'kind of life' that should be the goal of their imaginary village (fairness, respect, and treating others the way you'd want to be treated) and leads to a practical understanding of 'ethics' expressed in two principles: 'Do no harm' and 'Treat others appropriately.' Socrates offers the image of an 'ethical yardstick'—something we can use to measure our actions and determine whether they're right or wrong.

One side is marked off in a way that tells us whether we're *doing any harm*; the other, marked in a way that tells us whether or not we're *treating others appropriately*.

Socrates now directs the conversation to specifics of the CEO's behavior. Part of *treating people appropriately* is to keep promises. So, he asks, what did the CEO promise the company? Most importantly, the executive says, to earn a good return for shareholders because of the risk they assume in investing money without any guarantees. Socrates argues that employees invest something even more valuable than money—the days of their lives. Therefore, he claims, they should be seen as important as stockholders.

Chapter 5

Socrates continues the discussion of whether or not the CEO kept a promise with the company by shifting the topic to executive compensation. He describes how American CEOs make significantly more than chief executives in other countries. In the United States, CEOs earn about 350 times more than the average worker. By contrast, in the United Kingdom, the ratio is 80:1.

Socrates suggests that part of the problem is that current and former CEOs on board compensation committees fail to see they have a *conflict of interest*. He claims that such high compensation is a sign that the CEO has *broken a promise* to make as much money for the company as possible *and* to treat everyone appropriately at the same time. The unfair pay ratio is a second reason for saying the CEO's actions have been ethically wrong.

Chapter 6

The dialogue continues around the question of whether or not the CEO has done anything that violates the ethical requirement to *treat others appropriately*. Pointing to the fact that so few women rise to the top tier in corporations or serve on boards of directors, Socrates argues that this is because of a 'glass ceiling,' not a talent shortage.

Next, he objects to the fact that the CEO also serves as Chair of the Board. He argues that this is a *conflict of interest* and undermines the board's responsibility to exercise oversight of the company's management.

Shifting to whether or not the principle of *do no harm* has been violated, Socrates rejects the idea that the financial meltdown was an 'act of God.' He sees it, instead, as the result of greed, short term thinking, and negligence which produced considerable harm through the resulting recession and the loss of jobs, homes, and people's money.

Socrates argues that all of this shows that the CEO's statement that she "did nothing wrong" was incorrect. The CEO concedes the second hand. Socrates signals that he is willing to give her a chance to make back the money she's just lost.

Chapter 7

Socrates explains that all the CEO has to do to keep the money is to finish the conversation. The discussion will be about how she should operate in the future. First, Socrates suggests that the CEO's ethics and compliance office doesn't play a strong enough role in evaluating strategic decisions. Next, pointing out that ethical analysis is as technically sophisticated as financial analysis, he encourages the CEO herself—as well as other senior managers and board members—to become proficient in the relevant technical skills. Socrates then suggests some ways that the CEO might integrate ethics more effectively into the company's day to day operations. In particular, he suggests that at each company meeting, the following questions get asked: When we look at our mission statement and list of company values, are we keeping our promise? Do our *actions* match what our *words* say we're committed to? Are we treating everyone involved in this matter *appropriately*? Is there anyone who *will* get hurt or *could* get hurt by what we're doing? Are we keeping the risk of harm at a reasonable level?

When the CEO turns around, Socrates isn't there.

Chapter 8

The CEO makes a major gaff at a Senate hearing in Washington, D.C. Once again, it goes viral on the internet. Socrates reappears as the driver of her limousine and takes her to his beach house in Maryland for another series of conversations. He says that some of the comments she just made show that she is still blind to the *ethical* dimensions of a number of issues.

Socrates suggests that the CEO's bank bears some responsibility for the negative consequences that come from the actions of some of the bank's client companies: a company that manufactured one of the weapons used in a school massacre; a company that's very profitable, was very generous with its senior executives, but insisted its union employees take a pay freeze; and a petroleum company that spent millions of dollars of its profits to derail anything to do increasing public awareness about the threat of global climate change. He also objects to public statements the CEO has made about climate change ("the threat has been exaggerated") and the economy ("wealth inevitably trickles down").

Chapter 9

Socrates reveals that the real reason behind this new conversation is that he wants to recommend the CEO for a new position. But first he needs to reassure himself about her abilities. Socrates says that their initial roles in this discussion will be that Socrates will take a skeptical attitude about business ethics, and the CEO must show where he's wrong. Socrates begins by arguing that ethics in general is "rubbish." He endorses the 'emotive theory of ethics.' He rejects ethics as an arbitrary and subjective way that people use to feel better about themselves. He goes on to explain why he thinks that grounding ethics in cultural norms, laws, or religions makes no sense. One of his central points is that there is so much disagreement in these perspectives.

Chapter 10

Socrates continues his critique of ethics, grounding his comments in the idea that, in the world of nature, the strong dominate the weak. The weak use concepts like fairness, respect, and equality to make a virtue of their own weaknesses. The CEO recognized this as the same argument Callicles offers in Plato's *Gorgias*—that the law of nature is that the strong prevail. He says that the weak, in response, concoct conventional ideas of morality and virtues like compassion and moderation and band together to rein in their superiors. Plato's Socrates replies with the idea that 'vice harms the doer.' That is, when 'superior' people like Callicles operate without any restraint, they ultimately pay a serious penalty—their ability to be satisfied or to stop themselves is compromised.

The CEO points out that 'vice harms the doer' can be seen in contemporary cases of very talented people who become embroiled in scandal and destroy their lives through seriously compromised cognitive and affective abilities. Put more prosaically, they're undone by their own greed and stupidity. The CEO and Socrates reflect on the syndrome and its causes. Socrates points out the similarities between the phenomenon they've been discussing and addiction. Wondering about the origin of a mechanism in humans in which 'vice harms the doer,' Socrates engages in speculation from the perspective of evolutionary psychology.

Chapter 11

This chapter is a continuation of the CEO's attempt to demonstrate an objective, rational, logical foundation to ethics. Returning to the example of the simple 'village' from their earlier conversation, the CEO focuses on the goal of providing the villagers with a particular 'kind of life' or 'quality of life.' In an attempt to define these ideas more precisely, the CEO grounds them in the notion of *a rudimentary sense of satisfaction with life*—that is, the experience people have when their most basic needs are met. This will be the foundation of her defense of ethics. She claims that these needs have an *objective* basis, because they are the conditions necessary in order for any human being to grow, develop, or flourish in a healthy way. These needs are both tangible and intangible.

Chapter 12

This chapter is a further continuation of the CEO's attempt to demonstrate an objective, rational, logical foundation to ethics. As a way of explaining the relationship between 'basic human needs' and a 'decent life,' she appeals to utopian theory—specifically, B. F. Skinner's *Walden Two*. She claims that the basic assumption of utopian theory is that human beings are all configured in a way that determines the conditions that have to be met in order for us to have a life that is even rudimentarily satisfying. She is using this claim as a foundation for ethics. She differentiates between tangible and intangible needs, considers what life would be like without having them satisfied and offers her daughter's "TJS" ("that just sucks") criterion.

Socrates asks how any of this connects with ethics. The CEO answers, "When we say that an action is *ethically negative*—wrong, bad, ethically unjustifiable, whatever language you like to use—that's shorthand for saying that the action prevents or at least makes more difficult our getting one of these *basic needs* met. Conversely, to say that an action is *ethically positive*—right, good, ethically defensible—*that's* shorthand for saying the action promotes or protects the satisfaction of these basic needs."

The CEO summarizes her argument for why "ethics isn't rubbish" and gives a brief explanation for why "business ethics isn't rubbish."

Chapter 13

The second day at Socrates' beach house begins with a review of the CEO's defense of business ethics. She and Socrates explicitly reject the idea that there can be a separate set of rules about right and wrong for business. The CEO distinguishes between 'maximum profits' and 'optimum profits,' and she argues that the latter is most in keeping with the 'job' of business. She backs up her claim by discussing the case of Apple and Proview. First, she summarizes John Stuart Mill's teleological approach to ethics (the ethical character of an action is determined by its consequences; utilitarianism; pleasure and pain; the importance of qualitative differences; treating others as an end and never simply as a means). When she applies this perspective to the Apple/Proview case, she argues that the long term costs of deception in business outweigh the benefits.

Chapter 14

After reviewing the value of Mill's approach, Socrates says two surprising things. First, he argues that it's important not to think that good ethics always gets rewarded with profits. Second, he cites examples of high quality good being produced by questionable means. This leads him to conclude that any defense of the idea that 'business ethics isn't rubbish' that relies only on utilitarianism won't work.

The discussion now shifts to the competing, deontological perspective on ethics by Immanuel Kant. The CEO outlines Kant's main ideas (the ethical character of an action is determined by its intrinsic character; ethics based on reason alone; freedom, autonomy, and dignity) and offers his discussion of the 'false promise' as relevant to the Apple/Proview case. Socrates replies that the CEO's analysis ignores two elements of Kant's thinking: his charge to treat people "never *simply* as a means"; and his claim that his principles apply "whether *in your own person* or in the person as another." He draws out the implications of these points: Is it possible to treat someone both as a means and an end? Are there limitations on how we can treat ourselves?

Chapter 15

Socrates explains the significance of the fact that Kant bases his ethics on *reason alone*. Using Kant's example of the false promise, Socrates shows that the formal, logical problem with a lie is that it is a contradiction. He explains that the importance of a purely rational standard has to do with which kind of evidence to trust when we make decisions. He briefly reviews the epistemological approaches of empiricism and rationalism. Returning to Kant's example of the false promise, Socrates illustrates Kant's formulation of the categorical imperative that says, 'act as if the *maxim* of your action were to become through your will a *universal law of nature*.' He then has the CEO apply this approach to the Apple/Proview case.

Chapter 16

Socrates shifts the topic to *responsibility*. Specifically, he asks whether the CEO and/or her bank have any moral responsibility for any harm that can be connected with the actions of the bank's client companies. The first example he raises is a gun company that manufactured a weapon used in a massacre of school children. The CEO has participated in meetings on Capitol Hill in which the gun company has lobbied against gun control legislation. Socrates' perspective is simple and straightforward. The bank's actions are part of a causal chain that ended with mass murder of children. Because the bank facilitated the production and sale of these weapons, it shares at least some responsibility for the tragic outcome. The CEO rejects this position, arguing that if her bank didn't do business with this company, another bank would. The only difference in the outcome would be that the bank's stakeholders would be hurt. Socrates also objects to the fact that the gun company CEO threatened to close part of its operation if the Senator voted the wrong way. Socrates calls this extortion, while the CEO sees it as an appropriate use of leverage to protect jobs and profits. For Socrates, this is just one example of how corporate resources can be used in a way that undermines the overall 'job' of the 'village.'

Chapter 17

Socrates continues his argument that the bank shares some responsibility for the consequences of the gun company's actions. He offers what he considers to be a simple set of criteria for responsibility: knowing what we're doing, freely choosing what we do, and understanding the likely consequences of our actions.

Relying on Mill's perspective, the CEO again points out that if her bank didn't handle the gun company's business, another bank would. She'll agree with Socrates' point of view only if her bank's actions are powerful enough to make a practical difference. That is, she says, "I'll agree I share some of the responsibility if you can say, 'If I do A, then B will happen, but that if I *don't* do A, then B *won't* happen.'" Socrates uses symbolic logic to represent her argument, and then a truth table to show that her argument is invalid.

He next has her apply Kant's 'maxim/universal law of nature' approach to the issue, suggesting this also shows her argument fails to pass muster. Then, relying on Mill's idea about the *qualitative* differences in pleasures and pains, Socrates asks the CEO to imagine her own daughter being killed in a school shooting. His point is that the *high quality* of the pain produced by such a tragedy outweighs whatever larger amount of identifiable lower quality benefits are involved.

Chapter 18

After the CEO reflects on Goldman Sachs and corporate culture, Socrates turns her attention to another one of the bank's clients—Caterpillar. This is a highly successful company. But while its executives were generously rewarded, lower-level employees have experienced wage freezes, pension freezes—even pay cuts. Socrates asks, "If the 'job of business' isn't *to make money,* but *to do its share in supporting the 'kind of life' we want in the village,* do practices like this do so?"

In approaching this question, Socrates introduces the novel idea of "return on infrastructure." He argues that citizens who authorize the use of public money to provide for a community's infrastructure—ways to protect health and safety, public utilities, means of communication, transportation, education, and social stability—would do so only with an understanding the money is used to benefit everyone in the community and provide the 'kind of life' the community aims for. That is, Socrates claims that no one would agree that after public money has built an infrastructure, it would be fine for businesses to become so successful they could leave the community, while leaving the citizens of that community to deal with the consequences. The CEO replies this is simply the way global business operates.

Chapter 19

Socrates brings his focus back to Caterpillar. He recounts the history of the company. While pointing out how successful the company has been, he expresses some reservations about how they operate. Socrates points out that his concern is whether or not Caterpillar has delivered an appropriate 'return on infrastructure' connected with the public infrastructure on which their success has been based—particularly the benefits they've received from the United States having such a strong (and expensive) military. Citing the company's anti-union stance, Socrates then changes the subject and tells about his great-grandfather's experience working for Pinkerton during labor strife in the 19th century. Returning to Caterpillar's general strategy, he again asks whether they deliver an appropriate 'return on infrastructure.' He explains, "I do not believe that the municipalities that Caterpillar left would think the company gave them a reasonable *return on infrastructure,* contributed appropriately to the 'kind of life' we all would like, and treated everyone involved—especially employees—with fairness and respect for their dignity. I'm sure the company's actions were all legal, but—given the perspective we've been taking—I think there are too many ways the company is not doing its 'job.' And, in my opinion, that means it's not operating according to the highest ethical standards."

Chapter 20

For the final day of the conversation, Socrates has arranged for two college students to join him and the CEO. Because Socrates thinks that some of the CEO's actions are undermining the quality of life people like Natalie and Sergio will be able to enjoy in the future, he wants representatives of their generation to take part.

The first topic Socrates brings up is global climate change. Again, he has complaints about the CEO's support for a client company. In this case, it's

ExxonMobil's financial support for individuals and organizations that denied that there was an urgent need to take action. And unlike the gun issue, the CEO has been very public in her skepticism about climate change. The discussion starts with Sergio outlining the scientific evidence behind the claim that the planet is warming and that humans are primarily responsible. Socrates points to ExxonMobil's actions that were designed to foster skepticism about the scientific consensus. And while he understands the business concerns that would lead the company to do that, he nonetheless argues that the company's defense of its financial interests and the public statements by the CEO violated the basic ethical principles of 'do no harm' and 'treat others appropriately.'

Chapter 21

Socrates asks Sergio to review the military implications of climate change that led his team to their topic in the business ethics competition: "One of the consequences of a warmer Arctic region is that corporations from a variety of industries—and from various nations—will be competing for the new resources. Given the strong likelihood of military conflict, what ethical responsibility do these companies have for preventing any possible harm?" The CEO initially reacts with skepticism that there could be a link between climate change and increased terrorism. Sergio details the ways that sea level rise, ice melting, precipitation, drought, extreme weather, and higher temperatures will produce population migrations, shortages of food and water, disease, damage to infrastructure, and social disruption. This will result in the military being involved in direct action, support to keep civil order, humanitarian assistance and dealing with civil unrest, political extremism, or terrorism. Accepting Sergio's argument, the CEO points out the direct impact of this on business by noting that virtually every industry will be seriously affected in some way.

Wanting to see what the CEO has retained from their earlier discussion, Socrates then challenges her to come up with an objective ethical analysis of her actions and ExxonMobil's. He asks: What makes the issues we're talking about qualify as *ethical* issues? Did the actions in question produce more good than harm? What's the intrinsic ethical character of the actions? She produces an analysis that applies the primary insights of Mill and Kant.

The conversation concludes with Socrates giving Sergio the opportunity to ask the CEO one specific question. After going back to the most important parts of the data, he asks, "With evidence so compelling and with so much at stake, why didn't people of your generation care enough about your kids and grandkids to consider that you might be wrong?"

Chapter 22

Socrates shifts the topic to another area in which he has reservations about the CEO's actions. In this case, he points to statements the CEO has made about the workings of the economy. She has argued that the wealth created from business activity will inevitably spread through the rest of society. "A rising tide floats all boats." Socrates claims this is simply not true, and he turns things over to Natalie, whose assignment was to determine whether the economy is doing its 'job.' She reviews data about GDP, unemployment, corporate profits, wages, the increased concentration of wealth at the top of the economy, and income disparity. Her conclusion: "According to standard markers—GDP, Dow Jones, corporate profits—we've had a strong economy over the last 50 to 60 years. However, the benefits have been concentrated at the very top." The discussion concludes by Socrates shifting the focus to "quality of life."

Chapter 23

Socrates calls up data that challenges the idea that the United States is the "best country on Earth." He cites statistics on poverty in the United States and comparisons among many nations on life satisfaction and prosperity. Figures on tax revenue as percentage of GDP lead him to the conclusion that countries with higher percentages than the United States also have higher quality of life. Shifting focus to the U.S. deficit, Socrates argues that the problem hasn't been government overspending, but not taking in enough revenue from wealthy individuals and corporations to cover the costs of government. He points out that some major corporations pay nothing in federal taxes.

The CEO objects that missing from the data which has been presented is anything about the *freedom* that capitalism in America gives us. Socrates replies that, in his opinion, the concentration of private wealth jeopardizes freedom because of the way that wealth translates into power in capitalism.

The discussion shifts back to whether or not wealth trickles down, and the CEO describes how this works from an international level. She explains that when a corporation can operate across nations, it's able to take advantage of lower costs for labor and materials, and to sell products to more markets. People in those countries benefit with new jobs and a better life. Socrates, however, characterizes international business too often as a 'race to the bottom.'

The discussion ends with Socrates letting Natalie put two questions to the CEO for her to consider: "If you still think that 'wealth trickles down,' what's your evidence?" and "If you end up as the CEO of a major multinational, are you willing to make a solemn promise that you will refuse to participate in anything that looks like a race to the bottom?" Then, referring back to their earlier use of Rawls' 'veil of ignorance' exercise, Socrates adds his own question for her to ponder: "Do you honestly think that any villager would freely agree to a system that created astonishing amounts of wealth and economic power for a small percentage of the villagers as long as some of it was used to create benefits for *other* villages but that the price would be paid in terms of the 'kind of life' *our* village was organized for in the first place? Wouldn't that simply be crazy?"

Chapter 24

The CEO takes the initiative and asks if the final topic will be Socrates explaining what he's meant by his incendiary comments about culture wars, class struggle, and cons. Socrates answers that it will, but that in order to do so, they'll begin by looking at the role of intellectual frameworks, unstated assumptions, and ideologies in determining what we consider *facts*—in particular, economic facts. Sergio illustrates this phenomenon by showing how Natalie, Wendy, and Socrates unwittingly used false assumptions to draw conclusions about a pod of dolphins they were observing. As a result, their inferences were false, even though they were certain they were objectively describing facts. Socrates' point is that apparently neutral economic data can tell very different stories, depending on the framework, perspective, or ideology used through which to view them. Socrates claims that the CEO views economic data through the lens of a series of beliefs that are the equivalent of a religion. Natalie was given the assignment ahead of time of identifying the elements of the "Business Creed." They constitute a conventional description of capitalism, the market, and wealth. However, after looking at the data she discovered about the economy, Natalie decides that most of these ideas are false. She concludes, "By the time I got to the end of my research, this just looked like a giant con to me."

Chapter 25

Illuminating the idea that facts can be interpreted very differently depending on the frame of reference used, Socrates explains how the workings of the economy—and the actions of many businesses—can be seen as being part of a "confidence game"— specifically, a "long con" that can be extended for years. Socrates labels this particular con "The Sheriff of Nottingham" because it "steals from the poor to give to the rich" while claiming that what's going on is aimed at bringing prosperity to the village. He details the way the con enriches a minority of the village while transferring all of the costs to the majority. He is particularly critical of the ploy in which the villagers are accused of being irresponsible because they ended up with a deficit—when, in reality, the debt is because the rich villagers were able to trick or strong-arm the village to reduce the amount they had to pay in taxes. After Natalie refers to an interview with the CEO of Goldman Sachs in which he says that people must simply "do with less," Socrates points out a particularly pernicious aspect of the con—the grifters are even treated as experts on what the village should do.

Socrates then asks Natalie and Sergio to report on another assignment he gave them—to come up with an alternative set of beliefs that would, in their mind, guarantee that the economy of the village would 'do its job' in securing the 'kind of life' they would want people to have. They describe the "Village Creed." As a final assignment, Socrates asks the CEO to apply Rawls' exercise again to this new Creed. Would she agree to this from behind the 'veil of ignorance'? She concedes some of its merits, from an ethical perspective.

As the group heads for Socrates' beach house, Socrates confesses that the company that asked him to interview the CEO had already decided to offer her the job after their original conversation. Socrates' assignment was simply to convey the offer.

Epilogue

Socrates reveals the name of the company and the location—London. When the group arrives at his beach house, the CEO's husband and daughter are there. Socrates has offered the family to stay there so that the CEO can decide whether or not to accept the offer. She does. Once in London, she reflects on her experience with Socrates.

DISCUSSION QUESTIONS

Chapter 1

In chapters 1 through 6, Socrates is going to challenge the statements the CEO makes to the reporter: "Everybody knows that business is about making money. We didn't break any laws! We didn't lie, cheat, or steal! We didn't do anything wrong!"

1. Before reading any of the conversation between Socrates and the CEO, how would you describe the object of business? The CEO says that "everybody knows" the whole point of business is "making money." Socrates will challenge that. What do you think?

2. The CEO's basis for claiming "We didn't do anything wrong!" is "We didn't break any laws! We didn't lie, cheat, or steal!" Is this a reasonable defense in your opinion? From your perspective, what makes something "wrong"? In particular, what makes something wrong *in business*? Should the rules about right and wrong be different in business than in, for example, government, education, or one's personal life?

Chapter 2

1. Socrates' argument is based on the idea that humans have organized our societies so that we can enjoy a certain "kind of life." Every component of society—government, education, business, and the like—is subservient to that goal. Socrates claims that the job of the different elements of human society is to do its part to give its members a life in which we get what we need and are treated properly. What do you think?

2. What's your reaction to Socrates' argument about the *job of business*? He rejects the idea that profit is the point of business. He sees it just as a means to an end. What do you think?

3. Socrates cites the example of a hospital that makes money by compromising the care of its patients. He claims that it's both a bad hospital and a bad business. The CEO's first response is that it's a bad hospital but a good business. What's your opinion?

4. Taking a swipe at the CEO's own performance, Socrates says that "businesses like banks and other financial institutions—like the one you run—are *supposed* to meet our need for having a stable and secure financial foundation for the entire economy. And if a bank isn't doing that—even if it's making piles of money—*it isn't doing its job*! It's like a hospital that's making money but not curing people." Alluding to the meltdown of the financial services industry, Socrates is clearly suggesting that the banks didn't do their job. Is Socrates' criticism fair?

Chapter 3

1. The CEO judges the first 'hand' to be a draw. Do you agree?

2. Socrates offers John Rawls' idea of a 'veil of ignorance' as a good test of whether something is fair and reasonable. Do you think it's as good an objective measure as Socrates claims?

3. Socrates uses the 'veil of ignorance' to revisit the question of the 'job' of business. He says, "Think about what you'd *agree* to as the 'rules of the game' or 'terms of the deal' of any 'business' in our society.... I say that no matter what kind of business we imagine, no rational person would ever agree to 'terms of the deal' that didn't promise some specific benefit that he or she wanted. No rational person would agree that profit could ever be more important than the good or service the business is supposed to deliver. Anyone who made such a deal would be a fool." If you agreed with the CEO that the job of business is to make money, does this argument change your mind? Why or why not?

4. Socrates asks the CEO to use the 'veil of ignorance' exercise on the matter of individual freedom. She proposes, "People can do whatever they want as long as it doesn't directly or indirectly hurt anyone else in the village." Is that what you would come up with? If not, what standard would you draw up from behind the 'veil of ignorance'?

Chapter 4

1. The CEO's initial position is that "wrong" means breaking the law, lying, cheating, or stealing. What's your reaction to this as a standard for determining unethical behavior in business?

2. Socrates offers what he sees as a simple, practical, and commonsense ethical yardstick. He says, "Think of one side of the yardstick as being marked off in a way that tells us whether we're *doing any harm*: physical harm, emotional harm, short term harm, long term harm, harm that can be repaired, harm that can't, and so on. Think of the other side of the yardstick as being measured off in a way that tells us whether or not we're *treating people appropriately*: fairness, equality, honesty, keeping promises, helping people when they need it, and the like." He boils this down to two principles: *Do no harm* and *Treat others appropriately*. What's your reaction to this? Is Socrates leaving out anything important? Do ethics need to be more complicated than that?

3. Socrates grounds his two basic ethical principles in what he considers to be a practical understanding of the 'kind of life' people would want in the 'village' he and the CEO imagine. Does this seem like a reasonable basis for ethics—rather than laws, religious teaching, social norms, cultural traditions, or personal opinion?

4. Socrates begins the part of the dialogue that will explore the question of whether the CEO did anything wrong by asking what the executive promises the company. The CEO answers that the most important part of the promise is to advance the interests of stockholders. They invest their money without any guarantees, so their risk should be rewarded. Socrates argues that employees invest something even more valuable than money—the irreplaceable days of their lives. Therefore, he claims, they should be seen as important as stockholders. Do you agree with his argument?

Chapter 5

1. Socrates takes the CEO to task about her compensation on the basis of how chief executives are paid in other countries. Is that a fair criticism, or is he comparing apples and oranges?

2. What do you think is a reasonable ratio between the highest paid person at a company and the average salary? Between the highest and lowest paid people at a company?

3. The traditional formula in capitalism is that reward should be associated with risk. Following this logic, stockholders should receive a higher return on their investment than bondholders, for example. CEOs, however, risk none of their own money. They risk *other people's money*. Why, then, should senior executive compensation be so high?

4. What is your reaction to Socrates' claim that one way a Board should deal with the high cost of American CEOs is to bring in someone from a different country—who is equally talented and would accept a lower salary? That's an accepted practice in running other parts of the business. Why not senior management as well?

5. What is your explanation for why U.S. CEOs' compensation is so much higher than in other countries? What facts can you muster to back up your claim?

Chapter 6

1. Socrates suggests that if there was no 'glass ceiling'—that is, if there was no discrimination against women—the number of women in the C-suite and on boards would reflect their share of the population. He offers the example of women in leadership positions in education to counter the CEO's claim that the reason is 'lack of talent.' What's your reaction to this part of the discussion?

2. Socrates objects to the fact that the CEO is also the Chair of the board of directors. This is a common arrangement in business. However, from the perspective of good corporate governance, it is no longer considered a 'best practice.' Do you agree with Socrates' objection?

3. The CEO's willingness to take credit for the positive consequences that flow from the bank's actions while denying responsibility for any negative consequences is common in business. Socrates claims that this position is illogical. He also argues that the CEO's claim that the economic meltdown was the equivalent of an 'act of God' is, at best, inaccurate. He sees it as more of a rationalization of negligent behavior. With whom do you agree? Is Socrates oversimplifying things? Is the CEO dodging responsibility?

4. Socrates argues that the 'act of God' claim is a 'false analogy.' Can the same be said of his 'deer hunting' example?

5. By conceding the 'second hand' of their wager, the CEO is admitting that some of her actions actually were wrong. Do you agree that she lost this 'hand'?

Chapter 7

1. One of the reasons Socrates says that the CEO's ethics program isn't enough of a priority is that the Chief Ethics Officer makes half that of the Chief Counsel. Do you agree that this would affect how important ethical versus legal issues would be taken in the company?

2. Socrates also says that the Chief Ethics Officer should be involved in discussions of corporate strategy. Do you agree?

3. Socrates claims that the skills required for ethical analysis are as technical and sophisticated as those needed for financial analysis. What are those skills? Do you agree? During this discussion, Socrates refers to 'ethical vision' and says that '*ordinary* ethical vision' isn't enough to identify and resolve difficult ethical issues. What's he talking about? Do you agree?

4. Citing one company's practice for ensuring that safety is a priority, Socrates suggests that an analogous practice for making ethics a priority is that in each

meeting someone should make a point of asking if there are any ethical issues that need to be addressed. Considering that this could lead to decisions that reduce profitability, do you think that this suggestion is practical?

5. Another of Socrates' suggestions is that the CEO should find ways to reward ethical behavior at the company. He claims that, in business, people take something more seriously if they're rewarded for it. The CEO responds with the claim that she should simply be able to expect people to be honest. What do you think?

6. Socrates makes a point of lecturing the CEO about the importance of humility. In an age of CEO superstars with larger-than-life egos, is Socrates' perspective realistic or practical? Is arrogance a necessary trait to run a business?

Chapter 8

1. Socrates makes a number of statements about encouraging the CEO to take ethics more seriously. But do his actions suggest a double standard? It could be argued that in the conversation at her office, he violated the CEO's privacy by digging up personal information on her and that he strong-armed her into the conversation by setting up the situation so that he could threaten to fire her. Then, it looks like he's almost kidnapping her. Is Socrates doing anything unethical? Does it matter if his intentions are good?

2. One of Socrates' assumptions is that the bank shares some responsibility for the negative consequences of the actions of their client corporations. That is, he argues, that the bank facilitates questionable actions. But if the CEO's bank didn't do business with these companies, another bank would. Do you agree?

3. Socrates also criticizes the CEO for using her position to advance something of a personal agenda. He mentions statements she'd made about the economy and her denial of global warming. These statements get attention because she holds such a prominent position. However, she is clearly making claims in areas that fall outside her expertise. Should people in her position feel greater constraints than the rest of us when it comes to freedom of expression?

Chapter 9

1. Playing devil's advocate, Socrates levels an assault on ethics. He argues that, overall, it's a meaningless enterprise full of contradictory claims, special pleading, and rationalization. One of his first specific points is that ethics is: "Rubbish, rubbish, rubbish! If there were something *real* to ethics, don't you think that 2,000 years of philosophers brooding and arguing about this would have produced something? Do you know the only thing that philosophers agree on about ethics? That anyone who doesn't see things their way is wrong!" Philosophers do perennially disagree. Does this mean, as Socrates claims, that there's nothing substantive about what they say?

2. Socrates argues that one of the reasons there's no agreement about ethics is that it's really all based on our emotions. He cites A. J. Ayer's 'emotive theory of ethics.' What's your reaction?

3. Modern democratic societies put considerable emphasis on the importance of respecting the fact that people see many things differently. We value the insights of individual conscience. When it comes to ethics, Socrates rejects this. He says, "But *sincerity* doesn't guarantee that what we do is right. In fact, all sincerity does is let me show that ethics is rubbish. If all that it takes for an action to be right is for me to *believe* it's right, then *anything* can be justified." Do you agree?

4. Socrates systematically rejects cultural traditions, social norms, law, or religion as the source of reasonable standards about right and wrong. Religion and law, in particular, are treated in our society with a respect totally absent in Socrates' comments. Are his criticisms justified?

5. The CEO responds by saying that "as examples of thoughtful attempts to identify how we should and shouldn't treat each other, these different outlooks provide us with 'grist for the mill,' shall we say. It's not the *judgments* per se—whether something's acceptable or not from a legal or religious perspective—that are important. It's the *reasons behind* the judgment." Do you agree? What *reasons* would count as acceptable?

Chapter 10

1. The ancient Greek distinction between *physis* (what comes from nature) and *nomos* (what is a product of human convention) lets Callicles dismiss ethical ideals as artifacts made up by the weak to protect themselves against their superiors. He claims that the 'law of nature' is that the strong should dominate. Do you agree that this is the 'law of nature'? In the world of nature, what counts as 'strength'? Think broadly.

2. Callicles claims that ethics is the result of inferior people making virtues out of their own weaknesses. What's your reaction?

3. What's your first reaction to the idea that 'vice harms the doer'?

4. The Socratic idea that 'vice harms the doer' identifies two specific abilities that are compromised in someone who engages in seriously unethical behavior. One is cognitive (the ability to perceive reality and, in particular, assess risk accurately); the other, affective (the ability to be satisfied). Or, as the CEO puts it, these people become so stupid and greedy that they're the authors of their own destruction. Can you think of any examples of this?

5. Take an example of a contemporary scandal. Come up with a plan that would have ensured that the person you're thinking of could have gotten away with what they were doing? Why weren't they able to come up with the same plan? Is this evidence that 'vice harms the doer' is a genuine phenomenon?

6. Evolutionary psychology is a relatively new field, and there is debate about the claims of experts in this discipline. Nonetheless, it does provide an interesting tool for speculating about why 'vice harms the doer' would exist in contemporary humans. What do you think of the idea that it has evolved as an evolutionary mechanism to reveal anti-social behavior?

Chapter 11

1. The CEO recalls a class from business school in which the professor warned his students of the danger of 'number fixation' and the need for them to develop 'ethical night vision.' Does the concept of 'ethical night vision' make sense to you? Can you think of some aspect of life in which it is possible to enhance your apparently *subjective* ability to perceive dimensions of something or to improve your judgment? Could this apply to judgment about things like fashion, music, or food, for example?

2. What is your reaction to the CEO's claim that "*simply because of the nature of the cloth from which we're cut*—there is a set of necessary conditions that must be met in order for any human being to grow, develop, or flourish in a healthy way"? Humans all over the planet appear to have widely different desires. Is there really

a biologically determined baseline of conditions that are absolutely necessary in order to think that life is satisfying in even the most rudimentary way?

3. The CEO distinguished between tangible and intangible needs. Do you agree? Can you spell these needs out more than she does? How do you draw the line between a need and a want?

Chapter 12

1. At the start of this chapter, the CEO claims that she will show Socrates "a way to evaluate the ethical character of actions that isn't *arbitrary* and *emotional* and that is distinctly different from other ways that we evaluate actions: *legal, profitable, religiously orthodox,* and the like. I'm saying I can show you a meaningful, logical, rational, and objective way to label actions *right, wrong, ethically acceptable, ethically unacceptable*—whatever terms you like to use." In your opinion, did she succeed?

2. The CEO appeals to utopian theory—specifically, to B. F. Skinner's *Walden Two*—for support that a particular set of conditions will produce a sense that life is basically good. Have you read any other descriptions of ideal societies? Plato's *Republic*? Thomas More's *Utopia*? Edward Bellamy's *Looking Backward*? Charlotte Perkins Gilman's *Herland*? Ernest Callenbach's *Ecotopia*? Do they make the same assumption? How similar are the conditions they provide for the inhabitants of their ideal communities?

3. The CEO divides 'basic human needs' into tangible and intangible.

   Tangible: life; physical health, and safety; emotional health and safety; absence of pain and suffering; being cared for when we need assistance; the skills and knowledge necessary to operate in the village; social interaction and access to relationships; and rest.

   Intangible: freedom in action and thought; fairness; equality; honesty; privacy; respect for our dignity as persons.

   What's your reaction to this list? Is anything missing? Do you think that some of these 'needs' are actually 'wants'? Do you agree with the CEO that if our life lacks any of these, we would experience a fundamental dissatisfaction with our life? That is, she says that even though we might be able to cope with having this need unfulfilled, it would still bother us.

4. What's your reaction to the *T-J-S* ("this just sucks") criterion? Does it work as well as the CEO thinks in backing up her claims?

5. Socrates asks how the idea of basic human needs connects with ethics. The CEO answers, "When we say that an action is *ethically negative*—wrong, bad, ethically unjustifiable, whatever language you like to use—that's shorthand for saying that the action prevents or at least makes more difficult our getting one of these *basic needs* met. Conversely, to say that an action is *ethically positive*—right, good, ethically defensible—*that's* shorthand for saying the action promotes or protects the satisfaction of these basic needs." What's your reaction?

6. Do you find the CEO's 90-second defense of business ethics persuasive? If not, where does her argument go wrong?

Chapter 13

1. Both Socrates and the CEO reject the idea that business operates according to a separate set of rules about right and wrong than those that apply in one's personal life, for example. What's your reaction to that?

2. The CEO distinguishes between 'maximum profits' and 'optimum profits' and says that the latter is what businesses should aim at. Do you accept the distinction? Do you agree with her position?

3. What is your reaction to the strategy Apple allegedly used with Proview? Do you see this as 'clever gamesmanship,' or outright fraud, or something in the middle?

4. The CEO appeals to John Stuart Mill's version of utilitarianism. What is your overall reaction to his main ideas? (All actions are morally neutral. Actions become right or wrong depending on their results. Pleasure and pain are the factors that determine whether an action is ethically positive or negative. The best actions are those that produce the greatest happiness. Some pleasures are better than others, and some pains are worse than others. A small amount of high quality pain can outweigh a large amount of low quality pleasure.)

5. The CEO argues that Mill's perspective suggests that Apple's actions were wrong because they produced more harm than good. (Be sure to notice her point about the long term, practical impact of deception in business.) Do you agree?

Chapter 14

1. Socrates begins this part of the discussion with a surprising claim: good ethics don't inevitably get rewarded with profit. What's your reaction to this?

2. Then he basically dismisses utilitarianism by suggesting it has a fatal flaw—that the benefits of a particular action can be so spectacular that they outweigh even a fair amount of high quality harm involved in producing them. Can you identify any examples of that currently going on? Do you agree with Socrates that this means that utilitarianism is faulty? Maybe Socrates is wrong.

3. The CEO responds to Socrates' criticism by appealing to Immanuel Kant's approach. What is your overall reaction to his main ideas? (Actions are intrinsically right or wrong. Ethically acceptable actions treat people with respect for their dignity and, therefore, treat them as ends in themselves.)

4. The CEO argues that Kant's perspective suggests that Apple's actions were wrong because they treated the people at Proview as means to an end. Do you agree?

5. Socrates points out two elements of Kant's statements the CEO has overlooked: his charge to treat people "never *simply* as a means"; and his claim that his principles apply "whether *in your own person* or in the person as another." Do you agree that it's possible to treat someone as both a means and an end? Give an example. Kant says that the way the CEO treats *herself* is ethically questionable because she'd never ask someone else to treat themselves in such a way. Does this limitation that Kant places on our freedom make any sense? Shouldn't we be able to choose exactly how we live?

Chapter 15

1. By attempting to base ethics on reason alone, Kant puts 'ethics' in the same 'intellectual ballpark' as mathematics and logic. In your mind, does that make ethics a stronger or weaker intellectual enterprise?

2. Kant's approach to ethics doesn't talk about *hurting* people, but standards for *appropriate* and *inappropriate treatment*. Does this perspective strike you as stronger or weaker than utilitarianism? Considering how different Mill's and Kant's approaches are, does it makes sense to you to say that for an action to be ethically defensible, it has to be justifiable from *both* perspectives?

3. Identify the maxims of two actions—one that you think is ethically defensible, the other that you think is wrong. Does Kant's 'universal law of nature' version of the categorical imperative illustrate the ethical character of these actions?

4. In terms of what we often think about as characteristics of unethical actions— people being hurt, threatened, lied to, manipulated, and the like—'act as if the *maxim* of your action were to become through your will a *universal law of nature*' seems pretty 'thin' or 'antiseptic.' Is this a strength or weakness?

5. Socrates suggests that Kant's technical, rational approach might keep from getting our judgment clouded by irrational 'intuition' or 'gut feel'—factors that are regularly appealed to by many people in business. What do you think of his example from Wall Street? Does it make sense to make a business decision based on the *rejection* of fear, uncertainty, and doubt? Isn't a strategy like that likely to be self-destructive?

Chapter 16

1. What is your initial reaction to Socrates' general claim that the CEO's bank shares in the responsibility for the outcome of the actions of the bank's corporate clients. Considering that banks are critical to the functioning of companies, do they deserve part of the credit—and part of the blame—for the benefits and harms that result from their clients' actions?

2. Socrates' argument is actually pretty simple. The bank is a key link in a causal chain. The CEO's initial reply is similarly straightforward. If her bank weren't that link, another bank would be. It wouldn't affect the outcome. What do you think of their initial positions?

3. Socrates points out that the CEO apparently was using her position as CEO to endorse a position rejected by an overwhelming majority of Americans. In a democracy, should corporate strategies take popular opinion into account?

4. Socrates also objects to the fact that the gun company's CEO threatened to close part of its operation if the Senator voted the wrong way. Socrates calls this extortion, while the CEO sees it as an appropriate use of leverage to protect jobs and profits. What do you think?

5. What is your opinion about what should happen to the painting Socrates refers to? What is your opinion of the museum's legal defense?

Chapter 17

1. Socrates offers a simple understanding of when we're *morally responsible* for something. He says, "Did I know what I was doing? Did I freely choose what I did? And did I know—or could I reasonably be expected to know—the likely consequences of my action? If I can answer 'yes' to all three, then I'm responsible— at least to some extent—for the consequences of my action." Do you agree?

2. He also claims that if we freely choose to let ourselves get into a state where we can't control our actions—whether through alcohol, drugs, or just a bad habit of giving into our temper—we're still responsible for what we do. Do you agree?

3. Socrates uses a truth table to show that the CEO's argument is invalid—even though it seems like it should make sense. Did you find Socrates' demonstration persuasive?

4. Socrates has the CEO apply Kant's 'maxim/universal law of nature' approach to the issue. Do you agree with the way she identifies the maxim of the action involved? Do you agree that it fails Kant's test?

5. Wanting to demonstrate the importance of Mill's idea about the importance of the *qualitative dimensions* of benefits and harms, Socrates asks the CEO to imagine that her daughter is killed in a school shooting. His point is that the *high quality* of the pain produced by such a tragedy outweighs whatever larger amount of identifiable lower quality benefits involved. How is this relevant to his argument that the CEO's bank is at least partially responsible for any harm produced by the weapons produced by the gun company?

Chapter 18

1. The CEO reflects on Greg Smith's critique of Goldman Sachs, recalling that he said during his 12 years with the company, Goldman's culture went from being about "teamwork, integrity, a spirit of humility, and always doing right by our clients" to making money—even at the expense of the clients. Smith also wrote, "You don't have to be a rocket scientist to figure out that the junior analyst sitting quietly in the corner of the room hearing about 'muppets,' 'ripping eyeballs out' and 'getting paid' doesn't exactly turn into a model citizen." Goldman's CEO and COO replied by calling Smith "disgruntled." They admitted that the company was "far from perfect," but said that "where the firm has seen a problem, we've responded to it seriously and substantively." What's your reaction to this exchange?

2. Smith is referring to the 'culture' of Goldman Sachs, but similar criticisms have been made for years against Wall Street. For example, movies that celebrate greed and dishonesty—like *Wall Street*, *Boiler Room*, and *The Wolf of Wall Street*—supposedly enjoy cult status among many people in the industry. There are regular critiques about the large bonuses in this industry and the sense of entitlement among traders and analysts. It could be argued that the 'culture' prevalent on Wall Street was as much to blame for the meltdown as any other factor. What do you think?

3. Socrates introduces the novel concept of "return on infrastructure." He argues that citizens who authorize the use of public money to provide for a community's infrastructure—ways to protect health and safety, public utilities, means of communication, transportation, education, and social stability—would do so only with an understanding the money is used to benefit everyone in the community and to provide the 'kind of life' the community aims for. His point is that in the same way that investors are entitled to a reasonable return on their investment, any community that uses public money to build and support the infrastructure everyone uses should also get a good return. What's your reaction to this idea?

4. Socrates focuses on the way that a business's success could hurt the community in which it was founded. If it becomes so successful it moves to a different community, the people left behind must deal with the consequences—lost jobs, lost tax revenue, the ongoing cost of the infrastructure, etc. The CEO notes that this is simply the way global business operates. What's your reaction to their disagreement?

5. Socrates puts a series of questions to the CEO: "Would any rational, self-interested villager freely *agree* to spend the community's money on something that will benefit their village only until you've made enough money to shift the benefits to other villages, and leave them in the dust while you personally end up with great wealth over the long term? Villages spend public money as an *investment in their future*. Do you really think they'd agree to invest in your business when the terms of the deal are essentially that they'll help you get started until you decide to take the money and run? Is that the 'kind of life' they're trying to support? One

in which villagers get to use public money to benefit themselves personally while they undermine the village and make life worse for the people they leave behind?" Using Rawls' 'veil of ignorance' exercise, what would you freely agree to about whether any restrictions should be put on people or organizations that benefit from the infrastructure built by public funds?

Chapter 19

1. This chapter begins with Socrates' response to the CEO's comment made at the end of the preceding chapter: "We rely on the workings of the market. The benefits trickle down. It ultimately all works out to everyone's benefit." Socrates' stunt with the cards shows how strongly he believes this simply isn't true. This topic will be thoroughly explored in later chapters, but what's your initial reaction? Who's right?

2. Socrates continues pressing the CEO on the idea of 'return on infrastructure.' He says that "it could be argued that the region that originally provided the critical infrastructure is not getting a fair return on their investment or a reasonable share of the wealth they helped to create. ... Critics of the company would obviously say that the company isn't doing its 'job.' They'd say that Illinois and the United States paid for the infrastructure that let Caterpillar prosper—everything from police, fire departments, hospitals, and schools to the military. And when the company had enough money, it moved many jobs out of Illinois and out of the United States to places where the costs are lower. That sure looks a lot like 'you pay for the infrastructure, and I'll take the money and run' to me. I can't imagine any rational, self-interested village *freely agreeing* to terms like that." Is this a fair criticism of the company? As long as Caterpillar didn't break any laws, and as long as they delivered a good return for investors, did they act inappropriately?

3. One of Socrates' most unusual points is that international companies like Caterpillar—especially companies whose products depend on petroleum—benefit greatly from the powerful (and expensive) American military. He argues that companies like Caterpillar have even more responsibility to pay for the infrastructure than businesses in other industries. Do you agree?

4. Socrates points to the disparity between the pay of senior executives and workers at Caterpillar—despite how successful the company has been. Is there any reason the company should "share the wealth" if they can keep costs down through an aggressive stance towards the unions?

Chapter 20

1. Socrates brings Natalie and Sergio into the conversation because he believes that on certain issues—like global climate change—their interests are more important than those of people his age. Do you think that your generation's interests are taken into account as well as they should be on matters with a long term impact?

2. What is your reaction to the concept of "rights of future generations"? How do those rights compare to the rights of people currently alive? Are "future generations" a legitimate "stakeholder" who should be considered in business decisions?

3. Sergio argues that since about 1990, there has been a consensus among climate scientists that global climate change is real and increasing. In the United States, at least, this claim was aggressively contested by a number of people in the business community. Looking at the data, what is your reaction to how this matter has been handled?

4. Socrates criticizes the CEO for taking a public position on a topic on which she has no technical expertise. She's an executive, not a scientist. However, her words are given more weight because of her position. It is common in the United States that the press highlights the opinions of celebrities of all stripes—athletes, entertainers, executives—on topics that have nothing to do with the areas in which they excel. What do you think of this phenomenon?

5. Socrates argues that the actions of the CEO and ExxonMobil are ethically questionable. He claims that her speeches and the company's actions concealed the truth about a serious threat and thereby slowed the pace at which the evidence for climate change was seen as legitimate by the American public. The result is that future generations are being bequeathed a more dangerous future. Socrates asks the CEO, "In light of the fact that the evidence of the threat was clear and scientifically established, was it wrong for you and your client to try to get people to think the issue was still debatable? And because these actions contributed to delaying appropriate action being taken to deal with the danger, are you responsible for the resulting increase in the harm experienced by future generations?" What do you think?

6. Socrates also objects to the fact that future generations are being asked to shoulder the burden of a problem they had no hand in creating, while present generations enjoy the benefits of our current lifestyle. Does this raise any serious issues around fairness?

Chapter 21

1. What is your reaction to the national security implications of global warming? Do you think this aspect of climate change has been represented appropriately in public discussion?

2. Pick a company or industry. Identify in as much detail as you can how business will be affected by the impacts of climate change that the military experts point to.

3. What do you think of the CEO's analysis of the case? What do you think her analysis shows? What do you think it says about the ethical defensibility of her actions or those of companies like ExxonMobil?

4. Sergio's final question to the CEO is: "With evidence so compelling and with so much at stake, why didn't people of your generation care enough about your kids and grandkids to consider that you might be wrong?" Is this a fair question?

Chapter 22

1. The ideas that 'wealth trickles down' and that 'a rising tide floats all boats' are heard so frequently in discussions about business and the economy that it might seem odd that Socrates would challenge them. If you, your friends, or professors believe these ideas about how the economy works, what data have you been basing your opinion on?

2. Socrates claims that it simply isn't true that the economy works this way. Natalie says that her data show that we've had a strong economy over the last 50 to 60 years, but the benefits have been concentrated at the very top. What's your reaction to that? Is her analysis accurate? Is there any way in which her data are biased towards a particular conclusion?

3. If you accept her data, what do you think of the ethical character of the actions of people who have repeatedly said that 'wealth trickles down'? Are they

misinformed and simply repeating what others have told them? Is there anything ethically questionable about that? Could they be lying?

4. Socrates ends this chapter with a question designed to set up the next topic of discussion. He asks Natalie, "How do you think the United States rates in terms of 'quality of life'?" She answers, "I have no doubt that we're at the very top." The CEO concurs: "I agree with Natalie. We're the best country on Earth." What do you think? What data do you have that support your conclusion?

Chapter 23

1. Do Socrates' statistics on poverty in the United States and comparisons among many nations on life satisfaction and prosperity support his challenge to the idea that the United States is not "the best country on Earth"?

2. Socrates claims that a higher percentage of GDP going to government translates into higher prosperity, satisfaction, and quality of life. What conclusion do you draw from the fact that countries like Sweden, Finland, Norway, and Denmark are both significantly more socialistic than the United States and have higher "life satisfaction" scores?

3. Socrates agrees with the CEO that a government should operate in a way which is fiscally responsible. However, he identifies the problem as wealthy individuals and corporations being allowed to pay less than they should. There are major, wealthy corporations that pay no federal taxes to the U.S. government. What's your reaction?

4. The CEO points out that Socrates is failing to account for the *freedom* produced by capitalism. Does she have a good point? Socrates responds by citing Milton Friedman as a way of suggesting that concentrations of *economic* power are as dangerous as concentrations of *political* power. What's your reaction to this?

5. The CEO responds to the challenge to show how wealth 'trickles down' by taking an international perspective. What would you say to the claim that so much high quality good is done by moving jobs from a country like the United States to a developing nation that it is not simply ethically defensible, but ethically *required*? What is your reaction to Socrates' claim that the strategy the CEO describes is simply a 'race to the bottom'?

6. How would you answer Socrates' question to the CEO: "Do you honestly think any villager would freely agree to a system that created astonishing amounts of wealth and economic power for a small percentage of the villagers as long as some of it was used to create benefits for *other* villages but that the price would be paid in terms of the 'kind of life' *our* village was organized for in the first place? Wouldn't that simply be crazy?"

Chapter 24

1. Socrates claims that unstated assumptions—which sometimes we aren't even aware we make—affect what we accept as facts about the world around us. Sergio illustrates this with the way the group describes the behavior of a pod of dolphins. He points out that their inferences are false and based on false assumptions. Can you think of any other examples of how false assumptions have led people to incorrect conclusions about something, that is, where the "facts" many people believed about something turned out to be false?

2. Sergio suggests that the pursuit of profit can be a factor in keeping people in business from questioning fundamental assumptions about aspects of their operations. He cites the example of dolphins and companies that make money by using them in shows. What's your reaction to this? Can you think of other examples where the fact that something is so profitable may be keeping people working in that industry from recognizing ethical issues?

3. What is your reaction to Socrates' claim that, for executives like the CEO, their beliefs about business are the equivalent of a religion? What do you think of the 'beliefs' in "Business Creed"? What is your reaction to Natalie's complaint that the data don't support its claims? If you think she's wrong on any point, what data can you point to that show this?

4. Natalie makes a particularly disturbing point about the negative consequences the developing nations have experienced by adopting the way of life the developed nations have exported that is supposed to be "the good life"—but isn't. She points to skyrocketing rates of diabetes, obesity, and heart disease that came with the Western version of 'prosperity' and says that this suggests something different. She asks, "How can it make any sense to say that *wealth* is more important than *health*?"

5. In the next chapter, Socrates explains how the way the economy operates to the benefit of a few makes it look similar to a 'confidence game.' Before hearing his argument, what's your reaction to the idea?

Chapter 25

1. What do you think of "The Sheriff of Nottingham"? Socrates is not seriously suggesting that there is an actual conspiracy to pull off such a con. His point is that when we use the frame of reference of a confidence game to examine the data about how the economy works, it's a surprisingly disturbing fit. What's your reaction to this?

2. Socrates is particularly critical of the part of the con in which the villagers are accused of being irresponsible because they ended up with a deficit—when, in reality, the debt is because the rich villagers were able to trick or strong-arm the village to reduce the amount they had to pay in taxes. Is this an accurate accusation by Socrates or a clever way to rationalize the villagers' fiscal irresponsibility?

3. What do you think of Blankfein's assessment—that is, that people of your generation, in particular, will have to do with less in the future? How does fairness factor into all of this?

4. Referring to people like Blankfein, Socrates points out a particularly pernicious aspect of the con—the grifters are even treated as experts on what the village should do. Is this a fair criticism by Socrates? Wouldn't Wall Street CEOs actually be the best experts in this area?

5. Is the criticism of the way the billionaire CEO, who was running for mayor of New York City, operated his supermarkets fair? Is he doing anything ethically inappropriate? Isn't the situation just the ordinary workings of the market and nothing nefarious?

6. What do you think of the 'Village Creed'? Think of Rawls' 'veil of ignorance' exercise. Is this something you could freely agree to as the terms for running the village? From an ethical standpoint, how does this compare to the way business and the economy currently operate?

SOURCES AND REFERENCES

Chapter 3

John Rawls, *A Theory of Justice*, Cambridge, MA: Harvard University Press, 1971. See "The Veil of Ignorance," pp. 136–142.

Thomas Hobbes, *Leviathan*, "Chapter XIII: Of the Natural Condition of Mankind as Concerning Their Felicity, and Misery" in The English Works of Thomas Hobbes of Malmesbury; Now First Collected and Edited by Sir William Molesworth, Bart. (London: Bohn, 1839–45). 11 vols. Vol. 3.

Chapter 5

On executive compensation, see the following.

AFL-CIO, "CEO to Worker Pay Gaps around the World." http://www.aflcio.org /Corporate-Watch/Paywatch-Archive/CEO-Pay-and-You/CEO-to-Worker-Pay -Gap-in-the-United-States/Pay-Gaps-in-the-World.

Lucian Arye Bebchuk and Yaniv Grinstein, "The Growth of Executive Pay," Harvard Law and Economics Discussion Paper, No. 510, *Oxford Review of Economic Policy*, Vol. 21, pp. 283–303, 2005. Bebchuk (Harvard) and Grinstein (Cornell) found that from 1993 to 2003, aggregate compensation paid by public companies for the top five executives grew from less than 5% to more than 10% of aggregate corporate earnings. Yet the authors found no equivalent increase in performance to justify such an expense ($350 billion).

The Bottom Line: Connecting Corporate Performance and Gender Diversity (New York: Catalyst, 2004), accessed September 25, 2014, http://www.catalyst.org/knowledge /bottom-line-connecting-corporate-performance-and-gender-diversity.

Graef S. Crystal, *In Search of Excess: The Overcompensation of American Executives*, New York: W. W. Norton, 1991.

Chapter 9

A. J. Ayer, *Language, Truth and Logic* (London: Penguin Books, 1936). For the "emotive theory of ethics," see "6. Critique of Ethics and Theology," pp. 104–126.

Chapter 10

David M. Buss, ed. *The Handbook of Evolutionary Psychology* (Hoboken, NJ: John Wiley & Sons, 2005).

Robin Dunbar, *Grooming, Gossip, and the Evolution of Language* (Cambridge, MA: Harvard University Press, 1998).

Thomas Hobbes, *Leviathan*. Ch. 13.

Plato, *Gorgias*.

Chapter 12

B. F. Skinner, *Walden Two* (New York: Macmillan, 1948). On Skinner's minimal requirements for "the Good Life," see Chapter 20.

United Nations, "The Universal Declaration of Human Rights" (United Nations: New York, 1948), accessed September 25, 2014, http://www.un.org/en/documents /udhr/.

Chapter 13

Jeremy Bentham, *An Introduction to the Principles of Morals and Legislation* (Oxford: Clarendon Press, 1907). Chapter 1, "Of the Principle of Utility 1."

John Stuart Mill, *Principles of Political Economy with Some of Their Applications to Social Philosophy*, ed. William James Ashley (London: Longmans, Green and Co., 1909, 7th ed.). Book V. On the Influence of Government, Chapter XI. Of the Grounds and Limits of the Laisser-faire or Non-interference Principle, § 11.

John Stuart Mill, *Utilitarianism*. Seventh edition. (London: Longmans, Green, and Co: 1879). Chapter II. "What Utilitarianism Is."

Proview Electronics Co. Limited, Et Al Vs. Apple, Inc., Et Al. Category: Fraud— Unlimited. No. 112CV219219, Superior Court of the State of California in and for the County of Santa Clara. February 17, 2012, accessed September 25, 2014, www .sccaseinfo.org/pa6.asp?full_case_number=1-12-CV-219219.

Michael D. Young, "Where deception is still king: Apple, iPad, and the still murky world of negotiation ethics," *Advocate: Journal of Consumer Attorneys Association of Southern California*, August 2012, accessed September 25, 2014, http://www .judicatewest.com/files/articles/105_08.pdf.

Chapter 14

Immanuel Kant, *Critique of Pure Reason*, translated by Norman Kemp Smith (New York: Macmillan, 1929) A7.

_____, *Fundamental Principles of the Metaphysics of Morals*, 1785, trans. Thomas Kingsmill Abbott, http://www.gutenberg.org/cache/epub/5682/pg5682.html.

Texaco, Inc. v. Pennzoil Co., 729 S.W.2d 768 (Tex. App. 1987).

Debra Whitefield, "Settles Dispute over Purchase of Getty Oil: Texaco Agrees to Pay Pennzoil $3 Billion," *Los Angeles Times*, December 20, 1987.

The Sarbanes-Oxley Act of 2002, accessed September 25, 2014, http://www.sec.gov /about/laws/soa2002.pdf.

Chapter 15

Susan Cain, *Quiet: The Power of Introverts in a World That Can't Stop Talking* (New York: Crown Publishing, 2012), p. 169.

Immanuel Kant, *Fundamental Principles of the Metaphysics of Morals*, 1785, trans. Thomas Kingsmill Abbott, italic added. http://www.gutenberg.org/cache /epub/5682/pg5682.html.

Chapter 16

Tom Mashbert, "Family Seeks Return of a Matisse Seized by the Nazis," *The New York Times*, April 5, 2013, accessed September 25, 2014, http://www.nytimes .com/2013/04/06/arts/design/rosenberg-family-asks-norwegian-museum-to -return-a-matisse.html.

Joe Nocera, "The Gun Report, 1 Year Later," *The New York Times*, February 3, 2014, accessed September 25, 2014, http://www.nytimes.com/2014/02/04/opinion /nocera-the-gun-report-1-year-later.html?_r=0.

Chapter 17

Aristotle, *Nicomachean Ethics*, Book III, 5.
Kant, *Fundamental Principles of the Metaphysics of Morals*.
Joe Nocera, "The Gun Report: 1 Year Later."

Ray Rivera and Alison Leigh Cowan, "Gun Makers Use Home Leverage in Connecticut," *The New York Times*, December 23, 2012, accessed September 25, 2014, http://www.nytimes.com/2012/12/24/nyregion/gun-makers-based -in-connecticut-form-a-potent-lobby.html.

Chapter 18

Lloyd C. Blankfein and Gary D. Cohn, "Goldman Memo: We Were Disappointed to Read Assertions," *The Wall Street Journal*, March 14, 2012, accessed September 25, 2014, http://blogs.wsj.com/deals/2012/03/14 /goldman-memo-we-were-disappointed-to-read-assertions/.

Steven Greenhouse, "At Caterpillar, Pressing Labor While Business Booms," *The New York Times*, July 22, 2012, accessed September 25, 2014, http://www.nytimes .com/2012/07/23/business/profitable-caterpillar-pushes-workers-for-steep-cuts .html.

Jessica Silver-Greenberg, "Dimon Says JPMorgan Made an 'Egregious Mistake'," *The New York Times*, May 13, 2012, accessed September 25, 2014, http://www.nytimes .com/2012/05/14/business/dimon-says-jpmorgan-made-an-egregious-mistake .html?_r=0.

Greg Smith, "Why I Am Leaving Goldman Sachs," The New York Times, March 14, 2012, accessed September 25, 2014, http://www.nytimes.com/2012/03/14 /opinion/why-i-am-leaving-goldman-sachs.html.

Chapter 19

Caterpillar, Inc., "The Story of Caterpillar," accessed September 25, 2014, http://pdf .cat.com/cda/files/89616/9/StoryofCaterpillar042004.pdf.

"Caterpillar CEO Blasts Illinois Business Climate, Quinn Once Again on Defense," *Huffington Post*, February 13, 2012, accessed September 25, 2014, http://www .huffingtonpost.com/2012/02/13/caterpillar-ceo-blasts-il_n_1273263.html.

James R. Hagerty and Alistair MacDonald, "As Unions Lose Their Grip, Indiana Lures Manufacturing Jobs," *The Wall Street Journal*, March 18, 2012, accessed September 25, 2014, http://online.wsj.com/news/articles/SB100014240529702047 95304577223602514988234.

Chapter 20

Steve Coll, *Private Empire: ExxonMobil and American Power* (New York: Penguin Press, 2012).

Intergovernmental Panel on Climate Change. See the IPCC's Assessment Reports issued regularly beginning in 1990, accessed September 25, 2014, http://www.ipcc.ch/publications_and_data/publications_and_data_reports .shtml#1.

Elizabeth Kolbert, *Field Notes From a Catastrophe: Man, Nature, and Climate Change* (New York: Bloomsbury USA, 2006).

Mark Lynas, *Six Degrees: Our Future on a Hotter Planet* (New York: National Geographic, 2008).

Michael E. Mann, *The Hockey Stick and the Climate Wars: Dispatches from the Front Lines* (New York: Columbia University Press, 2012).

Images:

Hurricane Sandy Destruction: Leonard Zhukovsky/Fotolia

Map: Palmer Z Index Short-Term Conditions. NOAA, http://www.ncdc.noaa.gov
/sotc/drought/2012/6
Chart: Global Temperature and Carbon Dioxide, http://www1.ncdc.noaa.gov/pub
/data/cmb/images/indicators/global-temp-and-co2-1880-2009.gif and http://
www.ncdc.noaa.gov/indicators/
Chart: Atmosphere CO2 at Mauna Loa Observatory, http://www.esrl.noaa.gov
/gmd/ccgg/trends/
Chart: Ice Core Data. Based on data from http://www.grida.no/publications/vg
/climate/page/3057.aspx and http://www.esrl.noaa.gov/gmd/ccgg/trends/

Chapter 21

National Intelligence Council, "National Intelligence Assessment on the National
Security Implications of Global Climate Change to 2030," (Washington D.C.: NIC,
2008).
"National Security and the Threat of Climate Change," (Alexandria, VA: The CNA
Corporation, 2007), pp. 6–7.

Chapter 22

On income inequality in the United States, see, for example, Chad Stone, Danilo
Trisi, Arloc Sherman, and William Chen, "A Guide to Statistics on Historical
Trends in Income Inequality," Washington D.C.: Center of Budget and Policy
Priorities, 2014.
Paul Davidson and John Waggoner, "Economy Leaves Wages Behind," USA Today,
May 6, 2013, 1A, 2A.
Blake Ellis, "Average Student Loan Debt: $29,400," CNN Money, December 4, 2012,
http://money.cnn.com/2013/12/04/pf/college/student-loan-debt/.
Paul Solman, "Will We Ever Get to Full Employment?" PBS Newshour, April 25, 2013,
accessed September 25, 2014, http://www.pbs.org/newshour/making-sense
/will-we-ever-get-to-full-employment/.

Images:

US Gross Domestic Product, GDP History US From FY 1950 to FY 2013. U.S.
Department of Commerce, Bureau of Economic Analysis, http://www.bea.gov
/iTable/iTable.cfm?ReqID=9&step=1#reqid=9&step=3&isuri=1&904=2014&903=5
&906=a&905=1950&910=x&911=0
Dow Jones, 1950–2014 http://www.davemanuel.com/where-did-the-djia-nasdaq
-sp500-trade-on.php.
Chart: Corporate Profits After Tax (CP), Federal Reserve Bank of St. Louis, https://
research.stlouisfed.org/fred2/series/CP/https://research.stlouisfed.org/fred2
/series/CP/.
Chart: Unemployment, Labor Force Statistics from the Current Population Survey,
http://data.bls.gov/timeseries/LNU04000000?years_option=all_years&periods
_option=specific_periods&periods=Annual+Datahttp://data.bls.gov/timeseries
/LNU04000000?years_option=all_years&periods_option=specific_
periods&periods=Annual+Data
Chart: Profits are higher, Federal Reserve Bank of St. Louis.
Chart: Inflation-adjusted wages flat, Bureau of Labor Statistics
Chart: Income Concentration at the Top Has Risen Sharply in Recent Decades,
Source: Center on Budget and Policy Priorities, http://www.cbpp.org/cms
/?fa=view&id=3629http://www.cbpp.org/cms/?fa=view&id=3629

Income Concentration at the Top, based on data from Center on Budget and Policy Priorities, http://www.cbpp.org/cms/?fa=view&id=3629http://www.cbpp.org/cms/?fa=view&id=3629

Chart: Corporate Profits After Tax (CP), Federal Reserve Bank of St. Louis, https://research.stlouisfed.org/fred2/series/CP/.

Chapter 23

Victor Fleischer, "Overseas Cash and the Tax Games Multinationals Play," *The New York Times*, October 3, 2012, accessed on September 25, 2014, http://dealbook.nytimes.com/2012/10/03/overseas-cash-and-the-tax-games-multinationals-play/.

Milton Friedman, *Capitalism and Freedom* (Chicago: University of Chicago Press), pp. 2–3, 9.

Bonnie Kavoussi, "Facebook Paid No Income Taxes in 2012: Report," *Huffington Post*, February 15, 2013, accessed on September 25, 2014, http://www.huffingtonpost.com/2013/02/15/facebook-taxes_n_2694368.html.

David Kocieniewski, "G.E.'s Strategies Let It Avoid Taxes Altogether," *The New York Times*, March 24, 2011, accessed on September 25, 2014, http://www.nytimes.com/2011/03/25/business/economy/25tax.html.

_____. "Biggest Public Firms Paid Little U.S. Tax, Study Says," November 3, 2011, accessed on September 25, 2014, http://www.nytimes.com/2011/11/03/business/280-big-public-firms-paid-little-us-tax-study-finds.html.

Nelson D. Schwartz and Charles Duhigg, "Apple's Web of Tax Shelters Saved It Billions, Panel Finds," *The New York Times*, May 20, 2013, accessed on September 25, 2014, http://www.nytimes.com/2013/05/21/business/apple-avoided-billions-in-taxes-congressional-panel-says.html.

For information on "quality of life index," "life satisfaction index," "Legatum Prosperity Index see:

http://www.economist.com/media/pdf/QUALITY_OF_LIFE.pdf

http://www.economist.com/news/21566430-where-be-born-2013-lottery-life

http://www.oecdbetterlifeindex.org/topics/life-satisfaction/#/11111111511

http://webapi.prosperity.com/download/pdf/The_2012_Legatum_Prosperity_index_Rankings.pdf

http://stats.oecd.org/Index.aspx?QueryId=21699

Images:

NUMBER IN POVERTY: 1959–2012, United States Census Bureau, http://www.census.gov/hhes/www/poverty/data/incpovhlth/2012/figure4.pdf.

Chart: U.S. Poverty Rates by Race or Ethnicity: 1959–2010, Institute for Research on Poverty, http://www.irp.wisc.edu/faqs/faq3/Figure1.png.

Chart: Poverty rates by sex and age, United States Census Bureau, http://www.census.gov/hhes/www/poverty/data/incpovhlth/2012/figure6.pdf

Table: Revenue Statistics—Comparative tables, based on data from http://stats.oecd.org/Index.aspx?QueryId=21699.

Revenue and Expenditures as a Percent of GDP (1950–2010), source: The U.S. Deficit / Debt Problem: A Longer-Run Perspective, Daniel L. Thornton, Federal Reserve Bank of St. Louis, http://research.stlouisfed.org/publications/review/12/11/Thornton.pdf

Chart: Income Tax Rates, Top bracket, Tax Rate (Percent), based on data from http://www.ntu.org/tax-basics/history-of-federal-individual-1.html

Corporate taxes as percentage of GDP 1946-2013, based on data from Federal
Reserve Bank of St. Louis, http://research.stlouisfed.org/fred2/graph/?chart
_type=line&recession_bars=on&log_scales=&bgcolor=%23e1e9f0&graph
_bgcolor=%23ffffff&fo=verdana&ts=12&tts=12&txtcolor=%23444444&show
_legend=yes&show_axis_titles=yes&drp=0&cosd=1929-01-01&coed=2013-01-01&
width=670&height=445&stacking=&range=&mode=fred&id=FCTAX
_GDPC1&transformation=lin&nd=&ost=-99999&oet=99999&scale=left&line
_color=%234572a7&line_style=solid&lw=2&mark_type=none&mw=1&mma=
0&fml=a&fgst=lin&fq=Annual&fam=avg&vintage_date=&revision_date=

Chapter 24

Anna Bernasek, "The Typical Household, Now Worth a Third Less," *The New
York Times*, July 26, 2014 accessed September 25, 2014, http://www.nytimes
.com/2014/07/27/business/the-typical-household-now-worth-a-third-less.html.

Thomas Fuller, "Prosperity in Vietnam Carries a Price: Diabetes," *The New York Times*,
June 9, 2013 accessed September 25, 2014, http://www.nytimes.com/2013/06/05
/world/asia/diabetes-is-the-price-vietnam-pays-for-progress.html.

Steve Sternberg, "World Prospers, Hearts Suffer," *USA Today*, November 18, 2002,
accessed September 25, 2014, http://usatoday30.usatoday.com/news
/health/2002-11-17-global-heart-1dcover_x.htm.

John Upton, "Where Is the Worst Air in the World?" Slate.com, March 5, 2013,
accessed September 25, 2014, http://www.slate.com/articles/health_and_science
/medical_examiner/2013/03/worst_air_pollution_in_the_world_beijing_delhi
_ahwaz_and_ulaanbaatar.html.

Thomas I. White, *In Defense of Dolphins: The New Moral Frontier* (Oxford: Blackwell,
2007).

World Health Organization, "Database: Outdoor Air Pollution in Cities," accessed
September 25, 2014, http://www.who.int/phe/health_topics/outdoorair
/databases/cities-2011/en/.

Chapter 25

Scott Pelley, "Goldman Sachs CEO: Entitlements Must Be Contained," CBS News,
June 12, 2013, accessed September 25, 2014, http://www.cbsnews.com/news
/goldman-sachs-ceo-entitlements-must-be-contained/.

Trevor Zink, 2014. *Net Green: The Impact of Corporate Social Responsibility on the Natural
Environment and Employee Satisfaction*. Dissertation, University of California at
Santa Barbara. Ann Arbor: ProQuest/UMI.

Epilogue

Douglas Adams, *The Hitchhiker's Guide to the Galaxy* (New York: Pocket Books, 1979),
p. 156.